GENERATIONS OF

CAPTIVITY

IRA BERLIN

GENERATIONS OF
CAPTIVITY

A History of African-American Slaves

THE BELKNAP PRESS OF HARVARD UNIVERSITY PRESS

Cambridge, Massachusetts, and London, England

2003

Library of Congress Cataloging-in-Publication Data

Berlin, Ira, 1941–
Generations of captivity : a history of African-American slaves / Ira Berlin.
p. cm.
Includes bibliographical references (p.) and index.
ISBN 0-674-01061-2 (alk. paper)
1. Slavery—United States—History.
2. Slaves—United States—History.
I. Title.

E441 .B47 2003
973'.0496073—dc21   2002028142

Credits

Page 1: "Marché D'esclaves" from Chambon, *Le Commerce de L'Amérique par Marseille* (1764). Courtesy of the John Carter Brown Library at Brown University. *Page 21:* "The Castle of St. George d'Elmina" from William Bosman, *Nauwkeurige Beschryving . . .* (1704). Courtesy of the John Carter Brown Library at Brown University. *Page 51:* "The Plantation," artist unknown (c. 1825). Gift of Edgar William and Bernice Chrysler Garbisch, 1963. Reproduced by permission of The Metropolitan Museum of Art. All rights reserved. *Page 97:* "A Sunday Morning View of the African Episcopal Church of St. Thomas in Philadelphia," lithograph by David Kennedy and William Lucas (1829). Reproduced by permission of The Historical Society of Pennsylvania. *Page 159:* "Slave Trade, Sold to Tennessee," from Lewis Miller, *Sketchbook of Landscapes in the State of Virginia, 1853.* Reproduced by permission of the Abby Aldrich Rockefeller Folk Art Center, Colonial Williamsburg Foundation, Williamsburg, Virginia. *Page 245:* "Arrival of Contrabands at Fortress Monroe, Virginia," from *Frank Leslie's Illustrated Newspaper,* June 8, 1861. Courtesy of the Freedmen and Southern Society Project, University of Maryland. *Pages viii–ix, 22, 52, 98:* Graphito. *Page 160:* Meridian Mapping.

For my brothers, Bruce and Alan
They ain't heavy

MAPS

CONTENTS

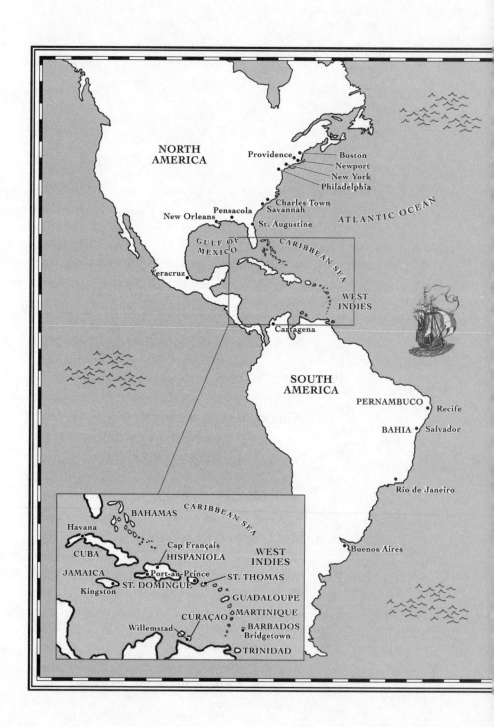

NORTH
AMERICA

Providence
Boston
Newport
New York
Philadelphia

Charles Town
Pensacola
Savannah
New Orleans
St. Augustine

GULF OF
MEXICO

CARIBBEAN SEA

ATLANTIC OCEAN

Veracruz

WEST
INDIES

Cartagena

SOUTH
AMERICA

PERNAMBUCO
Recife

BAHIA
Salvador

Rio de Janeiro

CARIBBEAN SEA

BAHAMAS

Havana

CUBA

Cap Français
HISPANIOLA

Port-au-Prince

WEST
INDIES

Buenos Aires

JAMAICA

ST. THOMAS

Kingston
ST. DOMINGUE

GUADALOUPE

MARTINIQUE

CURAÇAO

Willemstad

BARBADOS
Bridgetown

TRINIDAD

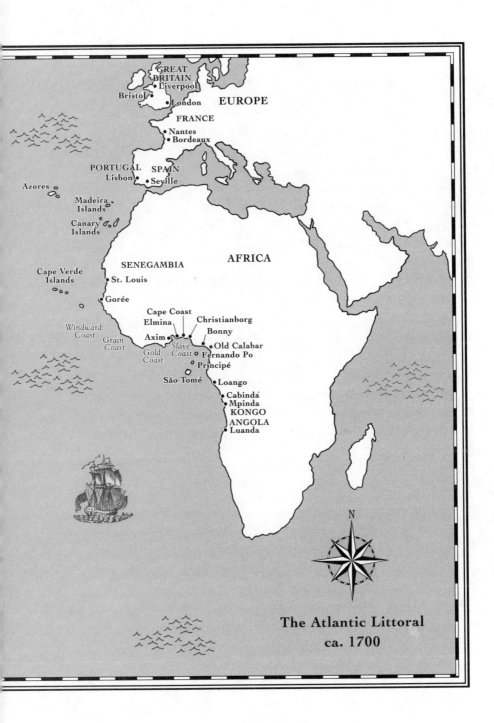

GREAT
BRITAIN
• Liverpool
Bristol •
• London   EUROPE

FRANCE
• Nantes
• Bordeaux

PORTUGAL   SPAIN
Lisbon •   • Seville

Azores

Madeira
Islands

Canary
Islands

SENEGAMBIA   AFRICA

Cape Verde
Islands   • St. Louis

• Gorée

Cape Coast
Elmina   Christianborg
Windward   Bonny
Coast
Axim •   • Old Calabar
Grain
Coast   Slave   • Fernando Po
Gold   Coast
Coast   • Príncipe

São Tomé   • Loango

• Cabinda
• Mpinda
KONGO
ANGOLA
• Luanda

N

The Atlantic Littoral
ca. 1700

PROLOGUE

SLAVERY AND FREEDOM

No one knew slavery better than the slave, and few had thought harder about what freedom could mean. In January 1865 General William Tecumseh Sherman and Secretary of War Edwin M. Stanton met in Savannah to query an assemblage of former slaves and free people of color on just these subjects. The response of Garrison Frazier, a 67-year-old Baptist minister who served as spokesman for the group, offers about as good a working definition of chattel bondage as any, and as clear an understanding of the aspirations of black people as can be found. "Slavery," declared Frazier, "is receiving by the *irresistible power* the work of another man, and not by his *consent*." While freedom, Frazier continued, "is taking us from the yoke of bondage, and placing us where we could reap the fruits of our own labor, take care of ourselves and assist the Government in maintaining our freedom."[1]

Frazier's last remark—calculated to reassure the general and the secretary—spoke to the minister's appreciation of the political realities of the moment. But his definition of slavery—irresistible power to arrogate another's labor—drew on some three hundred years of experience in bondage on mainland North America. Slavery, of necessity, rested on force. It could be sustained only when slaveowners—who, with reason, preferred the title "master"—enjoyed a monopoly on violence, backed by the power of the state. Without irresistible power, slavery quickly collapsed—an event well understood by all those who came together at that historic meeting in Savannah.

Frazier also correctly emphasized the centrality of labor to the enslavement of himself and his people. Plantation slavery did not have its origins in a conspiracy to dishonor, shame, brutalize, or otherwise reduce black people's standing on some perverse scale of humanity—although it did all of those at one time or another. Slavery's moral stench cannot mask the design of American captivity: to commandeer the labor of the many to make a few rich and powerful. Slavery thus made class as it made race, and in entwining the two processes it mystified both.

No history of slavery can avoid these themes: violence, power, and labor, hence the formation and reformation of classes and races. The study of slavery on mainland North America is first the study of enormous, hideous violence that a few powerful men wielded to extort the labor of others and thereby attain a place atop American society. The history of slavery, as Thomas Jefferson observed, was "a perpetual exercise of the most boisterous passions, the most unremitting despotism."[2] Violence, as Jefferson also understood, begat more violence as slaves refused to surrender what they believed was rightfully theirs. Born of a violent usurpation, slavery would—and perhaps could only—die in the same bloody warfare.

The contest between master and slave proceeded on uneven terrain. By definition, relations between masters and slaves were profoundly asymmetrical, with slaveowners holding a disproportion of power and slaves having hardly any. For three centuries, slave masters mobilized enormous resources that stretched across continents and oceans and employed them with great ferocity in an effort to subdue their human property. Slaves, for their part, had little to depend upon but themselves. Yet even when their power was reduced to a mere trifle, slaves still had enough to threaten their owners—a last card, which, as their owners well understood, they might play at any time.

Despite the uneven nature of the contest, slave masters never quite carried the day. While slaveowners won nearly all the great battles, slaves won their share of skirmishes, frustrating the masters' grand design. Although denied the right to marry, they made families; denied the right to an independent religious life, they established churches; denied the right to hold property, they owned many things. Defined as property and condemned as little more than beasts, they refused to surrender their humanity. Their small successes and occasional victories, moreover, positioned them to win the last battle. In the end, it was they—not their owners—who sat at the table with the conquering general and triumphant secretary of war. Yet, even then—as Garrison Frazier and the others understood—the contest had not ended, for freedom, like slavery, was not made but constantly remade.

Generations of Captivity tells the story of the making and remaking of slavery over the course of nearly three centuries in the portion of North America that became the United States. The emphasis is on the slave. Although slavery was a relationship—hence understanding its working requires an appreciation of slaveowners (large and small), white nonslaveholders, free people of color, and Native Americans—the slave was central to drama. The emphasis is also on change. For too long, scholars have taken the slaves' legal status as chattel property and their social standing at the extreme of subordination as evidence that slaves stood outside history. Depicted as socially dead, they became "absolute aliens," "genealogical isolates," "deracinated outsiders," "prepolitical," or unreflective "sambos" who were known for who they were rather than what they did.[3] Appreciating the ongoing struggle between slaves and slaveowners gives the lie to such assumptions. Knowing that a person was a slave does not tell everything about him or her. Put another way, slaveholders severely circumscribed the lives of enslaved people, but they never fully defined them. The slaves' history—like all human history—was made not only by what was done to them but also by what they did for themselves.

All of which is to say that slavery, though originally imposed and maintained by violence, was negotiated. Although disfranchised, slaves were not politically inert, and their politics—even absent an independent institutional basis—was as active as any. The ongoing contest forced slave-owners and slaves, even as they confronted one another as deadly enemies, to concede a degree of legitimacy to their opponent. No matter how reluctantly given—or, more likely, extracted—such concessions were difficult for either party to acknowledge. Masters presumed their own absolute sovereignty, and slaves never relinquished the right to control their own destiny. But no matter how adamant the denials, nearly every interaction of master and slave forced such recognition, for the web of interconnections necessitated a coexistence that fostered grudging cooperation as well as open contestation. The refusal of either party to concede the realities of master-slave relations only added to slavery's instability. No bargain could last for very long, for as power slipped from master to slave and back, the terms of slavery were negotiated and then renegotiated.

Central to those negotiations was the labor slaves performed, for when, where, and especially how slaves worked determined, in large measure, the course of their lives. But if the study of slavery is first a branch of labor history, it is also more. Slaves, no less than any other workers, did not live on bread alone. Family, language, and spirituality infused the patches of tobacco and the fields of rice and indigo, just as exploitation and compensation informed the spiritual language of brush-arbor sermons and the vernacular of field chants. The weight of time alone—whether calculated as a portion of a day, a year, or a lifetime—does not automatically elevate labor in the field or workshop over any of the other manifestations of human existence emanating from the quarter, household, and church. It is precisely in connecting the quarter, household, and church to the field and the workshop that the slaves' experience can be made comprehensible. Study of the workplace offers only a practical point of entry to their social organization, domestic arrangements, religious beliefs, and medical practices, along with their music, cuisine, linguistic and sartorial style, and much else.

Over time, slaves transformed their experience—drawn from, among other things, work habits, musical style, and religious beliefs—into a culture that joined them together as a class and distinguished them from their owners. The slave experience provided the basis of institutions that had no standing in law but a powerful presence in life. It enfranchised leaders who articulated aspirations that reached beyond life's daily trials. It became the foundation of collective action, for it entailed both responsibilities and obligations. It nourished the hope that there would be something better—if not for the present then for the future.

The history of slavery in the United States—the republic and the colonies that preceded it—can be divided into five parts, here generously denominated as "generations." It began with the charter generations, cosmopolitan men and women of African descent who arrived in mainland North America almost simultaneously with the first European adventurers. Their knowledge of the larger Atlantic world, the fluidity with which they moved in it, and their chameleonlike ability to alter their identity moderated the force of chattel bondage, allowing a considerable proportion of these initial arrivals to gain their freedom and enjoy a modest prosperity.

Those who followed—the plantation generations—were not nearly as fortunate. Stripped of family and kin, these peoples of the African interior faced the full force of the plantation revolution. Their catastrophic confrontation with large-scale staple production—tobacco in the Chesapeake at the end of the seventeenth century and rice in lowcountry South Carolina and Georgia at the beginning of the eighteenth century—debased African and African-American life. Members of the plantation generations worked harder, died earlier, and escaped slavery less frequently than their predecessors. Whether measured by the many who died or the few who survived, the plantation generations' history was one of impoverishment, degradation, and loss. Yet, in equal measure, it is also the story of survival, resistance, and cultural reconstruction amid the imposition of planter dominance.

Hope was restored at the end of the eighteenth century as a series of egalitarian revolutions spread through the Atlantic. But while thousands of members of the revolutionary generations secured their freedom, reconstituted their families, remade their religious life, and attained a modicum of prosperity, many more were condemned to yet another century of captivity.

The division between the enslaved many and the free few increased during the nineteenth century as members of the migration generations were propelled from the southern seaboard across the continent. Their divided history—as tens of thousands went south to construct a new slave society in the southern interior and hundreds fled north to create a free one—set the stage for the Great Jubilee and the emergence of the freedom generations.

Tracing the generations of African and African-American captivity across the centuries requires sensitivity to place as well as time. The geography of slave life changed with its history. Whereas the charter generations' history can be understood by viewing slavery from Dutch New Netherland, English Chesapeake, French Louisiana, and Spanish Florida, changes in American society—mostly in the eighteenth century—require that the plantation and revolutionary generations be viewed on a larger canvas: the North, the Chesapeake, lowcountry South Carolina and Georgia, and the lower Mississippi Valley. The westward expansion of the United States in the nineteenth century necessitates yet another geography of slavery. The migration generations are divided not merely north and south but between the old seaboard South and the new southern interior. As with many other aspects of American life, the Civil War created—perhaps for the first time—a common African-American experience.

Each chapter of *Generations of Captivity* begins with the region that best exemplifies the generational experience. Thus, "Charter Generations" (chapter 1) starts with black life in Dutch New Netherland (present-day New York), not because of any chronological primacy in the history of European and African settlement in mainland North America but because the character of the charter generations was most fully evident in seventeenth-century New Netherland. For like reasons, "Plantation Generations" (chapter 2) begins with the tobacco revolution in the Chesapeake, "Revolutionary Generations" (chapter 3) with emancipations in the northern states, and "Migration Generations" (chapter 4) with the cotton and sugar revolutions in the southern interior. By beginning where change was most evident and then inspecting various permutations, each chapter elaborates how the very same processes—initial settlement, the advent of staple production, social revolution, forced migration, and civil war—followed a different course in different places; hence the use of the plural when discussing the various "generations" of people of African descent.

This complex matrix of space and time suggests that the idea of "generation" might be both too precise and too diffuse, as generations overlap in ways that militate against sharp boundaries. Slave children could no more escape the experience of their parents than they could deny that of their own children. Thus, the lives of the charter generations impinged on those of the plantation generations, just as the memories of the plantation generations echoed in the revolutionary generations, or the ideas of the migration generations invaded those of the freedom generations. But exploring these connections—the instinctive imitations, conscious reproductions, or determined repudiations—has some advantages. Such generational linkages expose the crooked path whereby slave life changed over the course of nearly three centuries. Slaves were different people in 1650 than they would be in 1750 or 1850, but they always carried something of their forebears into the future. Like all history, the generational experiences could be recalled, reformulated, or reconstructed to suit contemporary needs. In the 1770s, members of the revolutionary generations instituted freedom suits on the basis of the charter generations' mixed ancestry. Members of the freedom generation recalled the promises made during the revolutionary years. No understanding of slavery can ignore the force of change or the ability of men and women to reconstruct the past in their own image.

Two theoretical distinctions undergird slavery's ever-changing history and geography. The first, drawn from the study of slavery in antiquity, distinguishes between societies with slaves and slave societies.[4] Societies with slaves were not societies in which, as one apologist for slavery in the North observed, "even the darkest aspect of slavery was softened by a smile."[5] Superficially, slavery in such societies might appear milder, as slaveowners—not driven by the great wealth sugar, tobacco, rice, or cotton could produce—had less reason to press their slaves. Moreover, slaveholdings in societies with slaves were generally small, and the line between slave and free could be remarkably fluid, with manumission often possible and sometimes encouraged. But neither mildness nor openness defined societies with slaves. Slaveholders in such societies could act with extraordinary brutality precisely because their slaves were extraneous to their main business. They could limit their slaves' access to freedom expressly because they desired to set themselves apart from their slaves.

What distinguished societies with slaves was the fact that slaves were marginal to the central productive processes. In societies with slaves, slavery was just one form of labor among many. Slaveowners treated their slaves with extreme callousness and cruelty at times, because this was the way they treated all subordinates, be they indentured servants, debtors, prisoners of war, pawns, peasants, or perhaps simply poor folks. In societies with slaves, no one presumed the master-slave relationship to be the exemplar.

In slave societies, by contrast, slavery stood at the center of economic production, and the master-slave relationship provided the model for all social relations: husband and wife, parent and child, employer and employee. From the most intimate connections between men and women to the most public ones between ruler and ruled, all relationships mimicked those of slavery. As Frank Tannenbaum observed, "Nothing escaped, nothing, and no one."[6] Whereas in societies with slaves slaveholders were just one portion of a propertied elite, in slave societies they were the ruling class. In slave societies, nearly everyone—free and slave—aspired to enter the slaveholding class, and upon occasion some former slaves rose into the slaveholders' ranks. Their acceptance was grudging, as they carried the stigma of bondage in their lineage and, in the case of American slavery, color in their skin. But the right to enter the slaveholding class was rarely denied, because slaveownership was open to all irrespective of family, nationality, color, or ancestry.

Historians have outlined the process by which societies with slaves in the Americas became slave societies.[7] The transformation generally turned upon the discovery of some commodity—gold being the ideal, sugar being a close second—that could command an international market. In pursuit of that market, slaveholders capitalized production and monopolized resources, muscled other classes to the periphery, and consolidated their political power. The number of slaves increased sharply, generally by direct importation from Africa, and enslaved people of African descent became the majority of the laboring class, sometimes the majority of the population. Other forms of labor—family labor, indentured servitude, wage labor—declined, as slaveholders drove small farmers and wage workers to the margins. These men and women sometimes resisted violently, in the North American mainland most famously in Bacon's rebellion.[8] But mostly they voted with their feet and migrated from slave societies, much as the "redlegs" deserted Barbados in the wake of the sugar revolution of the mid-seventeenth century, the small planters and drovers fled low-country Carolina in the wake of the rice revolution of the early eighteenth century, and the yeomanry abandoned the blackbelt for the hill country of the southern interior and the flatlands of the Midwest in the wake of the cotton revolution of the early nineteenth century.

In the absence of competitors, slaveholders solidified their rule. Through their control of the state, they enacted—or reinvigorated—comprehensive slave codes in which they vested themselves with near-complete sovereignty over their slaves, often extending to an absolute right over the slave's life. The new laws sharply reduced the latitude slaves previously enjoyed and extended the deference slaves must show to their owners at all times, without question. The prerogatives that slaves once openly maintained—to travel, to meet among themselves, to hold property, and to trade at market—were also severely circumscribed or abolished, although they survived at the pleasure of individual slaveowners. That done, slaveholders narrowed the slaves' access to freedom, so that the previously permeable boundaries between bondage and liberty became impenetrable barriers.

Finally, slaveholders elaborated the ideology of subordination, generally finding the sources of their own domination in some rule of nature or law of God. Since slavery in the New World became exclusively identified with people of African descent, the slaveholders' explanation of their own domination generally took the form of racial ideologies. But African descent and the pigmocracy that accompanied it was only one manifestation of the slaves' subordination. Even where slaveowner and slave admittedly shared the same origins, masters construed domination in "racial" terms.[9]

Whereas elements of the process by which societies with slaves were transformed into slave societies were everywhere the same, the process was always different, except for its inherent brutality. Some societies with slaves passed rapidly into slave societies, so that the earlier experience left hardly a mark. Others moved slowly and imperfectly through the transformation, backtracking several times, so that the process was more circular than linear. Yet other societies with slaves never completed the transition, and some hardly began it. Moreover, slave societies did not always stay slave societies. The development of slavery did not necessarily run in one direction; slave societies also became societies with slaves as often as the opposite.

As one marker of slavery's history, the transformation of societies with slaves to slave societies provides a clue to yet another. A second marker in the evolution of slavery—the arrival of freedom—had an effect that was as powerful as the first. Freedom came to American slaves in two great revolutionary climacterics. The first—the democratic revolutions of the late eighteenth century—hit slavery hard. The Declaration of Independence in the American colonies, the Declaration of the Rights of Man in France, and the emergence of an independent Haitian Republic on Hispaniola undermined the ideological foundation upon which slavery rested, and the wars that accompanied these ideological upheavals provided slaves with new leverage to contest their owners' power.[10] Some slaves secured their liberty, and portions of the new United States became identified with freedom. But slavery was nothing if not resilient. It not only survived the egalitarian forces unleashed in the Age of Revolution but also grew strong on them. It would take another revolution—what Charles Beard called in another context the Second American Revolution—to finally bring slavery down.

The history of freedom, like the history of slavery, was never the same from time to time and place to place. Geography, demography, and economy informed the process of emancipation just as they tempered the course of enslavement. Free societies were as different as the slave societies they replaced. But as with the transition from societies with slaves to slave societies, historians have identified general processes by which freedom supplants slavery.

Whether in Vermont or Barbados, Jamaica or Brazil, emancipation followed the same course. Evidence of slavery's weakening grip—in whispers of distant abolition or rumblings of military mobilization—emboldened slaves and panicked slaveowners. The conflict between slave and master intensified, as each bolstered the ideological foundations of its claim—freedom for slaves, mastership for owners. Seemingly harmonious relations between slaves and owners turned factious and violent. The patina of rationalizations that sustained the slave regime fell away. Complacent slaves became insolent, and benevolent masters turned vicious, as the irreconcilable differences that underlay slavery became manifest. Both declared themselves betrayed, charging the other with ingratitude.

With the arrival of freedom, former slaves seized the moment to remake their lives. They took new names, found new residences, reconstituted their families and churches, established new institutions like schools and benevolent associations, strove for material independence, and created the political organizations to protect and advance that independence. Against the onrushing tide of change, former masters hastened to reconstruct the old regime on new ground, sometimes conceding what they could not resist, sometimes asserting their old power in novel ways, and sometimes redefining the terms of conflict by creating new mechanisms of domination. Among the latter was a redefinition of the terms of superordination and subordination. In the color-coded slave societies of the Americas, these inevitably included new definitions of race. Without slavery to order society, blackness and whiteness gained in importance.

Meanwhile, the people caught between the former slaves and former masters hurriedly repaired to safe ground, trying to preserve what they once had even as they searched for ways to seize the moment. Former free people of color—adrift in a world that promised equality but stripped of their former privileged status—hedged between their old allegiance and the new possibilities that accompanied universal freedom. While some moved into positions of leadership among the newly freed, others re-treated to anonymity, waiting for the storm to subside. Similarly, white nonslaveholders—bereft of the special status their white skin once pro-vided—watched the changes carefully, some seeing advantages in the de-feat of the old planter class (scalawags in the American context) and some becoming the shock troops of revanchist masters (klansmen).[11]

In the United States, the two emancipations—the partial liberation of the Revolution and the total liquidation of the Civil War—unleashed the latent egalitarian impulses in American society. But while the process by which slave societies were transformed into free ones followed the same course during these two uprisings, they were never precisely the same from place to place. After the American Revolution, freedom—and slav-ery—took different forms in the North, Chesapeake, lowcountry, and lower Mississippi Valley. After the Civil War, freedom—following slavery's final demise—took a different shape in the former free states and the for-mer slave states. Indeed, within each of these vast domains, freedom gained new meanings dependent upon the demographic balance of white and black, the resilience of the old class structures, the nature of the crop, and the course of the military conflict by which freedom arrived. No less than slavery, freedom had a history that changed with time and place.

The coincidence of slavery's destruction with the revolutions that made the American Republic in 1776 and then remade it in 1861 reveals the ex-tent to which slavery was woven into the fabric of American life. For most of its history, the American colonies and then the United States was a so-ciety of slaves and slaveholders. From the first, slavery shaped the Ameri-can economy, its politics, its culture, and its most deeply held beliefs. The American economy was founded upon the production of slave-grown crops, the great staples of tobacco, rice, sugar, and finally cotton that were sold on the international market and made some men extraordinarily wealthy. That great wealth allowed slaveholding planters a large place in the establishment of the new federal government in 1787, as planters were quick to translate their economic power into political power. Between the founding of the Republic and the Civil War, the majority of presidents—from Washington, Jefferson, Madison, Monroe, and Jackson through

Tyler, Polk, and Taylor—were themselves slaveholders, and generally substantial slaveholders. The same was true for the Supreme Court, where two slaveholding Chief Justices—John Marshall and Roger Taney—ruled over a slaveholding majority. And so too with the Congress—indeed, politics during the antebellum period revolved around the struggle between North and South for control of Congress.

The power of the slaveholder class, represented by the predominance of slaveholders in the nation's leadership, gave it a large hand in shaping American culture and the values associated with American society. It was no accident that a slaveholder penned the founding statement of American nationality and that freedom became the nation's transcendent marker. Men and women who drove slaves understood the meaning of chattel bondage—as did the men and women who were in fact chattel bondsmen and bondswomen. Just as it was no accident that Thomas Jefferson wrote "all men are created equal," it is most certainly no accident that the greatest spokesmen for the realization of that ideal—from Richard Allen through Frederick Douglass, W. E. B. DuBois to Martin Luther King, Jr.—were former slaves and the descendants of slaves. Only by understanding the generations of Americans who spent their lives in captivity can we fully appreciate the generations of Americans who struggled for freedom.

The historicization of slavery—and freedom—reveals how the critical changes in the nature of slavery have been employed to make history. Whether it is recalling the promises of the Revolution ("all men are created equal") or the Civil War ("forty acres and a mule") or remembering the Middle Passage from Africa or the Second Middle Passage from Virginia, the history of slavery has itself been used to make slavery's history. For some three hundred years, Americans have situated their own history in terms of the struggle between freedom and slavery—and freedom's triumph. It thus should not be surprising that even at the beginning of the twenty-first century, one hundred and thirty plus years after slavery's legal demise, slavery continues to play a part in American life, as Americans discover that their national buildings were constructed by slaves, their great cities are underlaid with the bones of slaves, and their greatest heroes and heroines were slaveowners and slaves. Coming to terms with slavery's complex history is no easier in the twenty-first century than it was in centuries past.

In presenting a history of slavery in mainland North America from its ill-defined beginnings to its fiery demise, *Generations of Captivity* reprises and extends my earlier study, *Many Thousands Gone: The First Two Centuries of Slavery in North America*. The short five years since the publication of *Many Thousands Gone* have witnessed a vast outpouring of new research in this field.[12] To take only the crudest of measures, more than two hundred books have been submitted for the Gilder Lehrman Institute's Frederick Douglass Award for the best study on slavery. The journal *Slavery and Abolition*'s annual bibliography of scholarly articles and conference papers regularly runs over thirty tightly packed pages. *Generations of Captivity* draws on this new scholarship to deepen understanding of the charter, plantation, and revolutionary generations.

Generations of Captivity also addresses the large, and largely unanswered, question posed by recent studies of slavery in colonial and revolutionary North America, including my own. At the beginning of the nineteenth century (the point at which *Many Thousands Gone* concludes), the markers that are most closely identified with slavery's history in the United States—cotton cultivation, residence in the blackbelt, and African-Christian spirituality—hardly existed. In 1800 few American slaves grew cotton, few resided in the Deep South, and most did not identify with Christianity—no matter how latitudinous the definition of Christian belief. Yet in 1865, when with the ratification of the Thirteenth Amendment to the Constitution black people completed their wartime exodus from slavery, all of these elements were in place. Most slaves grew cotton, resided in the Deep South, and professed Christianity.

Little in the vast literature of nineteenth-century slavery in the United States explains the plantation revolutions that transformed tobacco and rice growers into cultivators of cotton and sugar, the Second Middle Passage that forcibly transferred nearly one million men and women from the seaboard to the interior, and the sudden willingness of men and women whose ancestors resisted Christianity for more than two centuries to embrace it and make it their own. Although there is a rich and growing monographic literature on each of these subjects—upon which much of this book rests—none of the great studies of nineteenth-century slavery make these rapid and often traumatic changes in black life the central element in slavery's history between the Revolution and the Civil War.

"The rigid and static nature of ante-bellum slavery, 1830–1860," wrote Kenneth M. Stampp nearly fifty years ago in his classic study *The Peculiar Institution*, "makes it possible to examine it institutionally with only slight regard for chronology." Eugene D. Genovese in his *Roll, Jordan, Roll*, another foundational text, and almost all other scholars—even those critical of Stampp and Genovese—have followed Stampp's lead. These seminal works—now more than a generation old, eons on the revisionist clock—have been elaborated and critiqued by a host of specialized studies of agricultural practice, domestic relations, manumission, material culture, plantation architecture, religious conventions, slave hire, underclass resistance, westward migration, and dozens of like subjects. While they are premised on a society in flux, the full force of these accumulated changes on slave society has yet to be measured. As a result, even the best recent overviews of antebellum slavery also remain riveted to the relationship between master and slave. Indeed, it was precisely such an attachment that sent scholars who were interested in slavery's evolution, including myself, to the seventeenth and eighteenth centuries, years in which free people were enslaved and Africans became African Americans. It now appears that the period of slavery's most rapid change in mainland North America was not its first two hundred years but the half century preceding the Civil War.[13]

Many Thousands Gone connected the evolution of slave life in mainland North America during the seventeenth and eighteenth centuries to slavery's long transit from the eastern end of the Mediterranean across the Atlantic to the Americas. It viewed the charter generations as an outgrowth of the historic meeting of Africa, Europe, and the Americas. It considered the plantation generations to be an extension of the imposition of staple production first in the Mediterranean, then the Atlantic islands, Brazilian mainland, and the Windward and Leeward islands of the Caribbean. It understood the revolutionary generations as a product of the massive social upheavals that turned the Atlantic world upside down at the end of the eighteenth century.

Viewing the lives of nineteenth-century American slaves through this same Atlantic lens emphasizes how antebellum slavery remained part of slavery's long history and continued its Atlantic connections. For more than a millennium, the creation of new slave societies transformed old ones. The growth of plantation slavery in Madeira and the Canary Islands transformed slavery in the Mediterranean, just as the expansion of plantation production to São Tomé and Principé altered slave life in Madeira and the Canaries. Likewise, the rise of plantation slavery in seventeenth-century Barbados remade the lives of masters and slaves in Pernambuco, and its growth in Jamaica reconfigured slavery in Barbados.[14]

From this perspective, the lightning-like expansion of plantation slavery in the southern interior of the United States caused a thunderclap in the older slave-exporting seaboard states, north as well as south. It changed them in the same ways that the process of plantation succession had earlier transformed slavery in the Mediterranean and the Atlantic. Slaveholders transferred slaves to areas of greater profitability, which became slave societies par excellence. Older, less productive areas reverted to societies with slaves. As the level of exploitation increased in the former, labor discipline intensified, and slave mortality and morbidity increased. Manumission became increasingly selective and rare. Something of the opposite happened in the older areas, where labor discipline grew flaccid, the slaves' material circumstances improved, and the possibilities of manumission and even emancipation grew. Everywhere, slaves and slaveholders reformulated their lives, as both created new ideologies to deal with the trauma of change. And everywhere, as always, new definitions of race arose.

Incorporating the nineteenth-century United States into the history of Atlantic slavery also clarifies many of the issues central to the study of antebellum America. It provides a fuller understanding of the divisions within American slave society, especially the east-west division between the expansive southern interior and the declining seaboard South. It casts new light on everything from the transformation of slave law to the evolution of slave music. Most importantly, it illuminates how the struggle between master and slave moved onto new ground—articulated in the language of domesticity—during the nineteenth century. In short, it places the vexed matter of paternalism—or what Eugene D. Genovese and Elizabeth Fox-Genovese called "seigneuralism"—in the context not only of the historic affinity of traditional elites for familial metaphors but also in the context of the massive forced migration which informed every aspect of black life during the middle years of the nineteenth century.[15] The Second Middle Passage shredded the planters' paternalist pretenses in the eyes of black people and prodded slaves and free people of color to create a host of oppositional ideologies and institutions that better accounted for the realities of the endless deportations, expulsions, and flights that continually remade their world. The historicization of the study of antebellum slavery, like the historicization of its colonial and revolutionary antecedents, clarifies one of the great controversies of slave historiography, in seeing planters' defense of slavery (and the slaves' counter) as a product not of slavery itself but of a particular moment in slavery's history.

In writing about antebellum slavery, I have also taken the opportunity to join the debate over slavery and freedom in the free states. New studies make it evident that the nineteenth-century North remained part of what Don Fehrenbacher called a "slaveholding republic" long after the region made a commitment to slavery's liquidation. Indeed, after reviewing the evidence, I think it remains an open question when, prior to January 1, 1863, the North became a free society. For that reason, slavery is just as essential to understanding the history of the antebellum North as it is to understanding the history of the colonial and revolutionary North. By including the North in *Generations of Captivity*, I wish to suggest that the antebellum United States might be better understood not as a nation sharply divided between slavery and freedom but as a nation of slaves and slaveholders, one portion of which was undergoing a slow transformation to freedom. Although the triumph of free labor and its underpenning ideologies was critical to the transformation of northern society and the struggle between North and South, the slowness of its development reveals how deeply the "free states" were enmeshed in the slaveholding republic.[16]

Generations of Captivity concludes with a short reprise of the destruction of slavery and the emergence of the freedom generation amid the Civil War. While this epilogue hardly does justice to the complicated history of slavery's end and the reconstruction of African-American life in the first years of freedom, it connects the expectations black people carried from three hundred years of slavery to the revolutionary possibilities presented by wartime emancipation. It demonstrates that former slaves had no desire to deny or escape their slave past but to use it to construct a better life for themselves and their posterity. That lesson, above all others, is the legacy of the generations of captivity.

1

CHARTER GENERATIONS

't Casteel St. George d' Elmina, aan d'eene

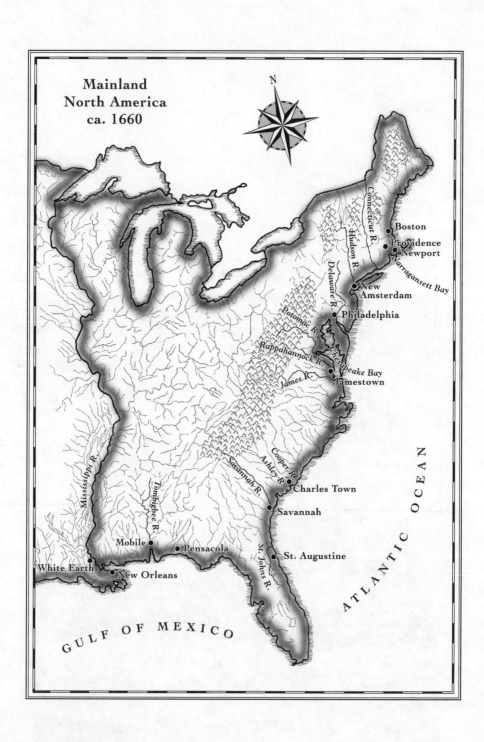

**Mainland
North America
ca. 1660**

N

Connecticut R.

Boston

Hudson R.

Providence
Newport

Narragansett Bay

Delaware R.

New
Amsterdam

Potomac R.

Philadelphia

Rappahannock R.

Chesapeake Bay

James R.

Jamestown

Cooper R.

Ashley R.

Savannah R.

Charles Town

Mississippi R.

Savannah

Tombigbee R.

St. Johns R.

St. Augustine

Mobile

Pensacola

ATLANTIC OCEAN

White Earth

New Orleans

GULF OF MEXICO

BLACK LIFE on mainland North America originated not in Africa or America but in the nether world between the two continents. Along the periphery of the Atlantic—first in Africa, then Europe, and finally in the Americas—it was a product of the momentous meeting of Africans and Europeans and then their equally fateful rendezvous with the peoples of the New World. Although the countenances of these "Atlantic creoles" might bear the features of Africa, Europe, or the Americas in whole or part, their beginnings, strictly speaking, were in none of those places.[1] Instead, by their experience and sometimes by their person, they had become part of the three worlds that came together in the Atlantic littoral. Familiar with the commerce of the Atlantic, fluent in its new languages, and intimate with its trade and cultures, they were cosmopolitan in the fullest sense.

Atlantic creoles traced their beginnings to the historic encounter of Europeans and Africans on the west coast of Africa. Many served as intermediaries, employing their linguistic skills and their familiarity with the Atlantic's diverse commercial practices, cultural conventions, and diplomatic etiquette to mediate between the African merchants and European sea captains. In so doing, some Atlantic creoles identified with their ancestral homeland (or a portion of it)—be it African or European—and served as its representatives in negotiations. Other Atlantic creoles had been won over by the power and largess of one party or another, so that Africans entered the employ of European trading companies, and Europeans traded with African potentates. Yet others played fast and loose with their mixed heritage, employing whichever identity paid best. Whatever strategy they adopted, Atlantic creoles began the process of integrating the icons and beliefs of the Atlantic world into a new way of life.[2]

The emergence of the Atlantic creoles was only a tiny outcropping in the massive social upheaval that joined the peoples of the eastern and western hemispheres. But it was representative of the small beginnings that initiated the monumental transformations, as the new people of the Atlantic soon made their presence felt. Some traveled broadly as bluewater sailors, supercargoes, interpreters, and shipboard servants. Others were carried to foreign places as exotic trophies to be displayed before curious publics eager for a glimpse of the lands beyond the sea. Some were even sent to distant shores with commissions to master the ways of the newly discovered "other" and retrieve the secrets of their knowledge and wealth. A few entered as honored guests, took their place in royal courts as esteemed councilors, and married into the best families.[3]

Atlantic creoles first emerged around the trading factories or *feitorias* established along the coast of Africa in the fifteenth century by European expansionists. Finding trade more lucrative than pillage, the Portuguese Crown began sending agents to oversee its interests in Africa. These official representatives were succeeded in turn by private entrepreneurs, or *lançados,* who, with the aid of African potentates, established themselves sometimes in competition with the Crown's emissaries. Portuguese competitors were soon joined by other European nations, and the coastal factories became a commercial rendezvous for all manner of transatlantic traders. What was true of the nominally Portuguese enclaves also held for those later established or seized by the Dutch (Fort Nassaw and Elmina), Danes (Fredriksborg and Christianborg), Swedes (Carlsborg), French (St. Louis), and English (Fort Kormantse).[4]

The growth of the small fishing villages along Africa's Gold Coast during the sixteenth and seventeenth centuries suggests something of the change that followed the arrival of European traders. Between 1550 and 1618, Mouri (where the Dutch constructed Fort Nassau in 1612) grew from a village of 200 people to 1,500 and then to an estimated 5,000 to 6,000 at the end of the eighteenth century. In 1555, Cape Coast counted only twenty houses; by 1680 it had 500 or more. Axim, which had 500 inhabitants in 1631, expanded to between 2,000 and 3,000 by 1690. Among the African fishermen, craftsmen, village-based peasants, and laborers attached to these villages were an increasing number of Europeans. Although the mortality and transiency rates in these enclaves were extraordinarily high even by the standards of early modern port cities, permanent European settlements developed from the corporate employees, merchants and factors, stateless sailors and soldiers, skilled craftsmen, occasional missionaries, and sundry transcontinental drifters.[5]

Established in 1482 by the Portuguese and captured by the Dutch in 1637, Elmina was one of the first of these factories and a model for those that followed. A meeting place for African and European commercial ambitions, Elmina—the Castle São Jorge da Mina and the town that surrounded it—became headquarters of the Portuguese and later Dutch mercantile activities on the Gold Coast and, with a population of 15,000 to 20,000 in 1682, the largest of some three dozen European outposts in the region.[6]

The peoples of the enclaves—long-term residents and wayfarers alike—soon joined together, geographically and genetically. European men took wives and mistresses among African women, and before long the children born of these unions helped people the enclave. Elmina sprouted a substantial cadre of Euro-Africans (most of them Luso-Africans), men and women of African birth but shared African and European parentage, whose swarthy skin, European dress and deportment, acquaintance with local norms, and multilingualism gave them an insider's knowledge of both African and European ways but denied them full acceptance in either culture. By the eighteenth century, they numbered several hundred in Elmina. Along the Angolan coast they may have been even more numerous.[7]

People of mixed ancestry and tawny complexion composed but a small fraction of the population of the coastal factories, but few observers failed to note their existence—which itself gave their presence a disproportionate significance. Africans and Europeans alike sneered at the creoles' mixed lineage and condemned them as haughty, proud, and overbearing. When they adopted African ways, wore African dress and amulets, or underwent circumcision and scarification, Europeans declared them outcasts (*tangosmaos* or *reneges* to the Portuguese). When they adopted European ways, wore European clothing and crucifixes, employed European names or titles, and comported themselves in the manner of "white men," Africans denied them the right to hold land, marry, and inherit property. Although the *tangosmaos* faced reproach and proscription, all parties conceded that the creoles were shrewd traders. Their reputation attested to their mastery of the fine points of intercultural negotiations and the advantage in dealing with these knowledgeable entrepreneurs. Despite their defamers, some rose to positions of wealth and power, compensating for their lack of lineage with knowledge, skill, and entrepreneurial derring-do.[8]

Not all *tangosmaos* were of mixed ancestry, and not all people of mixed ancestry were *tangosmaos*. Color was only one marker of this culture-in-the-making, and generally the least significant one.[9] From common experience, conventions of personal behavior, and cultural sensibilities compounded by shared ostracism, Atlantic creoles acquired interests of their own, apart from those of their European and African antecedents. Of necessity, they spoke a variety of African and European languages, weighted strongly toward Portuguese. But from the seeming babble emerged a pidgin lingua franca that enabled Atlantic creoles to communicate with all. In time, their pidgin evolved into a creole, borrowing its vocabulary from all parties and creating a grammar unique unto itself. Derisively called *fala de Guine* or *fala de negros*—literally "Guinea speech" or "Negro Speech"—by the Portuguese and black Portuguese by others, this creole lingua franca became the language of the Atlantic.[10]

Although jaded observers condemned the culture of the enclaves as nothing more than "whoring, drinking, gambling, swearing, fighting, and shouting," Atlantic creoles attended church (usually Roman Catholic), married according to the sacraments, raised children conversant with European norms, and drew a livelihood from their knowledge of the Atlantic commercial economy. In short, they created societies of their own, *of* but not always *in* the societies of the Africans who dominated the interior trade and the Europeans who controlled the commerce of the Atlantic. By the mid-nineteenth century, they would station themselves on all corners of the Atlantic world, establishing branches of their families in Europe and the Americas so their children felt as comfortable in Bahia as in Birmingham, Lisbon as in Lagos. During the seventeenth and eighteenth centuries, however, their world centered on the Atlantic itself.

Operating under European protection, always at African sufferance, the enclaves developed governments with a politics as diverse and complicated as the peoples who populated them. Their presence created political havoc, enabling new men and women of commerce to gain prominence and threatening older, often hereditary hierarchies. Intermarriage with established peoples allowed creoles to fabricate lineages that gained them full membership in local elites, something that creoles eagerly embraced. The resultant political turmoil promoted state formation along with new class relations and ideologies.[11]

New religious forms emerged and then disappeared in much the same manner, as Europeans and Africans brought to the enclaves not only their commercial and political aspirations but all the trappings of their cultures as well. Priests and ministers sent to tend European souls made African converts, some of whom saw Christianity as a way to both ingratiate themselves with their trading partners and gain a new truth. Missionaries sped the process of Christianization and occasionally scored striking successes. At the beginning of the sixteenth century, the royal house of Kongo converted to Christianity. Catholicism, in various syncretic forms, infiltrated the posts along the Angolan coast and spread northward. Islam filtered in from the north.

Whatever the sources of the new religions, most converts saw little cause to surrender their own deities. They incorporated Christianity and Islam to serve their own needs and gave Jesus and Mohammed a place in their spiritual pantheon. New religious practices, polities, and theologies emerged from the mixing of Christianity, Islam, and polytheism. Similar syncretic formations influenced the agricultural practices, architectural forms, and sartorial styles as well as the cuisine, music, art, and technology of the enclaves. Like the stone fortifications that greeted visitors, these cultural innovations announced the presence of something new to those arriving on the African coast, whether they traveled by caravan from the interior or sailed by caravel from the Atlantic.[12]

The business of the creole communities was trade—brokering the movement of goods through the Atlantic world. Although island settlements such as Cape Verde, Principé, and São Tomé developed indigenous agricultural and sometimes plantation economies, the comings and goings of African and European merchants dominated life even in the largest of the creole communities, which served as both field headquarters for great European mercantile companies and collection points for trade between the African interior and the Atlantic littoral. Depending on the location, the exchange involved European textiles, metalware, guns, liquor, and beads for African gold, ivory, hides, pepper, beeswax, and dyewoods. The coastal trade or cabotage added to the mix. Everywhere, slaves were bought and sold, and over time the importance of commerce-in-persons grew.

As societies engaged in the trade in slaves, the coastal enclaves became societies with slaves. African slavery in its various forms—from pawnage to chattel bondage—was practiced in these towns. Both Europeans and Africans held slaves, imported and exported them, hired them, used them as collateral, and traded them. At Elmina, the Dutch West India Company owned some 300 slaves in the late seventeenth century, and individual Europeans and Africans held others. Along with slaves appeared the inevitable trappings of that particular form of domination—overseers to supervise slave labor, slave catchers to retrieve runaways, soldiers to keep order and guard against insurrections, and officials to adjudicate and punish transgressions beyond a master's reach. Freedmen and freedwomen, who had somehow escaped bondage, also enjoyed a considerable presence. Former slaves mixed Africa and Europe culturally and sometimes physically.[13]

Mirroring developments on the coast of Africa, a cadre of Atlantic creoles emerged in Europe. By the mid-sixteenth century, some ten thousand black people lived in Lisbon, where they composed about 10 percent of the population. Seville had a slave population of 6,000 (including a minority of Moors and Moriscos). As the centers of the Iberian slave trade, these cities distributed African slaves throughout Europe. Many found their way to the most distant corners of the continent. By the end of the sixteenth century, they were numerous enough in England for Elizabeth to order their expulsion from the kingdom.[14]

Whether they resided in Europe or Africa, it was knowledge and experience far more than color that set the Atlantic creoles apart from the Africans who brought slaves from the interior and the Europeans who carried them across the Atlantic, on one hand, and the hapless men and women upon whose commodification the slave trade rested, on the other. Maintaining a secure place in such a volatile social order was not easy. The Atlantic creoles' liminality, particularly their lack of identity with any one group, posed numerous dangers. While their intermediate position made them valuable to African and European traders alike, it also made them vulnerable: they could be ostracized, scapegoated, and on occasion enslaved. Maintaining independence amid the shifting alliances between and among Europeans and Africans was always difficult. Inevitably, some failed.

Debt, crime, heresy, immorality, official disfavor, or bad luck could mean enslavement—if not for the great traders, at least for those on the fringes of the creole community.[15] Placed in captivity, Atlantic creoles might be exiled anywhere around the Atlantic—the islands along the coast, the European metropoles, or the plantations of the New World. In the seventeenth century and the early part of the eighteenth, most slaves exported from Africa went to the sugar plantations of the Atlantic islands and the Americas. Enslaved Atlantic creoles might be shipped to Pernambuco, Barbados, or Martinique and later Jamaica and Saint Domingue— all expanding centers of New World staple production. But transporting them to these hubs of the plantation economy posed dangers, which American planters well understood. The distinguishing characteristics of

Atlantic creoles—their linguistic dexterity, cultural plasticity, and social agility—were precisely those qualities that the sugar planters of the New World feared the most. For their labor force, planters desired youth and strength, not experience and wisdom. Too much knowledge might be subversive to the good order of the plantation.

Simply put, men and women who understood the operations of the Atlantic system, including the slave trade, were too dangerous to be trusted in the human tinderboxes created by the sugar revolution. Rejected by the most prosperous New World regimes, Atlantic creoles were frequently exiled to marginal slave societies where would-be slaveowners, unable to compete with plantation magnates, snapped up those whom the grandees had disparaged as "refuse" for reasons of age, illness, or criminality. And in the seventeenth century, few New World slave societies were more marginal than those of mainland North America.[16] Atlantic creoles were among the first Africans transported to the mainland. They became black America's charter generations.

Atlantic creoles began arriving in the Americas in the sixteenth century. Some accompanied the conquistadors, marching with Balboa, Cortés, De Soto, and Pizarro. Others traveled on their own, as sailors and interpreters in both the transatlantic and African trades. Yet others crisscrossed the ocean several times, as did Jerónimo, a Wolof slave, who was sold from Lisbon to Cartagena and from Cartagena to Murica, where he was purchased by a churchman who sent him to Valencia. A "*mulâtress*" wife and her three slaves followed her French husband, a gunsmith in the employ of the French Compagnie des Indes, from Gorée to Louisiana, when he was deported for criminal activities.[17] Wherever they went, Atlantic creoles employed their distinctive language, planted their unique institutions of the creole community, and propagated their special outlook. Within the Portuguese and Spanish empires, they created an intercontinental web of *cofradias,* so that by the seventeenth century the network of black religious brotherhoods stretched from Lisbon to São Tomé, Angola, and Brazil.[18] Although no comparable institutional linkages existed in the Anglo- and Franco-American worlds, there were numerous informal connections between black people in New England and Virginia, Louisiana, and Saint Domingue. Like their African counterparts, Atlantic creoles of European, South American, and Caribbean origins also became part of black America's charter generations.

NEW NETHERLAND

The Dutch were the main conduit for carrying such men and women to the North American mainland in the early seventeenth century. Juan (Jan, in some accounts) Rodrigues, a sailor of mixed racial ancestry who had shipped from Hispaniola in 1613 on the *Jonge Tobias,* offers a case in point. The ship, one of several Dutch merchant vessels vying for the North American fur trade before the founding of the Dutch West India Company, anchored on the Hudson River sometime in 1612 and deposited Rodrigues either as an independent trader or, more likely, as ship's agent. When a rival Dutch ship arrived the following year, Rodrigues promptly shifted his allegiance, informing its captain that, despite his color, "he was a free man." He served his new employer as translator and agent, collecting furs from the native population. When the captain of the *Jonge Tobias* returned to the Hudson River, Rodrigues changed his allegiance yet again, only to be denounced as a turncoat and "that black rascal." Barely escaping with his life, he took up residence with some friendly Indians.[19]

Other people of color followed Juan Rodrigues to Dutch America, especially to the small settlement on the Hudson. Some of these Atlantic creoles arrived as slaves, particularly following the Dutch victories over the Portuguese on the west coast of Africa in the 1640s, the subsequent wars, then civil strife, and finally Portuguese restoration.[20] While such slaves might be sent anywhere in the Dutch empire between New Netherland and Pernambuco, officers of the West India Company in New Amsterdam made known their preference for such creoles—deeming "Negroes who had been 12 or 13 years in the West Indies" to be "a better sort of Negroes."[21] A perusal of the names scattered through archival remains of New Netherland reveals something of the nature of this transatlantic transfer: Paulo d'Angola and Anthony Portuguese, Pedro Negretto and Francisco Negro, Simon Congo and Jan Guinea, Van St. Thomas and

Francisco Cartagena, Claes de Neger and Assento Angola, and—perhaps most telling—Carla Criole, Jan Creoli, and Christoffel Crioell.[22]

These names trace the tumultuous experience that propelled their bearers across the Atlantic and into slavery in the New World. They suggest that whatever tragedy befell them, Atlantic creoles did not arrive in the New World as deracinated chattels stripped of their past and without resources to meet the future. Unlike those who followed them into slavery in succeeding generations, transplanted creoles were not designated by diminutives, or derisively named after ancient notables or classical deities, or burdened with tags more appropriate to barnyard animals than to human beings. Instead, their names provided concrete evidence that they carried a good deal more than their dignity to the Americas.

To such men and women, New Amsterdam—a fortified port controlled by the Dutch West India Company—was not radically different from Elmina or Luanda, save for its smaller size and colder climate. Its population was a farrago of petty traders, artisans, merchants, soldiers, and corporate functionaries, all scrambling for status in a frontier milieu that demanded intercultural exchange. On the tip of Manhattan Island, Atlantic creoles rubbed elbows with sailors of various nationalities, Native Americans with diverse tribal allegiances, and pirates and privateers who professed neither nationality nor allegiance. In the absence of a staple crop, their work—building fortifications, hunting and trapping, tending fields and domestic animals, and transporting merchandise of all sorts—did not set them apart from workers of European descent, who often labored alongside them. Such encounters made a working knowledge of the creole tongue as valuable on the North American coast as in Africa. Whereas a later generation of transplanted Africans would be linguistically isolated and de-skilled by the process of enslavement, Atlantic creoles found themselves very much at home in their new environment. Rather than losing their skills, they discovered that the value of their gift for intercultural negotiation appreciated. The transatlantic journey did not break creole communities; it only transported them to other sites.

Along the edges of the North American continent, creoles found that their cultural and social marginality was an asset. Slaveholders learned that the ability of creoles to negotiate with the diverse populace of seventeenth-century North America was as valuable as their labor, perhaps more so. While their owners employed creoles' skills on their own behalf, creoles did the same for themselves, trading their knowledge for a place in the still undefined social order. In 1665, when Jan Angola, accused of stealing wood, could not address the New Amsterdam court in Dutch, he was ordered to return the following day with "Domingo the Negro as interpreter," an act familiar to Atlantic creoles in Elmina, Lisbon, San Salvador, or Cap Françis.[23]

To be sure, slavery bore heavily on Atlantic creoles in the New World. As in Africa and Europe, it was a system of exploitation, subservience, and debasement that rested on force. Yet Atlantic creoles were familiar with servitude in forms ranging from unbridled exploitation to corporate familialism. They had known free people to be enslaved, and they had known slaves to be liberated; the boundary between slavery and freedom on the African coast was permeable. Servitude generally did not prevent men and women from marrying, acquiring property (slaves included), enjoying a modest prosperity, and eventually being incorporated into the host society. Creoles transported across the Atlantic had no reason to suspect they could not do the same in the New World. If the stigma of servitude, physical labor, uncertain lineage, and alien religion branded them as outsiders, there were many others in North America—men and women of unblemished European pedigree prominent among them—who shared those taints. That black people could and occasionally did hold slaves and servants and employ white people suggested that race—like lineage and religion—was just one of many markers in the social order.

The experience of Atlantic creoles provided strategies for containing the abuse and degradation of slavery and even winning freedom. Although the routes to social advancement were many, they generally involved re-attachment to a community through the agency of an influential patron or, better yet, an established institution that could broker a slave's incorporation into the larger society.[24] Freedom was measured by the degree of communal integration, not by ability to secure individual autonomy. Along the coast of Africa, Atlantic creoles often identified with the ap-

pendages of European or African power—whether international mercantile corporations or local chieftains—in hopes of relieving the stigma of
otherness, be it enslavement, bastard birth, paganism, or race. They employed this strategy repeatedly in mainland North America, as they tried
to clear the hurdles of social and cultural difference and establish a place
for themselves. By linking themselves to the most important edifices of
the nascent European-American societies, Atlantic creoles struggled to become part of a social order where exclusion or otherness—not subordination—could threaten all other gains. To be inferior within the sharply
stratified world of the seventeenth-century Atlantic was a common and
therefore understandable experience; to be the "other" and excluded posed
unparalleled dangers.

The black men and women who entered New Netherland between
1626 and the English conquest in 1664 exemplified the ability of people of
African descent to integrate themselves into mainland society during the
first century of settlement, despite their status as slaves and the contempt
of the colony's rulers. Far more than any other mainland colony during
the first half of the seventeenth century, New Netherland rested on slave
labor. The prosperity of the Dutch metropole and the opportunities presented to ambitious men and women in the far-flung Dutch empire denied New Netherland its share of free Dutch immigrants and limited its
access to indentured servants. To populate the colony, the West India
Company scoured the Atlantic basin for settlers, recruiting German Lu-
therans, French Huguenots, and Sephardic Jews. But these newcomers
did little to satisfy the colony's need for laborers. As a result, by 1640
about one hundred blacks were living in New Amsterdam, composing
roughly 30 percent of the port's population and a still larger portion of the
labor force. Their proportion diminished over the course of the seventeenth century but remained substantial. At the time of the English conquest, some three hundred slaves made up one fifth of the population of
New Amsterdam, giving New Netherland the largest urban slave population on mainland North America.[25]

The diverse needs of the Dutch mercantile economy strengthened the
hand of Atlantic creoles in New Netherland during the initial period of

settlement. Caring only for short-term profits, the company, the largest slaveholder in the colony, allowed its slaves to live independently and work on their own in return for a stipulated amount of labor and an annual tribute. Company slaves thus enjoyed a large measure of independence, which they used to master the Dutch language, trade freely, accumulate property, identify with Dutch Reformed Christianity, and—most important—establish families. During the first generation, some twenty-five couples took their vows in the Dutch Reformed Church in New Amsterdam. When children arrived, their parents baptized them as well. Participation in the religious life of New Netherland provides but one indicator of how quickly Atlantic creoles mastered the social intricacies of the new continent. In 1635, less than ten years after the arrival of the first black people, black New Netherlanders understood enough about the organization of the colony and the operation of the company to travel to the company's headquarters in Holland and petition for wages.[26]

Many slaves gained their freedom. This was not easy in New Netherland, although there was no legal proscription on manumission. Indeed, gaining freedom was nearly impossible for slaves owned privately and difficult even for those owned by the West India Company. The company valued its slaves and was willing to liberate only the elderly, whom it viewed as a liability. Even when manumitting such slaves, the company exacted an annual tribute from adults and retained ownership of their children. The latter practice elicited protests from both blacks and whites in New Amsterdam. To the West India Company's former slaves, who were unable to pass their new status on to their children, this "half-freedom" appeared to be no freedom at all.[27]

Manumission in New Netherland was calculated to benefit slave owners, not slaves. Its purposes were to spur slaves to greater exertion and to relieve slaveowners of the cost of supporting the elderly, whose infirmities rendered them more burden than asset. Yet, however compromised the attainment of freedom, slaves did what was necessary to secure it. They accepted the company's terms and agreed to pay its corporate tribute. But they bridled at the fact that their children's status would not follow their own. Half-free blacks pressed the West India Company to make their status hereditary. Hearing rumors that baptism would assure freedom to their children, they pressed their claims to church membership. A Dutch prelate complained of the "worldly and perverse aims" of black people who "wanted nothing else than to deliver their children from bodily slavery, without striving for piety and Christian virtues."[28] Although conversion never guaranteed freedom in New Netherland, many half-free blacks achieved their goal. By the time of the English conquest, about one black person in five had achieved freedom in New Amsterdam.[29] Some free people of African descent prospered, and building on small gifts of land that the West India Company provided as freedom dues, a few entered the landholding class.[30]

By the middle of the seventeenth century, black people participated in almost every aspect of life in New Netherland. In addition to marrying and baptizing their children in the Dutch Reformed Church, they sued and were sued in Dutch courts and fought alongside Dutch militiamen against the colony's enemies. Black men and women—slave as well as free—traded independently and accumulated property. Black people also began to develop a variety of institutions that reflected their unique experience and served their special needs. They stood as godparents to one another's children, suggesting close family ties, and they rarely called on white people—owners or not—to serve in this capacity. At times, established black families legally adopted orphaned black children, further knitting the black community together in a web of constructed kinship.[31] The patterns of residence, marriage, church membership, and godparentage speak not only to the material success of Atlantic creoles but also to their ability to create a community among themselves.

THE CHESAPEAKE

If the likes of Paulo d'Angola and Anthony Portuguese, Pedro Negretto and Francisco Cartagena made their presence felt in the Dutch port of New Amsterdam, they also could be found in the colonies to the south where the English ruled and the population was overwhelmingly rural.

The story of Anthony Johnson, sold to the English at Jamestown in

1621 as Antonio a Negro, reveals something of the history of Atlantic creoles in the Chesapeake region. During the dozen years following his arrival, Antonio labored on the Bennett family's plantation on Virginia's middle peninsula, where he was among the few who survived the 1622 Indian raid that all but destroyed the colony, and where he later earned an official commendation for his "hard labor and known service." His loyalty and industry also won the favor of the Bennetts, who became Antonio's patron as well as his owner, perhaps because worthies like Antonio were hard to find among the rough, hard-bitten, often sickly men who comprised the mass of servants and slaves in the region. Whatever the source of the Bennetts' largesse, they allowed Antonio to farm independently while still a slave, marry, and baptize his children. Eventually, he and his family exited bondage. Once free, Antonio a Negro anglicized his name to Anthony Johnson, which was so familiar to English speakers that no one could doubt his identification with the colony's rulers.[32]

Johnson, his wife Mary, and their children—who numbered four by 1640—followed their benefactor to the eastern shore of Virginia, where the Bennett clan had established itself as a leading family and where the Johnson family began to farm on its own. In 1651 Anthony Johnson earned a 250-acre headright, a substantial estate for any Virginian, let alone a former slave. Johnson's son John did even better than his father, receiving a patent for 550 acres, and another son, Richard, owned a 100-acre estate. When Anthony Johnson's plantation burned to the ground in 1653, he petitioned the county court for relief. Reminding authorities that he and his wife were long-time residents of the eastern shore and that "their hard labors and knowne services for obtayneing their livelihood were well known," he requested and was granted a special abatement of his taxes.

Like other men of substance, Johnson and his sons farmed independently, held slaves, and left their heirs sizable estates. As established members of their community, they enjoyed rights in common with other free men and frequently employed the law to protect themselves and advance their interests. Still, when Anthony Johnson's slave, a black man named John Casar (sometimes Casor, Cassaugh, or Cazara), claimed his freedom and gained sanctuary with Robert and George Parker, two neighboring white planters, Johnson did not immediately attempt to retrieve his property. The Parkers had already exhibited considerable animus toward the Johnson family, accusing John Johnson of "fornication and other enormities." Antagonizing rancorous white men of the planter class was a hazardous business, even if Johnson could prove they had conspired to lure John Casar from his household. At length, however, Anthony Johnson decided to act. He took the Parkers to court and won Casar's return, along with damages against the Parkers.[33]

Johnson and the Parkers wrestled over Casar because labor—whether European, Native American, or African in origin—was the key to success on the mainland, as ambitious men scrambled for status, land, and yet more labor. In their rush to seize the main chance, planters might trample their workers, but they made little distinction among their subordinates by age, sex, nation, or race. While the advantages of this peculiar brand of equality may have been lost on its beneficiaries, it was precisely the shared labor regimen of African, European, and Native American that allowed some black men like Anthony Johnson to escape bondage and join the scramble that characterized life in the seventeenth-century Chesapeake.[34]

The Johnsons were not unique in the region. Creoles like John Francisco, Bashaw Ferdinando (or Farnando), Emanuel Driggus (sometimes Drighouse; probably Rodriggus), Anthony Longo (perhaps Loango), and Francisco a Negroe (soon to become Francis, then Frank, Payne and finally Paine) could be found throughout the region and most especially on the eastern shore. The number remained tiny. In 1665 the free black population of Virginia's Northampton and Accomack counties amounted to less than twenty adults and perhaps an equal number of children. But as the black population of the region was itself small, totaling no more than 300 on the eastern shore and perhaps 1,700 in all of Maryland and Virginia, the proportion of black people enjoying freedom was substantial. And, perhaps more importantly, it was growing. In Northampton County, free people of African descent made up about one fifth of the black population at mid-century, rising to nearly 30 percent in 1668, not radically different from New Amsterdam.[35]

As elsewhere, Atlantic creoles in the Chesapeake ascended the social order and exhibited a sure-handed understanding of the local hierarchy and the complex dynamics of patron-client relations. Although still in bondage, they began to acquire the property, skills, and personal connections that became their mark throughout the Atlantic world. They worked provision grounds, kept livestock, traded independently, and married white women as often as they married black.[36] More important, they found advocates among the propertied classes—often their owners—and identified themselves with the colony's most important institutions, registering their marriages, baptisms, and children's godparents in the Anglican Church and their property in the county courthouse. They sued and were sued in local courts, and they petitioned the colonial legislatures and governors.[37]

The experience of Atlantic creoles in the Dutch colony of New Netherland and the English colonies of Virginia and Maryland was repeated across mainland North America prior to the advent of the plantation. But it was never repeated in quite the same way, so that while the story of the charter generations had one melody, it was played in many different keys.

In places as different as Canada and lowcountry South Carolina, Atlantic creoles hardly had a chance to make an imprint. Mathieu Da Costa, a man of African descent sometimes in the employ of the Dutch and sometimes the French, may have alighted in Port Royal on the St. Lawrence River in the first years of the eighteenth century. But his visit was so brief that historians are still searching for evidence of his presence.[38] The charter generation had a more substantial presence in pioneer Carolina, but the rapid advent of large-scale rice production truncated its development there; Atlantic creoles had hardly a chance to leave their mark on the lowcountry.

THE LOWER MISSISSIPPI VALLEY

In the lower Mississippi Valley, however, the failure of the plantation revolution extended the charter generation's life to nearly a century. Atlantic creoles entered the great valley much as they entered the seaboard colonies, irregularly, with none of the system that characterized the international trade. Perrine, a black cook, arrived with other *engagés* from Lorient in 1720. Raphael Bernard, the black manservant of a wealthy French emigré, followed his master from France for 200 francs and the promise of a new suit. When his owner failed to respect the bargain and abused him to boot, he sued and recovered his back wages. John Mingo, a fugitive from South Carolina, traveled half a continent to Louisiana, where a patron assisted him in securing legal freedom, a small plot of land, and the right to purchase a slave woman whom he had taken for his wife. When Mingo quarreled with his erstwhile benefactor over the terms of the arrangement, he also sued, and, although his larger claim was disallowed, Mingo won the right to purchase his wife. Louis Congo, a slave whose name suggests his origins, gained his freedom playing upon the colony's need for an executioner. In return for assuming that gruesome task, his employer freed Louis Congo and allowed him to live with his wife (although she was not liberated, as he had demanded) on land of his own choosing.[39]

Perhaps the best known of these Atlantic creoles was Samba, a Bambara.[40] Working for the Compagnie des Indes as an interpreter (*maître de langue*) at Galam, upstream from St. Louis on the Senegal River during the 1720s, Samba Bambara—as he appears in the records—traveled freely along the river between St. Louis, Galam, and Fort d'Arguin. By 1722 he received permission from the compagnie for his family to reside in St. Louis. When his wife dishonored him, Samba Bambara called on his corporate employer to exile her from St. Louis and thereby bring order to his domestic life. But despite his reliance on the company, Samba Bambara allegedly joined with African captives in a revolt at Fort d'Arguin, and, when the revolt was quelled, he was enslaved and deported. Significantly, he was not sold to the emerging plantation colony of Saint Domingue, where the sugar revolution stimulated a nearly insatiable demand for slaves. Instead, French officials at St. Louis exiled Samba Bambara to Louisiana, a marginal military outpost far outside the major transatlantic sea lanes and with no staple agricultural economy.

Just as the port of New Amsterdam shared much with Elmina, the port of New Orleans on the Mississippi mirrored St. Louis on the Senegal in the 1720s. As the headquarters of the Compagnie des Indes in mainland North America, the town housed a familiar collection of corporate functionaries, traders, and craftsmen, along with growing numbers of French *engagés* and African slaves. New Orleans was frequented by Indians, whose canoes supplied it much as African canoemen supplied St. Louis. Its taverns and back-alley retreats were meeting places for sailors of various nationalities, Canadian *courreurs de bois,* and soldiers—the latter no more pleased to be stationed on the North American frontier than their counterparts welcomed assignment to an African factory. Indeed, the soldiers' status in this rough frontier community differed little from that on the coast of Africa.[41]

Suggesting something of the symmetry of the Atlantic world, New Orleans was no alien terrain to Samba Bambara, save for the flora and fauna. Despite the long transatlantic journey, once in the New World, he recovered much of what he had lost in the Old, although he never escaped slavery. Like the Atlantic creoles who alighted in New Netherland and Jamestown, Samba Bambara employed skills on the coast of North America that he had learned on the coast of Africa. Drawing on his knowledge of French, various African languages, and the ubiquitous creole tongue, the rebel regained his position with his old patron, the Compagnie des Indes, this time as an interpreter swearing on the Christian Bible to translate faithfully before Louisiana's Superior Council. Later, he became an overseer on the largest "concession" in the colony, the company's massive plantation across the river from New Orleans.[42]

Like his counterparts in New Amsterdam, Samba Bambara succeeded in a rugged frontier slave society by following the familiar lines of patronage to the doorstep of his corporate employer. Although the constraints of slavery eventually turned him against the company on the Mississippi, just as he had turned against it on the Senegal River, his ability to transfer his knowledge and skills from the Old World to the New, despite the weight of enslavement, suggests that the history of Atlantic creoles in New Amsterdam—their ability to escape slavery, form families, secure property, and claim a degree of independence—was no anomaly.

Much like their counterparts on the seaboard, Samba Bambara, Louis

Congo, John Mingo, Raphael Bernard, and Perrine understood their rights, and—given their familiarity with the Atlantic world, its languages, religions, and legal codes—they did not hesitate to exercise them. In this the French *Code Noir* provided a small assist. This compilation of laws and regulations was first promulgated in 1685, ostensibly to protect black slaves in French colonies from abuse, and was reissued in 1724 to cover Louisiana. The Louisiana *Code* was weighted against manumission and discouraged self-purchase. It required manumitted slaves to defer to their former owners, punished free black people more severely than white ones, and barred interracial marriage. Still, free people of African descent enjoyed many of the same legal rights as other free people, including the right to petition. People of color—like Raphael Bernard and John Mingo—employed those rights to advance their interests, much as their counterparts in Dutch New Netherland and English Virginia did. Occasionally they used the law to improve their collective status. During the 1720s, they successfully petitioned for the removal of a special head tax on free blacks and sued individual white colonists for transgressions of various sorts.[43]

The presence of Atlantic creoles, eager for freedom and knowledgeable in the ways of the law, frustrated Louisiana planters, impatient to launch their own plantation revolution. During the 1720s, after more than two decades of failure, they had at last succeeded in muscling Indians off some of the best land. Having imported some five thousand slaves directly from Africa and established new discipline on the estates, their most fervent aspiration was near realization. But an alliance of Natchez Indians and African slaves smashed the nascent plantation complex. The staple economy based on tobacco and indigo collapsed, the slave trade was closed, the Compagnie des Indes surrendered its charter, and Louisiana resumed its position of marginality in the Atlantic world.

The Natchez rebellion and the subsequent failure of the plantation revolution did not overthrow slavery, but it breathed new life into the charter generation in Louisiana. As the market economy foundered, the slaves' economy expanded, along with the subsidiary rights to travel freely, trade independently, hire their own time, and hold property—rights with no foundation in law but universally accepted in practice. Through the middle years of the eighteenth century, the slaves' independent production played a larger and larger role in the economic life of the colony. Before long, black people began to exit slavery, often taking up the role of soldiers in defense of the white minority. The free black population grew slowly under the French, who remained fearful of black freedom. But after the Spanish took control of Louisiana in 1763, the slaves' access to freedom via manumission and self-purchase expanded, and the charter generation found themselves on more secure, if still shaky, ground.

Not until the great rebellion in Saint Domingue eliminated the world's largest sugar producer and allowed Louisiana planters to transform themselves into plantation moguls was the charter generation dismantled. Though a mere blink in the history of Canada and South Carolina, the charter generation had lasted nearly a century in the lower Mississippi Valley.

FLORIDA

Whereas the history of Louisiana documents the longevity of the charter generations, the history of Florida suggests something of their resilience. The very changes that truncated the charter generation in South Carolina and compressed its history into a few decades at the end of the seventeenth century assured its survival—even its prosperity—in Florida.

The rapid expansion of the English settlement in South Carolina deepened the fears of Spanish officials in Florida. In their search for allies against the growing menace to the north, they could find only one reliable group of friends—their own slaves and those of the Carolinians. Atlantic creoles, appreciative of the fine differences between European Protestants in South Carolina and European Catholics in Florida, were also quick to recognize that the enemy of their enemy could be a friend. An alliance was sealed which spurred the growth of creole society in Florida.

Spanish raiders took the first steps toward that alliance in 1686 when, in assaulting Edisto Island, they carried off some dozen slaves. The governor of South Carolina demanded their return, along with those "who run

dayly into your towns," but Spanish officials peremptorily refused. Instead, they put the fugitives to work for wages, instructed them in the ten-
ets of Catholicism, and allowed them to marry—in short, providing runaways with all the accoutrements of freedom except its legal title.[44]

That was quick in coming. In 1693 the Spanish Crown offered freedom
to all fugitives—men as well as women—who converted to Catholicism.
Thereafter, Spanish officials in Florida provided "Liberty and Protection"
to all slaves who reached St. Augustine, and they consistently refused to
return runaways who took refuge in their colony.[45]

The broad promise of liberty was not always kept, however. Some fugitives were sold in St. Augustine to local planters and others were shipped
to Havana. Nonetheless, the promise itself transformed Florida into a
magnet for Carolina slaves. As the news spread, fugitives fled to Florida,
often requesting baptism into the "True Faith." Spanish officials delighted
in the former slaves' choice of religion, smugly observing that they "want
to be Christians and that their masters did not want to let them learn the
doctrine nor be Catholics."[46]

But much as they might celebrate the runaways' desire for the true religion, Spanish officials did not allow their enthusiasm to blind them to the
special skills these Atlantic creoles carried. Their knowledge of the countryside, linguistic facility, and ability to negotiate between the lowland's
warring factions in a manner their forebears had made famous throughout
the Atlantic littoral made the fugitives ideal allies against the English enemy. Former Carolina slaves no sooner arrived in Florida than they were
enlisted in the militia and sent to raid the plantations of their old owners,
assisting black men and women—many of them friends and sometimes
family—in escaping bondage. When these periodic raids boiled over into
outright warfare, the runaways were incorporated into the black militia,
fighting against the English in the Yamasee War and defending St. Augustine against an English assault in which the invaders almost reached the
walls of the city.[47]

The stream of fugitives grew with the expansion of slavery in South
Carolina during the first decades of the eighteenth century.[48] Armed with

the profits of rice production, South Carolina slaveholders entered the international slave market, purchasing laborers by the boatload. Charles Town became the largest mainland slave market, as Africans disembarked on its wharves by the thousands. Generally deemed "Angolans," most were drawn from deep in the interior of central Africa. But some were Atlantic Creoles, with experience in the coastal towns of Cabinda, Loango, and Mpinda. Many spoke Portuguese, which, as one Carolinian noted, was "as near Spanish as Scotch is to English," and some were practicing Catholics.

At the end of the fifteenth century, when the royal house of Kongo converted to Christianity, Catholicism in various syncretic forms entered broadly into the life of the Kingdom of the Kongo. During the next two centuries it spread through the efforts of Portuguese missionaries and, later, an indigenous Kongolese priesthood. Leaders of the Kongolese church corresponded with Rome and traveled to Europe to receive the endorsement of Christ's vicar. Seeing no reason to surrender their own native deities, converts incorporated them into the Christian belief system, giving Kongolese Catholicism its unique character.[49]

Despite these embellishments, the Kongolese were knowledgeable believers who knew their catechism, the pantheon of saints, and the symbols and rituals of the Cross. The arrival of these children of Christ in Charles Town had little effect on South Carolina slaveholders, who doubtless would have disapproved of their brand of Christianity if they noticed it at all. But if planters paid little attention to the beliefs of saltwater slaves as they put them to work in the rice fields, the presence of a Catholic sanctuary less than three hundred miles south of Charles Town did not escape the slaves' notice.

No doubt the Church's presence in Florida made Spanish St. Augustine even more attractive to enslaved Catholics. During the 1720s and 1730s, they and other slaves—many newly arrived in South Carolina—defected in increasing numbers. In 1733 Spanish authorities reiterated their offer of freedom, prohibiting the sale of fugitives and commending black militiamen for their service in the struggle against the British. Five years later, the governor requested that the fugitives previously sold to Havana be returned to Florida and freed. Word of the new edicts may have enticed others to flee the Carolinas.[50]

In 1739 a group of African slaves initiated a mass exodus, slaying several dozen whites who stood in their path. Pursued by South Carolina militiamen, the defectors confronted their owners' soldiers in pitched battles at Stono, only fifty miles from the Florida line.[51] Although most of the Stono rebels were captured or killed, others successfully escaped to Florida. Once they arrived, it became difficult for their owners to retrieve them, as Spanish officials would not surrender their co-religionists. The escapees, who had already been baptized and knew their catechism, were quickly integrated into black life in St. Augustine, although they prayed, as one Miguel Domingo told a Spanish priest, in Kikongo.[52]

The former Carolina slaves did more than pray. As their numbers grew, black militiamen took an ever more active role in the border warfare against their former owners. The former slaves' presence and the Spaniards' promise of freedom, military commissions, and even "A Coat Faced with Velvet," augmented the small but steady stream of runaways to Florida. Among those enlisted in the militia was one Francisco Menéndez, a former slave who may have adopted the name of one of St. Augustine's most powerful magistrates. Menéndez's heroics in repelling an English attack on St. Augustine in 1728 had won a special commendation from the Spanish Crown, along with the promise of freedom. When he was not freed, Menéndez and many of his fellow militiamen petitioned the governor of Florida and then the Bishop of Cuba for their liberty, which they eventually received.[53]

To better protect St. Augustine, the governor of Florida established a black settlement to the north of the city. Gracia Real de Santa Teresa de Mose, a walled fort surrounding some ramshackle huts, was both a barrier against another English incursion and an agricultural settlement. The governor assigned a priest to instruct the newly arrived slaves and resident free blacks. Although the Spanish military supervised the town, the governor placed Menéndez in charge. Whatever their agricultural objectives and religious aspirations, the black men and women stationed at Mose understood that their future was tied to the strategic mission of the settlement. They pledged to "shed their last drop of blood in defense of the Great Crown of Spain and the Holy Faith."[54]

Under Captain Menéndez, Mose became the center of black life in colonial Florida, as well as a base from which former slaves—sometimes joined by Indians—raided South Carolina. The settlement of some one hundred free black men and women was also the last line of defense against English assaults on St. Augustine, which came with a vengeance following the Stono rebellion. A bloody struggle at Mose eventually forced the black population to evacuate, and Spanish forces would not recapture the fort until reinforcements arrived from Cuba. However devastating to the fort itself, the militia's extraordinary bravery won Menéndez yet another commendation, this one from the governor of Florida, who declared that the black captain "had distinguished himself in the establishment, and cultivation of Mose."[55]

Menéndez was quick to capitalize on his fame. Writing in the language of patronage, he reminded the king that his "sole object was to defend the Holy Evangel and sovereignty of the Crown" and requested remuneration for the "loyalty, zeal and love I have always demonstrated in the royal service." In his petition to the king, Menéndez requested a stipend worthy of a militia captain.[56] To secure his royal reward, Menéndez took to the sea as a privateer, hoping eventually to reach Spain and collect his due.

Instead, a British ship captured the famous "Signior Capitano Francisco." Although his captors stretched him out on a cannon and threatened him with emasculation for alleged atrocities during the siege of Mose, Menéndez had become too valuable to mutilate. The British sailors gave him two hundred lashes, soaked his wounds in brine, and commended him to a doctor "to take care of his Sore A-se." Menéndez was then carried before a British admiralty court on New Providence Island, where "this Francisco that Cursed Seed of Cain" was ordered sold into slavery. Yet even this misadventure could not undo the irrepressible Menéndez. By 1752, perhaps ransomed out of bondage, he was back at his familiar post in Mose.[57]

While Menéndez sought his fortune at sea, black men and women, joined by new arrivals—many of them Atlantic creoles from Spain, Cuba, and Africa—entered more fully into the life of St. Augustine. Free blacks continued to work for the Crown as trackers, soldiers, sailors, and privateers. Others worked independently as artisans, laborers, and domestics. They purchased property and, upon occasion, assisted others out of bondage, steadily increasing the proportion of black people who enjoyed freedom.[58]

Within St. Augustine, Florida's charter generation expanded in new directions. The disproportionately male former fugitives intermarried with the Native American population and newly arriving slaves from Mexico, Cuba, and Spain. As their Atlantic connections grew, old hands and new arrivals created a tight community whose lives revolved around the militia and the church. In 1746 black people composed about one quarter of St. Augustine's population of 1,500. Like the charter generations in the Chesapeake and New Netherland, they sanctified their marriages and baptized their children in the established church, choosing godparents from among both the white and black congregants. That the church was Catholic rather than Anglican or Dutch Reformed was less important than that membership knit black people together in bonds of kinship and certified incorporation into the larger community. Militia membership—with its uniforms, flags, and martial rituals—served a similar purpose by amplifying communication between black people and the colonial state. Much like Atlantic creoles elsewhere on the mainland, Florida's charter generation became skilled in pulling the lever of patronage, in this case royal authority. Declaring themselves "vassals of the King and deserving of royal protection," they continually put themselves in the forefront of service to the Spanish Crown with the expectations that the Crown would reciprocate.[59]

Hoped-for rewards were not always forthcoming, as all "vassals of the King" were not equally favored. Beginning in 1749, a new governor of Florida forced black people in St. Augustine to return to Mose, much against their will, as they had enjoyed the cosmopolitan life of the city, where their ability to converse in several European, Indian, and African languages gave them credentials as cultural brokers in a multicultural society.[60] Although protests about the primitive conditions at Mose and pleas for permission to return to St. Augustine went unanswered, Spanish officials did not forget the colony's black defenders—at least as long as the English threat in South Carolina and later Georgia (established in 1732) loomed over Florida and the Spanish-controlled islands to the south. In 1763, when the English wrested control of Florida from Spain, black colonists retreated to Cuba with His Majesty's subjects, where the Crown granted them land, tools, a small subsidy, and a slave for each of the colony's leaders.[61] The evacuation shattered the achievement of creole culture in Spanish Florida, however. Far more than their counterparts in the Chesapeake or the northern colonies, Florida's charter generations had been incorporated as full—if yet unequal—participants in the life of mainland society. With the English occupation, South Carolina planters moved south en masse, bringing with them the social order of the plantation and obliterating the century-old history of the society that Atlantic creoles had created in Spanish Florida.

Atlantic creoles' ability to trade freely, profess Christianity, gain access to the law, secure freedom, and enjoy a modest prosperity shaped popular understanding of black life in the era prior to the plantation. But the possibilities of large-scale commodity production threatened the open, porous slave system that developed in the early years of European and African settlement. It would soon sweep the charter generations away, leaving only fragments of their history upon which future Americans might ponder a world that once was.

2

PLANTATION GENERATIONS

Mainland
North America
ca. 1763

N

MASSACHUSETTS

NEW YORK

NEW
HAMPSHIRE

Boston
MASSACHUSETTS
Providence • Newport
CONNECTICUT RHODE ISLAND

PENNSYLVANIA

New York

NEW
JERSEY
Philadelphia

Annapolis
Alexandria

DELAWARE

MARYLAND

VIRGINIA

Williamsburg
Norfolk

Great
Dismal
Swamp

NORTH CAROLINA

SOUTH
CAROLINA

GEORGIA

Wilmington

Georgetown
Charles Town

LOUISIANA
(SPAIN)

Savannah

Natchez
Pointe
Coupée

(CLAIMED BY
SPAIN & GEORGIA)
Mobile

WEST FLORIDA
Pensacola

Baton Rouge
New Orleans

St. Augustine
EAST FLORIDA

ATLANTIC OCEAN

GULF OF MEXICO

THE FIRST BLACK PEOPLE to arrive in mainland North America bore—or soon adopted—names like Anthony Johnson, Paulo d'Angola, Juan Rodrigues, Francisco Menéndez, and Samba Bambara. Although enslaved, they established families, professed Christianity, and employed the law with great facility. They traveled widely and enjoyed access to the great ports and from there the larger Atlantic world. Throughout the mainland, they spoke the language of their enslaver or the ubiquitous creole lingua franca. They participated in the exchange economies of the pioneer settlements and accumulated property, gaining reputations as shrewd and knowledgeable traders in the manner of creoles throughout the Atlantic littoral. A considerable portion of these first arrivals—fully one-fifth in New Amsterdam, St. Augustine, and Virginia's eastern shore—gained their freedom. Free men often served as soldiers, and some attained modest privilege and authority.

Their successors were not nearly as fortunate. They worked harder and died earlier. Their family life was truncated, and few men and women claimed ties of blood or marriage. They knew—and wanted to know—

little about Christianity and European jurisprudence. They had but small opportunities to participate independently in exchange economies and rarely accumulated property. Most lived on large estates deep in the countryside, cut off from the larger Atlantic world. Few escaped slavery. Only rarely were they allowed to bear arms, let alone serve in organized militia. Their names reflected the contempt in which their owners held them. Most answered to some European diminutive—Jack and Sukey in the English colonies, Pedro and Francisca in places under Spanish rule, and Jean and Marie in the French dominions. As if to emphasize their inferiority, some were tagged with names usually assigned to barnyard animals. Others were designated with the name of some ancient deity or great personage like Hercules or Cato as a kind of cosmic jest: the most insignificant with the greatest of name. Whatever they were called, they rarely bore surnames—marks of lineage that their owners sought to obliterate and of adulthood that they would not tolerate.[1]

The degradation of black life in mainland North America had many sources, but the largest was the growth of the plantation, a radically different form of social organization and commercial production controlled by a class of men whose appetite for labor was nearly insatiable. Drawing power from the metropolitan state (England, the Netherlands, France, and Spain), planters transformed societies with slaves into slave societies in mainland North America. In the process, they redefined the meaning of race, investing color—white and black—with a far greater weight in defining status than heretofore. Blackness and whiteness took on new meaning.

The plantation revolution came to mainland North America in fits and starts. Beginning in the late seventeenth century in the Chesapeake, planters moved unevenly across the continent over the next century and a half, first to lowland South Carolina in the early eighteenth century and then, after failing to establish a plantation regime in the colonies north of the Chesapeake, to the lower Mississippi Valley. During the nineteenth century, the plantation revolution swept across the interior of the southern United States. By the time it had run its course, slave societies dedicated to cultivating tobacco in the Chesapeake, rice in lowcountry South Carolina and Georgia, sugar in the lower Mississippi Valley, and cotton across the breadth of the southern interior stood at the heart of the nation's society and economy.

The trajectory of the plantation revolution was always the same, although the variations produced strikingly different slave societies. The Chesapeake set the pattern for the mainland and also revealed how time and circumstance gave slavery a new meaning.

THE CHESAPEAKE

The new regime arrived in the Chesapeake with shot and cannon. The transformation from a society with slaves to a slave society began when in 1676 planters smashed Nathaniel Bacon's motley army of small holders and indentured servants, black and white.[2] Following their victory, planters slowly replaced indentured servants with slaves as their main source of plantation labor. Caring little about the origins, color, and nationality of those who worked their fields, they enslaved Indians where they could, under new legislation that declared "all Indians taken in warr be held and accounted slaves dureing life."[3] Red peoples were fit—however uneasily—into a system of racial categorization that increasingly admitted only white or black. But the Native American population dwindled rapidly in the seventeenth-century Chesapeake, and Africans soon became the object of the planters' desire. During the last five years of the century, tobacco planters in the region purchased more slaves than they had in the previous twenty. The number of black people, almost all of them slaves, lurched upward; the Middle Passage had come to the Chesapeake. For many whites, it seemed as though the region would "some time or other be confirmed by the name of New Guinea."[4]

Increased reliance on slave labor soon outstripped West Indian supplies. Planters turned from the Atlantic littoral to the African interior as their primary source of slaves. During the 1680s, some 2,000 Africans were carried into Virginia. This number more than doubled in the 1690s, and it doubled again in the first decade of the eighteenth century. Nearly 8,000 African slaves arrived in the colony between 1700 and 1710, and the Chesapeake briefly replaced Jamaica as the most profitable slave market in British America. The proportion of the Chesapeake's black population born in Africa grew steadily. At the turn of the century, newly arrived Africans far outnumbered descendants of the charter generation, constituting nearly 90 percent of the slave population.[5] Some eighty years after the first black people arrived at Jamestown and forty years after the legalization of slavery, African importation profoundly transformed black life in the region.

In the first decades of the eighteenth century, men and women marked by ritual scarification (which slaveowners called "country markings" or "negro markings"), filed teeth, and plaited hair were everywhere to be seen.[6] Their music—particularly drums—filled the air with sounds that frightened European and European-American settlers; their pots, pipes, and other material aspects of their lives left a distinctive mark on the landscape. The language of black America turned from creole to the languages of the African interior—probably various dialects of Igbo. An Anglican missionary found "difficulty of conversing with the Majority of Negroes themselves," because they have "a language peculiar to themselves, a wild confused medley of Negro and corrupt English, which makes them very unintelligible except to those who have conversed with them for many years." Whereas Atlantic creoles had beaten on the doors of the established churches to gain a modicum of recognition, the new arrivals showed neither knowledge of nor interest in Christianity; Jesus disappeared from African-American life, not to return for most people of African descent until well into the nineteenth century. The religious practices of the new arrivals, dismissed as idolatry and devil worship by the established clergy, placed them outside the pale of civilization as most European and European-Americans understood it. Africa had come to the Chesapeake.[7]

The Africanization of the labor force marked a sharp deterioration in the conditions of slave life. With an eye for a quick profit, Chesapeake planters imported males disproportionately. Generally men outnumbered women more than two to one on slaveships entering the region; this sexual imbalance soon manifested itself in the plantation population, as the numbers of men and women, which had previously been roughly equal, swung heavily toward men. The sharply skewed sex ratio made it difficult for the newly arrived Africans to form families, let alone establish the deep lineages that framed so much of life in Africa. The familial linkages that had bound members of the charter generation in the Chesapeake attenuated. In dividing their labor force by age and physical ability but rarely by sex, planters ignored the special needs of women during pregnancy and undermined the ability of the slave population to reproduce itself. As direct importation drove birth rates down, it pushed mortality rates up, for the dismal conditions of the transatlantic journey left transplanted Africans weakened and vulnerable to New World diseases. Fertility remained low and mortality high in the Chesapeake, and the number of slaves grew slowly, if at all, by natural means. Whereas Anthony and Mary Johnson, like other members of the charter generations, had lived to see their grandchildren, few of the newly arrived Africans would produce even one new generation. Indeed, within a year of their arrival, one-quarter of the "New Negroes" would be dead.[8]

African enslavement and the Middle Passage left the newly arrived mentally drained as well as physically weak. Planters, determined to break the spirit of the new arrivals, stripped them of ties to their homeland. Among the first objects of the planters' assault were the names Africans carried to the New World, and with them the lineage that structured much of African life. Writing to his overseer from his plantation on the Rappahannock River in 1727, Robert "King" Carter, perhaps the richest of the Chesapeake's new grandees, explained the process by which he initiated Africans into American captivity. "I name'd them here & by their names we can always know what sizes they are of & I am sure we repeated them so often to them that every one knew their names & would readily answer to them." Carter then forwarded his slaves to a satellite plantation or "quarter," where his overseer repeated the process, taking "care that the negros both men & women I sent . . . always go by ye names we gave them." In the months that followed, the drill continued, with Carter again joining in the process of stripping the newly arrived Africans of the signature of their identity.[9]

Renaming was only the first of numerous indignities visited upon newly arrived Africans. Generally, Chesapeake planters distrusted Africans, with their strange tongues and alien customs, and gave them little responsibility. Whenever possible planters put the newly arrived African slaves to work at the most repetitive and backbreaking tasks in some upland quarter, denying them access to positions of skill that Atlantic creoles frequently enjoyed. Planters made but scant attempt to see that the new arrivals had adequate food, clothing, or shelter, because the open slave trade made "New Negroes" cheap, and the new disease environment inflated their mortality rate no matter how well they were tended. Residing in desolate, unhealthy, sex-segregated barracks on the rude frontier, African slaves lived a lonely existence isolated from the mainstream of Chesapeake life, without families or ties of kin. Often they were separated by language from supervisors and co-workers alike. The physical separation denied the new arrivals the opportunity to find a well-placed patron and enjoy the company of men and women of equal rank. The planters' purpose—to strip away all family ties upon which the enslaved person's identity rested and leave them totally dependent upon their owners—was nearly realized.[10]

The slaves' world narrowed. The ability of the charter generations to move unimpeded through the countryside had nourished a broad view of the world, as it allowed them to interact openly with planters and servants, Europeans and Indians. The wide social networks fostered a sense of self-assurance, even bravado. Planters were determined to curb that freedom of movement and break the confidence which was so much a hallmark of the Atlantic creoles and their descendants. New laws required slaves to carry a pass when they left the estate of their owner even on the most routine business and denied them the right to meet in groups of more than four, and then only for brief periods of time. Even more novel than the legislation itself was the determination of the planter-controlled judiciary to enforce it, as county courts fined those who allowed their slaves "to goe abrod."[11]

But restrictions on movement were only one small indicator of change. Whereas members of the charter generations slept and ate under the same roof and worked in the same fields as their owners, the new arrivals lived in a world apart. In like fashion, the ties between black slaves and white servants atrophied. The social distance between white and black became all but unbridgeable, for not only did blacks sink, but whites also rose in aspiration, if not in fact. Their strivings were well served by distinguishing themselves from African slaves. No matter how low their status, white servants and small holders were distinguished from slave society's designated mudsill by their pale skin. This small difference became the basis of allegiance among the lower ranks and the foundation upon which the entire social order rested.[12]

The nature of the slave trade in the Chesapeake reinforced the isolation of the quarter. Upon entering the Chesapeake, slaveships peddled their human cargo in small lots at the numerous tobacco landings that lined the bay's extensive perimeter. Planters rarely bought more than a few slaves at a time, and larger purchasers like King Carter frequently acted as jobbers, reselling their slaves to upstart planters. Once purchased, African slaves were denied even the fragile communities that shipmates had created in the cramped, terrifying journey to the New World.[13]

The dynamics of the international slave trade further reduced the possibility of reconstituting a single African nationality in the Chesapeake. Between 1683 and 1721, roughly half of the slaves the Royal African Company sent to Virginia (and whose point of departure is known) sailed from Senegambia, near the Niger Valley. But the departure ports were collection points for slaves of many nations and provide only the roughest guide to lineages, village allegiances, and ethnic affiliations by which Africans identified themselves. In addition, most slavers made other stops along the African coast and in the Caribbean, where they purchased some slaves and sold others. Moreover, independent traders, who worked outside the control of the African Company and whose points of origin are unknown, also brought slaves to Virginia, creating a somewhat different mix.

During the second and third decade of the eighteenth century, the source of most of the slaves entering the Chesapeake changed. So-called Callabars who derived from the Nigerian hinterland via captiveries on the Bight of Biafra made up about 40 percent of the arrivals. In the following decades, the trade shifted southward, so that the largest group of African slaves—although still not the majority—originated not from the Slave Coast but from Angola. Through the entire period, the majority came from ports as distant from one another as Senegambia and Angola. Perhaps because of the miscellaneous and changing nature of the trade into the Chesapeake, planters rarely took note of the nationality of their slaves, describing them simply as Africans or New Negroes. "If they are likely young negroes, it's not a farthing matter where they come from," declared one Virginia slaveowner upon the completion of a purchase in 1725. The slave trade to the Chesapeake scattered various nations.[14]

Few Atlantic creoles could be found among these diverse arrivals to the Chesapeake. The touchstones of the charter generations—linguistic fluency, familiarity with the commercial and legal practices of the Atlantic, knowledge of European conventions and institutions, and (occasionally) partial European ancestry—vanished in the plantation age. Most saltwater slaves derived from the interior of Africa, where they worked as peasant farmers and pastoralists. They had little preparation for what was to come: capture, transport to the coast, journey across the Atlantic, and arrival in the New World. Unmediated by a common pidgin or creole language, newly arrived Africans often stood mute before their enslavers, estranged from the new land and the white men, who—like King Carter—asserted their domination by repeating some unfathomable gibberish.

A social order based on bondage required raw power to sustain it. During the early years of the eighteenth century, planters mobilized the apparatus of coercion in the service of their new regime. Although Chesapeake slavery (and servitude) had always rested upon force, with maimings, brandings, and beatings occurring commonly in the seventeenth century, the level of violence escalated on the plantation, lengthening the physical and social—if not moral—distance between master and slave. Chesapeake slaves faced the pillory, whipping post, and gallows with far greater regularity and in far larger numbers than ever before.

Even as planters employed the rod, the lash, the branding iron, and the fist with increased regularity, they invented new punishments that would humiliate and demoralize as well as correct. Planter William Byrd forced a slave bedwetter to drink "a pint of piss," and Joseph Ball placed a metal "bit" in the mouth of persistent runaways. But beyond the dehumanizing affronts, there were the grotesque mutilations. In 1707 King Carter requested court permission to chop off the toes of "two Incorrigible negroes . . . named Barbara Harry & Dinah." County officials readily granted him "full power to dismember," a penalty applied to white men only for the most heinous crimes. It was not the last time Carter would mutilate his slaves, nor was this the harshest penalty Chesapeake slaves would be assessed in the planters' campaign to terrorize those whom they deemed their human property.[15] Visible to all, the theater of terror—with its army of black amputees hobbling across the Chesapeake landscape—affirmed the power of the master class and their willingness to use it.

The state ratified the planters' actions and affirmed even their right to take a slave's life without fear of retribution. After 1669 the death of a slave "who chance to die" while being corrected by his or her owner or upon orders of an owner no longer constituted a felony in Virginia. Such legislation, which soon became general throughout the region, stretched the masters' authority far beyond anything previously enjoyed. In the years to follow, Chesapeake lawmakers expanded the power of slaveholders and diminished the rights of slaves even further. The Virginia slave code, enacted in 1705, recapitulated, systematized, and expanded these sometimes contradictory statutes, affirming the slaveholders' ascent.[16]

Confined to the plantation, African slaves faced a new harsh work regimen as planters escalated the demands they placed on laborers in the tobacco fields. With the decline of white servitude, slaves could no longer take refuge in the standards established for English servants. During the eighteenth century, slaves worked more days and longer hours, under closer supervision and with greater regimentation, than servants ever had worked in the seventeenth. Although the processes of production changed little, slaveholders reduced the number of holidays to three: Christmas, Easter, and Whitsuntide. Saturday became a full workday, and many slaves worked Sundays as well. Planters shortened or eliminated the midday break and in many places extended the workday into the evening, requiring slaves to grind corn and chop wood after sundown. Winter, previously a slack season, now filled with an array of new tasks: grubbing stumps, cleaning pastures, repairing buildings. Shorter winter days did not save slaves from the new regimen, as some planters required that they work at night, often by firelight.

Although they worked harder and longer than had English servants, African slaves rarely received the allotment of food, access to shelter, and medical attention traditionally due white laborers. The customary rights accorded English workers lost their meaning as the field force became increasingly African. Slaves might protest, but their appeals stopped at the plantation's borders. Whereas slaveholders in the seventeenth century had petitioned the courts to discipline unruly slaves, in the eighteenth century planters assumed absolute sovereignty over their plantations. The masters' authority was rarely questioned, and, unlike white servants, African slaves had no court of last resort.[17]

Having enslaved black people and confined the remaining white servants to a subordinate place in Chesapeake society, the grandees knit themselves together through strategic marriages, carefully crafted business dealings, and elaborate rituals. The result was a style of life which awed common folk and to which lesser planters dared not aspire. By mid-century, the great planters had forged an interlocking directorate, tied together by family loyalties, business partnerships, political allegiances, and grand displays at taverns, courthouses, and cotillions. Although Chesapeake planters were famous for their intramural disputes, their rule was complete. They would not be challenged until the evangelical awakenings of the late eighteenth century—and then only briefly.

Meanwhile, the grandees steadily expanded their holdings and tightened their grip on colonial legislatures and county courts. Their plantations became the seats of small empires, as much factories as farms, which extended to mills, foundries, weaving houses, and numerous satellite plantations. Planters took on the airs of gentlemen, along the English model, making much of their sociability and cultivating a sense of stewardship. Their large mansions with accompanying "Kitchins, Dayry houses, Barns, Stables, Store houses, and some . . . 2 or 3 Negro Quarters" became the hub of the planters' universe. The home plantation, declared the tutor on one such estate, was "like a Town; but most of the Inhabitants are black." The great plantation towns—Carter's Grove, Corotoman, Sabine Hall, Shirley, Stafford Hall, and eventually Doohoregan, Monticello, and Mount Vernon—dominated the countryside and symbolized the rule of the planter class.[18]

As planters consolidated their power, a new sense of mastership began to emerge. They no longer looked upon themselves as mere patrons of their slaves and other subordinates, willing perhaps to extend favors in return for loyalty and labor. From their new position atop Chesapeake society, planters began to spin out a vision of social relations that emphasized deference and authority. Preoccupied, if not obsessed, with their numerous dependents, they reshaped their self-image into that of metaphorical fathers, whose benevolence could elevate those who accepted their rule and whose harsh retribution would chasten and humble those who challenged it. "I must take care to keep all my people to their Duty, to see all the Springs in motion and make everyone draw his equal Share to carry the Machine forward," wrote William Byrd in 1726. The vision of themselves as prime movers of all things, fathers writ large, became the ideological foundation of the planters' world.[19]

The consolidation of the planters' power and the emergence of the paternalist ideology meant many things for slaves, but its first meaning was work. Regimented labor was all-encompassing. During the seventeenth century, few planters owned more than one or two laborers, and most planters worked in the field alongside their slaves and servants in a manner that necessarily promoted close interactions. African importation and the general increase in the size of holdings permitted planters—along with their wives and children—to withdraw from the fields. They hired overseers to supervise their slaves and, sometimes, stewards to supervise their overseers. The work force was divided by age, sex, and ability. There were few economies of scale in tobacco culture, and planters—believing close supervision increased production—kept work units small by dividing their holdings into "quarters." But the small units rarely meant slaves worked alongside their owners. To squeeze more labor from their workers, planters also reorganized their work force into squads or gangs, often plac-

ing agile young workers at the head of each gang, to serve as the paceset-
ter. Slaves found their toil subject to minute inspection, as planters or
their minions monitored the numerous tasks that tobacco cultivation necessitated. The demands placed on slaves grew steadily throughout the
eighteenth century—particularly in the older, settled areas—as planters
tried to compensate for the diminishing yields that followed tobacco's
steady exhaustion of the soil. Slaves worked harder and longer, as slaveholders purchased new lands to maintain the older level of production. As
slaves suffered, planters prospered from the increased productivity, and
the size of slave-grown crops far exceeded those previously brought to
market.[20]

The time slaves spent working their owners' crop meant time lost tending their own gardens and provision grounds. The slaves' independent
economy shriveled as the great planters expanded their domain. Whereas
seventeenth-century planters had gladly allowed slaves to feed and clothe
themselves, the new grandees—eager to cloak themselves in the patriarch's
mantle and to maximize the time slaves spent in their fields—issued
weekly rations and seasonal allotments of clothing, taking pride in the largess they bestowed on "their people." Plantation slaves generally maintained gardens, raised barnyard fowl, and hunted and fished to supplement their allowance. But few of them grew tobacco in provision grounds
to compete with their owners or brought hogs or cattle to market for their
own benefit.[21] Under such conditions, the slaves' economy only rarely
reached beyond the boundaries of their owners' estates. Such petty trade
could rarely generate the income necessary to purchase freedom, as members of the charter generations had been able to do.[22]

Evidence of the degradation of slave life was everywhere. Violence,
isolation, exhaustion, and alienation often led African slaves to profound
depression and occasionally to self-destruction. However, most slaves refused to surrender to the dehumanization that accompanied the plantation revolution. Instead, they contested the new regime at every turn—
protesting the organization, pace, and intensity of labor and challenging
the planters' definition of property rights.

Slaves answered the planters' ruthless imposition with an equally desperate, often bloody, resistance. During the first decades of the eighteenth century, the Chesapeake was rife with conspiracies and insurrectionary plots. In 1709 and 1710, 1722, and then for three successive years beginning in 1729, planters uncovered broad-reaching conspiracies to, in the words of Virginia's governor, "levy Warr against her majesty's Governmt," as black people struck back at the new oppressive regime.[23]

Resistance required guile as well as muscle. The imposition of the new regime had begun with the usurpation of Africans' names, but slaves soon took back this signature of their identity. While slaves answered to the names their owners imposed on them, many clandestinely maintained their African names. If secrecy provided one shield, seeming ignorance offered another. In the very stereotype of the dumb, brutish African that planters voiced so loudly, newly arrived slaves found protection, as they used their apparent ignorance of the language, landscape, and work routines of the Chesapeake to their own benefit. Observing the New Negroes on one Maryland estate, a visitor was "surprised at their Perseverance." "Let an hundred Men shew him how to hoe, or drive a Wheelbarrow, he'll still take the one by the bottom, and the Other by the Wheel." Triumphant planters had won the initial battle by gaining control over Chesapeake society and placing their imprint on the processes of production. But slaves answered that the war would be a long one.[24] Much as they might yearn for a quick, violent confrontation with their owners, slaves learned that numbers alone and the planters' near monopoly of physical force—particularly their ability to call upon the authority of the metropolitan state—made victory in hand-to-hand combat a doubtful prospect. A more subtle strategy was required.

In lieu of open rebellion, many transplanted Africans joined together to distance themselves from the source of their oppression. Rather than embrace Chesapeake society in the manner of the charter generation, Africans moved in the opposite direction—sometimes literally. Runaways fled toward the mountainous backcountry and lowland swamps to establish maroon settlements. They generally traveled in large bands that included women and children, despite the hazards such groups entailed for a successful escape as they tried to recreate the only society they knew free from white domination. Weather and topography conspired against the long-term viability of fugitive settlements in the Chesapeake.[25]

Yet, like all of the slaves' weapons, the practice of withholding labor—by malingering but especially by running away—had to be employed with surgical care. Chronic runaways faced brutal physical reprisals and, if they survived, were eventually sold to some distant place. Slaves thus calculated exactly how this weapon could be employed. Truants rarely fled in the winter. They almost always maintained ties with compatriots on their home estate, who supplied food, clothing, and information. If possible, they avoided remaining at large so long as to be "outlawed," a circumstance that upped the ante in this most dangerous game and might bring reprisals that put the entire plantation community at risk.[26]

The new plantation regime left little room for free blacks, even those descendants of the charter generation who had long enjoyed freedom. Chesapeake planters relied upon white nonslaveholders as overseers and artisans, slave catchers and militiamen. With the emergence of this new middle caste of white workers to oversee slaves, lawmakers systematically carved away those privileges of the free black members of the charter generation that contradicted the logic of racial slavery. Only by fixing "a perpetual Brand upon Free-Negros & Mulattos by excluding them from that great Priviledge of a Freeman," declared the governor of Virginia in 1723, could white planters "make the free-Negros sensible that a distinction ought to be made between their offspring and the Descendants of an Englishman, with whom they never were to be Accounted Equal."[27]

Opportunities for black people to escape slavery or enjoy liberty all but disappeared in the Chesapeake in the eighteenth century. In the same motion that slaveowning legislators degraded the free people's legal standing, they narrowed the avenues to freedom, denying slaveholders the right to free their slaves and slaves to buy their freedom.[28] As the door to freedom slammed shut, free people of color like the Johnsons fled the region. Those who could do so passed into white society, a difficult task at which only a few succeeded. Yet others joined the remnants of declining Indian tribes to create what twentieth-century anthropologists would describe as "tri-racial isolates"—peoples of diverse origins (African, European, and

Native American) who refused to identify with any one group.[29] By mid-eighteenth century, free people of African descent constituted a small—and shrinking—share of the black population, probably not more than 5 percent.[30]

Those black men and women who maintained their freedom could scarcely hope for the opportunities an earlier generation of free people of color had enjoyed in the Chesapeake. Occasionally, they tried to reclaim the privileges of the charter generation, but planter-controlled legislatures and courts tossed aside their petitions, which were more supplication than demand. The transformation of the free black population in the century between 1660 and 1760 measured the changes that accompanied the plantation revolution in the Chesapeake.[31] Planters celebrated the equation of black with slavery, for the close connection made it easy for white planters to treat all black people the same. Slaves, meanwhile, began to forge new communities as "Africans," an identity none had previously considered or even knew existed. The birth of an African identity and the degradation of free people of African descent were part of the same process of transforming a society with slaves into a slave society.

Lowcountry South Carolina, Georgia, and Florida

The plantation revolution in lowcountry South Carolina, Georgia, and Florida followed the pattern established on the Chesapeake, but time and circumstances sped the arrival of a slave society and gave it a distinctive shape. Beginning in the last decade of the seventeenth century, the discovery of exportable staples—first naval stores (rosin, turpentine, tall oil, and pitch) and then rice and indigo—permanently altered the character of lowcountry South Carolina. Spurred by the riches that rice produced, planters consolidated their place atop lowcountry society, banished the white yeomanry to the hinterland, expanded farms into plantations, and carved even larger plantations out of the inland swamps and coastal marshes. Before long, African slaves began pouring into the region; and sometime during the first decade of the eighteenth century, white numerical superiority gave way to the lowcountry's demographic distinction: a black majority.

Slaves became the mainspring of the lowcountry's working class, and Africans became the dominant group in the slave population. They also composed an ever larger share of the total population. By the 1720s, slaves outnumbered whites by more than two to one throughout the region, and in the heavily settled plantation parishes surrounding Charles Town, black slaves made up a three to one majority. That margin grew steadily during the 1730s, so that by 1760, black people made up 60 percent of the population in all but three lowcountry parishes, and the South Carolina countryside, in the words of one visitor, "look[ed] more like a negro country than like a country settled by white people."

Georgia, where authorities in London had reined in the planters' ambition, remained slaveless until mid-century. But once freed of the restrictions on slavery, planters—"stark Mad after Negroes"—imported them in large numbers, giving lowland Georgia counties considerable black majorities. East Florida followed a similar path of development after the British assumed control in 1763 and allowed South Carolina and Georgia slave masters to expand the plantation order southward. By 1770 more than one Florida estate boasted "no white face belonging to the plantation but an overseer."[32]

Slaves not only changed in number but also in kind. As in the Chesapeake, the new arrivals overwhelmed the charter generation, whose numbers had never been large in the region. Although some creoles with origins in the Caribbean and other portions of the Atlantic littoral continued to dribble into the lowcountry, their numbers dwindled to a small fraction of the whole. Indian slaves increased at first, as lowcountry planters—following a path pioneered in the Chesapeake—grabbed the most available laborers. Whereas the Indian wars in the Chesapeake yielded few slaves, the struggle with the Tuscaroras and the Yamassees in the lowcountry allowed planters to incorporate large numbers of captured Indians into the plantation labor force. By the second decade of the eighteenth century, South Carolina counted some 1,500 enslaved Indians.[33]

The enslavement of native peoples failed to satisfy the needs of the rapidly expanding rice economy, however. For that, lowcountry planters turned to Africa, and Charles Town took its place as the center of the low-land slave trade, quickly becoming the mainland's largest transatlantic slave market. Whereas slave imports had rarely exceeded 300 per year prior to 1710, by the 1720s they numbered more than 2,000 men and women annually, and 4,000 annually by the 1770s. The lowcountry had become the chief terminus for the Middle Passage to mainland North America.[34]

The flood of new arrivals swamped the Native American population, in much the same manner that enslaved Africans had earlier swamped the charter generation of Atlantic creoles. Native American slaves soon vanished from the census, as planters lumped Indian slaves together with Africans. This terminological shell game suggests how little planters dwelled upon matters of origins, nationality, or race in their haste to satisfy their need for labor. Having identified slavery with African ancestry, they simply transformed Native Americans into African Americans.

Whereas lowcountry planters cared little about the provenance of the native slaves, they became keenly attuned to the physical and cultural origins of the saltwater arrivals. Lowcountry planters, in contrast with slave-owners in the Chesapeake, developed preferences far beyond the usual demands for healthy males. Both buyers and sellers dwelled upon the regional and national origins of their human merchandise, disparaging the qualities of slaves from the Bight of Biafra or the so-called Callabars and celebrating the virtues of Gambian people (sometimes referred to as Coromantees) above all others. "Gold Coast or Gambia's are best, next to them the Windward Coast are prefer'd to Angola's. There must not be a Callabar amongst them," observed a Charles Town merchant in describing the most salable mixture. Some planters based their choices on long experience and a considered understanding of the physical and social character of various African nations. Others acted upon preferences drawn from shallow ethnic stereotypes: Coromantees revolted; Angolans ran away; Callabars destroyed themselves.

Still, even with their enormous resources, lowcountry slaveholders could not bend the international market to their will. Despite their preferences for Gambians, slaves deriving from central Africa—the much maligned Angolans—composed a far larger proportion of the African arrivals early in the eighteenth century. Later in the century, slaves from Senegambia and the Windward Coast constituted the bulk of the forced migrants.[35]

The pattern—far more than the content—of the lowland slave trade shaped the evolution of slave society in the lowcountry. While African slaves arrived in the Chesapeake through a multiplicity of inlets and creeks, they poured into the lowcountry through a single port. Almost all of the slaves in Carolina and later in Georgia and East Florida—indeed, 40 percent of pre-revolutionary black arrivals in mainland North America—entered through the port of Charles Town. The large uni-centered slave market that snapped up the new arrivals assured the survival not only of the common denominators of West African life but also of many of its particular national forms. Planter preferences, shipboard ties, or perhaps the chance ascendancy of a single nation allowed specific African cultures to reconstitute themselves within the plantation setting.

Some slaveowners controlled the trade on both sides of the Atlantic. Planter-merchant Richard Oswald, who owned a slave factory on the Sierra Leone River, shipped slaves directly to his Florida estate, making much of his ability to keep his imports together. Common national identities also drew slaves together across plantation boundaries, and when fugitives escaped, planters knew they would likely be found with their former compatriots. March, who spoke "very broken English though he has been many years in the province," fled to a plantation "where he frequently used to visit a countryman of his." Ties of language, experience, and memory bound slaves together much as they did other immigrants, forced and free.[36]

Whatever their origins, the destination of Africans entering the lowcountry was the plantation. As the black majority grew, so did the size of these estates. By 1720 three-quarters of the slaves in South Carolina resided on plantations with ten or more slaves. At mid-century over a third of all lowcountry slaves resided on estates with fifty slaves or more, and in some places the number was larger still. At the time of the American Revolution, for example, more than half of the slaves in the Georgetown District lived on plantations of over fifty slaves, and more than one-fifth lived in units of one hundred slaves or more.[37] By any measurement, South Carolina, then Georgia, and finally East Florida had surpassed the Chesapeake as a slave society.

Yet the differences between slave society in the Chesapeake and the lowcountry were measured in more than numbers. Rice cultivation—which stretched from Cape Fear in North Carolina to the St. John River in East Florida—accounted for much of the lowland's distinctive development, shaping slavery in the lowcountry much as tobacco shaped it in the Chesapeake.[38] Rice made enormous demands on those who cultivated, processed, and milled it. Massed on sprawling plantations, slaves labored in large, well-ordered gangs under close supervision, according to the seasonally dictated routine of rice production. For a large portion of the year, slaves worked knee deep in stagnant muck under a boiling sun. In August—even after the fields were drained and the crops laid-by—there was little respite. The rice had to be processed, and lowcountry plantations—like those in the Chesapeake—were factories as much as farms.

Almost as soon as the harvest was complete, the cycle began again. Slaves prepared the land for the next year's crop, cleared and extended the ditches and canals, rebuilt and augmented the embankments and dams, and repaired the trunks and floodgates. However tedious and demanding tobacco cultivation, it never approached the exertion demanded by rice. In 1775, a Scotch visitor first mistook a rice field for "that of our green oats." On closer inspection he discovered there was "no living near it with the putrid water that must lie on it, and the labour required for it is only fit for slaves, and I think the hardest work I have seen them engaged in."[39]

Indigo, a rapidly growing weed that could be processed into a much-valued blue dye, accompanied and complemented the ascendancy of rice. It was an equally demanding crop whose short season and delicate nature required careful attention. After planting in the spring, indigo needed little tending until the harvesting of the leaves in July, August, and occasionally September. But processing indigo was, if anything, even more arduous than rice. As fast as the leaves were harvested, slaves carried them to a series of great vats or tubs where they fermented while slaves kept up a continuous pumping, stirring, and beating. The decaying indigo, with its rotten odor, attracted clouds of flies that only slaves could be forced to tolerate. In time, the putrefied leaves were removed and the bluish liquid drained into a series of vats where slaves beat the liquid with broad paddles. The process was repeated several times before the blue liquid was set with lime at just the right moment—a great skill, by all accounts. After the sediment precipitated, the liquid was filtered and drawn off, leaving a dense blue mud, which was then strained, dried, cut into blocks, and dried again in preparation for shipping. This demanding and delicate process required both brute strength and a fine hand to create just the right density, texture, and brilliance of color. But slaves had little time to admire their handiwork, for like rice, indigo was a hard master.[40]

The relentless demands of rice and indigo, on one hand, and the ready availability of Africans, on the other, made for a deadly combination. Weakened by the rigors of the Middle Passage, the harsh labor regimen, and a new disease environment, slaves died by the thousands in the lowcountry's swamps. As long as the slave trade remained open and profits allowed slaveholders to maintain—indeed, increase—their labor force, they skimped on food, clothing, medical attention, and housing, often packing newly arrived slaves into grim barracks where cramped conditions promoted the spread of disease. The sickle-cell trait provided some immunity against malaria, but Africans had no more protection than Europeans from yellow fever, pleurisy, pneumonia, and a variety of subtropical diseases endemic to the region.

With men composing about two-thirds of imports, slaves found it difficult to establish normal domestic relations and impossible to establish the complex extended households and deep lineages that characterized family life in Africa. The women, underfed and confined to strenuous field labor, conceived at low rates and miscarried at high ones. The slave population of the lowcountry experienced no natural increase in the 1720s—a time when slaves were beginning to reproduce in the Chesapeake. The birth rates of lowcountry slaves continued to fall during the middle years of the eighteenth century, while mortality rates rose sharply, so that only the continued importation of Africans allowed the slave population to grow. Even with the reemergence of a new creole population after mid-century, the low fertility and high mortality of saltwater slaves ransomed the growth of the slave population to the continued importation of Africans. Not until the 1760s did the slave population begin again to reproduce naturally. "Plantation agriculture," one historian has observed, "brought the demographic regime of the sugar islands to lowcountry South Carolina."[41]

The inauguration of the plantation regime also meant a loss of independence for slaves. The casual and open exchanges between master and slave during the pioneer years disappeared, as did the possibility of enlisting slaves as soldiers. In the place of such open-handed interactions stood fear and contempt, as planters attempted to master their slaves. Saltwater slaves found themselves tagged with names whose whimsical nature suggested their owners' disdain. One slave trader and planter, Henry Laurens, denominated some of his new slaves with place names like Senegal, Pondicherry, and Quebec and gave others names with a classical ring, such as Othello and Claudius. One man became King Cole.[42]

However eccentric the matter of naming slaves, the process by which Africans were bent to the demands of the new regime turned deadly serious when it came to matters of discipline. As in the Chesapeake, an escalation in the level of violence accompanied the imposition of a plantation economy. Christian missionaries decried the "profane & Inhumane practices," as planters turned to the lash, the faggot, and the noose to discipline slaves unfamiliar with the requirements of rice and indigo. Even punishment for "small faults" took on a monstrous quality, as when one planter placed miscreants in a "coffin where they are almost crushed to death," keeping them "in that hellish machine for Twenty Four hours." Such atrocities disturbed a few clerics, but planters embraced terror as a critical element in sustaining their dominion over a people who, as one slaveholder professed, were "created only for slavery."[43]

The state—which was nothing less than the planters themselves—naturally affirmed this judgment. In 1690 South Carolina lawmakers held slaveholders and their agents to be legally blameless for the death of a slave as a result of "correction." Even if the slave died as a result of "wilfulness, wantonness, or bloody mindedness," the murderer would face a maximum penalty of three months in jail and a fine of £50 to be paid to the owner. But since the murderer was often the owner, the financial penalty could hardly be considered onerous. As one student of slave law has noted, "There was no capital murder of slaves in South Carolina."[44]

The transplanted Africans who might be subjected to such abuse made no pretense of trying to adapt to the planters' ways. Slave unrest grew with every new wave of harsh discipline and terror. The first decades of the eighteenth century were alive with rumors of insurrection and outbursts of violence, as slaves lashed back at the lords of the plantation. Although the extent of the violence and the depth of the conspiracies cannot be measured with precision, there can be no doubt about what happened at Stono, where a group of Florida-bound fugitives turned on their pursuers with bloody results.[45] The Stono rebellion marked the transformation of the lowcountry into a slave society. The following year, the South Carolina legislature, borrowing from Barbadian law, wrote its own slave code, giving planters near total power over their human property.

Stono was an equally significant landmark in the slaves' efforts to reformulate Africa in America. During the second third of the eighteenth century, a new African-American culture began to emerge in the lowlands. Its development followed much the same course as it had in the Chesapeake, but the differences between the two regions—geographic, demographic, economic, and social—sent African-American culture in different directions. Domestic and religious life were the most obvious manifestations of the slaves' determination to maintain the ways of the Old World in the New. The polygamous practices of the largely male population scandalized Anglican missionaries, as did the unwavering antagonism of African slaves to Christianity. Writing from Savannah in 1754, an Anglican missionary discovered that black people clung to "the old Superstition of a false Religion." Even when a handful of Africans demonstrated an interest in Christ's way, their reformulations of Christian eschatology appalled the mission men.

The Reverend Francis Le Jau, perhaps the most resolute of the Anglican missionaries, found that his prize convert "put his own Construction upon some Words of the Holy Prophet's . . . [respecting] the several judgmts. That Chastise Men because of their Sins." Indeed, his pupil's claim "that there wou'd be a dismal time and the Moon wou'd be turn'd into Blood, and there would be dearth of darkness" frightened Le Jau and many others who heard the pronouncement. Such specters reinforced the planters' adamant opposition to the Christianization of their slaves, and for all his effort, Le Jau touched but a handful of the thousands of slaves in his parish. Facing reluctant masters and slaves, no lowcountry missionary did any better. Christianity made few inroads into the slave quarters, and the slaves' sacred world remained rooted on the east side of the Atlantic.[46]

The expression and elaboration of the plantation allowed slaves to create a world of their own. The charter generations' shallow roots in the lowcountry had permitted planters to impose the plantation regime with little opposition, and the charter generations' small size meant that the new black arrivals could quickly create their own universe, based on African precedents. The slave quarter, standing at the center of these huge agricultural factories—the most highly capitalized enterprises in mainland North America during the eighteenth century—was the heart of African-American life in the countryside, and increasingly, slaves put their stamp on it. Planters may have designed their estates, but slaves built them—literally. The small houses in the quarter, constructed of a sea-shell muck of the slaves' own making or bricks fired in the plantation kiln, gave the quarter the appearance of a separate village or "Negro town," as more than one visitor observed.

The seclusion of life in the "Negro town" and its emulation of the texture, if not the form, of an African village imparted a sense of propriety, so much so that some lowcountry planters urged a return to the older barracks-style housing. What these planters feared as "too much liberty" was the emergence of a black community. The residents not only labored together but lived "in separate houses," "converse[ing] almost wholly among themselves." Isolated from the interaction of master and slave that characterized plantation relations in the great plantation towns of the Chesapeake, lowcountry slaves re-created, as best they could, Africa in America. The institutional presence of the plantation village bespoke the increasing permanence of black life in the rural lowcountry.[47]

As slaves formulated their lives in the overwhelmingly black countryside, the lowcountry grandees retreated to the region's cities, expanding the social and cultural distance between themselves and their slaves along with the physical distance. The streets of Charles Town—and, later, of Beaufort, Georgetown, Savannah, Darien, and Wilmington—sprouted great new mansions, as the wealthiest people on the North American mainland fled the malarial lowlands and its black majority. Although the cities of the lowcountry would eventually develop their own black majorities, they remained—even then—bastions of whiteness compared with the countryside.

By the 1740s, urban life in the lowcountry had become attractive enough that men who had made their fortunes in rice and slaves gave little consideration to returning to England, as West Indian slaveholders often did. Instead, through marriage and business connections, South Carolina's great planters, often joined by the most successful merchants, began to weave their disparate social relations into a close-knit ruling class, whose pride of place would become legendary. Charles Town, the capital of this new elite, grew rapidly. Between 1720 and 1740 the city's population doubled, and nearly doubled again by the eve of American independence, to stand at about 12,000. With its fine houses, great churches, and shops packed with luxury goods, Charles Town's prosperity bespoke the maturation of the lowland plantation system and the rise of a planter class.[48]

Ensconced in their new urban mansions, their pockets lined with the riches rice produced, planters ruled their lowcountry domains through a long chain of command: stewards located in the smaller rice ports, overseers stationed near or on their plantations, and plantation-based black foremen or, in a telling idiom, "drivers." Insulated from the labor of the field by this elaborate hierarchy, most planters could no more imagine working across a sawbuck from their slaves than they could envision enlisting them in the colony's militia. The time when black and white fought side by side against the Spaniards and the Yamassees had passed.

But the planters' withdrawal from the countryside did not breed the callous indifference of West Indian absenteeism. For one thing, absenteeism in the lowcountry generally meant no more than a day's boat ride between townhouse and country estate. The very complexity of rice and indigo production required constant attention not only of overseers and stewards but planters as well. Indeed, even as they established their urban households, lowcountry planters built new, larger houses on the plantation itself, often on the model of English country estates. They maintained a deep and continuing interest in their land, where they resided during the nonmalarial season.

Mastership-at-a-distance operated differently from either the client-patron relationship that framed the social order for the charter generation or the hands-on regime of resident planters in the Chesapeake. A handful of favorites might attract the attention of lowcountry planters, and troublemakers left their own mark, but the mass of slaves remained anonymous to the master. Observing their small armies of slaves only intermittently and usually from afar, the grandees hardly knew them as individuals. Their interaction with plantation hands was indirect at best, save for the regular accountings of births and deaths in the plantation record books.[49]

Separation from their estates, both organizationally and geographically, forced lowland planters to cede some of their authority to underlings. Whereas stewards and overseers—almost always white—were the primary beneficiaries of this downward spiral of command, slaves also gained some advantages. Planters occasionally allowed a slave man to rise to the rank of foreman or driver. Although black drivers officially reported to the resident white overseers, these young white men generally served for only a few years before striking off on their own and they rarely gained the planters' confidence. Their motives and morals troubled planters, who often bypassed them, allowing drivers to amass considerable authority. For all practical purposes, drivers directed the day-to-day plantation operations on some estates, balancing the contradictory interests of the owner, overseer, and the mass of field hands from whence they had emerged.[50]

While only a select few rose to the rank of driver, many benefitted from the task system, another consequence of the planters' long-distant relationship with the countryside. Under the task system, a slave's daily routine was sharply defined: so many rows of rice to be sowed, so much grain to be threshed, or so many lines of canal to be cleared. Such a precise definition of work suggests that city-bound planters found it difficult to keep their slaves in the field from sunup to sundown and conceded control over worktime in return for a generally accepted unit of output, especially when it could be measured from afar. With little direct white supervision, slaves and their black drivers conspired to preserve a portion of the day for their own use while meeting the planters' minimum work requirements. Together, they rolled back some of the harshest aspects of the plantation revolution.[51]

While plantation slaves struggled to build their world on such fragments, another development within the shadow of the plantation threatened to fracture black society. Although planters lived at a distance from most of their slaves, they maintained close, sometime intimate, relations with others. The slaveholders' great wealth and seasonal urban residence created a demand for house servants to make life comfortable, messengers to maintain the lines of communication between city and countryside, and boatmen to shuttle supplies to and from the estates. Within the great rice ports, both the economy and society rested on slaves who transported and processed plantation staples, satisfied the planters' taste for luxury goods, and serviced the ships that bound the lowcountry to the rest of the world.

Urban slaves, unlike their plantation counterparts, lived literally on top of or beside their owners and other white people in attics, backrooms, and closets. The comparative smallness of city houses, shared residence, and disproportionately large numbers of women—at a time when men dominated the plantation population—allowed urban slaves a measure of independence unknown to their rural counterparts. As domestics, laborers, and especially skilled tradesmen and tradeswomen, they moved freely through the towns, often as hirelings rented from one master to another. Sometimes they rented themselves, collecting their own wages and living independently of owner or hirer.[52] Mobile, skilled, and cosmopolitan, urban slaves improved their material condition and expanded their social life even while the circumstances of the mass of rural slaves deteriorated in the wake of the rice revolution.

In the rice ports, the slaves' wealth far exceeded the modest prosperity of even the most successful slaves in the Chesapeake and allowed them a degree of comfort and independence that challenged the slave master's understanding of slavery. The black men and women—some slaves, some slave hirelings, and some runaway slaves—who resided on the fringes of lowcountry towns (below the Bluff in Savannah and in Charles Town's Neck) were free in everything but name. Some took the name as well, working on their own, living apart from their owners, controlling their own family life, riding horses and brandishing pistols. These slaves forcibly and visibly claimed the privileges that white men and women had reserved for themselves.[53]

Perhaps no aspect of their behavior was more obvious and, hence, more galling to city-bound planters as the slaves' elaborate dress. While plantation slaves—men and women—worked stripped to the waist, wearing no more than loin cloths (thereby confirming the planters' image of savagery), urban slaves appropriated their owners' taste for fine clothes—and often the garments themselves. Tooling around Charles Town in their finery, displaying pocket watches, and sporting powdered wigs, they aroused the ire of countless self-proclaimed ladies and gentlemen who viewed the slaves' finery as an affront to their exclusive claim to the symbols of civilization. Grand jury presentments offered a seemingly interminable list of laments about the "excessive and costly apparel" worn by slaves, particularly slave women. Lowcountry legislators enacted various sumptuary regulations to restrain what they considered the slaves' penchant for dressing above their station. The South Carolina Assembly even considered prohibiting masters and mistresses from giving their old clothes to their slaves. But hand-me-downs were not the problem as long as the slaves' independent economic enterprises prospered.[54]

Cash in hand endowed urban slaves with the means to distance themselves from the control of a master. Beyond their owner's eye, they associated as they wished. Funerals became just one of many occasions for "meeting in large bodies in the night," and, at least in one instance, "rioting in a most notorious manner and breaking the Lord's day." In what one appalled white observer labeled "a County-Dance or Rout, a Cabel of [sixty] *Negroes*" met on the outskirts of Charles Town, feasted on

"Tongues, Hams, Beef, Geese, Turkies and Fowls, drank bottled liquors of all sorts . . . the men copying (or *taking off*), the manners of their masters and the women those of their mistresses."[55]

Such independence was the first outcropping of a community in the making. Slaves established cook shops, groceries, and taverns to cater to their own people. These illicit establishments became notorious interracial meeting grounds, where white sailors and journeymen fraternized with city-bound slaves and the movement of liquor and sex transcended racial lines. Interracial gangs of thieves appeared to be as endemic in the cities of the lowcountry as they were in ports all around the Atlantic rim. Although urban officials redoubled their efforts to terminate such ventures, they continually failed.[56]

Alongside these illicit enterprises were a handful of legal—if not entirely respectable—ones sponsored by the Society for the Propagation of the Gospel (SPG) and other missionaries, occasionally with the aid of reformist planters. In Charles Town and Savannah, Anglican ministers and various missionaries who were associated with the SPG found willing converts among the assimilationist-minded populace. So too did the first stirrings of evangelical Christianity, which was brought to the lowcountry by George Whitefield and his most zealous converts, the planters Hugh and Jonathan Bryan. The promise of equality in the sight of God received an enthusiastic reception among the slaves of the rice ports. But for precisely the reason slaves were attracted to the evangelical promise, lowcountry lawmakers came down hard on the few men who dared to offer Christ's words to all comers. Slaveholders were leery, and the interest urban slaves manifested in Christianity fueled their suspicions.[57]

The incongruous prosperity of urban slaves and their attachment to Christianity, along with other manifestations of European-American society, also disturbed more than a few people of African descent, for the division between city and countryside marked a growing fissure within black society. On the plantations, the mass of black people, physically separated and psychologically estranged from the European-American world, had begun to create a new African-American culture, informed by the continued arrival of saltwater slaves. Urban slaves took a different course, perfecting their English, mimicking the planters' sartorial style, and welcoming Jesus. From their clothes, separate residences, and mastery of numerous artisanal skills, they were confident they could compete as equals on the planters' own ground. Barred from white society, this emerging colored elite wanted no part of life on the plantations.[58] When they could not be part of white society, these skilled, privileged urbanites began to create a society of their own in which white people played little part. Their success also reflected the creation of a slave society, if one which differed from that of the Chesapeake.

THE NORTH

No such division between countryside and plantation developed in the North or the lower Mississippi Valley, where English, French, and Spanish efforts to establish a plantation economy fell flat during the eighteenth century. This was not for want of trying. In the North, particularly the middle colonies, agriculturalists of all sorts along with urban businessmen turned to slave labor to meet the growing demand for workers. As war disrupted the supply of European indentured servants and military enlistment siphoned young white men from the labor force, the numbers and the importance of enslaved workers increased. In some colonies, growth of the enslaved black population outstripped that of the free white population, reaching 15 percent of the total.[59] This general expansion revealed the trend but concealed its full impact, for slavery scored its greatest gains in the most economically productive portions of the North. By mid-century, slaves became the single most important source of labor in the North's most fertile agricultural areas and in its busiest ports. Although the development of slavery in the North stopped short of the transformation initiated by the tobacco and rice revolutions, it nonetheless reshaped the lives of black people, both deepening the nightmare of slavery and buffering its worst effects.

The northern commitment to slavery emerged first in the great port cities, where slaveownership became nearly universal among the urban elite and commonplace among the middling sort. The upper orders of white

society became fully invested in slavery. On the eve of American independence, nearly three-fourths of Boston's wealthiest quartile of property-
holders held slaves. A like proportion could be found in New York, Philadelphia, Providence, and Newport. From a position at the top of colonial
society, one visitor noted that there was "not a house in Boston" that "has
not one or two" slaves—an observation that might be applied to every
northern city with but slight exaggeration.[60]

As their numbers increased, slaves moved from the periphery of urban
productivity, as servants in gentry homes, to its center, as workers in artisan shops. By the early decades of the eighteenth century, slaves were no
longer simply an appendage to a mixed labor force but a central element
in many trades. For the largest urban employers—particularly those connected to the maritime trades—bonded labor became commonplace. But
slaves could be found in the smallest shops, and the presence of slaves—
often practicing crafts that had previously been the province of white
workers, free and unfree—drew increasingly noisy rebukes from those
who felt the sting of slave competition.[61]

The expansion of slavery followed a similar trajectory in the countryside. Indeed, the rapid growth of rural slavery eclipsed its development in
the cities of the North. Throughout the grain-producing areas of Pennsylvania, northern New Jersey, the Hudson Valley, and Long Island—the
North's bread basket—bondage spread swiftly during the eighteenth century, as farmers turned from white indentured servants to black slaves. By
mid-century slavery's tentacles reached into parts of southern New England, especially the area around Narragansett Bay, where large slaveholders—many of whom had originated in Barbados—took on the airs of a
planter class. In these places, slaves constituted as much as one-third of
the labor force, and sometimes more than half.[62]

With the expanding demand for slaves, would-be slaveowners who
had depended on occasional, chance arrivals from the West Indies turned
to direct African imports.[63] The influx of saltwater slaves—disproportionately, adult men—made Africans an increasingly visible portion of
the slave population and sensitized white northerners to the differences
among black people from various parts of the continent. Notions of Afri-

can nationality emerged as white northerners learned to distinguish be-tween Igbos and Angolans, much as had their southern counterparts, and black northerners identified with their countrymen.[64]

The transformation of the slave trade was but a harbinger of the trans-formation of slavery itself, as the forces unleashed by the Middle Passage made themselves felt in the North. Direct African importation brought with it higher mortality, lower fertility, stricter discipline, and the other degradations of African-American life that accompanied the open slave trade throughout the Americas. The sexual imbalance among the new-comers wreaked havoc on domestic life in the North, undermining black people's attempts to form stable communities and putting their very exis-tence at risk.

Disease had a particularly unfortunate impact on men and women with no exposure to the contagions of the New World—not even from a brief stop in the West Indies—or to the North's cold, damp winters. Ailments like measles and whooping cough, which Europeans usually sloughed off in childhood encounters, killed people of African descent by the hun-dreds. The deadly effect of disease was compounded by poor diet, insuf-ficient clothing, and inadequate shelter. Unable to resist a whole new pha-lanx of microbes, the morbidity and mortality of African slaves rocketed upward, as it did elsewhere on the continent in the wake of the plantation revolution. The crude death rate of black people in Boston and Philadel-phia during the 1750s and 1760s was well over 60 per thousand, nearly one-third to a half more than the death rate of white people.[65]

As the slaves' mortality rose, their reproduction rate fell. In the north-ern colonies, Africans had difficulty finding mates, establishing families, conceiving, and producing healthy infants. The problem was not new. From the beginning of settlement, northern slaveholders, unlike their counterparts farther south, showed little interest in creating an indige-nous slave population. From their perspective, the discomfort and ex-pense of sharing their cramped quarters with slaves outweighed the profits offered by a self-reproducing labor force. Northern slaveholders discour-aged their slaves from marrying and did not provide accommodations for slave families to reside in the same abode. They routinely separated husbands from wives and parents from children and only reluctantly extended visitation rights. Seeing but small advantage in the creation of an indigenous, self-reproducing slave population, northern slaveholders sold slave women at the first sign of pregnancy. Such practices constrained the development of residential family units and diminished the chances that black men would assume the roles of husbands and fathers and black women the roles of wives and mothers. Grandparenthood became unknown to most northerners of African descent. The attenuation of familial ties by distance and time, along with the difficulties created by small units, frequent sale, and meddling slaveowners, made a normal family life by the standards of colonial American society, African society, or European society nearly impossible.[66] Over the course of the eighteenth century, African-American family life fell into greater and greater disarray.[67] Domestic life, which had been the hallmark of the charter generation throughout the North, became increasingly difficult for slaves to sustain in the eighteenth century.

It was a vicious cycle. Unable to reproduce, the black population drifted demographically toward the aged. Old people were susceptible to disease, and their susceptibility increased over time, for slaveowners showed no desire to pay for the medical treatment of unproductive hands. This older, enfeebled, disease-ridden population had little hope of—and perhaps little interest in—reproducing itself. With deaths towering over births, slaves could not sustain their numbers. Close observers like Benjamin Franklin understood that it would take "a continual Supply . . . from Africa" to maintain slavery. In its demographic outline, northern slavery at mid-century bore a closer resemblance to the plantation colonies to the south during the beginnings of African importation than to the bondage of the charter generation.[68]

The slave family may have been disorganized and slaves themselves wracked by disease, but their growing number and their increased centrality to the northern economy provoked slaveholders to demand new controls over slave life. In the middle years of the eighteenth century, northern lawmakers—taking a page from southern statute books—updated, refined, or consolidated the miscellaneous regulations that had been enacted during the seventeenth century and issued more comprehensive slave codes. In every case, legislators strengthened the hand of the slave-owner at the expense of the slave and free black. Black people—free and slave—found their mobility curbed, their economies limited, and their punishments stiffened. Occasionally, they resisted in the manner of the charter generation, challenging the new strictures in court or in law. But they rarely succeeded and instead found their access to freedom circum-scribed.[69]

New York, Pennsylvania, New Jersey, and then the New England colo-nies curtailed manumission by requiring slaveholders to post heavy bonds for the good conduct of former slaves and to support those who fell to public charity.[70] Slaveholders, desperate for labor, needed few such obsta-cles to discourage them from donning the emancipator's garb. The pro-portion of black people enjoying freedom in the North shriveled. In 1724, according to one estimate, about 7 percent of the black population of New York was free, a sharp decline from 1664, when nearly 20 percent of black New Yorkers had secured their liberty.[71]

As their numbers declined, free blacks saw their prosperity wane. The disappearance of black landowners from the property rolls made it easy for whites to equate blackness with bondage. Lawmakers reinforced this presumption by circumscribing the liberty of free blacks. Various north-ern colonies barred free blacks from voting, mustering in the militia, sit-ting on juries, and testifying in court. Some jurisdictions required free blacks to carry special passes to travel, trade, and keep a gun or a dog. Elsewhere, people of African descent were judged, along with slaves, in special courts; and for certain offenses free blacks could be punished like slaves. Often lawmakers contrived legislation to force free blacks into bondage.[72]

Black life in the North increasingly resembled that of the plantation South. Nothing revealed this more dramatically than the names by which slaves were called. Africans who entered the North in the eighteenth cen-tury were labeled—as one opponent of slavery observed—"with such like Names they give their Dogs and Horses." Classic appellations, assigned to slaves in jest, became as common in the slave quarters of the North as in the colonies to the south. Moreover, unlike members of the charter generation, northern slaves of the eighteenth century rarely had two names, just as they rarely registered their marriages, baptized their children, selected godparents, or held property of any sort. Indeed, some northern colonies barred free black people from owning property.[73] Rather than hold property, free people of color were becoming little more than property.

As the North took on the trappings of a slave society, black people—free and slave—turned to the task of creating their own world. This transformation took two forms, beginning with an explosive attempt to break the chains of bondage—most prominently by revolt in New York in 1712 and again 1741. But slaveholders answered the slave rebels with deadly, unrestrained force. Insurrectionists and conspirators—indeed, suspected insurrectionists and conspirators—were executed and dismembered in grotesque public displays that left no doubt of the fate of those who dared to challenge slavery.[74]

As the slaveowners' overwhelming power became manifest, northern slaves followed their southern counterparts in rejecting the incorporative strategy of the charter generation and in recasting black life apart from that of their enslavers. While members of the charter generation had moved quickly to adopt English or, in New Netherland, Dutch names, African arrivals struggled to hold on to the emblems of their homeland. When Quasho Quando's owner attempted to rename him Julius Caesar, Quando simply refused to accept the new identifier, despite his owner's threats. Whereas the charter generation had connived to gain admission to Christian churches to formalize their marriages and baptize their children, the new arrivals kept their distance from the Cross. By the middle of the eighteenth century, after decades of proselytization, less than a tenth of the black population of New York City subscribed to Christianity. The proportion was doubtless smaller in rural parts.[75]

The rejection of Christianity was but one indicator of the reorientation of black culture spurred by the importation of African slaves. A large number of African immigrants, although probably a minority of the whole, had a powerful effect on the native population, infusing black society with knowledge of the African homeland and homeways. Sometimes it was just the presence of African men and women walking the streets of northern cities and the byways of the countryside bearing ritual scars and speaking the language of a land most black northerners knew only from second- and third-hand accounts. At other times, newly arrived Africans reawakened black Americans to their African past by providing direct knowledge of West African society. In 1769 "Congamochu, alias Squingal" "talked much of his wives, and country" before he ran off.[76]

African Americans soon began to fold their African inheritance into their own evolving culture. In Andover and Plymouth, Massachusetts, black people employed construction methods reminiscent of West Africa, designing their homes in the traditional African pattern. As suggested by the houses they built, black northerners were often highly conscious of their African connections. They called themselves "Sons of Africa" and adopted African forms to maximize their independence, to choose their leaders, and, in general, to give shape to their lives.[77]

Perhaps the most visible manifestation of the new African-American society was celebration of Election and Pinkster days, festivals of great merrymaking that drew black people from all over the countryside. "All the various languages of Africa, mixed with broken and ludicrous English, filled the air, accompanied with the music of the fiddle, tambourine, the banjo, [and] drum," recalled an observer of the festival in Newport. Drawing upon their own resources and those of their owners, black men and women, dressed in all manner of finery "with cues, real or false, heads pomatumed and powdered, cocked hat," paraded in horse and carriage, marched in formation, danced with "the most lewd and indecent gesticulation," and sang with "sounds of frightful dissonance." Although such garish sensuality offended some white men and women, it attracted others.[78]

Yet the new culture was still a reflection of a society with slaves. The expansion of slavery stopped short of transforming the North into a slave society. Even in the middle colonies, where slavery's expansion had its greatest impact, northern farmers did not reorganize production on the plantation model or inaugurate a system of gang labor. For the most part, northern slaves remained jacks-of-all-trades, engaging in all aspects of work in the countryside. They continued to labor in small groups in which indentured servants and wage workers, white and black, had a substantial presence. Their importance grew from the force of their numbers, not from a change in the kind of work they performed. While the greatly expanded slave population allowed black people—slave and free—to unite as never before, and while the influx of Africans awakened black northerners to their African origins, no distinctive African-American culture emerged in the North. By the 1760s, when availability allowed, farmers and artisans turned back to European labor—either indentured servants or wage workers. But its flirtation with the plantation revolution nonetheless permanently transformed northern society, drawing it more fully into the orbit of the Atlantic economy as a supplier of slaves to the colonies in the South. The North still remained a society with slaves but one in which the institution of slavery was deeply embedded.

The Lower Mississippi Valley

So too did the lower Mississippi Valley, where the successive efforts of the French and then Spanish to create a slave society foundered on the absence of a commodity to sell on the international market. If the plantation revolution touched the northern colonies indirectly, it affected the lower Mississippi Valley—the colonies of Louisiana and West Florida—hardly at all. Following the Natchez revolt of 1729, the nascent plantation order unraveled, as the importation of Africans ceased. The French Crown stripped the Company of the Indies of its control of Louisiana, severing the ties between Africa and the lower Mississippi Valley. After 1731 only one African slaver arrived in Louisiana until the Spanish—who took effective control of Louisiana in 1769—reopened the slave trade in the 1770s. Although West Indian slaves continued to dribble into the colony through ongoing trade with the sugar islands, their numbers were never substantial. While the tobacco and rice revolutions transformed the seaboard colonies in quick order, the lower Mississippi Valley devolved from a slave society into a society with slaves. A polyglot labor force replaced the dwindling African majority, and, most importantly, some black people began to exit slavery, as the line between slavery and freedom became increasingly permeable.

Under the new French regime, the slave society continued its devolution into a society with slaves. Planters, who understood they were dependent upon an indigenous slave population, moderated their demands on plantation labor and allowed slaves to engage in production of their own as gardeners, provisioners, and marketers. In quick order, slaveowners replaced barracks with small outbuildings, giving the quarter a village-like appearance. They encouraged family formation and eased the slaves' work load—particularly that of women, so that pregnancies might be carried to term. Slaves took advantage of the new circumstances and joined together as man and wife. With increased frequency, plantation inventories listed men and women as couples and women as "sa femme."

Before long, the black population began to increase by natural means. By the 1740s, the differences between the creole majority in Louisiana and the African-born population in the sugar islands had become a matter of common knowledge on both sides of the Atlantic. "This species survives almost entirely by procreation," one French official wrote from New Orleans in 1741. "In effect, among the approximately 4,000 blacks of all types and ages, two thirds are Creole. That is the difference between this country and the French West Indies where there is very little natural reproduction among slaves."[79]

Critical to the slaves' success in reproducing themselves was the collapse of the staple-based economy during the middle years of the eighteenth century. Slaveholders in post-Natchez Louisiana continued to grow tobacco for export but without notable success, as European markets preferred the Chesapeake leaf.[80] They did but slightly better with indigo and rice, which failed to compete with the lowcountry products. Stagnation of its export economy stifled the development of plantations in Louisiana and West Florida. Rather than massing on large rural estates, the black population gravitated to the port of New Orleans. As the century progressed, slavery in the lower Mississippi Valley increasingly became an urban-centered institution. By 1763 one-quarter of the black population of Louisiana resided on small tracts in districts around New Orleans.[81]

Whereas slavery in the lowcountry, the Chesapeake, and even the north-ern colonies migrated from the cities to the countryside and became iden-tified with agricultural production during the eighteenth century, the trend was just the opposite in the lower Mississippi Valley.

The growing urban focus also informed developments in the country-side, where planters turned to the production of lumber, naval stores, and cattle. These commodities found a far readier reception in Saint Domingue, Martinique, and other Caribbean islands than either of the old standbys, although they never generated the level of return that plant-ers identified with staple production. In the absence of bonanza profits, agriculture became less a way of making money—big money—and the harsh regime of former years mellowed.

Freed from devotion to a single crop and released from the narrow al-ternatives of plantation life, slaves worked at a variety of trades. When one Louisiana planter described his slave as "a black-smith, mason, cooper, roofer, strong long sawyer, mixing with these a little of the rough carpen-try with the rough joinery," no one thought this bondsman unusual.[82] Many slave men moved from the fields to the forest, where they felled the great cypress trees, hewed shingles, collected pitch and tar, and tended cattle and various draft animals. Lumbering and cattle-raising were ardu-ous and dangerous, to be sure, but they allowed slaves to work at their own pace far from their owners' eyes.

Other aspects of the new work regimen operated to the slaves' advan-tage. Slave lumbermen, many of them hired out for short periods of time, carried axes and, like slave drovers and herdsmen, were generally armed with knives and guns—necessities for men who worked in the wild and hunted animals for food and furs. Woodsmen had access to horses, as did slaves who tended cattle and swine. Periodic demands that slaveowners disarm their slaves and restrict their access to horses and mules confirmed that many believed these to be dangerous practices, but they did nothing to halt them.[83] In short, slave lumbermen and drovers were not to be trifled with. Their work allowed considerable mobility and latitude in choosing their associates and bred a sense of independence, not something planters wanted to encourage. Slaves found it a welcome relief from the old plantation order.

As the slaveholders' economy faded, the slaves' economy flourished. Black men and women became full participants in the system of exchange that developed within the lower Mississippi Valley, trading the produce of their gardens and provision grounds, the fruits of their hunting and trapping expeditions, and a variety of handicrafts with European settlers and Indian tribesmen. Many hard-pressed planters turned to the production of foodstuffs for internal consumption and sometimes for export to Saint Domingue and Martinique. To cut costs, they encouraged and sometimes required slaves to feed themselves and their families by gardening, hunting, and trapping on their own time. Indeed, some slaveholders demanded that their slaves not only feed themselves but also provide their own clothes and purchase other necessities. Such requirements forced slaveowners to cede their slaves a portion of their time to work independently. "It is because the slaves are not clothed that they are left free of all work on Sunday," argued one advocate in an affirmation of the slaves' right to maintain gardens, market produce, and work independently on Sunday. "On such days some of them go to the neighbors' plantations who hire them to cut moss and to gather provisions. This is done with the tacit consent of their masters who do not know the where-abouts of their slaves on the said day, nor do they question them, nor do they worry themselves about them and are always satisfied that the negroes will appear again on the following Monday for work."[84]

With the promise of such independence—the right to travel freely, earn money from overwork, hire themselves out, and sell the products of their own labor—slaves accepted the burden of subsisting themselves. Plantation slaves established substantial gardens and raised barnyard fowl, crafted baskets and pottery, and hunted and fished, while refusing to relinquish their claim to a regular allowance from their owner. Eager to enrich the family diet and gain still greater control over their own lives, slaves pressed their owners to expand the time they could spend working for themselves. By mid-century, according to one account, slaves labored independently for as much as three of the thirteen hours of daylight in addition to Sundays. Some slaves gained Saturdays as well. Others worked long into the evening so they could extend their noontime break. "In this way," according to a Spanish officer, "they have time to attend for a short while to their crops and to their poultry, hogs, etc." Slaveholders gave the slaves' property de facto recognition by paying slaves for commodities they had produced on their own time and de jure recognition by protecting their property in court against theft. The slaveowners' actions deepened the slaves' sense of proprietorship over their own labor.[85]

In the lower Mississippi Valley as throughout mainland North America, the slaves' modest prosperity attracted a host of traders, shopkeepers, and peddlers—both Native American and European—who were eager to exchange their wares for those the slaves produced. Small crossroads taverns and groceries sprang up to purchase those wares, but slaves preferred to sell their goods themselves, generally in the bustling market at the great entrepôt of the Mississippi Valley, New Orleans, and its satellites of Mobile and Pensacola. There urban slaves—women working as domestics and marketers, men as laborers, teamsters, boatsmen, and artisans—developed an even more vigorous independent economy. "Those who live in or near the capital," reported an acute observer of slave life in Louisiana, "generally turn their two hours at noon to account by making faggots to sell in the city; others sell ashes, or fruits that are in season."[86]

Slaves who worked the great wharves and streets of the port cities or visited its markets carried away much besides a few sols or pesos earned from peddling their chickens and eggs. Market day broke the isolation of rural life and became social occasions of the first rank. Free from the direct oversight of an owner or *commandeur,* plantation slaves mixed openly among themselves and with the black residents of the city, selling and trading goods and gossip. Once the haggling had ended, the merriment began as slaves turned to more joyful pursuits, from religious observance to drinking, dancing, and gaming. Dressed in their finest attire, some pious men and women headed directly for the cathedral that dominated the city's main square, as the Catholic Church—unlike the established Protestant denominations—welcomed them. Others gravitated toward the back alleys and more secular pursuits. In the rear of the city, away

from the river, a regular rendezvous developed on the site of the slaves'
Sunday Market. *Place de Nègres,* later renamed Congo Square, soon became a gathering spot where black people celebrated their African past
and planned for an American future.[87]

The independence found in the streets of New Orleans was reinforced
by the expanding role of black men in Louisiana's militia. Playing off European-American vulnerability to foreign invasion and domestic insurrection, black militiamen gained special standing fighting the white man's
battles—first for the French during the Natchez rebellion and then for the
Spanish, who had long experience employing black soldiers. As soldiers
on behalf of the French and later the Spanish Crown, slave and free black
warriors not only tamed European interlopers and hostile Indians but also
disciplined plantation slaves and captured runaways. In the process, they
became a political, cultural, and sometimes a physical extension of European-American society. However grossly discriminated against, their service in the white man's cause enabled them to inch up the colony's social
ladder.

To assure a ready supply of colored militiamen and guarantee their loyalty, Spanish officials encouraged the growth of the free colored population (as free people of African descent were called, often regardless of
color). Unlike the French *Code Noir,* which discouraged manumission by
requiring slaveowners to obtain permission of the colony's highest governing body—the Superior Council—before they could free their slaves,
Spanish law allowed slaveowners to manumit with little more than a trip
to the local court house.[88] Given the opportunity, numerous slaveholders
made the journey. Between 1769 and 1779, the first decade after Spain
took effective control of Louisiana, slaveholders registered 320 deeds of
manumission in New Orleans, many times the number issued during the
entire period of French rule.[89]

Manumission began inside the slaveowners' household. Among the first
to be freed were the lovers and children of the slaveowners themselves.
During the first decade of Spanish rule, numerous masters freed their
slave wives, and the children they bore, for reasons of "love and affection."
More than half of the voluntary manumissions under Spanish rule were

children, and three-quarters of these were of mixed racial origins. Most of the adults were women. In short, given the opportunity, slaveholders freed their families as a matter of course.[90]

But manumission was not confined to family members. Close living conditions, particularly in the cities, allowed some slaves—generally house servants, artisans, and tradesmen and women of various sorts—to gain the attention and respect of their owners. Slaveholders also awarded these privileged slaves freedom, although again manumitters favored females over males. Women and girls made up nearly two-thirds of the slaves freed.[91]

Spanish officials also loosened strictures on self-emancipation, simplifying the purchase of freedom. Whereas the *Code Noir* made slave masters responsible for inaugurating slave freedom, the *Siete Partidas* and the *coartación*—the latter an amalgam of customary practices that had gained the force of law in Spanish America in the eighteenth century—gave slaves the power to initiate their own emancipation through negotiations with their owners. Once the process of self-purchase began, it transcended the relationship between master and slave, and the slaves' right to freedom could not be denied, even in the face of an owner's opposition.

If a slaveowner refused to negotiate freedom, the slave—or any interested party, for that matter—could petition the governor's court and have a *carta de libertad* issued, thereby requiring the owner to manumit when the stipulated price was paid. The *carta*, moreover, remained in force no matter how many times a slave was sold or traded, and any contribution the slave had made toward freedom had to be recognized by future owners. Owners who refused to negotiate with their slaves could be carried before a judicial tribunal, which would fix a price for slaves to buy themselves.[92] Unlike most of the regulations that defined slaves' rights, Spanish officials enforced the law respecting manumission, often in the face of the owners' steadfast opposition. With no special friend at law, slaveowners generally avoided official adjudication and settled with their slaves out of court.[93]

As Louisiana slaves grasped the implications of Spanish law and—most importantly—came to appreciate the willingness of Spanish officials to enforce it, more and more slaves took advantage of the new opportunities. Although master-inspired manumissions outnumbered those initiated by slaves during the first decade of Spanish rule, the proportion of slave-initiated manumissions steadily increased over the course of this period. Drawing upon their own resources and joining together with free people of color—many of them just a step removed from slavery—slaves opened negotiations to buy their own liberty and that of their families and friends. If owners rejected the slaves' proposals to buy their way out of bondage, slaves did not hesitate to invoke their legal rights.[94]

Still, the right to purchase freedom, no matter how fully elaborated, liberated not a single slave. Rather, it was the expansion of the slaves' independent economy during the post-Natchez years which gave people of African descent the opportunity to free themselves in large numbers. Drawing on the money they earned through jobbing, overwork, and the sale of produce and handicraft, Louisiana slaves—particularly those within easy reach of New Orleans—began to buy their way out of bondage in larger numbers than in any place in mainland North America. The free colored population, which had grown slowly under French rule, surged upward during the last third of the eighteenth century. In the first decade of Spanish rule, nearly 200 slaves initiated proceedings to purchase their freedom in New Orleans alone. As with master-sponsored manumission, a majority of the slaves who gained freedom through the courts were female, although they tended to be older and darker in color.[95] As a result, the free colored population increased dramatically after Spain took control of the colony, probably doubling the proportion of people of African descent who enjoyed freedom during the first decade.[96] In New Orleans, site of the greatest growth of the free community, this group grew from less than one hundred in 1771 to more than 315 in 1777.[97]

The collapse of staple production, the expansion of the slaves' economy, and the growth of the free colored population all signaled the re-emergence of a society with slaves in the lower Mississippi Valley. No Middle Passage Africanized the slave population there. But while the plantation revolution bypassed the region, it continued apace elsewhere on the North American mainland. In the Chesapeake, in lowcountry

South Carolina, Georgia, and East Florida, slave societies replaced societies with slaves, and a massive wave of new arrivals from the African interior swallowed the Atlantic creoles.

As connections between mainland black society and the larger Atlantic world attenuated, the expansion of the great estates and the growth of the African population made the plantation the locus of African-American life. Within the plantation, slaves struggled fiercely against the growing power of the planter class and their masters' determination to reduce black people to labor and little more. Countering the trauma of enslavement, towering rates of mortality, endless work, and omnipresent violence, slaves created new economies and societies to protect themselves from the harshest aspects of the slave regime and to provide a modicum of independence. Listening in on the growing debates between European-Americans and their European overlords, words like "freedom" and "liberty" attracted their attention, for they promised the reconstruction of black life on more favorable grounds. With the outbreak of revolutionary warfare first in the English seaboard colonies, then in continental Europe, and finally in the Caribbean, those possibilities became a new reality.

3

REVOLUTIONARY GENERATIONS

A Sunday Morning View of the African Episcopal Church of St Thomas in Philadelphia.—— Taken in June 1829

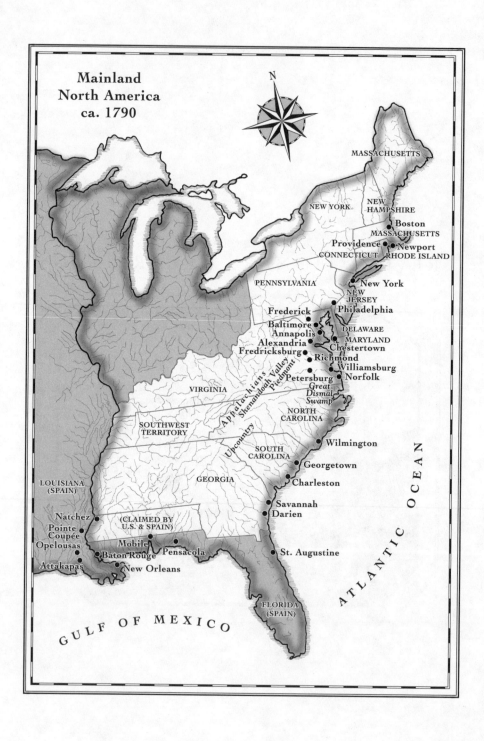

Mainland
North America
ca. 1790

N

MASSACHUSETTS

NEW YORK

NEW
HAMPSHIRE

Boston
MASSACHUSETTS

Providence
CONNECTICUT

Newport
RHODE ISLAND

PENNSYLVANIA

New York
NEW
JERSEY

Frederick

Philadelphia

Baltimore
Annapolis
Alexandria
Fredricksburg

DELAWARE

MARYLAND

Chestertown

Richmond
Williamsburg

Petersburg
Norfolk

VIRGINIA

Appalachians
Shenandoah Valley
Piedmont

Great
Dismal
Swamp

NORTH
CAROLINA

SOUTHWEST
TERRITORY

Upcountry

SOUTH
CAROLINA

Wilmington

Georgetown

GEORGIA

Charleston

LOUISIANA
(SPAIN)

Savannah
Darien

Natchez
Pointe
Coupée
Opelousas

(CLAIMED BY
U.S. & SPAIN)

Mobile

Pensacola

St. Augustine

Attakapas
Baton Rouge
New Orleans

ATLANTIC OCEAN

FLORIDA
(SPAIN)

GULF OF MEXICO

THE AGE OF the great democratic revolutions—the American, the French, and the Haitian—marked a third transformation in the lives of black people in mainland North America, propelling some slaves to freedom and dooming others to nearly another century of captivity. The War for American Independence and the revolutionary conflicts it spawned throughout the Atlantic gave slaves new leverage in their struggle with their owners. Shattering the unity of the planter class and compromising its ability to mobilize the metropolitan state to slavery's defense, the revolutionary era offered slaves new opportunities to challenge both the institution of chattel bondage and the allied structures of white supremacy.

In many instances, the state—whether understood as the planters' former British, French, and Spanish overlords or their own representatives—turned against the master class. As the slaveholders faltered, so did the support once rendered them by nonslaveholders. Some abandoned long-standing ties with planters, to fashion new connections among themselves. A few formed alliances with slaves. The emergence of such combinations compelled slave masters—now divided into Loyalist and Patriot factions—to make previously unimagined concessions, occasionally extending to freedom. Such concessions, no matter how skillfully parried, eroded the planters' position atop slave society and opened the way for some slaves to secure their freedom and others to improve their lot.

Yet, slaveholders did not surrender their power easily. In most places, they recovered their balance, sometimes overwhelming their opponents and sometimes acquiescing just enough to revitalize their shaken institution. At the end of the revolutionary era, there were many more black people enslaved than at the beginning. Even then, however, slaveowners could not recreate the status quo antebellum. The shock of revolution profoundly altered slavery.[1]

To a large degree, warfare itself—the intensity of the fighting and the internal divisions it created—shaped the slaves' ability to challenge the old order. Where the fighting remained distant and invading armies were little more than rumors, masters generally parried the slaves' threat. But where rival armies clashed and occupied large portions of the countryside, creating civil disorder and social strife, the advantage fell to the slaves. Often slaves found opportunities for freedom amid the chaos of war, camouflaging themselves among the tramping soldiers and occasionally taking up arms and becoming soldiers themselves.

The turmoil of war marked only the beginning of the slaveholders' problems. The invocation of universal equality—most prominently in the American Declaration of Independence and the French Declaration of the Rights of Man—further strengthened the slaves' hand. The Patriots' loud complaints of enslavement to a distant imperial tyrant and insistence on the universality of liberty overflowed the narrow boundaries of the struggle for political independence. How can Americans "complain so loudly of attempts to enslave them," mused Tom Paine in 1775, "while they hold so many hundreds of thousands in slavery?" Others, including many slaveholders, echoed Paine's unsettling query. Compelled by the logic of their own answers, some rebellious Americans moved against slavery.[2]

Revolutionary ideology was only one source of the new spirit of liberty and equality. In English North America, an evangelical upsurge that presumed all were equal in God's eyes complemented and sometimes reinforced revolutionary idealism, and placed new pressure on slaveholders. The evangelicals despised the planters' haughty manners and high ways and welcomed slaves into the fold as brothers and sisters in Jesus Christ. Black men and women who joined—and occasionally led—the evangelical churches considered temporal freedom an obvious extension of their spiritual liberation, and many white congregants enthusiastically agreed.[3]

The war and the libertarian ideology that accompanied it extended beyond the boundaries of the newly established United States, deeply affecting the rest of mainland North America. As the fighting spread to the lower Mississippi Valley and from there to the Gulf Coast, planters in those regions found themselves on the defensive, their position threatened by international rivalries among imperial powers and eroded by internal divisions. Events in France, Spain, mainland South America, and the islands of the Caribbean initiated new assaults on slavery and widened these breaches.

No place was touched more deeply than the French colony of Saint Domingue on the island of Hispaniola, where *gens de couleur,* seized by notions of liberty, equality, and fraternity, pressed their case for full citizenship. Planters denounced the free people of color as presumptuous upstarts and imprisoned their leaders, executing many after torture and mutilation. Driven to the brink, the free people took up arms and, when defeat loomed, armed their slaves, who needed no primer on revolution. The dispute between free people—white and brown—quickly escalated into a full-fledged slave insurrection, pitting white against black, free against slave. Interventions by the British and Spanish advanced the cause of the slave, as one belligerent after another bid for the slaves' support. By the time France tried to retake the colony and reimpose slavery, an independent Haiti had emerged under Toussaint L'Ouverture.[4] Saint Domingue's long shadow reached the deepest recesses of mainland society.[5]

As the realities of worldwide revolution manifested themselves, the ground for negotiation over slavery expanded, sometimes in legislative caucuses, sometimes in courtrooms, and sometimes directly between slaves and their owners. Slaves and masters positioned themselves to take advantage of the new circumstances. With the wind of revolution at their backs, slaves pressed to fulfill the expectations of the new era, if not with freedom, then at least with a greater measure of control over their lives and labor. Bracing against this gale of change, slaveowners labored to deflate the slaves' soaring expectations and, when possible, increase their control by extracting still greater drafts of labor. If the bloody events filled slaveholders with dread, they induced slaves to act with ever greater urgency.

THE NORTH

Nowhere on mainland North America did events and ideas of the Age of Revolution fall with greater force on black society than in the northern colonies. Emboldened by their own claim as freedom's champion, some white Americans joined slaves and free blacks in a condemnation of slavery. Emancipation came quickly in northern New England, particularly in areas where slaves were numerically few and economically marginal. Vermont freed its slaves by constitutional amendment and Massachusetts and New Hampshire by legal processes so obscure that historians continue to puzzle over slavery's demise.[6] But in southern New England and the Middle Atlantic states—where black people were more numerous and slavery more deeply entrenched—slaveholders resisted efforts to eliminate chattel bondage. Instead, they sought ways to protect their property by enforcing long-neglected slave codes and implementing new harsh restrictions.[7] In such places, the war itself proved the greatest solvent to the master-slave relation.

The massive movement of troops—particularly the British occupation and subsequent Patriot reoccupation of the great seaboard cities—and the resultant dispersal of civilian populations greatly disrupted the routines on which the slaveholders' power rested. Numerous owners transferred their slaves to friends and neighbors for safekeeping. Others tried to remove or "refugee" slaves (as the process became known) to distant places where they might be safe from confiscation or sequestration from one or the other belligerent.[8] Neither course had the desired effect. Even as slaveowners labored to shore up their faltering institution, black men and women fled bondage by the thousands. Generally, they headed for the war zone, where they found cover amid the chaos of armies on the move. Those willing to do the dirty work of war—cleaning camps, washing laundry, moving materiel, providing sex—found soldiers aplenty willing to provide shelter, sanctuary, and sometimes freedom in return for the slaves' labor. Once begun, the flood of fugitives proved difficult to stop, and it continued long after the fighting ended.

Successful flight struck slavery a mighty blow. Nothing strengthened the slaves' hand more than the example of former slaves. Although free people of color quickly acquired interests of their own—and calculated them carefully before committing themselves to slave or slaveowner—their very existence demonstrated the possibilities of freedom far better than any revolutionary tract. Free people of color, moreover, were not content simply to lead by example. Most espoused the cause of universal freedom and the liberation of family, friends, and indeed anyone who had shared with them the bitter fruits of bondage.

The wartime erosion of slavery encouraged direct assaults against the institution itself when peace returned. The heady notions of universal human equality that justified American independence gave black people a powerful weapon with which to attack chattel bondage, and they understood that this was no time to be quiet. "It is the momentous question of our lives," declared black Philadelphians in 1781. "If we are silent this day, we may be silent for ever."[9] Black people made themselves heard, denouncing the double standard that allowed white Americans to fight for their own freedom while denying that right to others. Indeed, slaves and free blacks not only employed the ideas of the Revolution but also its very language. Declaring that "they have in Common with all other men a Natural and Unalienable Right to that freedom which the Grat Parent of the Unavers hath Bestowed equalley on all menkind and which they have Never forfuted by any Compact or agreement whatever," black Bostonians amplified the idea respecting the "Naturel Right of all men" that was familiar to "every true patriot."

Such words could not be ignored easily by those who had marched under the banner of Jefferson's declaration. Numerous northern slaveholders yielded to the logic of the Revolution and freed their slaves or allowed them to purchase their liberty. In 1780 the revolutionary government of Pennsylvania, spurred by reminders that slavery was "disgraceful to any people, and more especially to those who have been contending in the great cause of liberty themselves," legislated a gradual emancipation. Other northern states followed, so that by the first years of the nineteenth century every state north of the Chesapeake enacted some plan for emancipation. The free black population of the North grew from a small corps of several hundred in the 1770s to nearly 50,000 in 1810. The Revolution thus reversed the development of northern slavery, first liquidating the remnants of a slave society, then revivifying the North as a society with slaves, and finally initiating the transformation into free states.

But the gradualist legislation assured that the demise of slavery in the North would be a slow, tortuous process. In 1810 there were still some 27,000 slaves in these so-called free states. For most northern slaves, more than a generation passed before they exited chattel bondage, and more than two generations went by before they extricated themselves from the various snares—legal, extralegal, and occasionally illegal—that allowed former owners and other white people to delay their freedom and control their lives and labor. In New York and New Jersey, the largest slaveholding states in the North, emancipation legislation left some black people locked in bondage or other forms of servitude until the mid-nineteenth century and beyond. Even then, former slaves faced a forest of proscriptive statutes and discriminatory practices as white lawmakers limited the legal rights of former slaves and as white employers created new forms of subordination that kept black people dependent.[10]

Black people who escaped slavery often found themselves living in circumstances that suspiciously resembled the old. Following the gradualist laws and conditional manumissions—which delayed manumission well into adulthood—many manumitters required their slaves to agree to long-term indentureships as part of the price of freedom, thereby reviving an older system of subordination and providing masters with a profitable exit from slaveownership. Even without prompting from their former owners, poverty forced freed people to indenture themselves or their children to white householders, many of whom were slaveholders or former slaveholders. Often newly emancipated black people left bondage and entered servitude in the same motion. The status and circumstances of black people made it easy for former masters to treat former slaves much as they had prior to emancipation and encouraged the notion that black free people were little more than slaves without masters. The logic of racial subordination hardened racial stereotypes.[11]

Slavery's slow demise had powerful consequences for African-American life in the North. It handicapped efforts of black people to secure households of their own, to find independent employment, and to establish their own institutions. It gave former slaveowners time to construct new forms of subordination that prevented the integration of black people into free society as equals. Indeed, in many places, free blacks continued to be governed by the same regulations as slaves—subjected to curfews and travel restrictions and denied the right to vote, sit on juries, testify in court, and stand in the militia. Finally, slavery's protracted demise created divisions within black society itself—between those who had early exited bondage and those who remained locked in slavery's grip until its final liquidation.

Legal freedom, however imperfect and slowly realized, was freedom nonetheless. Emancipated men and women began a historic reconstruction of black life, altering the relationship between black and white and among black people and transforming the meaning of race. Former slaves commonly celebrated emancipation by taking new names, as both a symbol of personal liberation and an act of political defiance. This gesture of self-definition reversed the enslavement process and confirmed the free blacks' newly won liberty, just as the loss of an African name had earlier symbolized enslavement. In taking new names, former slaves fused the processes of emancipation and creolization: they claimed their freedom and obliterated lingering reminders of the past, in slavery *and* in Africa.

Many freed peoples replaced the derisive names that slaveowners had forced upon them with Biblical and common Anglo-American names, shrugging off connections with slavery and Africa in the same motion. In place of Caesar and Pompey, Charity and Fortune, Cuffee and Phibbee stood Jim and Bett, Joe and Sarah, William and Rebecca. And—as if to emphasize the new self-esteem that accompanied freedom—freedpeople usually elevated their names from the diminutive to the full form: Jim became James and Bett became Elizabeth. In bondage, most black people had no surname; freedom allowed them the opportunity to select one. The black Freemans, Newmans, Somersets, and Armsteads scattered throughout the North suggests how a new name provided an occasion to celebrate slavery's demise. But most frequently, black people took familiar Anglo-American surnames—Jackson, Johnson, Moore, and Morgan. These names, like the singular absence of the names of the great slaveholding families, again suggest how black people identified with free society as they shucked off their old status.[12]

For many former slaves, another part of the process of securing freedom was establishing a new address. These freedpeople tried to escape the stigma of slavery by leaving their owner's abode for a new residence. Fleeing the memory of slavery and the subtle subordination that the continued presence of a former master entailed was reason enough to abandon old haunts. For others, however, freedom required a return to the site of their enslavement. But whether they fled from their old residence or returned to it, the process of emancipation set thousands of black people in motion.

For former owners, this massive migration was just additional evidence of the chaotic character of black life in freedom. But most newly freed blacks knew where they were going. The great thrust of post-revolutionary black migration in the North was from country to city, as former slaves escaped the poverty, isolation, and insecurity of the rural North. Augmenting this stream of cityward migrants were refugees from the south, as one southern state after another made manumission contingent upon removal.[13] To these mainland migrants were added several hundred, perhaps as many as a thousand, black refugees who had been caught in the insurgency that transformed Saint Domingue into the world's first black republic. Many in the North echoed the sentiment of one white New Yorker who complained that "whole hosts of Africans now deluge our city."[14]

With their numbers swollen by the influx, black northerners, who had always been disproportionately urban, became even more so. The black populations of Philadelphia, New York City, and Boston grew considerably faster than those of Pennsylvania, New York State, and Massachusetts.[15] This vast movement of people also shifted the sexual balance of black society. The disproportionate importation of African men had created a largely male slave population during the period prior to the Revolution. By the beginning of the nineteenth century, however, the sexual balance had shifted in the urban North. In 1806 black women outnumbered black men four to three in New York City. Among people who were still enslaved the imbalance was even more pronounced. The sexual disequilibrium in northern cities grew thereafter. Notably absent were urban males in their late teens and twenties, many of whom had been sold south and some of whom had gone to sea, as the maritime industry became the largest single employer of black men. In the countryside, the black population remained heavily male.[16]

Along with other baggage that former slaves brought to the cities of the North was a powerful desire to escape the drudgery that accompanied slavery and to improve their material circumstances. Yet, emancipation did little to elevate the status of former slaves and, in many ways, weakened the place of black men and women in the northern economy. As slavery waned in the North, black people moved from the artisan shop to the merchant household, severing the ties between black men and the most lucrative urban work.[17] Slave craftsmen had difficulty finding work at their old trades once they were free, as white employers refused to hire free blacks for any but the most menial tasks. At best, such work was hard, dirty, irregular, and unremunerative. Often it could be demeaning, as when black laborers swept streets and disposed of night soil. The female majority reinforced the identification of black women with domestic labor, as they rarely worked outside the service trades.[18]

As former slaves dropped to the bottom of the occupational hierarchy, they had few friends to slow their descent. In the North, revolutionary ideology promised freedom but made no provision for former slaves to be trained in a craft and offered no guarantees of steady work or a living wage. After freeing their slaves, slaveowners expressed almost no concern for their fate. Having lost the guarantee of subsistence, most black people scrambled to survive.[19]

Nonetheless, some black men and women found a niche in the middle ranks of American society, entering the professions and mechanical trades and securing small proprietorships. A handful became merchants and manufacturers of the first rank. But the service trades—work that had been identified with slavery—provided the primary occupational refuge. To white northerners, catering food, cleaning stables, cutting hair, and driving coaches seemed fitting roles for newly freed black men and women, since it kept black people at the service of white people. Although some free blacks saw in such work only painful reminders of the past, others saw opportunities. Many of the most successful black businessmen and women opened their own barber shops, catering establishments, coal yards, oyster houses, and stables.[20]

Economic independence provided the basis of family security, and no goal stood higher among the newly freed people than establishing a household under their own control. Given the opportunity, newly freed slaves legitimated relations that previously had no standing in law, joining together to celebrate weddings and to register their marriages in official records often of their own making. The legitimatization of long-standing relationships allowed black people a freer hand in performing familial duties, as husbands and wives, parents, sons and daughters.

But giving family life a basis in fact as well as in law was generally the last step in a long process. Before a family could be united under one roof, spouses, parents, and children had to be located, an arduous task amid the flight of so many slaves. Wartime disorder assured that post-revolutionary reconstruction would be slow, tedious, and—for many—incomplete. Free people continued to reside in the households of their former owners and other white employers. Because many of these employers refused to lodge complete families, husband and wives, parents and children were often forced to reside under different roofs. Only as they gained a competency could black people begin to form independent households. Even then, black households commonly held multiple families or included boarders among their residents.[21]

As black men and women set up housekeeping on their own, the residential distribution of black people shifted. In the great seaports, many black people left their owners' neighborhoods for the same reasons they had abandoned the countryside—to escape the daily reminders of their former status. But no single area of residential concentration emerged in any northern city, so that the new pattern of residence was hardly a ghetto. Instead, clusters of three or four black families congregated in older commercial areas that were residentially undesirable or in the outlying districts where rents were cheap. Although the majority of residents of such neighborhoods were white, the high concentration of black people made them centers of the nascent African-American community.[22]

Black communities soon sported a host of institutions—churches, schools, fraternal organizations, and friendly societies—which addressed the problems of newly freed slaves. Many of these institutions rested upon the informal, clandestine associations black people had created in slavery. Others drew on the experiences former slaves gained interacting with white abolitionists, who had assisted their passage from slavery. Yet others were a product of the novel circumstances of freedom: the need for a whole range of services—from maternal care to burial—as well as the freedpeople's desire to articulate their own moral and social commitments.

The new organizations marked the emergence of a leadership class that came of age with freedom.[23] Many of these leaders owed their liberty to the changes unleashed during the Age of Revolution, and they shared the optimism that accompanied independence. Generally wealthier, more literate, and better connected with white people than most former slaves, these upward-striving and self-consciously respectable men and women assumed positions of leadership in the growing free black population and pressed for equality. Standing in the vanguard of the liberation of their people, they became the slaves' advocate and the great champions of universal freedom.

Pointing to the Declaration of Independence, they petitioned for a ban on the slave trade, demanded that rights to manumission be enlarged, and pressed for a general emancipation. Where gradual emancipation laws had been enacted, they labored to speed slavery's demise. When Pennsylvania slaveholders attempted to amend the Emancipation Act of 1780 in order to re-enslave many of those who had recently been freed, black petitioners successfully urged the state legislature not to return former slaves to "all the horrors of hateful slavery" after restoring "the common blessings they were by nature entitled to." And once freedom was achieved, black men and women demanded complete equality, attacking limitations on their right to sit on juries, testify in court, and vote.[23]

Proud of their achievements and certain their experience provided a guide that would elevate the entire race, these new leaders did not hesitate to lecture "their people" on the importance of hard work, temperance, frugality, and piety. Rejecting the saturnalia of Election Day, they established new forms of sociability and political action, celebrating not the coronation of surrogate kings and queens but their own exodus from bondage with grand parades and long orations. Disciplined political caucuses, with their careful adherence to parliamentary rules, and precisely worded memorials, with their classical references, demonstrated to all who would listen that free men and women of color were not a heathen, uncivilized people but respectable, propertied men and women worthy of citizenship in the republic.[24]

Much of their intended audience hardly heard the message. Outside of a small circle of abolitionists, white northerners ignored the black petitioners, dismissed their petitions, threw eggs at their parades, and ridiculed their claim to citizenship. More importantly, many of their black compatriots also paid them no mind. Eager to enjoy the immediate rewards of liberty, these new arrivals to freedom spent their wages on new frocks and waistcoats. While the respectables met in the quiet decorum of their sitting rooms to debate the issues of the day, the newcomers joined together in smoke-filled gaming houses and noisy midnight frolics. Their boisterous lifestyle, colorful dress, plaited hair, eelskin queues, and swaggering gait scandalized the respectables, who saw such behavior as a calumny upon the race and a special threat to their own efforts to secure full recognition. The newcomers sneered at their pretensions.

But on one thing nearly all black people agreed. The universal adoption of the term "African" in the designation of African-American institutions marked the final creation of an African nationality in the New World. If black people in the North no longer called themselves or named their children in the traditional African manner, they nevertheless celebrated their origins on the placards that adorned the largest buildings and the biggest organizations in the black community. The Free African Society of Philadelphia introduced its articles of incorporation with the words: "We, the free Africans and their descendants." Some spoke earnestly about returning to Africa, although few actually made the journey.[25] The acceptance of "African" as the institutional designation also denoted the passing of distinctive national identities—the descendants of Africa were no longer Igbos, Coromantees, or Gambians. Henceforth, all people of African descent in the United States would be one people.[26]

THE CHESAPEAKE

As in the northern colonies, the struggle for political independence—both the war itself and the changes that accompanied the establishment of an independent republic—transformed African-American life in the Upper South (as the Chesapeake region and its western extension into Kentucky, Tennessee, and Missouri came to be known). But unlike slavery in the North, slavery in the Upper South did not crack under the blows of revolutionary republicanism and evangelical egalitarianism. The slave society that had emerged in the wake of the plantation revolution of the late seventeenth century hardly faltered, even as the region's periphery—most prominently the area around Baltimore—devolved into a society with slaves. Thousands of slaves gained their liberty in the Upper South, and the greatly enlarged free black population began to reconstruct black life in freedom. But the expansion of slavery, and with it a host of new forms of racial dependency, more than counterbalanced the growth of freedom. Upper South planters emerged from the Revolution burdened by the threat of eventual emancipation but deeply committed to maintaining slavery as long as possible.

The nature of the war itself in the Upper South helped preserve slavery. Black people understood the importance of the revolutionary conflict to their prospects for freedom, and they found a willing ally in Virginia's governor, Lord Dunmore, who, in return for freedom, accepted their offer of military service in the King's cause. But in December 1775, Dunmore's Ethiopian Regiment was defeated at the battle of Great Bridge, forcing the governor and his black allies to evacuate the region. Thereafter the Chesapeake became a minor theater of the war; armed conflict did not return until 1783. Still, Dunmore's Proclamation and the occasional raid on Patriot plantations stirred slaves throughout the Chesapeake, allowing several thousand to seize their freedom.

When the British evacuated Yorktown, they took some of these slaves—several hundred—with them. Many were betrayed and given to soldiers as bounties or to Loyalist planters in compensation for property confiscated by the Patriots.[27] But the British also allowed some slaves to make their way to freedom in the North, Canada, and the West Indies. These outposts of African-American life were the beginning of a diaspora whereby people of African descent but American birth would repeople the Atlantic, this time from west to east. In all, more than 5,000 Upper South slaves escaped bondage during the war, and perhaps an equal number remained free in the South.[28]

This loss of a tiny fraction of the region's slave population hardly affected the long-term development of the Upper South. By refugeeing some slaves, disciplining others, and renegotiating basic labor arrangements with still others, Chesapeake planters kept their holdings intact even as slavery collapsed in the states to the north. In time, they even recovered some fugitives from places as distant as St. Augustine and New York, dragging them back into captivity from freedom's doorstep. More significantly, over the course of the war, the number of slaves in the Upper South grew by natural means. In spite of wartime turbulence that increased mortality and allowed some escapes, the Chesapeake's slave population continued to grow at an annual rate of about 2 percent. Between the beginning of the Revolution and the dawn of the new century, the slave population of the Chesapeake expanded by two-thirds and the region emerged as the major exporter of slaves.[29]

The steady growth of the Upper South's slave population had a profound effect on the institution of slavery. It frustrated nascent emancipationist sentiment and affirmed the planters' commitment to slavery. It allowed many nonslaveholders to enter the slaveholder's ranks, solidifying support for chattel bondage among those who previously had no direct interest in the institution. Perhaps most important, the growing number of slaves promoted the belief that the region was overpopulated. George Washington spoke for his class when he observed that it was "demonstratively clear that . . . I have more working Negros by a full moiety, than can be employed to any advantage in the farming system."[30]

Enjoying a surfeit of bound labor, Chesapeake planters became vocal opponents of the African slave trade, smugly condemning both Lower South planters who were impatient to repopulate their plantations and northern merchants who were eager to supply them with Africans. The opposition of Chesapeake slaveholders to the international slave trade— but not to slavery per se—allowed them to initiate a new inter-regional trade consonant with their needs.[31] The internal slave trade, or Second Middle Passage, proved to be a source of enormous profit to slaveowners in the Upper South—what one Maryland newspaper called "an almost universal resource to raise money."

While planters invested their quick cash in new comforts and new economies, slaves found their lives thrown into disarray, their families dismembered, and their communities set adrift. At century's end, men and women whose ancestors had worked the tobacco fields of the Chesapeake for a century or more were soon growing hemp in Kentucky and Tennessee, cotton in the southern interior, and sugar in the lower Mississippi Valley. An estimated 115,000 slaves left the tidewater region between 1780 and 1810. Although forced migration of slaves during this period—called by contemporaries the "Georgia trade"—would be dwarfed by the massive intercontinental trade of the nineteenth century, its traumatic effects resonated throughout the slave quarter.[32]

The war and independence reordered the region's economy by unseating tobacco monoculture and putting in its place a new regimen of mixed farming—corn, wheat, dairy, and, in some cases, vegetables and fruits. The dynamic element in the new agricultural mix was wheat, the demand for which increased as the European crisis set in motion by the French

Revolution deepened.[33] Wheat cultivation altered the rhythm of the work year, the daily routine, the division of labor, and the nature of the task. Wheat required steady workers only during planting and harvesting; for the remainder of the year, workers had little to do with the crop. Wheat also sped the switch from hoe to plow and, concomitantly, the employment of draft animals, which needed pens and barns, pasturage in the summer, and forage in the winter. A variety of new plantation-based occupations arose: stockminder, dairy maid, herdsman, and of course plowman. Finally, wheat required a larger, more mobile, more skilled labor force than tobacco monoculture to transport the grain to market, store it, mill it, and reship it as bulk grain, flour, or bread. The wagons in which wheat was shipped, the animals that pulled them, and the bridles and harnesses the animals wore all required maintenance.[34]

Slaves performed most of these new tasks. On the plantations and farms, they sowed, mowed, plowed, broke flax, pressed cider, sheared sheep, and did dozens of other chores. Off the estates, they drove wagons, sailed boats, serviced inns and taverns, and labored in a variety of enterprises. Planters established cooperages, flour mills, iron works, smithies, and tanneries, creating still other employment for their slaves and increasing the proportion of slaves employed in nonagricultural pursuits. Yet, despite the many specialties in the new economy, most skilled slaves were not required to specialize in just one task. They moved from job to job over the course of the year to meet their owners' increasingly diverse demands.

Movement became the defining feature of black life in the postwar Chesapeake. Those who were not sold south shifted from place to place with greater frequency after the war. Often their owners hired them out, sometimes by the year, sometimes by the month, week, or day, and sometimes by the job. Such movement often came as a welcomed relief from the narrow confines of plantation life. The slaves' increased mobility was not simply a product of a changing economy; it also exemplified their willingness to seize advantages in the new order to remake their lives.[35]

The new economy broke the isolation of slave life on Chesapeake plantations in other ways as well. White workers also cultivated wheat and other small grains. Slaves who had worked only among their own suddenly found themselves laboring alongside white men and women, hired by the day or the job.[36] The re-creation of a mixed labor force returned the Chesapeake to its seventeenth-century agricultural beginnings, when white and black worked side by side. While the world of the Atlantic creoles could not be reproduced quite as easily as this new propinquity, the interaction of white and black field hands suggested new possibilities to a generation of slaves who had previously labored for white men but seldom beside them.

As they adjusted their labor force, slaveholders tried to reclaim prerogatives that had been lost during the tumult of war. Styling themselves "improving farmers," planters introduced new managerial techniques to rationalize production and increase the profitability of their estates—all in the name of a new enlightened age.[37] From the slaves' perspective, such progressive agriculture doubtless looked like much of the same, and "improvement" was just the masters' euphemism for working their slaves harder and longer. At Mount Vernon, George Washington set a pace that left slaves' time for little but work, ordering his overseers to have them "at their work as soon as it is light—work 'till it is dark—and be diligent while they are at it . . . The presumption," he emphasized, "being, that, every Labourer (male or female) does as much in the 24 hours as their strength, without endangering their health, or constitution, will allow of." While Washington disdained the lash and offered a variety of incentives to encourage his slaves to meet his imposing standard of industry, he also implemented a system of close supervision. "If the Negroes will not do their duty by fair means, they must be compelled to do it," declared the leader of the new republic.[38]

Slaves resisted this intensification of labor under the new regimen much as they had resisted it under the old, frustrating and infuriating those who had been charged with its implementation. As masters like Washington contrived to speed the pace of work, slaves conspired to maintain what they had come to understand as the traditional stint. More than one overseer felt like James Eagle, who supervised slaves on a Maryland plantation, when he complained that the slaves under his direction "Get much more

Dissatisfied Every year & troublesome for they say that they ought all to be at there liberty & they think that I am the Cause that they are not." Eventually, Eagle quit, muttering about being unable to "Conduct my business as I ought to do."[39]

Eagle's frustration reveals the advantages that some slaves found in the new order. The growing size and density of the black population made it easier for slaves to maintain an active community life. The rural isolation of the early eighteenth century was a thing of the past. The very mobility that introduced uncertainty into slave life also gave slaves a fuller knowledge of the world beyond the plantation's borders. In addition, the new economy permitted a growing number of slaves to escape backbreaking field labor entirely and move into artisanal positions previously reserved for white men and women. The plantations and farms of the Upper South began to house many more skilled workers and many fewer field hands.[40]

The host of skills required by mixed farming created a market for short-term labor, and slaves were as quick as their owners to see profit—and a measure of freedom—in meeting that demand. Artisans, boatmen, and wagoners had far greater control over their lives than field hands or domestics. But "jobbing" was just a small part of the slaves' economy. Entering the marketplace, slaves sold items of handicraft and produce from their gardens, along with their labor, and thereby accumulated property of their own.[41] The slaves' economy grew rapidly in the manufactories—iron forges and furnaces especially—where payment for overwork was but one of many incentives that slaveowners employed to compensate skilled workers.[42]

The expansion of the slaves' economy opened the door for a reformulation of the master-slave relationship. Slaves proved to be tough bargainers. They tenaciously protected what they understood to be rightfully theirs, and they believed that additional assignments should be compensated. Few slaveholders dared to challenge the slaves' right to market goods produced on their own time, and some slaveholders regularly purchased produce from their slaves—affirming the slaves' right to a portion of their own labor. The reinvigoration of the slaves' economy entangled masters and slaves in endless negotiations, which sometimes resolved amicably but often dissatisfied one or the other party, and sometimes both.[43]

For the most part, the slaves' economy was a family economy. Whether working in the gardens and grounds, making items of handicraft, or earning a few dollars in "overwork," everyone labored to supplement the family's diet, improve their clothing, or add to their stock of household items. To go beyond subsistence required not only adult working hands but the labor of those whom even slaveholders had not yet tapped. The very young and the very old became the backbone of the slaves' own workforce. Their mobilization made new demands on family life and created new tensions. But it also provided the glue that held families together and extended kinship beyond the household.

Changes in both the masters' and the slaves' economies affected men and women differently. In general, most of the positions requiring skill or demanding mobility went to men, leaving the work force in the field even more disproportionately female than before the war. This new sexual division of labor threatened family life, as members were forcibly removed through apprenticeship, rental, and especially sale to the southern interior.[44] The number of families in which parents and children shared a residence declined among the revolutionary generation, and it became, as an English visitor observed, the "usual practice for the negroes to go to see their wives on the Saturday night." Although slaves regained considerable control over their domestic lives in the years following the Revolution—in their choice of marriage partners and supervision of their own children—the separation of husbands and wives and parents and children introduced another element of instability in the domestic lives of slaves.[45]

Alterations in the structure of family life were paralleled by changes in religious life. The evangelical awakenings, led primarily by Baptists and Methodists, which had begun prior to the Revolution, re-ignited in the 1780s. Even more than in the pre-revolutionary period, the movement's rough egalitarianism became harnessed to a growing antislavery sentiment and a willingness to allow slave and free black members to participate in some aspects of church governance and discipline. Attracted by the social inversion implicit in this radical reading of the Bible—a savior who loved all equally, and a God who promised vengeance on the wicked and ever-lasting glory to the good—the enslaved, the impoverished, and the de-spised flocked to the evangelical standard. Indeed, within the white popu-lace, evangelical preachers were the most determined opponents of slavery. Whether it was the hope of eternal life or temporal equality that drew slaves to the church, black men and especially black women came in un-precedented numbers.[46] Although only a small fragment of the black pop-ulation embraced Christianity, this cadre of awakeners represented Chris-tianity's first beachhead in African-American life since the demise of the charter generations. In blending Christianity with the sacred world their parents, and sometimes grandparents, had carried from Africa, these new converts to Christianity created a creed which emphasized that all were equal in the sight of God, and they employed it to redress their owners' authority.

The evangelicals' antislavery moment soon passed. The preachers' op-position to slavery faltered under pressure from planters and from their own quest for respectability. But the slaves who had accepted Christ as their savior maintained their commitment to evangelical Christianity's spiritual and social promise. Although still but a tiny portion of the slave population—not more than 10 percent at the turn of the century, accord-ing to a generous estimate—black converts filled churches and camp meetings and made up a substantial minority of Baptist and Methodist congregations. Black believers took to the pulpit themselves, and a small number of black ministers could be found scattered throughout the re-gion, preaching openly to black and, occasionally, mixed churches. They and their followers would provide the shock troops in the Christianization of black life.[47]

Like many ambitious black men and women, black preachers gravitated toward the growing towns and cities of the region: Alexandria, Chester-town, Frederick, Fredericksburg, Norfolk, Petersburg, Richmond, and, most importantly, Baltimore.[48] In all of those places, artisans stood at the heart of economic change, and black men composed a large faction of these skilled workers. While newly freed slaves were being ousted from northern workshops, black men and women were becoming the backbone of the Chesapeake's urban industrial workforce, some as slaves and some as slave hirelings.[49] Towns became great emporiums in which everything was for sale, and among the commodities that might be purchased was freedom.

Wheat culture and its concomitant urbanization spurred the growth of the free black population—perhaps the single most important development in black life in the Upper South. The proportion of black people enjoying freedom had declined steadily during the eighteenth century, as manumission nearly ended and the charter generation failed to reproduce itself. But the changes that accompanied the Revolution—the war, the transformation of the countryside, and the growth of towns—reversed the downward slide of African-American liberation, and free blacks became the fastest growing element in the region's population. With slaves gaining their freedom through military service, successful flight, freedom suits, self-purchase, and grants of manumission, the Chesapeake's free black population doubled and doubled again in the three decades following the Revolution. By the end of the first decade of the nineteenth century, there were over 108,000 free black people in the Upper South. Better than 10 percent of the black population enjoyed freedom.[50]

Growing numbers altered the character of the free black population. As men and women gained their freedom in roughly equal numbers, the sexual imbalance of the free black community, which had long weighed heavily toward women, readjusted toward equilibrium.[51] Most of these newly freed blacks had darker skin than those in the first wave, who were the product of relations between white and black, generally the indentured European servant women and African slave men. As large-scale indiscriminate manumission and the successful escape of many fugitives darkened the free black population, the balance between mulatto and black free people may have tilted toward the latter.[52] Since most runaways were young men and women, the growing number of successful fugitives infused the free black population with a large group of restless youths. By the beginning of the nineteenth century, free people of African descent were no longer a tiny group of mulattoes and cripples, as it had been in the years immediately before the Revolution. It included more people of unmixed racial origins, the vigorous young as well as elderly former slaves.

As in the North, freedom arrived in the Upper South under the heavy burden of slavery's continuing presence, and new forms of dependency emerged as quickly as old ones were liquidated. In the countryside, many free blacks continued to reside with their former masters, suffering the oversight of an owner even after they were no longer owned. Planters came to appreciate the advantages of control without responsibility. They held tight to the spouses and children of former slaves, using them as a lever to gain access to the labor of free blacks. Some planters sold or rented small plots of land to former slaves to secure the benefit of their labor during planting and harvest. In the cities, "term slavery"—whereby black people were to receive their freedom at some distant time—provided a means for owners to exact the labor of men and women while they were young and vigorous and then make them responsible for themselves in old age. Much like gradual emancipation and apprenticeship in the northern states, contingent manumission and term slavery delayed the arrival of freedom and strengthened the master's hand.[53]

But if the continued threat of slavery weighed heavily on those who gained their freedom, newly freed blacks accepted the challenge. They worked assiduously to free their kin, since slaves could rarely buy their way out of bondage on their own—belying the term "self-purchase." Much the same could be said about successful flight, in that few people escaped bondage without assistance from family or friends. It was precisely the determination of newly freed slaves to aid those still in bondage—particularly their kin—that made them untrustworthy in the eyes of slaveholders and their white allies. Newly freed blacks faced heightened proscription, ostracism, and discrimination. To the new forms of subordination that equated free blacks with slaves, lawmakers affixed additional burdens to distinguish free black people from free whites. Rights identified with citizenship and manhood—voting, sitting on juries, testifying in court, attending the militia, owning dogs, and carrying guns—were denied black men. A pass system prevented black men and women from traveling freely and required them to register annually with county authorities. Many of these restrictions had long existed, but the new legislation reinforced them, reminding all that freedom would not mean equality.[54]

The straightjacket of new forms of subordination did not prevent former slaves from celebrating emancipation, however. As a first gesture in declaring their new status, free blacks in the Upper South, like their northern counterparts, chose to change their own names. With freedom, day names (Friday, Tuesday) and place names (London, Paris) became less prominent among people of African descent, and common Anglo-American names became the norm. The classical names of slave times made their final exit among free people, as did the various diminutives with which slaves had been tagged. The aspiration for full manhood and womanhood was also manifest in the selection of surnames, which became nearly universal among free blacks during the first decade of the nineteenth century. Although Upper South free blacks took the names of former masters with greater frequency than did their northern counterparts, such names were never the rule. Indeed, census enumerators identified a disproportionately large number of black people who celebrated their liberation by declaring themselves Freeman, Freeland, and Liberty.[55]

As in the North, a new address often accompanied a new name. But there was no rural evacuation of the Upper South, as most newly liberated slaves were unwilling to abandon friends and relatives still in slavery. The majority of free blacks remained in the countryside. Still, a distinct cityward migration caused urban officials in the Upper South to join their northern counterparts in bemoaning the "large numbers of free blacks flock[ing] from the country to the towns." Without exception, the free black population of every Upper South city grew faster than in the hinterland and generally faster than the urban white and slave populace. As the balance of the region's free black life swung to the cities, the proportion of the urban black population that enjoyed freedom likewise increased, so that the cities tilted toward freedom following the Revolution.[56]

The achievement of household independence lagged far behind the arrival of freedom, however, as newly freed men and women continued to reside with slaveholders, many of whom had been their owners. The slow rate of household formation pointed to the difficulty free blacks had in earning a living. In the countryside, free blacks generally worked as farm hands. A few entered into sharecropping agreements, and a handful even negotiated tenantries, hoping to ascend the agricultural ladder to land-ownership. However hard they labored, few black croppers and tenants joined the landowning class. In Baltimore County, as favorable an environment as free blacks might find in the region, black property owners composed only 4 percent of the landowners in 1790.[57]

Whereas blacks became increasingly marginal to the northern economy in the years following emancipation, free blacks—and slaves—grew more important in the Upper South. The continued presence of slavery, which stymied the aspirations of black people for an independent domestic life, strengthened their place in the urban economy. Behind the shadow of slave labor, particularly the growing use of hired slaves, free blacks maintained their place in the artisanal crafts and urban services. The occupational niches free blacks occupied in the Upper South—barbering, catering, drayage, and shoemaking—were much the same as in the North, but they were considerably larger. Still, urban free blacks, for the most part, remained poor and propertyless, pushing a broom or shouldering a shovel for a living.[58]

Poor or not, free blacks began to create a society worthy of their new status. A leadership class soon emerged from within the ranks of the black artisans and shopkeepers, much as it did in the North. Men like Daniel Coker in Baltimore, Christopher McPherson in Richmond, and Ceasar Hope in Williamsburg were as much a product of the transformation of black life in the Upper South as were Richard Allen in Philadelphia and Prince Hall in Boston. Like Allen and Hall, the new leaders of the Upper South eagerly pressed for full citizenship. Indeed, Upper South blacks stepped beyond those in the northern states, entering into the partisan electoral arena. In 1792 Thomas Brown, a veteran of the Revolution, offered himself to Baltimore's electorate, declaring that his candidacy for the Maryland House of Delegates would "represent so many hundreds of poor Blacks as inhabit this town, as well as several thousands in different parts of the state."[59]

Before long, the institutional scaffolding of African-American life, from schools to cemeteries, all bore the name "African." As in the North, the African church occupied a central position in this new social structure.[60] But the sharp divisions between the respectables and the poor, so evident in post-emancipation black society in the North, never emerged in the Upper South. To be sure, there was a powerful tavern culture along the docks and in the back alleys of the new towns that challenged the aspirations of the upward-striving, church-going respectables; poor free blacks and slaves marched to a different drummer than did the likes of Coker and Hope. But the continued existence of slavery in the Upper South muted these differences within black society. Many free people of color— men and women—married slaves and lived, worked, and prayed with them. Independent African churches were usually joint ventures of free and slave. The ability of free people to hold property propelled them into positions of leadership in these organizations, but slaves participated fully and often took leadership roles as deacons and ministers. Everyday experience reinforced these ties between free and slave peoples. Measured by church membership, family formation, wealth distribution, and aspirations, black society was much more of one piece in the Upper South—despite the formal divisions of free and slave—than in the North. As perhaps nowhere else in the United States, the fate of free and slave blacks was entwined.

LOWCOUNTRY SOUTH CAROLINA, GEORGIA, AND EAST FLORIDA

The revolutionary changes that mobilized the North to move from a slave to a free society and stimulated the expansion of the free black population in the Upper South resonated differently in the Lower South—South Carolina, Georgia, and Florida and, as settlement spread west, Alabama and Mississippi. The War for Independence greatly disrupted plantation life, but the Patriot victory affirmed the power of the planter class and armed it with new weapons to protect and expand slavery. Unlike in the North, the region's leading men did not associate in abolition societies and press for the liquidation of slavery after the war. Indeed, they did not even muse about the possibility of slavery's eventual demise, as did slaveholders in the Upper South. Nowhere in the Lower South did lawmakers scheme to invent new forms of racial subordination to keep control of their laborers, such as apprenticeship, contingent manumission, or term slavery. Nowhere did the features of a society with slaves re-emerge. Instead, planters repaired the damage the war had wrought, extended their domain to the upcountry in the foothills of the Blue Ridge, reopened direct trade with Africa, and consolidated their status as the region's ruling class. By the beginning of the nineteenth century, slavery in the Lower South was primed for a half century of explosive growth.

The War for American Independence ripped the fabric of society in the Lower South. As nowhere else on the North American continent, the Revolution became a bitter civil war filled with savage, fratricidal violence. Loyalist partisans backed by the might of the world's greatest military power and Patriot forces supported by the revolutionary army bloodied each other for more than seven years. Throwing aside military conventions, the combatants resorted to ambush, assassination, arson, butchery, pillage, and plunder, assaulting each other with growing ferocity. Between the Loyalists and Patriots stood thousands of men and women who desired nothing more than to stay out of harm's way. When they could not, many turned Tory and initiated their own war of all-against-all, forming bands of guerrillas and banditti who had no permanent allegiance but to their own narrow interests. Such savage warfare exposed slaves to unspeakable atrocities, but it also revealed the rifts within the planter class.[61]

Slaves quickly took advantage of these divisions. Many gained their freedom aiding one belligerent or the other. The British were the first to offer an exchange of freedom, and thousands of slaves volunteered for what one called "the king's service." General-in-Chief Henry Clinton promised "full security to follow . . . any Occupation which [they] shall think proper within British lines." The Patriots were not far behind, although their promise of freedom never enjoyed the same official sanction. Other slaves simply abandoned their owners and set off on their own. Before he ran off in the fall of 1775, Limus boldly announced his determination to be his own man. "Though he is my Property," reported Limus's stunned owner, "he has the audacity to tell me, he will be free, that he will serve no Man, and that he will be conquered or governed by no Man." With that, Limus was gone.[62]

Perhaps like Limus, many runaways found refuge in swollen maroon colonies or the ports of Charles Town (now Charleston) and Savannah, particularly after the British occupied them. Still others found no need to run, since their masters abandoned them. By fleeing the disorder of the countryside, fearful masters allowed slaves to claim their liberty on their old estates.

The slaves' seizure of freedom panicked lowcountry slaveholders. Reading every challenge to their authority as the beginning of an insurrection, they thrashed wildly against the "deep laid Horrid Tragick Plan for destroying the inhabitants of this province without respect of persons, age or sex." When they could, they refugeed their slaves to some safe haven in the Floridas, Louisiana, and the West Indies. When they could not, they instituted a reign of terror, enacting new restrictive slave codes and enforcing old ones with a vengeance.

Scapegoats were numerous. Thomas Jeremiah, a successful free black pilot in Charleston—called by South Carolina's royal governor "one of the most valuable, and useful men . . . in the Province"—was arrested for conspiring to lead slaves into an alliance with the British. When the governor protested the gross miscarriage of justice, Charleston's Committee for Safety brazenly threatened to hang Jeremiah on the doorpost of the executive mansion. The governor thereafter held his tongue, but his silence did nothing to save Jeremiah, who was hanged and then burned.[63]

No successful insurrection placed the bottom rail on top, but thousands of slaves gained their freedom, escaping to the lowland swamps, upcountry, Spanish Florida, and the greater Atlantic. Their success induced slaveowners to append a novel notice to the standard runaway advertisement: "If they will return to their duty they will be forgiven." Such pathetic

pleas revealed how wartime events had compromised the masters' authority and reduced the great planters to supplicants.[64] At war's end, many of
these fugitive slaves—perhaps as many as 20,000—left the lowcountry
when the retreating British evacuated Savannah and Charleston. Thousands more remained at large. When Thomas Pinckney, South Carolina's
representative to the Continental Congress, returned home, he discovered
his plantation empty of slaves except for a handful of pregnant women
and old people. Pinckney's experience was no exception.[65]

Freedom brought few immediate benefits to the escapees. The war scattered friends and separated families. Those who took refuge in army
camps, whether Loyalist or Patriot, found themselves exploited, battered,
and sometimes re-enslaved. Often, they were the lucky ones, for the
camps were rife with disease and death, which turned them into little
more than charnel houses. Even those who avoided the army encampments and remained in the countryside—working for themselves or for
their owners—discovered that reformulating plantation life in the midst
of a civil war was no easy task. Departing owners stripped plantations of
livestock, draft animals, agricultural implements, and supplies, and forag-
ing soldiers and other marauders took much of the rest. Periodic raids by
soldiers, bandits, and partisan gangs forced slaves to take to the woods for
fear they would be kidnapped, abused, or worse.[66] Plantations became the
killing grounds of the war, and their residents died by the thousands.

Nonetheless, amid the carnage, slaves began to make their lives anew on
the old estates. Some simply quit work, since, according to one disillu-
sioned planter, they were "now perfectly free & live upon the best produce
of the Plantation."[67] Others renegotiated the terms under which they
would labor, in the process altering the relationship between master and
slave. As slave discipline evaporated, slaveholders bowed to the slaves' demands, allowing them to enlarge their gardens and provision grounds and
grow crops to feed their families rather than to make their owners rich.

From the planters' perspective, such concessions came easily enough, as
wartime disruption and the British blockade made it all but impossible to
market the region's great staples in any case. Rice production slipped
badly, and indigo all but disappeared from the plantation regimen when

the Continental Congress prohibited its export to England. With few markets for their staples and with foodstuffs in short supply, slaveholders saw wisdom in their slaves' demands. The slaves' gardens and provision grounds grew at the expense of the owners' fields. If planters saw advantages in harnessing the slaves' economy for their own purposes, slaves welcomed the chance to increase the time they spent feeding and clothing themselves. Although neither master nor slave embraced the new order, both found advantages in the changes the war had brought.[68]

Among the crops that benefited from the new collaboration was cotton, which had occupied a negligible place in the pre-war economy. Small amounts had always been grown in South Carolina and Georgia, and it had long been a favorite in the slaves' gardens and provisions grounds. Planters grew long-staple "sea island" cotton but showed little interest in the short-staple variety with its difficult-to-remove seeds. But with imported cloth in short supply and patriotic homespun suddenly in favor, the production of cotton for internal consumption increased rapidly. Planters purchased tools for cleaning and carding the cotton fibers, spinning thread, and weaving cloth, and occasionally they put women and children to work in special weaving houses. The coalescence of interest established important precedents that, much to the slaves' eventual distress, planters would draw upon in the postwar years. But for the short term, slaves welcomed the fact that their owners' fields had become more like their own gardens.[69]

Death, flight, and evacuation sharply reduced the slave population of the Lower South during the war years. Between 1775 and 1783, the number of slaves in Georgia fell from some 15,000 to 5,000, a loss of nearly two-thirds. In South Carolina the decline was numerically greater, totaling some 25,000, or approximately one-quarter of the pre-war slave population. In areas where the revolutionary struggle was particularly intense, the decline was even more precipitous. Since men were most able to escape and most liable for military impressment, the decline in the number of slave men may have been proportionally greater. While Washington and his fellow slaveowners bemoaned the excess of slaves in the Upper South, Lower South planters issued complaints of a different sort. Lowcountry delegates to the Constitutional Convention in 1787 denounced attempts by representatives from the Upper South to prohibit international trade in slaves, stating firmly that "South Carolina and Georgia cannot do without slaves."[70]

At war's end, returning slaveholders found their estates in disrepair, their fields barren, and their labor force depleted. They also confronted the new economic realities of American independence, which barred their products from numerous world markets and deprived them of the bounties the British imperial system had supplied.[71] But before they could begin rebuilding their shattered economy, reconstructing the labor force, and establishing new markets, planters had to restore order on their estates. Slaveowners who expected to operate as they had before the war faced new struggles, as slaves—who had greatly expanded their independence in their owners' absence—did not willingly surrender wartime gains.[72] Some fled as their owners approached, making it clear that the terms of their labor would have to be renegotiated before they would again submit to another man's rule. Others, armed and organized, maintained a military presence to resist reestablishment of the old order.

Twenty miles north of the mouth of the Savannah River, where some one hundred maroons established a fortified encampment, black irregulars raided neighboring estates, frustrating the reimposition of the plantation regime. When planters asserted their claim, black soldiers were equal to the challenge. Calling themselves "the King of England's soldiers," a group of black veterans of the siege of Savannah attacked the Georgia militia directly. As planters well understood, the presence of armed black men informed slaves of alternatives to plantation labor and increased general insubordination on the great estates. "If something cannot be shortly done, I dread the consequences," a white militia captain warned the governors of South Carolina and Georgia.[73]

Even more than in the states of the Upper South, the level of plantation violence in the Lower South appeared to rise sharply in the immediate postwar years, as slaves struggled to enlarge wartime gains in the face of the planters' attempt to reassert the old order. Violence did not diminish in the 1790s, as news of the great slave revolt in Saint Domingue passed from the Atlantic ports to the countryside. The subsequent arrival of refugees—white and black—and the interjection of revolutionary politics into the partisan divisions within the Lower South provided planters with first-hand accounts of a world turned upside down. Encouraged by Toussaint's victory, slaves were well in advance of their owners in these matters.[74]

Faced by the slaves' challenge, planters closed ranks and mobilized the authority of the state. They sent the militia—often led by veterans of the revolutionary army—against black irregulars and maroons, defeating them in pitched battles, beheading their leaders, and driving the maroons more deeply into the swamps. On the plantations, slaveholders confronted insubordination with the same overwhelming force, wielding the lash with special ferocity as they reestablished their sovereignty.[75] Slaves opposed their masters with ingenuity and determination, but the planters prevailed. They successfully revived staple production, consolidated their control over the lowcountry, and expanded the plantation system. During the 1790s, rice production equaled and then surpassed the greatest pre-war years, as slaveholders completed the transition from inland to tidal fields. In the upcountry, they introduced a new crop, short staple cotton.[76]

The success of planters in South Carolina and Georgia reveals the powerful role of the state in a slave society. In Florida, where Spanish officials had no such commitment to the plantation regime, the plantation economy languished, and many of the South Carolina and Georgia planters who migrated to Florida under pre-war British control returned home during the 1780s. Others left in the 1790s, perhaps disgusted when Spanish authorities provided a refuge for Georges (soon to be Jorge) Biassou, a leader of slave forces in Saint Domingue who broke with Toussaint and associated himself with the Spanish Crown in Santo Domingo. Biassou immediately took command of the black militia in Florida and forged an alliance with the communities of fugitive slaves through the marriage of his brother-in-law with the daughter of Prince Witten, a carpenter formerly of South Carolina.

The revival of the black militia with Jorge Biassou playing a role previously performed by Francisco Menéndez could hardly cheer planters who had emigrated from South Carolina and Georgia hoping to profit from the southward expansion of rice cultivation. Ill at ease in a society in which armed, disciplined black militiamen enjoyed such an important position, they began to decamp. When Florida's governor burned all the plantations north of the St. John's River rather than surrender them to an invading force of American adventurers, many of the remaining planters departed. The revival of plantation society in Florida would await the territory's incorporation into the United States in 1819.[77]

But even in South Carolina and Georgia, where slaveholders maintained a firm grip on the levers of power, the Revolution remade slavery. The prime element in the change was the emergence of cotton. Slaves who had gladly expanded their own cotton patches during the war found their owners transforming cotton from a garden crop grown for local consumption to a staple crop cultivated for export. In what one scholar called a "terrible irony," cotton took its place alongside rice and tobacco as a mainstay of the slaveholders' regime and as the crop that would precipitate slavery's greatest expansion.

Sea island cotton remained the principal crop of the estuarine region. But long-staple cotton could not be grown in the hilly interior, leaving tobacco and small grains as the most important upcountry exports. The successful development of a gin that could separate the sticky green seeds from the shorter fiber allowed cotton production to expand to the uplands. Between 1790 and 1800, South Carolina's annual cotton exports rose from less than 10,000 pounds to some 6,000,000, and most of it came from the upcountry.[78]

The resumption of staple production kindled the demand for slaves, as slave masters hustled to replace the laborers lost during the war and add new ones. When they could, they retrieved refugeed slaves and re-enslaved fugitives.[79] But retrieving slaves scattered by the war failed to satisfy the planters' needs, and they looked elsewhere to revitalize their labor force. Planters purchased many slaves from the North, where emancipation induced some slaveholders to sell off their slaves at bargain prices, and from the Upper South, where planters complained of an excess of slaves and the appearance of "Georgia traders" initiated a massive forced migration.[80] This Second Middle Passage—the domestic slave trade—would eventually bring millions of slaves to the Lower South, but in its infancy it could not meet the swollen demand. After some hesitation, Lower South planters turned again to Africa. Between the end of the Revolution and 1787 and again between 1803 and 1808, South Carolina reopened the international slave trade and reconnected mainland North America to the great forced migration of Africans. During this short period, South Carolina imported nearly 90,000 Africans. The influx allowed planters to more than recoup their wartime losses.[81]

With the resumption of staple production and the reconstitution of the labor force, planters reasserted their commitment to slavery. Armed with a new confidence, Lower South grandees enlarged their land holdings by purchasing the estates of departed Loyalists and by ousting small holders. Lowcountry plantations—already the largest, most capital-intensive and technologically advanced enterprises on the continent—grew still larger and more complex, as planters learned to monitor the estuarial flows necessary for tidal rice production. As they did, their plantation populations swelled to still greater proportions, and the slave majority increased far beyond the bounds established in pre-revolutionary years. By 1810, four of five residents in the South Carolina lowcountry were slaves, and in the three most productive rice-producing parishes the black population towered to over 90 percent.

Perhaps even more significant than the growing density of the lowland's slave population was the westward march of the plantation regime. By 1800, slaves composed one-third of the population of South Carolina's upcountry, an arena which had but few slaves prior to the Revolution. The Piedmont was fast on its way to becoming incorporated into the plantation regime.[82]

But try as they might, Lower South planters could no more recreate the pre-revolutionary social order than could their counterparts to the north. The ravages of war, the reordering of the labor force, and the rise of cotton had transformed the slave regime—and not always to the planters' liking. If most slaves had failed to secure their freedom during wartime, they nevertheless appreciated the changes that transpired and were not about to surrender these advantages. Exploiting their owner's eagerness to reestablish production, slaves worked to enhance their position on the post-revolutionary plantation. Control over the task offered one such opportunity, as did the slaves' tradition of marketing their own produce and handicraft. In the years following the Revolution, slaves built upon the old task system to maintain—and perhaps expand—control over a portion of their own time. As one observer reported from Georgia in 1806, once a slave had completed his task, "his master feels no right to call on him," leaving the slave to spend "the remainder of the day at work in his own corn field."[83]

The introduction of cotton to the upcountry and its rapid expansion at the turn of the century altered the terrain upon which slaves and slaveholders confronted one another, sometimes to the advantage of the master, sometimes to the slave. Most upcountry planters resided on their estates—in part because they could hardly afford not to but also because they appeared to have no taste for the absenteeism of the lowlands. The planters' presence reduced the distance between master and slave and eliminated the need for the many stewards, overseers, and drivers who mediated the master-slave relationship. Master and slave confronted each other directly, with no one to temper the violence. Upland cotton also called forth a new design for production. Gang labor, which was subordinate to tasking in the lowlands, became the dominant mode for organizing production. Indeed, the advantages of the gang in driving slaves led some lowcountry rice planters to experiment with it too.[84]

The introduction of short-staple cotton created other points of contention. The nature of cotton production allowed far fewer slaves to escape field labor, and carving new fields from the upland wilderness required muscle much more than skill. But here the advantages swung in favor of the slave, for planters were willing to pay slaves for the additional labor necessary to jump start the cotton economy. The opportunity for "overwork" expanded the slaves' economy, even as the master enlarged his own sphere.[85] As slaves and masters tried to find small advantages, the new regime took shape.

Establishing a new norm for work in the masters' fields did not resolve the ongoing struggle, for the slaves' independent productive labor also became a source of conflict. The war had allowed slaves to enter the marketplace more openly and aggressively than ever before—selling and trading with one another, with their owners, and with both white and black in the great rice ports. In the postwar years, the slaves' trading networks extended even further from their plantation base, perhaps because the physical mobility made possible by the war gave them a greater familiarity with the countryside. Slaves enjoyed a near monopoly control over the market in the rice ports, and they carried their independent productive activities to the upcountry.[86]

Planters squirmed uncomfortably as the slaves' participation in the market grew. Some attempted to subvert these entrepreneurial activities by establishing plantation-based stores. These stores harnessed the slaves' material aspirations to the masters' pecuniary advantage, pouring the profits of the slaves' economy into the pockets of the owning class. For other planters, however, such stores conceded far too much. Rather than regulate the slaves' independent productive activities, they wanted to quash them entirely.

The arrival of thousands of black newcomers—some from Africa, some from states to the north—complicated the struggle between master and slave. Creole slaves drawn from all over North America had worked under a variety of labor regimens. Saltwater slaves, who by 1810 composed more than one-fifth of the slaves in South Carolina, landed with no knowledge of the precedents established through long years of on-the-ground negotiations between slaves and owners. Masters and slaves contended for the allegiance of the new arrivals. Slaveholders used the occasion of the entry of new slaves to ratchet up labor demands, apply new standards of discipline, and create an order more to their liking; old hands countered these new demands by tutoring the newcomers in the contest between master and slave.

The reafricanization of the Lower South with the arrival of saltwater slaves informed all aspects of black life. This was especially true in the upcountry, where planters located most of the new arrivals. But no part of the Lower South was untouched by the reopening of the trade in African slaves, whose presence slowed and finally reversed the steady march of creolization. In South Carolina, the proportion of Africans in the slave population, which had declined to nearly 10 percent in 1790, increased sharply in the first decade of the nineteenth century, so that in 1810 one lowcountry slave in five had been born in Africa.[87] Once again, black society in the lowcountry was transformed from creole to African.

Most African slaves entered the region through Charleston, as in earlier years. Funneling the trade through a single port allowed for the maintenance of national groups and shipboard ties, increasing the impact of the recent arrivals. Between 1783 and 1787 large numbers of Africans came from the Gold Coast, and between 1804 and 1807 from Angola.[88] The ethnic coherence of the post-revolutionary trade re-emphasized the solidarities of the Old World. Once again, countrymarks and plaited hair became common on the estates of the Lower South, and some creoles may have adopted the style. From a cultural perspective, the smooth integration of Africans into established African-American life in the Lower South suggests how deeply African ways had already been incorporated into life in the quarter. From an institutional perspective, the steady increase of the native population suggests how quickly established African-American communities absorbed the newcomers. From a social perspective, the maintenance of African-American dominance within the black community suggests how fully creole society still guided the development of plantation life.

In the years following the Revolution, slave cemeteries appeared much more frequently on plantation plats, signaling planters' recognition of the permanency of the slaves' sacred grounds—an event that could be likened to the official recognition of an African graveyard in a northern city. Likewise, the paths and byways slaves employed to visit neighboring estates also gained greater prominence on plantation maps, as slaveholders acknowledged the limitations of sovereignty over their estates and accepted the inter-plantation connections among their slaves. In increasing numbers, slaves married across property lines, so that the ties of kinship that joined plantations together did the same for the countryside more generally. Just as the family had been the building block of the black community within the plantation, so the growing network of domestic relations linked plantations and expanded the black community beyond the bounds of individual estates. Although courtship patterns, bridewealth, the role of slave kin in producing bridewealth, and the responsibility of kin for the success of slave marriages remain unexplored subjects, the steady expansion in the region's internal economies suggests that the pattern of inheritance and larger kin relations grew as lineages expanded.[89] Not all planters found these changes to their liking, but the rapidity with which slaveholders reinitiated plantation production assuaged many hurts.

As if to acknowledge the slaves' dominion over their plantation environs, planters in the lowcountry retreated more completely to the rice ports. Their seasonal absenteeism assured that slaves would continue to have much to say about daily life on the plantation, and their urban residence provided a new arena for black people to build upon the independence they had won during the war. In Charleston, Savannah, and a host of other rice ports, slave artisans enlarged their role in the urban economies, as did various trades relating to the movement of goods, draymen, and boatsmen most especially. Hiring became a common practice and self-hire a given, despite numerous protests. Economic independence assured social independence. Slaves who were able to live and work on their own became their own masters and mistresses to a considerable degree. They collected wages, established residences, and governed their families apart from their owners.[90]

In the years following the Revolution, some black men and women—generally creoles, often artisans, and almost always urban-based—were able to translate de facto independence into de jure freedom. Increased manumission and self-purchase, along with the arrival of several hundred free colored refugees from Saint Domingue, swelled the number of free people of color. Although the increase never equaled that of Upper South or the North, it was substantial. Between 1790 and 1810, the number of free people of color in South Carolina and Georgia nearly tripled, to over 6,000. Although the total was but a tiny fraction of the black population, their presence was unmistakable.[91]

But it was not simply numbers and residence which distinguished free people of color in the Lower South. Manumission in the region was selective, with slaveholders freeing those slaves they knew best. House servants numbered large among the liberated, suggesting the intimate ties they established with their owners. Women composed the majority of manumitted adults, and the children who were freed tended to be of mixed racial origins. Generally, the freed women were house servants and artisans with whom slaveholders had domestic intercourse and perhaps sexual intercourse as well. When they did not free these favorites, slaveholders often placed them in positions from which they could buy their way out of bondage, giving those who purchased themselves the same social origins as the manumittees.[92]

Like most freed people in the Lower South, colored refugees from Saint Domingue were linked to the slaveholding class by trade, patronage, and blood. Many had fought alongside the slaveholders there, and a few had been substantial slaveholders themselves. These men and women, generally light-skinned and creole, separated the free colored population of the lowcountry rice ports even further from the world created by plantation slaves. Whatever aspects of language and culture free people of color shared with urban slaves—many of whom were just a step away from legal freedom—they had little in common with the newly arrived Africans who populated the plantations in ever-increasing numbers.[93]

Unlike free blacks of the Upper South and North, free people of color in the Lower South did not jettison the names of their former owners or shed their identification with the slaveholding class. Instead, they labored to preserve evidence of those connections, knowing full well that ties with wealthy planters could provide protection and perhaps even patronage. April Ellison, a South Carolina slave who had been freed by one William Ellison, petitioned the court to change his given name. "April" smacked too much of slavery, the former slave told the court. A change would "save him and his children from degradation and contempt which the minds of some do and will attach to the name of April." Ellison had no wish to surrender his surname, however. Keeping his master's (perhaps his father's) name would not only be a "mark of gratitude and respect" but would also "greatly advance his interest as a tradesman." The court concurred. Although rarely revealing their motives as fully as the former April Ellison, many lowcountry free people of color followed his practice. While few black Van Cortlands, Livingstons, and DeLanceys could be found in New York, many black Draytons, Hugers, Kinlochs, Manigaults, and Middletons could be located in Charleston.[94]

For much the same reason, former slaves continued to reside in close proximity to their former owners, not only in the same city or district but often in the same neighborhood. The nearly complete evacuation of the countryside that accompanied freedom in the North did not follow manumission in the Lower South. Free people were no more urban in 1810 than they had been two decades earlier. Former slaves in the Lower South did not stray far from the site of their enslavement, where a patron would be most effective.

Their strategy worked. Far more than in the North or even the Upper South, manumitters maintained an active interest in the welfare of their former slaves. Some smoothed the transition from slavery to freedom with small grants of cash, household furnishings, clothing, and occasionally even long-term annuities. More importantly, the interest of former owners assured free people of color a market for their services, as their old masters and mistresses continued to patronize their shops and encouraged friends to do the same. Many free people labored in the trades they had long practiced as slaves, and some even continued to work in the same crafts as those who had freed them. Their skill allowed them to accumulate substantial propertied estates.[95]

Identification with the slaveholding class brought free people of color in the Lower South a measure of physical security, economic prosperity, and social status. A close association with a white patron often stood as the only barrier between slavery and freedom. As the fate of Thomas Jeremiah revealed, free people of color, no matter how wealthy or well placed, were vulnerable—for whites presumed them to be more black than free. Without a patron—or, in Thomas Jeremiah's case, with the wrong patron—a free black was in mortal danger. The shield of clientage not only afforded protection but also assured others—the patron's allies and friends—of the reliability of the former slave. In a practical way, such patronage kept vigilantes from the freed people's doors and encouraged customers to enter their shops. Perhaps for that reason, the radical de-skilling that accompanied emancipation in the North had no analogue in the Lower South, and former slaves maintained their high occupational standing, continuing to work as artisans and tradesmen.[96]

Fragile economic advances based on ties with the slaveholding elite did not bring equality. Indeed, the middling position of free people precluded an open aspiration for equality. Their political affairs tended to be conducted in private, behind the curtain of clientage. When they did venture into the public arena, they did so with great circumspection. The free people's memorials were marked by neither angry invocations of the great principles of the Declaration of Independence nor ringing demands for equal justice of the sort that characterized the protestations of black northerners. Rather, their appeals for the opportunity to prove their accounts at law, testify in court, or travel freely had more the tone of supplications than demands.[97] In a society where planters and their white non-slaveholding allies interpreted any challenge to their rule as an incipient insurrection, free people of color dared not let their petitions take any other form. If newly freed blacks in Philadelphia quickly rushed to the rescue of their enslaved brethren when the legislature hinted that emancipation might be reconsidered, Charleston's free people of color watched silently as slavery expanded, and they occasionally joined in the process by purchasing slaves of their own. The hoped-for Jubilee, which northern blacks solemnized in annual Emancipation Day parades, remained a well-hidden wish in the Lower South, if it was a wish at all.

Rather than contemplate the fate of those still in slavery, free people turned to their own struggle to climb the racial ladder by emulating their benefactors' speech, dress, and deportment as best they could. In their pursuit of acceptance, slaveownership was not simply an economic convenience but indispensable evidence of the free blacks' determination to break with their slave past and of their silent acceptance—if not approval—of slavery. From the slaveholders' perspective, nothing more fully

demonstrated the free people's reliability than their entry into the slaveholding class.

During the early years of the nineteenth century, almost one-third of
Charleston's free black families joined the slaveholders' ranks. Most purchased family members, as a means of ensuring their freedom. But for
some, slaveholding was strictly business, as it surely was for the handful of
free black planters on the outskirts of the city. Black agriculturalists were
generally small holders, hardly more than prosperous farmers, but their
eagerness to emulate their white benefactors bespoke their highest aspiration. A few of the lightest-skinned managed to sneak quietly under the
largest barrier—that of color—to achieve that aspiration, becoming in all
matters white.[98]

Most free people of color, however, did not cross the colorline. Excluded from the parlors of the planters and repulsed by the culture of the
quarter, they had no choice but to form their own society at the interstices
of the Lower South's two great social formations. Perhaps no institution
spoke more to the reality of free people's aspirations than the Brown Fellowship Society, an exclusive caste-conscious mutual association founded
in Charleston in 1790. Limited to fifty "bona fide free brown men of good
character," the society became the institutional embodiment of the free
colored elite in South Carolina. Like similar benevolent associations and
burial societies in the North, it originated in the exclusion of free people
of color from white institutions. Unable to inter their dead in the graveyard of St. Philip's Episcopal Church, which many attended, leading free
people of color created their own burial ground under the maxim of
"Charity and Benevolence." The Brown Fellowship Society provided its
members and their families a final resting place and granted small annuities to support widows and children. The social hall became a meeting
place for the most successful free people, and its members undertook to
assist other free people. Its burial ground became a resting place "not only
for themselves, but for the benefit and advantage of others."[99]

Still, rather than draw the community together, as did African-
American friendly associations in the North, the Brown Fellowship Soci-

ety fragmented black society by excluding slaves and dark-skinned free people from membership. Before long, dark-skinned people established a similar association—the Humane Brotherhood. The color-consciousness that supported slavery had suffused the black community: what whites did to browns, browns would do to blacks. The racial pecking order assured that all free people of color would stand not with but above blacks. The racial unity that was so much a part of black society in the Upper South proved elusive in the Lower South.

As their numbers grew and their place in the Lower South solidified, the free people's world took shape. It was defined neither by the conflicting pulls of master and slave nor by the fissures of color, residence, or skill that divided free people. Rather, free people of color drew upon their own special experience in delineating and articulating their interests. Although planters would accuse them of being the agent of slaves and slaves would denounce them as the planters' surrogate, the interest they defended was their own. The transformation of black life in the Age of Revolution marked the emergence of a three-caste society in the Lower South.

THE LOWER MISSISSIPPI VALLEY

War and revolution altered slavery in the lower Mississippi Valley as well. The wars of the Age of Revolution reverberated throughout the region in the last quarter of the eighteenth century and the first decade of the nineteenth, threatening to wrest slaves from their masters. Echoes of the colonial rebellion in the newly proclaimed North American republic deeply affected Spanish Louisiana and British West Florida. Loyalist planters from South Carolina and Georgia, eager to protect their property from the lowcountry's bloody warfare, refugeed thousands of slaves into West Florida, marching some of them as far west as the Anglo-American enclave of Natchez on the Mississippi River. They were soon joined by others ejected from the nascent free states, where progress toward emancipation had placed slave property at risk, and from the West Indies, where a growing subsistence crisis required a reduction in the slave population. Although planters settled most of these slaves in the British colonies east of the Mississippi, they transferred some to the Spanish-controlled west bank. The influx of slaves reinvigorated the plantation economy on both sides of the divide.[100]

But the same wartime struggles that promoted the growth of slavery also undermined it. Once again, tramping armies—sometimes marching under the American, sometimes the British, and sometimes the Spanish flag—gave slaves the opportunity to seize their freedom. Maroon settlements, their residents well-armed and well-connected with neighboring plantations, became permanent fixtures in the interior of Louisiana and West Florida, where they forged connections with Native Americans.[101] Perhaps most important, the continual warfare enhanced the importance of the black soldiers, as all parties bid for their services. Spanish authorities, with a long tradition of employing black militiamen, were the most successful. The free colored militia participated in every military action undertaken by Spain during the 1770s and 1780s, distinguishing itself in the campaign against the British at Baton Rouge and Natchez in 1779. Colored militiamen also served in the expeditions against Mobile in 1780 and Pensacola the following year. When not fighting foreign enemies, Spanish officials employed these men to maintain the levees that protected New Orleans from floodwaters, to hunt maroons, and to extinguish fires, as arson had become a considerable menace in the revolutionary age. If anyone doubted the militia's utility, authorities quickly rushed to its defense. "The colored people have served during the late war with great valor and usefulness," asserted the governor of Louisiana, "and in time of peace they are the ones used to pursue the runaway negro slaves and destroy their camps, an activity virtually impossible for regular troops to accomplish because of the well-hidden sites."[102]

Official reliance on the colored militia ensured that the door to freedom—unlocked by the French following the Natchez revolt and opened wider by the Spanish in the 1770s—would be kept ajar in the Age of Revolution. But the sharp increase of manumission that had begun in the first decade of Spanish rule slackened as slaveholders lost their enthusiasm for freeing their slaves. Perhaps the pool of lovers and parents with slaves to free diminished. Perhaps the rising price of slaves induced slaveholders to reconsider their generosity. Or perhaps there was not much generosity or enthusiasm in the first place. In any case, whereas manumission increased as revolutionary egalitarianism took hold in the young American Republic, it sputtered in the lower Mississippi Valley. Unmoved by the principles that spurred emancipation in northern portions of the United States and manumission in the Upper South, Louisiana slaveholders freed their slaves at an ever slower rate during the last two decades of the eighteenth century. By the first decade of the nineteenth century, manumission was no longer the wellspring of the free black population.[103]

As slaveholders held tight to their property-in-persons, slaves took responsibility for freeing themselves. The proportion of slaves who purchased their own freedom or that of a loved one increased even as the rate of slaveholder-sponsored manumission slipped. Self-emancipation, which had accounted for one-fifth of the total acts of liberation in the 1770s, made up over three-fifths by the first decade of the nineteenth century and had become the dominant route by which slaves exited bondage in the lower Mississippi Valley. Aided by favorable Spanish laws, some 1,500 black people purchased their liberty or that of others in New Orleans between 1769 and 1803. The proportion of slaves freed through the activities of slaves, their friends and relatives, and their allies within the white community spiraled upward in the post-revolutionary period.[104]

Immigration from Saint Domingue augmented manumission, self-purchase, and successful flight. Despite the opposition of Spanish and later United States officials, the number of immigrants grew steadily throughout the first decade of the nineteenth century. Many of the free people of color who migrated first to Charleston, New York, and Philadelphia eventually found their way to New Orleans. In 1809 Spanish officials in Cuba, angered by Napolean's deposition of Ferdinand from the Spanish throne, ousted the large community of Saint Domiguean refugees from Havana. Once again the losers of the Haitian Revolution were set adrift. Many took refuge in New Orleans, and their numbers, over 3,000 strong, almost doubled the city's free colored population; by the end of the decade, they may have composed as much as 60 percent of Louisiana's free black community. In 1810, free people of color made up nearly 30 percent of the city, and a similar proportion of Mobile and Pensacola.[105]

As in the Lower South, the growth of the free black population was weighted toward cityfolks, creoles, women, and children. The largest increases took place in and around New Orleans and, to a lesser extent, the other Gulf ports. The free black population of New Orleans—which had tripled during the first decade of Spanish rule—more than doubled between 1777 and 1791, to stand at over 850. By the time the United States took control of Louisiana in 1803, over 1,800 people of color enjoyed freedom in the territorial capital. Over 37 percent of the black population was free, and people of African descent composed more than one-fifth of the city.[106]

As it grew in numbers, the free colored population grew lighter. Whereas the census counted little more than one-fifth of Louisiana's free people of African descent as mulattoes in 1769, more than two-thirds were so identified in 1791. Migration from Saint Domingue reinforced this somatic marker; the free people of color of Saint Domingue also tended to be light-skinned, their New World pedigrees reached back generations, and their family trees included people of Native American and European as well as African descent.[107]

As in the Lower South, these free people maintained their ties with the powerful white men and women who had sponsored or assisted their passage to freedom. To that end, former slaves kept their old surnames, linking them with the region's great slaveholding families. They maintained their membership in the militia and married and baptized their children in the Catholic Church, affirming their identification with the touchstone of European-American civilization in the region. Many former slaves continued to live with their former masters, patrons, or white employers, because, as in other parts of the mainland, newly freed slaves could not afford to establish separate households. Even when they left their former owners, freed people continued to reside near them, often calling upon them to stand as godparents at their children's baptism, to notarize their legal documents, and to give security bond for their business loans.[108] The strategy succeeded to a considerable extent, for with the arrival of freedom, black men and women maintained their economic standing in the lower Mississippi Valley. In many instances, they improved upon it, controlling—even monopolizing—some artisanal and retail trades. Skills and connections accumulated in slavery, and the continued patronage of former masters and mistresses thrust free people of color into the middle ranks of urban society.[109]

The free people's interstitial occupations—like their tawny color and their middling legal status—represented their position in the social order of the lower Mississippi Valley. They were uncomfortably sandwiched between white free people and black slaves—a third caste in a social order designed for two. The divisions so evident in the Lower South between slaves and free people and among free people of color—by color, residence, and aspiration—grew wider as free people secured their place in the lower Mississippi Valley and developed an interest of their own apart from either slaves or slaveowners.

But the free people's social position was unstable, subject to pulls and pushes from above and below. While some free people worked to free family and friends, others saw their elevation as dependent upon slavery. They staked their claim to equality not as abolitionists, in the manner of northern free blacks, but as partisans of the slaveholders' regime. To such men and women, nothing more fully demonstrated their rights as subjects or as citizens than their ability to own slaves. By demonstrating their allegiance to the slaveholder's ideal, slaveownership refuted the planters' oft-stated belief that free people of color were nothing more than slaves without masters. Like ambitious whites, free people of color bought and sold slaves, used slaves as bequests, donations, and gifts in marriage contracts, and employed slaves as collateral in mortgages and other transactions. If in the process, families were divided and men and women shipped to distant parts, black slaveowners—like white ones—accepted those consequences as an unfortunate necessity.[110] Presenting slave ownership as evidence of their political reliability, these free people of color rested their case for enfranchisement and equality.

Not all free people took this route. Rather than own slaves, others lived and worked with them, extending the camaraderie that joined free people of color to the mass of plantation slaves. Indeed, such men and women condemned the assimilationist aspirations of colored slaveholders, their willingness—as members of the militia—to hunt down maroons, and their desire for their daughters to be placed with some white gentlemen. Instead, they pressed for a general emancipation in which all would be free and equal. The possibility for free people to realize their most profound aspiration waxed and waned with the transformation of the lower Mississippi Valley.

The divergent tugs on free people's allegiance intensified with the settlement between Britain and the United States in 1783. In quick-fire order, changes that accompanied the Age of Revolution were joined to the plantation revolution, transforming the economics, politics, and society of the lower Mississippi Valley. In the process, the relationship of slave and slaveholder was remade, the place of free people of color redefined, and the meaning of race renegotiated.

With the end of the American Revolution, ambitious European and American planters and would-be planters flowed into the lower Mississippi Valley.[111] They soon demanded an end to the complaisant regime that characterized slavery in the long half century following the Natchez rebellion, and Spanish officials were pleased to comply. The Cabildo—the governing body of New Orleans—issued its own regulations, combining French and Spanish black codes, along with additional proscriptions on black life. In succeeding years, the state—Spanish (until 1800), French (between 1800 and 1803), and finally American (beginning in 1803)—enacted other regulations, controlling the slaves' mobility and denying their right to hold or inherit property, contract independently, and testify in court. Explicit prohibitions against slave assemblage, gun ownership, and travel by horse were added, along with restrictions on manumission and self-purchase. The French, who again took control of Louisiana in 1800, proved even more compliant, reimposing the *Code Noir* during their brief ascendancy. The hasty resurrection of the old code pleased slaveholders, and, although it lost its effect with the American accession in 1803, planters—in control of the territorial legislature—incorporated many of its provisions into the territorial slave code.[112]

Perhaps even more significant than the plethora of new restrictions was a will to enforce the law. Slave miscreants faced an increasingly vigilant constabulary, whose members took it upon themselves to punish offenders. Officials turned with particular force on the maroon settlements that had proliferated amid the warfare of the Age of Revolution. They dismantled some fugitive colonies, scattering their members and driving many of them more deeply into the swamps. Maroons unfortunate enough to be captured were re-enslaved, deported, or executed.[113]

Having made the Mississippi Valley safe for slavery, Spanish officials reopened the slave trade. For the first time since the 1720s, slaves entered the great valley in large numbers, as another Middle Passage delivered African exiles to the mainland of North America. The slave population, which had edged upward through natural increase for more than a half century, began to grow rapidly with the addition of newly imported slaves. The number in the Natchez District increased from about 500 in 1784 to over 2,000 in 1796. On the west bank of the Mississippi, the slave population expanded even more rapidly, from less than 10,000 to more than 20,000 between 1777 and 1788. In the next decade the number of slaves climbed another 25 percent to reach nearly 25,000 in 1806. Under American rule, the slave population in Louisiana exploded to almost 35,000 at the time of the 1810 census. Large-scale importation allowed the black population to keep pace with a rapidly growing white population, and the lower Mississippi Valley maintained its black majority into the nineteenth century.[114]

Planters put the newly arrived slaves to work growing tobacco and indigo, breathing new life into a plantation economy that had stagnated for more than half a century. But as in previous years, the boom could not be sustained. Within a decade, Louisiana tobacco lost its privileged position in the Mexican market and Louisiana indigo fell to insect infestation and bad weather. Once again, the staple economy collapsed. But as tobacco and indigo disappeared from the lower Mississippi Valley, two new crops took their place.[115]

With the destruction of Saint Domingue's plantation regime, Louisiana planters moved into the sugar business. Aided by an infusion of new capital and labor, partially derived from refugeed Saint Domingean planters, Louisiana suddenly became a center of sugar production. Between 1796 and 1800 at least sixty plantations converted from tobacco and indigo to sugar production. Although cane could be grown in just a small part of southern Louisiana—and then with greater risks than in Saint Domingue because of the shorter growing season—sugar flourished. By 1803 Louisiana produced more than 4,500,000 pounds of sugar, worth three-quarters of a million dollars. Sugar became king in lower Louisiana.[116]

But north of sugar country, another commodity aspired to royalty. In cotton, planters found an equally lucrative alternative to tobacco and indigo. The crop had long been grown on a small scale in the lower Mississippi Valley, but, like seaboard producers, planters had been stymied by seemingly intractable difficulties in separating the fiber from the seed. Tinkerers—many of whom took up residence in the Natchez District—solved the problem early in the decade, and, by the mid-1790s, Natchez mechanics were competing to produce the most efficient gin. Cotton production began to climb, so that between October 1801 and May 1802 New Orleans exported over 18,000 bales of cotton.[117]

Sugar and cotton changed the face of the lower Mississippi Valley, just as tobacco had earlier remade the Chesapeake and rice the lowcountry. Planters monopolized the rich flatlands, ousting small farmers and sending them into the hill country. Before long, the newly minted planters established their bona fides as a ruling class. They tamed bayous and prairies, making them into great estates with names like the Briars, Elgin, Linden, Montebello, and Stanton Hall. They married among themselves and filled their homes with fine furnishings and their barns with blooded stock. Some affected the manner of aristocrats, issuing edicts on proper treatment of slaves and adjudicating disputes between aggrieved slaves and harried overseers. But with the prices of sugar and cotton skyrocketing and with land to be cleared for new fields, few of the would-be grandees had the time for such niceties. The lower Mississippi Valley would remain a hard-scrabble frontier for another generation. The day of the patriarch had not yet arrived in the lower Mississippi Valley.[118]

Success in the plantation business rested upon constructing and disciplining a labor force that could meet the requirements of staple production. Planters began by amassing slaves, first by mobilizing their own slaves—creoles who were mostly native to the lower Mississippi Valley—and then by drawing upon the growing domestic trade in slaves, buying some from the North, the Chesapeake, and the lowcountry. A good many of those from the lowcountry were transshipments, who after a brief layover in the sugar islands or a few hours docked in Charleston's harbor embarked for New Orleans, Natchez, or Mobile. Finally, the sugar and cotton growers turned to Africa. Since few planters could rely on a single source, the slave population of the Mississippi Valley became an amalgam of various creole and African nationalities. Whatever preferences slaveholders had for particular slaves, the circumstances of the plantation revolution in the lower Mississippi Valley gave scant opportunity to exercise them, as slaves arrived from all directions.[119] The valley's slave population was a mix of creoles who had lived between New York and Louisiana and Africans who had resided between the Slave Coast and Angola.

Amid this influx of new laborers, Africans stood out. Their proportion in the slave population increased steadily during the last decade of the eighteenth century and the first years of the nineteenth, reafricanizing the lower Mississippi Valley. Of the 26,000 slaves who entered the region between 1790 and 1810—according to one estimate—more than two-thirds, or 18,000, derived from Africa. However, Louisiana planters did not want just any Africans but specific ones—men rather than women, and adults rather than children. They also preferred particular African nations. While they were able to meet their need for adult men, they had little luck bending the international market to their desires for particular nationals. The origins of the African imports was almost as diverse as that of the plantation generations in the eighteenth century.[120]

Africanization marked the arrival of the plantation revolution in the lower Mississippi Valley, and, as elsewhere on mainland North America, black life became debased. Slaves became little more than cogs in a vast agricultural machine. Planters showed little interest in fostering family life among their slaves. Almost all the men and women sold at Natchez during the last quarter of the eighteenth century were purchased as individuals, and only rarely as families or even as couples. Those few slaves who arrived as whole families, or as mothers with children, were often separated, even when the children had barely reached their teens. Planters wanted a labor force heavily weighted toward men, and the influx of slave men—

many of them African—upset the sexual balance of the long-established creole population, undermining the integrity of existing slave families and denying many the opportunity to form new unions. Men and women, particularly among the newly arrived, had difficulty finding spouses. The newcomers also faced a new disease environment which left them susceptible to a variety of ailments. Mortality rates increased and fertility fell as the new plantation order took shape.[121]

The new arrivals' weakened condition did not reduce the demands planters placed on them. If anything, the boom in sugar and cotton increased the slaves' burden, especially where new plantations had to be carved out of previously uncultivated land. Felling trees, rooting stumps, draining swamps, and breaking the prairie turf was brutal work that crushed some of the strongest men and women. As plantations emerged from the swamps and prairies, the planters' struggle to create a disciplined labor force took on greater urgency. The introduction of new crops provided planters with an occasion to ratchet up labor demands, much as had their counterparts in the Chesapeake and lowcountry following the introduction of tobacco and rice. Both sugar and cotton planters employed the gang system, a still novel form of organization for most slaves, whether native to the Mississippi Valley or newcomers to the region.[122] Planters imposed the order of a slave society on the mainland's oldest society with slaves, stretching the workday and adding new tasks to meet the unique demands of sugar and cotton.

Even among the uninitiated—men and women who were unaware of how a day's labor had been defined through years of tense negotiation—extracting such large drafts of labor required extraordinarily coercive measures. Violent confrontations between masters and slaves seemed to grow as the lower Mississippi Valley became a slave society. Wielding the lash with greater frequency if not greater force, planters struggled to bend slaves to the new order. Slaves resisted with equal ferocity. Unrest increased and rumors of rebellion boiled to the surface. During the 1790s and into the new century, the lower Mississippi Valley was alive with news of revolt, as one intrigue after another came to light. In 1791, 1795, and again in 1804 and 1805, planters uncovered major conspiracies.[123] They responded with the lash, mutilating many rebels and suspected rebels, deporting others, and executing still others, often after grotesque torture.

Yet behind this bloody façade, master and slave began to renegotiate the terms under which slaves lived and worked. Many of these involved the pace of labor; others originated in the organization of labor and the authority of the masters' subalterns, as overseers became a fixture on the largest estates. From the planters' perspective, the large units on which sugar and cotton were grown made movement from plantation to plantation—a prominent feature of slave life in eighteenth-century Louisiana—unnecessary and undesirable. But perhaps the most intense conflicts arose over the slaves' economy: their free Sundays and half-Saturdays, their gardens and provision grounds, and their right to sell their labor and market its product. Slaves in the lower Mississippi Valley had a long tradition of independent productive activities. Planters, who once saw advantages in allowing slaves to subsist themselves, pressed for an allowance society in which rations replaced gardens and the right to market.

Slaves, for their part, stood their ground as best they could and occasionally scored some victories. Writing in 1803, a French emigré noted that the cotton planters around Pointe Coupée had "abandon[ed] the land to their slaves." Plantation slaves maintained substantial garden plots, which they "cultivate[d] . . . at their own account, and get their food from it. They also raise and fatten hogs and fowls which they sell on their own account." By the end of the second decade of the nineteenth century, with the changes set in motion by the plantation revolution becoming a familiar routine, the internal economies initiated by the charter generation remained intact.[124] Slaves not only maintained the prerogatives of the old order but also found advantages to the new regime.

But whatever gains the slaves secured were achieved at considerable cost. Under the new regime, plantation slaves frequently worked from dawn to noon and then, after a two hour break, until "the approach of night." As the planters' demands intensified, the time left for slaves to work their gardens grew shorter. Sustaining them took an extraordinary commitment. The frantic pace at which slaves worked in their own plots was captured by an emigré from Saint Domingue in 1799, who observed that a slave returning from the field "does not lose his time. He goes to work at a bit of the land which he has planted with provisions for his own use, while his companion, if he has one, busies herself in preparing some for him, herself, and their children." "Many of the owners take off a part of that ration," noted another visitor. Slaves "must obtain the rest of their food, as well as their clothing, from the results of their Sunday labors." Planters who supplied their slaves with clothes forced them to work on Sunday "until they have been reimbursed for their advances," so that the cash that previously went into the slaves' pockets went to the masters'.[125]

The struggle over the slaves' economy took a distinctive direction in the new cotton region, which abutted Indian territory. Again, some slaves found profit in the new crop, as cotton's seasonal demands created opportunities for overwork. To increase the productivity during planting and harvest, planters established quotas. For work done "over and above that amount," noted one observer, "their good master pays them for their accoutrement." While participating in this new variant of the old economy, slaves enjoyed some success in maintaining their gardens, provision grounds, and petty exchange economies. However, when they ventured into the cotton business for themselves, slaves faced opposition from planters who feared the slaves' cotton would be confused with their own. In quick order, lawmakers enacted legislation that barred slaves from "raising and Vending cotton."

Native Americans, longtime partners with slaves in the exchange economies of the lower Mississippi Valley, also found themselves targeted by the new restrictive legislation, which not only prohibited trade between "slaves and Indians" but also prohibited the two from meeting except in the presence of "some reputable white person." As planters asserted their sovereignty and sealed off their estates from outside influence, they sought to shrink the slaves' world and isolate them from all but the masters' dominion.

Among those from whom slaves had to be sequestered were free people of color whose very existence, planters believed, was subversive in a slave society. If Spanish authorities found value in a free colored militia, "armed and organized," the newly invigorated planter class saw nothing but danger, especially in the wake of events in Saint Domingue. Much to the slaveholders' delight, the degradation of slave life increased the social distance between plantation slaves and urban free people of color. Nothing seemed to be further from the cosmopolitan world of New Orleans and the other Gulf ports than the narrow alternatives of the plantation, with its isolation, machine-like regimentation, and harsh discipline.[126] As free people of color strove to establish themselves in the urban marketplace and master the etiquette of a multilingual society, they drew back from the horrors of plantation life and from the men and women forced to live that nightmare.

The repulsion may have been mutual. Plantation slaves, many of them newly arrived Africans, little appreciated the intricacies of urban life and had neither the desire nor the ability to meet its complex conventions. Rather than embrace European-American standards, plantation slaves sought to escape them. Their cultural practices pointed toward Africa—as did their filed teeth and tribal markings. While free people of color embraced Christianity and identified with the Catholic Church, the trappings of the white man's religions were not to be found in the quarter.[127]

Planters, ever eager to divide the black majority, labored to enlarge differences between city-bound free people of color and plantation slaves. Rewarding with freedom those men and women who displayed the physical and cultural attributes of European Americans fit their purpose exactly, as did employing free colored militiamen against maroons or feting white gentlemen and colored ladies at quadroon balls. It was no accident that the privileges afforded to free people of color expanded when the danger of slave rebellion was greatest. Nor was it mysterious that the free colored population grew physically lighter as the slave population—much of it just arrived from Africa—grew darker. But somatic coding was just one means of dividing slave and free blacks. Every time black militiamen took to the field against the maroons or a young white gentleman took a colored mistress, the distance between slaves and free people of color widened.

Two migrations of the late-eighteenth and early-nineteenth centuries reinforced the division. Whereas reafricanization renewed the ties of plantation slaves with Africa and isolated them from the Gulf ports, the arrival of thousands of free people of color from Saint Domingue alienated colored peoples from the plantation and its hard-pressed residents. These colored refugees had even less in common with plantation slaves than did the native free people of color. Their shared history reaching back to the Natchez revolt had but slight meaning to the newcomers. Men and women chased from their homes and dispossessed of their property—often including slaves—by Toussaint's armies could hardly identify with the newly arrived Africans and the plight of the plantation slave.

Yet, if the growth of the plantation attenuated relations between free people of color and slaves in the lower Mississippi Valley, it never severed them. The upsurge of revolutionary egalitarianism that obliterated differences of status and color in the name of human equality restored connections between these two peoples of African descent. The successful establishment of a revolutionary republic under a proclamation that "all men are created equal," and the bloody enactment of those principles, provided an ideological umbrella under which slaves, free people of color, Indians, and even disaffected white men and women could band together.

The confluence of the plantation revolution of sugar and cotton and the democratic striving of the Age of Revolution made for new, explosive possibilities in the lower Mississippi Valley.[128] Revolutionary republicanism spread rapidly during the last decade of the eighteenth century, and planters soon found themselves surrounded by insurrection and intrigue. Challenging the new harsh regime in the countryside, plantation slaves schemed to break the masters' grasp. Runaways grew in number, and maroon colonies reappeared in the backcountry. Thus, even as slaveholders sealed off their plantations from outside influences and instituted the discipline necessary to create a plantation regime, the plantation regime shook.

Revolutionary activities took place at many venues. The primitive, frontier plantations, where newly arrived Africans reformulated their common African heritage, were the sites of many intrigues. Others took shape in the streets and back alleys of the port cities, where disenchanted black and white workers drank and gamed together. Yet other plots were hatched in the barracks, where white and black militiamen—mobilized against the very threat of revolution—had been joined together. Almost all the insurrectionists talked the language of the revolutionary age. But while some linked their cause directly to the revolutions in the United States, France, and Saint Domingue, others drew on their memory of Africa.[129]

The largest of the conspiracies, a plot devised at Pointe Coupée in 1795, touched on all of these themes. Led by newly arrived African slaves on the plantation frontier, it joined together Europeans of various nationalities, European Americans, free people of color, and even some Tunica Indians. The Pointe Coupée conspirators were familiar with the revolutionary events in Boston, Paris, and Cap Français, having worked alongside slaves imported from the North American seaboard and Saint Domingue. They had listened to a local school teacher recite "The Declaration of the Rights of Man." And they understood the rift between French planters and Spanish governors. At least one of the plotters had sued for freedom.

Many had access to guns or the possibility of purchasing guns. Asked how slaves could obtain the weapons necessary to secure their freedom, one conspirator laughed off the question, declaring, "Don't be like stupid cows. We have pigs and chickens, and we can sell them and buy guns, powder, and balls." Drawing material support from their own economies, the conspirators brought together the many threads of black life in the lower Mississippi Valley. The governor's investigation culminated in the execution of several dozen slaves, the banishment of at least three free people of color, and the imprisonment of several white men.[130]

Yet, despite the planters' deepest fears, for the most part free people of color kept their distance from slaves and anything that smacked of servile insurrection. Although individual free men may have been involved in the Pointe Coupée conspiracy, the leaders of the free colored community in New Orleans and its military arm played no role. When militiamen became involved in revolutionary activity, they acted from a deep sense of anger at their own subordination and their attraction to the "maxims of the new French constitution." But whatever the appeal of revolutionary ideals, free people exhibited little concern for the plight of the slave.

A close investigation of one free colored conspirator, militia lieutenant Pedro Bailly, exposed only discontent with white domination and a profound desire for equality, although his inquisitors were eager to find evidence of an alliance with slaves. Bailly was proud that his people—free people of color—had confronted their white tormentors in Saint Domingue, but there was no desire to see a repetition of Toussaint's triumph in Louisiana. He himself was a slaveholder, as was his father and many of his comrades.

If free people of color exhibited little sympathy for slaves, the "maxims of the new French constitution" and the events in Saint Domingue fed their own desire for enfranchisement and full incorporation into Louisiana society. The arrival of the Americans in 1803 only heightened their egalitarian aspiration. Understanding that the treaty which transferred Louisiana to the United States promised that the free inhabitants would enjoy "all the rights, advantages and immunities of citizens," free blacks believed they beheld a new and unfettered opportunity. "We are duly sensible that our personal and political freedom is thereby assured to us for ever," declared New Orleans free people in one of their numerous memorials to the new American rulers, "and we are also impressed with the fullest confidence in the Justice and Liberality of the Government towards every Class of Citizens which they have here taken under their Protection." To demonstrate their loyalty and to underline their willingness to defend their rights, free black militiamen "universally mounted the Eagle in their hats" and marched in force at the ceremony transferring Louisiana to the United States, an action that the American governor read more as a threat than a mark of patriotism.[131]

If Spanish authorities, who had sustained the free colored militia, doubted its loyalty in the Age of Revolution, Americans were certain the colored militiamen could not be trusted. "In a country like this, where the negro population is so considerable, they should be carefully watched," warned one American administrator. Although in time the American governor, William C. C. Claiborne—like his Spanish predecessors—came to appreciate the free people of color as a counterweight to the French planter class, initially he feared for the safety of Louisiana. The arrival of colored people from Saint Domingue who had served in that colony's police force, been politicized by the events of the 1790s, and participated in the great revolt deeply frightened Claiborne. The growth of pirate communities along Louisiana's coast, many of which welcomed the colored refugees from Saint Domingue, compounded Claiborne's uneasiness. Like his predecessors, Claiborne feared a replay of Saint Domingue, with French planters pushing free people of color into the arms of insurrectionary slaves.[132]

Planters were more than willing to play their role in the drama. Enfranchised by the creation of a popularly elected territorial legislature, they achieved far more power than they ever had under Spanish or even French rule, and they were quick to turn it on the free people of color. In 1806, within three years of American accession, the planter-dominated legislature contained the growth of the free black population, severely circumscribing the rights of slaves to initiate manumission. Thereafter slaves could be freed only by special legislative enactment.

That done, the legislature struck at the privileges free people of color had enjoyed under Spanish rule, issuing prohibitions against carrying guns, punishing free black criminals more severely than white ones, and authorizing slaves to testify in court against free blacks but not whites. In an act that represented the very essence of the planters' contempt for people of color, the territorial legislature declared that "free people of color ought never to insult or strike white people, nor presume to conceive themselves equal to whites, but on the contrary . . . they ought to yield to them on every occasion and never speak or answer them but with respect."[133]

With planters now in control, the free people's position in the society of the lower Mississippi Valley slipped sharply. Claiborne slowly reduced the size of the black militia, first placing it under the control of white officers and then deactivating it entirely when the territorial legislature refused to recommission it. The free black population continued to grow, but—with limitations on manumission and self-purchase—most of the growth derived from natural increase and immigration. The dynamism of the final decades of the eighteenth century, when the free black population grew faster than either the white or slave population, dissipated, prosperity de-clined, and the great thrust toward equality was blunted as the new American ruler turned its back on them.

In the years that followed, as white immigrants flowed into the Mississippi Valley and the Gulf ports grew whiter, American administrators found it easier to ignore the free people of color or, worse yet, let the planters have their way. Occasionally, new crises arose, suddenly elevating free people to their old importance. In 1811, when slaves revolted in Pointe Coupée, and in 1815, when the British invaded Louisiana, free colored militiamen took up their traditional role as the handmaiden of the ruling class in hopes that their loyalty would be rewarded.[134] But long-term gains were few. Free people of color were forced to settle for a middling status, above slaves but below whites.

The collapse of the free people's struggle for equality cleared the way for the expansion of slavery. The Age of Revolution had threatened slavery in the lower Mississippi Valley, as it had elsewhere on the mainland. Planters parried the thrust with success. As in the Upper and Lower South, African-American slavery grew far more rapidly than freedom in the lower Mississippi Valley during the post-revolutionary years. The planters' westward surge out of the seaboard regions soon connected with their northward movement up the Mississippi Valley to create what would be the heartland of the plantation South in the nineteenth century. As the Age of Revolution receded, the plantation revolution roared ahead, and with it the Second Middle Passage.

MIGRATION GENERATIONS

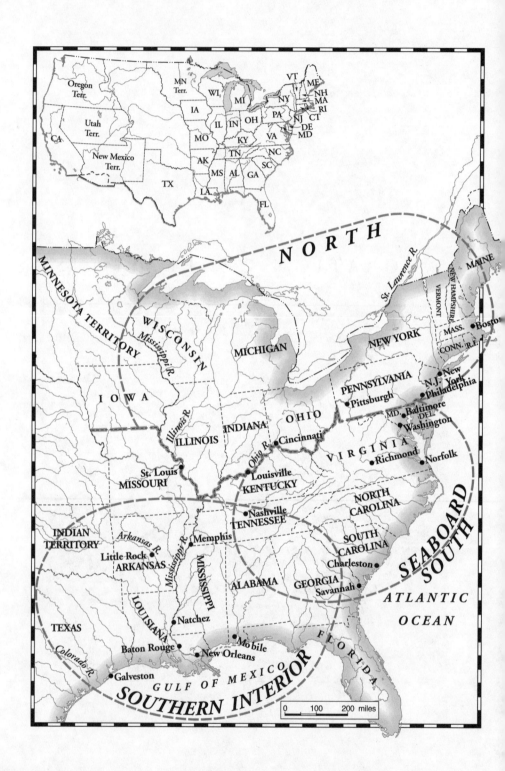

NORTH

St. Lawrence R.

MINNESOTA TERRITORY

WISCONSIN

Mississippi R.

MICHIGAN

MAINE

NEW HAMPSHIRE

VERMONT

MASS. • Boston

NEW YORK

CONN. R.I.

IOWA

Illinois R.

ILLINOIS

INDIANA

OHIO

PENNSYLVANIA

N.J. New York

• Pittsburgh

• Philadelphia

DEL.

MD. • Baltimore

• Washington

Ohio R.

Cincinnati

VIRGINIA

Louisville

• Richmond

• Norfolk

St. Louis

MISSOURI

KENTUCKY

Nashville

TENNESSEE

NORTH
CAROLINA

INDIAN
TERRITORY

Arkansas R.

• Memphis

Little Rock

ARKANSAS

Mississippi R.

MISSISSIPPI

ALABAMA

GEORGIA

SOUTH
CAROLINA

• Charleston

Savannah •

SEABOARD
SOUTH

ATLANTIC
OCEAN

TEXAS

LOUISIANA

• Natchez

Colorado R.

Baton Rouge •

• Mobile

New Orleans

FLORIDA

• Galveston

GULF OF MEXICO

SOUTHERN INTERIOR

0   100   200 miles

Oregon
Terr.

MN
Terr.

WI

MI

VT

ME

NY

NH
MA
RI

Utah
Terr.

IA

IL

IN

OH

PA

NJ CT

CA

MO

KY

VA

DE
MD

New Mexico
Terr.

TN

NC

AK

MS AL GA

SC

TX

LA.

FL

THE TRANSFORMATION of slavery set in motion during the Age of Revolution accelerated between 1810 and 1861. During that half century, thousands of men and women whose forebears had reconstituted African life along North America's Atlantic Coast were propelled across the continent in a Second Middle Passage. Driven by the cotton and sugar revolutions in the southern interior, the massive deportation displaced more than a million men and women, dwarfing the transatlantic slave trade that had carried Africans to the mainland. While the migrants struggled to reconstruct black society in a wilderness that stretched from upland South Carolina to Texas, those left behind in the seaboard South felt the powerful undertow of the forced evacuation, which disrupted their lives as fully as the lives of those transported west. Indeed, the changes wrought by the domestic slave trade incited yet another exodus from the South, as black people fled their native ground for the emerging free states.

The Second Middle Passage was the central event in the lives of African-American people between the American Revolution and slavery's final demise in December 1865. Whether slaves were themselves marched across the continent or were afraid that they, their families, or their friends would be, the massive deportation traumatized black people, both slave and free. Like some great, inescapable incubus, the colossal transfer cast a shadow over all aspects of black life, leaving no part unaffected. It fueled a series of plantation revolutions—cotton across the immense expanse of the Lower South, sugar in the lower Mississippi Valley, hemp in the upper valley—that created new, powerful slave societies. Although the magnitude of the changes and the vastness of the area effected—from the hills of Appalachia to the Texas plains—encouraged an extraordinary variety of social formations, no corner escaped the experience of the staple-producing plantation. Its presence resonated outside the region, eroding slavery on the seaboard South to such an extent that some portions of the Upper South—most prominently the border slave states of Delaware, Kentucky, Maryland, and Missouri—devolved from slave societies into societies with slaves. Finally, it accelerated the North's evolution from a society with slaves to a free society.

In each of these regions, the Second Middle Passage remade black life. Changes in the nature of production that accompanied the forced transfers bent men and women who once cultivated tobacco and rice to new labor regimens. Whether they grew cotton or sugar in the southern interior, were hired as farmers or manufacturers in the seaboard South, or took to the sea from some northern port, black men and women worked under new disciplines in circumstances foreign to their parents. But the transformation of black life extended beyond the workplace. Everywhere, black people reconstructed their families on new ground, redefining relations between husbands and wives, parents and children, and near and distant kin. In like fashion, they remade their sacred world, as men and women whose ancestors had ignored Jesus for nearly two centuries embraced Christianity. Relations between black and white, master and slave shifted, along with the ideologies that underpinned them. Divisions among people of African descent also grew, as men and women whose forebears had never known captivity distinguished themselves from those whose slave ancestry reached back to the sixteenth century. While many of the former restored their transatlantic connections, remaking the cos-

mopolitan world of the charter generations as agents of an expanding African-American diaspora, the latter—isolated in the southern interior and
blinded by the narrow alternatives of plantation life—were rooted in a
world that did not extend beyond the plantation gate.

As earlier, the transformation of black life in the nineteenth century
proceeded unevenly. Regional differences gave the migration generations a
different history in the greatly expanded southern interior, the older seaboard South, and the North.

THE SOUTHERN INTERIOR

Like a mighty torrent, the Second Middle Passage washed thousands of
black men and women across the continent, expanding slavery westward.
At the time of the Revolution, the slave regime was confined to a narrow
strip between the Atlantic seaboard and the Appalachian Mountains.
During the last decades of the eighteenth century, it breached the eastern-
most Blue Ridge range, inundated the Shenandoah Valley, and spilled
across the Cumberland Plateau into Kentucky and Tennessee. At the same
time, slaveowning planters enlarged their base at the mouth of the Mississippi River. The purchase of Louisiana from a beleaguered France, engi-
neered by Thomas Jefferson, created not an "empire for liberty," as Jefferson had promised, but an empire for slavery. With New Orleans and its
vast hinterland now under American rule, planters quickly occupied the
rich lands between the western Appalachian ranges and the Mississippi
River. The two great thrusts of slavery's expansion—one east to west from
the Chesapeake and lowcountry, the other south to north from the lower
Mississippi Valley—soon joined. Before long, slaveholders were casting
covetous eyes on the southwestern corner of the North American continent, a vision that they translated into reality with the successful American assault on Mexico in 1848.[1]

The territorial settlement that followed the Mexican War exposed the
federal government's long-established role as the agent of slavery's expansion. Federal diplomats who had wrested Louisiana from the French in
1803 took Florida from the Spanish in 1819. Between those two landmarks

in slavery's expansion, federal soldiers and state militiamen forcibly expropriated millions of acres of land from the Indians through armed conquest and defended the slave regime from black insurrectionists and foreign invaders. After defeating slave rebels in St. John the Baptist Parish, Louisiana, in 1811 and British invaders in New Orleans in 1814, federal soldiers turned their attention to sweeping aside Native peoples.

The conquest at the Battle of Horseshoe Bend in 1814 was followed by a series of one-sided treaties, as federal soldiers prepared the way for the eviction of Indians from territories east of the Mississippi. Pressed hard by westward-moving settlers, some Indians allied themselves with fugitive slaves. But in 1816 General Andrew Jackson liquidated this knot of resistance when he destroyed the Negro Fort on the Apalachicola River in the Florida panhandle. The dismantling of this emerging alliance between black and Native peoples ended a threat that had bedeviled the plantation regime throughout the eighteenth century.[2]

By the 1830s only fragments of the once-peaceful Indian nations remained scattered through the vast territory between the Appalachians and the Mississippi Valley. Some Native Americans mixed with white settlers and black maroons, creating yet other new peoples. Some climbed into the slaveholding class and in time attained the status of planters. Others served the nascent plantation regime as soldiers and slave catchers. Yet others lurked on the edges of plantation settlements, trading with slaves and serving as a market for stolen goods. Their long history of mixing with Anglo-American hunters and trappers and black fugitives created yet other social formations on this middle ground. These fugitive relationships, however, only revealed the marginality of Native people. By the fourth decade of the nineteenth century, Indians posed no threat to westward-moving planters.[3]

With the way cleared for slavery's expansion, federal agents began to distribute the government's newly acquired domain in a manner that favored planters, who grabbed the richest lands along the river bottoms. The pioneer farmers who had established a foothold in the nascent plantation region by simply squatting upon land from which Indians had been ousted soon found themselves on the defensive as the struggle over land resonated from territorial capitals to the national capital. Speculators, many of whom were substantial planters, preferred to sell to other planters, when they did not engross the property themselves. Migrating planters may have appreciated the work of the first arrivals in clearing the forests and breaking the prairie, but they had no intention of sharing the rich soils of the southern interior with drovers and dirt farmers. Their access to money and credit, knowledge of the law, and political influence enabled them to outbid, outmaneuver, and, if necessary, outmuscle aspiring yeomen.[4]

By dint of ambition, knowledge, and perhaps a strategic marriage, some smallholders climbed into the slaveholding class, transferring their capital from herding and subsistence farming into slave ownership. Many of them eventually found a place in the interstices between the great estates by supplying the plantations with foodstuffs and perhaps growing some cotton themselves. The most successful of these—holding between ten and twenty slaves—were particularly important in the period following settlement. Even when plantation society matured and the great planters consolidated their control, smallholders produced almost one third of the cotton and controlled nearly 40 percent of the slaves.

But few rose into the planter class, and most did not even reach the slaveowners' middling ranks. Many sold out, took a quick profit, and retreated to the hill country of north Georgia and Alabama, the wiregrass region of southeast Georgia, and the piney woods of Mississippi, northern Louisiana, and southern Arkansas. In so doing they followed the path of those who had earlier fled Barbados for lowland Carolina, and later those who fled lowland Carolina for the upcountry. As planters consolidated their control, only remnants of these pioneer settlements remained.[5]

Having seized the most fertile lands and prime riverine locations, planters made the region safe for slavery by securing political power. Without exception, territorial governors were appointed from the ranks of the planter class or those who would soon enter the planter class, and slaveholders populated the territorial and state legislatures as well as county courthouses and sheriffs' offices. Those legislatures imported slave codes from the established slave states, sometimes borrowing provisions that had first been enacted by Barbadian planters in the mid-seventeenth century at the start of the sugar revolution. Kentucky's slave code derived from that of Virginia, Tennessee's could be traced back to North Carolina, and Mississippi's to Georgia.[6] Upon entering the new territories, planters could be assured that their claim to property-in-persons would be protected, that their rights to discipline their slaves would be unchallenged, and that slaveholders and nonslaveholders alike would cooperate in the return of fugitives and the suppression of slave rebels. Behind the master class stood the power of the state in the form of militia, police juries, and patrols.

The cotton revolution in the southern interior—like earlier plantation revolutions in the Antilles, Chesapeake, and lowland South—came in a rush. Within less than a generation, the cultivation of short-staple cotton ceased to be an experiment. As the cultivation of cotton spread west from upcountry Carolina and north from Natchez to an area that became known as the blackbelt, cotton came to dominate the southern landscape, shaping its society and informing every aspect of its culture. While the changes were incremental, sweeping through Georgia, then Alabama and Mississippi, before reaching Arkansas and Texas, eventually no part of the southern interior was untouched. At the close of the War of 1812 the South had produced less than 300,000 bales of cotton per year. By 1820 that number had more than doubled, and by mid-century the harvest exceeded four million bales per year.[7]

With prime land and the law on their side—and the international demand for cotton spiraling upward—planters hastened to assemble a labor force. They used two methods. A minority—generally established planters and their kin or agents—marched west with their own slaves. Some packed up all their belongings, including their entire retinue of slaves—men and women, young and old. Others migrated in stages, with planter men pioneering alone, initially accompanied by a few trusted slave men to begin the hard work of taming the wilderness. Once they were settled, additional slaves followed. However, planters-in-transit carried only a small portion of the slaves who would eventually people the interior. Most would-be slaveholders depended upon smugglers, kidnappers, and traders to build their labor force.[8]

Desperate for workers, planters searched everywhere for "hands." Initially, some turned to Africa. Although the transatlantic slave trade had been terminated by congressional enactment in 1808, illegal slaving, especially through the Spanish colony of Florida prior to 1819 and the Mexican province of Texas, brought thousands of African and Caribbean slaves into the region. Just as Louisiana planters had earlier ignored the congressional prohibition on the importation of Africans into the Territory of Orleans, so planters in the southern interior skirted the new edict.[9] Transplanted Africans, with their ritual scars and fresh memories of their homeland, could be found scattered throughout western Georgia and Florida, Alabama, Mississippi, and Louisiana, just numerous enough to serve as reminders of the African past but too few in number to satisfy the expanding demand for slaves.

The rising price of slaves also encouraged the kidnapping of free blacks and the abduction of slaves who had been promised freedom by statutory emancipation or individual acts of manumission. Northern officials had little incentive to enforce post-revolutionary strictures barring the sale of slaves across state lines or statutes against kidnapping. The practice of plucking free people or soon-to-be-free people from the streets of northern cities or from isolated Chesapeake farms, often with the cooperation of corrupt sheriffs, occurred with frightening frequency during the first decades of the nineteenth century. Isabella Van Wagenen—still a slave in New York and not yet Sojourner Truth—nearly lost her son when he was sold to Alabama, in contravention of the law. With the aid of Quaker lawyers, she retrieved the boy, although not every black parent was as fortunate.[10]

Neither smuggling Africans nor kidnapping African Americans could satisfy the demand for laborers. Ultimately, they provided just a small fraction of the plantation labor force. Meanwhile, new men arriving on the cotton frontier were eager to buy their first slaves. Recently established planters, their wallets bulging from the sale of their first crops, wanted to buy more slaves. Grandees—hungry to expand their holdings—wanted yet more slaves. As the fields turned white with each new cotton crop, the planters' appetite for slaves grew beyond anything previously known on mainland North America. With federal officials—pressured by the British government—at last acting upon the constitutional provision against importation of Africans, slaveholders substituted a legal inter-regional trade for an illegal international one.

In the years immediately following the Revolution, "Georgia traders" had begun the process of transporting slaves from the North and the Chesapeake into the Carolinas, Georgia, Kentucky, and Tennessee. The internal trade was interrupted by the War of 1812, but the frenzied demand for cotton revived Georgia trading and spread it beyond the state for which it had been named. The Second Middle Passage had commenced.[11]

The internal slave trade became the largest enterprise in the South outside of the plantation itself, and probably the most advanced in its employment of modern transportation, finance, and publicity. It developed its own language: prime hands, bucks, breeding wenches, and fancy girls. Its routes, running counter to the freedom trails that fugitive slaves followed north, were similarly dotted by safe houses—pens, jails, and yards that provided resting places for slave traders as well as temporary warehouses for slaves. In all, the slave trade, with its hubs and regional centers, its spurs and circuits, reached into every cranny of southern society. Few southerners, white or black, were untouched.[12]

In the half century following the War of 1812, planters and traders expanded and rationalized the transcontinental transfer of slaves.[13] During the second decade of the nineteenth century, traders and owners sent an estimated 120,000 slaves from the seaboard to the west, with the states and territories of Georgia, Tennessee, Alabama, and Louisiana being the largest recipients. That number increased substantially during the following decade and yet again during the 1830s, when slave traders and migrating planters uprooted almost 300,000 black men, women, and children. By this time, though most of the slaves still derived from the Upper South—particularly Maryland and Virginia—their destination had moved further west. Alabama and Mississippi had become the largest recipients, with each receiving nearly 100,000 slaves during the 1830s. The Panic of 1837 and the subsequent decline in cotton and sugar production deflated the price of slaves and the trade slackened for a few years. But prices soon revived and with them the demand for slaves. Nearly one quarter of a million slaves left the seaboard for the interior during the 1850s, with more than half being taken west of the Mississippi River. The "mania for buying negroes" easily overwhelmed periodic bans against slave importation and did not cease until the arrival of Union troops.[14]

The Second Middle Passage, like the first, had a logic of its own. As with the transatlantic slave trade, planters developed a clear understanding of which slaves they wanted. For the most part, these were young men and women whose strength could be harnessed to turn the wilderness into plantations and whose fecundity would assure the continued viability of the slave regime. Young adults made up about half of the slaves traded, according to one estimate, and most of the rest were children. Slave traders evinced little interest in transferring slave families intact (except in the case of women with young children), but cotton planters appreciated the advantages of a self-reproducing labor force, and traders conveyed a rough balance of men and women. Smallholders seemed particularly partial to young women, who came at a lower price and offered the possibility of enlarging the slave force through reproduction. Summing up the conventional wisdom, veterans of the plantation business advised "it is better to buy *none in families*, but to *select only choice, first rate, young hands from 14 to 25 years of age,* (buying no children or aged negroes)."[15]

Planters also developed a clear understanding of which slaves they did not want. They demeaned as "refuse" those whom they believed could not withstand the rigors of the transcontinental journey—the aged and the broken. Westward-moving slaveholders also feared rebels or criminals, who were often the same in their eyes. Some of the first laws enacted by the territorial legislatures of Louisiana, Mississippi, and Alabama prohibited the entry of slaves with histories of disobedience or dishonesty. Eventually, Louisiana required imported slaves to be accompanied by certificates attesting to their "good moral character." Just as some eighteenth-century slave masters prized Igbos over Angolans, Coromontees over Callabars, some of their nineteenth-century counterparts desired Virginians over Carolinians. Over time these distinctions dissipated, as a shared understanding of race gave certain physical characteristics—"a prime hand," "a good breeder," "a yellow girl"—a greater weight than provenance.

As with the international slave trade, planters could not always get what they wanted; their attempts at various times to regulate the trade failed completely. Often planters got precisely those slaves they did *not* want, as seaboard slaveholders dumped "the dregs of the colored population" onto the new plantations of the west, as one Georgia newspaper noted. Some slave-exporting states systematically deported criminal slaves, and the importing states rarely enforced laws against their entry. A Methodist circuit rider echoed popular opinion when he noted that "the worst Negroes from the Carolinas and Va. are sent to the Miss. and sold for money."[16]

Still, if planters did not get everything they desired, they nonetheless shaped the character of the internal slave trade. Although the planters' views of slaves—whether young or old, Virginians or Carolinians—were grounded in stereotypes rather than any particular reality, their preferences mattered nonetheless. As a result of their choices, the southern interior became an extraordinarily youthful place. Men below the age of twenty-five composed nearly 39 percent of Alabama's slaves in 1820, a higher portion than in Virginia, where young men under twenty-five made up about 35 percent of all slaves. A comparison of Greene county in Alabama with Warwick county in the Virginia tidewater is even starker. A sexually balanced population emerged almost immediately in the cotton South, assuring the viability of the labor force.[17]

Although the presence—and rumored presence—of slaves from Africa provided a connection to an African homeland, too few Africans entered the interior to reafricanize the slave population. The vast majority of immigrants were African Americans, drawn from all over the North American continent. Slaves from the North, Chesapeake, and lowcountry mixed easily. While the "Savannah dialect" was distinguishable from the "brogue different from Negroes raised in Eastern Virginia" and some slaves bragged of their origins—claiming that "Virginny de best" and South Carolinians "eats cottonseed"—such regional chauvinism had no lasting effect on African-American life. Indeed, one of the consequences of the Second Middle Passage was to attenuate the regional distinctions that had characterized slave life during the seventeenth and eighteenth centuries. As a result of massive migration, by mid-century—if not earlier— the fault lines within African-American society generally ran north-south rather than east-west.[18]

The young black men and women ripped from the seaboard and transported to the interior comprised the shock troops of the cotton revolution. Their travail mirrored that of their grandparents and great grandparents who had been taken from Africa in the previous century. By the time they arrived at some forbidding piece of prairie that only the most optimistic owners believed could be converted into a great estate, would-be cotton cultivators—many barely more than children—had experienced all the nightmares of the Middle Passage. With little warning, they had been separated from everyone and everything they knew and loved. A lucky few traveled with their owner, whose concern for their well-being might extend beyond the pecuniary. Moving their entire operation west, such owners even occasionally purchased their slaves' relatives from other estates prior to their departure. They allowed slaves to transport their belongings, helped them maintain ties to friends left behind, and occasionally allowed them to return home to visit.[19] While these slaves faced the dangers that confronted all pioneers, they belonged to a fortunate minority. Most slaves were transported south by utter strangers, whose only interest in their survival derived from the profits to be turned by their eventual sale.

For these—the overwhelming majority of the deportees—the journey southward was traumatic and often deadly. Even before departing, slaves had experienced the humiliation of having their persons inspected in the most minute and intimate ways, with strange hands probing every crack and crevice of their bodies. Once under way, some traders moved their chattels by sea, with Norfolk to New Orleans being the most common route. But most slaves were forced to march the entire distance. "'Dem speckulators would put the chilluns in a wagon usually pulled by oxens and de older folks was chained or tied together sos dey could not run off." Shackled together "like so many fish on a trod," they tramped southward.[20]

The trek from the interior was long, arduous, and—for many slaves—rarely direct. Whether led by traders or owners, the coffles of slaves made many detours and stops. Meandering from town to town much as their seaborne counterparts in the African trade had earlier cruised from port to port and island to island, traders sold a few slaves and purchased others. Like the traders, slaveowners-in-transit were also on the make, bartering old hands for younger ones or selling slaves to finance their new ventures. Slaves purchased along the way rarely remained in one place for long and were often forced to relive the degrading protocols of sale. Their bodies greased to hide blemishes and hair painted to disguise age, they were again placed on the auction block to be poked, prodded, inspected, evaluated, and sent on their way.

Resale came quickly for some. Others remained just long enough to establish themselves, only to be suddenly uprooted by the death of their new owner, the settlement of an estate, or mere whim. A few were held in a state of limbo while speculators brokered a profitable deal. For some slaves, the auction block and pen were scenes from a recurring nightmare that had become a way of life. Anna Maria Coffee was sold eleven times, and she was just one of many who went back on the slave market repeatedly.

Grieving for their future, men and women often took their own lives. Others died when they could not maintain the feverish pace of the march. While the mortality rate of slaves during the Second Middle Passage never approached that of the transatlantic transfer, it surpassed the death rate of those who remained in the seaboard states.[21] Over time some of the hazards of the long march abated, as slave traders—intent on the safe delivery of a valuable commodity—standardized their routes and relied more on flatboats, steamboats, and eventually railroads for transportation. The largest traders established "jails," where slaves could be warehoused, inspected, rehabilitated if necessary, and auctioned, sometimes to minor traders who served as middlemen in the expanding transcontinental enterprise. But while the rationalization of the slave trade may have reduced the slaves' mortality rate, it did nothing to mitigate the essential brutality or the profound alienation that accompanied separation from the physical and social moorings of home and family.

Although slaves moving from the seaboard South—unlike their forebears caught in the transatlantic trade—shared a common language and could communicate easily, the Second Middle Passage was extraordinarily lonely, debilitating, and dispiriting. Capturing the mournful character of one southward marching coffle, an observer characterized it as "a procession of men, women, and children resembling that of a funeral." Indeed, with men and women dying on the march or being sold and resold, slaves became not merely commodified but cut off from nearly every human attachment. Surrendering to despair, many deportees had difficulties establishing friendships or even maintaining old ones. After a while, some simply resigned themselves to their fate, turned inward, and became reclusive, trying to protect a shred of humanity in a circumstance that denied it. Others exhibited a sort of manic glee, singing loudly and laughing conspicuously to compensate for the sad fate that had befallen them. Yet others fell into a deep depression and determined to march no further. Charles Ball, like others caught in the tide, "longed to die, and escape from the bonds of my tormentors."[22]

But many who survived the transcontinental trek formed strong bonds of friendship akin to those forged by shipmates on the voyage across the Atlantic. Indeed, the Second Middle Passage itself became a site for remaking African-American society. Mutual trust became a basis of resistance, which began almost simultaneously with the long march. Waiting for their first opportunity and calculating their chances carefully, a few slaves broke free and turned on their enslavers. Murder and mayhem made the Second Middle Passage almost as dangerous for traders as it was for slaves, which was why the men were chained tightly and guarded closely.

Like all slave rebellions, in-transit insurrections were rare and rarely successful, although an occasional triumph—like the revolt aboard the *Creole* in 1841, in which slaves being shipped from Norfolk to New Orleans seized the ship and forced the captain to sail to the Bahamas—put every trader on guard. The coffles that marched slaves southward—like the slave ships that carried their ancestors westward—became mobile fortresses, and under such circumstances, flight was far more common than revolt. Slaves found it easier—and far less perilous—to slip into the night and follow the North Star to the fabled land of freedom than to confront their heavily armed overlords.[23]

Like the parents and grandparents who hewed tobacco fields out of the Chesapeake frontier or claimed rice paddies from Carolina swamps, those who survived the long march faced extraordinary challenges upon arrival in their new home. They often found nothing in place but some surveyor's markers. Although planters carried some provisions or sent them ahead, these supplies rarely lasted long. Hungry and tired, pioneer slaves took on the backbreaking labor of clearing the land. "All I had to do," recalled one slave, was to "cut down trees and grub sprouts all day every day." As soon as a patch of ground was cleared, slaves began digging the earth to get their first crop in the ground, understanding that failure would be as disastrous for them as for their owners.

Perhaps the arduous routine served as a distraction from the homesickness that affected nearly everyone. Long after emancipation, former slaves remembered the deep melancholy of those first years. "Every time we look back and think 'bout home," recalled one Virginian who had been transported to Texas, "it make us sad."[24]

Death, a frequent visitor to the pioneer plantation, contributed to the slaves' melancholia. The long journey south, spartan frontier circumstances, exhaustion, inadequate nutrition, and bad water weakened the newly arrived slaves and diminished their ranks. The planters' preference for the rich river bottoms put slaves in harm's way, as low-lying areas swarmed with mosquitoes and other scourges. Diseases to which slaves had but weak immunities took their toll. Indeed, so deadly was the work of those first years that some planters preferred not to risk their valuable property. Rather than use their own slaves, they hired someone else's.

Hired hands performed the most arduous tasks, confronting extraordinary demands without even the minimum protections that accompanied ownership.[25]

The harsh conditions of frontier life strained the always contentious relations between masters and slaves. Already embittered at being separated from loved ones, slaves on the frontier grew "mean." Planters, eager to get on with the work at hand, often countered the slaves' discontent by pressing them with greater force, only to find that slaves called their bet and then raised the stakes, resisting with still greater force. As the struggle escalated, planters discovered that even their best hands became unmanageable. One planter noted that his previously compliant slaves evinced "a general disregard (with a few exceptions) of orders . . . and an unwillingness to be pressed hard at work."[26]

In the face of festering anger, planters struggled to sustain the old order. Drawing on lessons of mastership that had been nearly two hundred years in the making on the North American mainland, planters instituted a familiar regime: they employed force freely and often; created invidious divisions among the slaves; and exacted exemplary punishments for the smallest infraction. If they sometimes extended the carrot of privilege, the stick was never far behind.[27] The results were violent and bloody, as slave masters made it clear that slaves, by definition, had no rights they need respect. The plantation did not just happen; it had to be made to happen.

Planter authority did not transplant easily. Relations between masters and slaves teetered toward anarchy on the cotton frontier. In some places, negotiations between owners and owned became little more than hard words and angry threats. Rumors of rebellion seemed to be everywhere. "Scarcely a day passes," observed Mississippi's territorial governor in 1812, "without my receiving some information relative to the designs of those people to insurrect." While few rebelled, some joined gangs of bandits and outlaws who resided in the middle ground between the westward-moving planters and the retreating Indians. On the plantations, slave masters saw sabotage everywhere—in broken tools, maimed animals, and burned barns. Slaves regularly took flight to the woods, and a few, eager to regain the world they had lost, tried to retrace their steps to Virginia or the Carolinas. It was a doubtful enterprise, and success was rare. Recaptured, they faced an even grimmer reality than before.[28]

By the second or sometimes third year, the rough outlines of a field might be discerned and food might be more plentiful. But the workload did not abate, as planters demanded that their slaves, in the words of one slave pioneer, "whittle a plantation right out of the woods." Corn remained an important part of the plantation regimen, but cotton gained pride of place. Before long, the irregular rhythms of pioneer agriculture gave way to the regimented cadence of staple production. The shift was not an easy one. Facing an entirely new routine, many slaves—like a Virginia native carried to Alabama—"could not get used to cotton growing as he had been accustomed to wheat and tobacco." As they mastered a crop with which they had little previous experience, the migration generation confronted the full force of the cotton revolution.[29]

Would-be planters drove their slaves hard because cotton cultivation demanded unceasing attention. Although the crop required neither the painstaking care of tobacco nor the heavy labor of rice culture, its growing season was long and the various tasks nearly endless. From the time the ground was broken and the seeds dropped in late March or early April, the work never stopped. Once the young plants began to sprout, the cotton had to be "chopped" or thinned, a task which occupied slaves for much of the summer. When the grass was at last beaten back and the crop was laid by in the latter part of July or early August, field hands had a chance to rest. But planters made sure it was not for long, as workers turned to the fields of corn and peas. There was "no time of' de change of de seasons and after de crop was laid by. Dey was allus clearin' mo' lan' or sump'n'," one former slave attested.

When the bolls ripened in late August, picking began. It was a tedious process which often continued through Christmas into the new year. It was also painful, especially for new arrivals, as the sharp edges of the bolls cut deep gashes into the pickers' hands, slowing the work of drying, ginning, and baling. Even then the work was not done. "When I wuz so tired I cu'dn't hardly stan' I had to spin my cut of cotton befor' I cu'd go to sleep," recalled a former Mississippi slave. "We had to card, spin, an' reel at nite." Traveling through the cotton South at mid-century, Frederick Law Olmsted concluded that slaves labored "much harder and more unremittingly" than elsewhere. "Everything," Olmsted learned from one "benevolent" Mississippi planter, "has to bend, give way to large crops of cotton, land has to be cultivated wet or dry, negroes work, hot or cold."[30]

Planters used the novel circumstances that accompanied the introduction of cotton to ratchet up the level of exploitation once again, jettisoning the old standard task or generally agreed upon definition of the stint. The youth of the slave population guaranteed that there would be little memory of what had once defined a day's labor—a fact slaveholders were quick to recognize if they had not previously planned to exploit the inexperience of their labor force. One of the first casualties of the slaves' old routine was the loss of free Sundays and half-Saturdays. Slaves on the frontier faced a lengthening work day as well as night work. As slaveholders mobilized every available hand to get their first crop to market, slaves spent an increasing portion of their lives in the field.[31]

The fields in question were the owners', for the movement of slavery to the interior dismantled the complex systems of independent production that comprised the slaves' economy. The crushing demands of creating cotton fields left little time for slaves to establish gardens and provision grounds for themselves. Only a few of the slaves transferred to the interior—generally those conveyed by their owners—carried their own stock. Slaves lost the ability to raise and sell pigs and fowl, an important element in their economy nearly everywhere along the seaboard. Even when owners allowed slaves to carve out their own small fields or keep barnyard animals, slaves had difficulty locating a market for their produce. Thus, under the best of circumstances, they still had to create their independent economies anew, legitimating their right to a portion of their labor, finding the time to work on their own, and establishing a market for their goods.[32]

Among the innovations that confronted slaves in the cotton South was the introduction of sunrise-to-sunset gang labor and the near universality of white overseers. As tobacco growers, Chesapeake slaves had labored in small squads that were often coterminous with family lines and directed by a black foreman who was often a family elder. As rice cultivators, slaves generally worked by the task, under the immediate supervision of a black driver. Control over the allocation of labor allowed black supervisors to protect the weakest members of the plantation, particularly women and children. On the cotton frontier, by contrast, the lock-step discipline of the plantation gang forced all slaves to work at the master's pace and introduced a new, foreign mode of discipline. The disappearance of black foremen and drivers—who had once stood between masters or stewards and field hands—exposed slaves to the whim of white overseers, who had the impossible task of mediating between two constituencies with antagonistic interests. The overseers' dual responsibility for productivity and good order placed them on a collision course with the slaves they supervised. The results could be bloody, and overseers developed a reputation for brutality.[33] As they wielded the lash, slaves alternately pleaded for mercy, refused to work, broke tools, burned barns, turned truant, and responded to their abusers in kind.

The removal of black men—and occasionally women—from the managerial ranks in the cotton South reduced opportunities for slaves to rise within the plantation hierarchy. The occupational ladder was further truncated with the elimination of many of the skills that slaves had once practiced on the tobacco and rice plantations of the seaboard, for cotton cultivation demanded little artisanal labor. Field work required equipment no more sophisticated than a hoe or a simple plow. Once ginned and baled, cotton had only to be covered with a tarpaulin to protect it from the weather. Unlike tobacco, it required no barrels, hence no coopers; no barns and storage sheds, hence no carpenters and sawyers; no drays or wagons, hence no wagoners and carriage makers. Unlike rice, cotton required none of the complex hydraulic systems, fans, or mills, hence no engineers, machinists, and millers. The spread of cotton culture devastated the ranks of the slave artisanry, reducing many tradesmen and women to field hands and depriving them of the opportunity to pass their skills on to their children. For slave artisans, whose identity was in their work, the march south was doubly destructive.[34]

The primitive conditions of pioneer life reduced the number of slaves needed for domestic labor. If any slaves were taken out of the field to perform household chores, they were children. The field force, which had been heavily weighted toward women during the eighteenth century, regained its sexual balance, as planters' desire to maximize production blurred distinctions between slave women's and slave men's work. Men and women performed many of the same tasks, particularly on those plantations that relied on the hoe rather than the plow, although women were also put to the plow. "Make those bitches go to at least 100 [pounds of cotton] or whip them like the devil," one pioneer planter instructed his overseer.[35] The new demands of cotton pressed hard on all slaves, women no less than men, as the sexual division of labor took a new shape.

But the cotton South was only one of the places where slavery was being recast. A similar transformation was taking place on different terrain in the southernmost parishes of Louisiana, where sugar cultivation was expanding rapidly. The sugar revolution paralleled the cotton revolution, as planters monopolized the best land, ousted smallholders, imported slaves in large numbers, and ratcheted up the level of exploitation. But the magnitude of the change was greater in all respects, as the oldest, most desultory society with slaves in mainland North America was abruptly recast into the most robust of slave societies. Between 1810 and 1830, the slave population of the sugar South increased from under 10,000 to over 42,000. By 1860 it had more than doubled to nearly 90,000, with black majorities emerging in the most productive parishes.[36]

The sugar revolution differed from that in cotton, almost always to the disadvantage of the slave. The character of the slave trade in lower Louisiana spoke to these differences, for it was massive and continuous. The influx made New Orleans the great terminus of the interstate slave trade, serving the same function in the nineteenth century that Charleston had served in the eighteenth. The enormous numbers of slaves flowing into New Orleans gave sugar growers, some of the richest men in the United States, the ability to exercise their preferences. Whereas cotton planters purchased slaves for their youth and strength and early on established a sexually balanced labor force, sugar planters wanted young men to grow cane, and lots of them. Approximately two-thirds of the slaves brought to lower Louisiana were males. As a result, the slave population of the sugar region became weighted heavily toward men. In 1830 there were 130 men for every 100 women in the prime sugar-producing parish of St. Charles.[37]

Sugar slaves worked at a killing pace. Planters required them not only to grow the cane but also to process it, leaving little seasonal respite. The short growing season necessitated a relentless work regimen, lest a cold snap destroy the labor of an entire year. During grinding season in late fall, slaves worked nearly around the clock, with all hands seeming to operate on the double-quick. "On cane plantations in sugar time," noted Solomon Northup, a kidnapped black New Yorker who rose to the rank of driver on one Louisiana estate, "there is no distinction as to the days of the week."

New technologies added urgency to the already frenetic tempo of the plantation. At the beginning of the nineteenth century, slaves squeezed the cane through a set of rollers driven by human or animal power and collected the juice in kettles for evaporation and granulation. By mid-century the process had been mechanized, with steam engines driving the rollers and vacuum pans replacing the boiling pot. New processes of filtration and clarification removed impurities and produced a purer, light-colored liquid. The unceasing pace of the machines tied slaves to a hard master, perhaps even more unrelenting than their white overlords. The demands were usually lethal. According to one visitor to the sugar parishes, few slaves lasted more than seven years.[38]

The extreme demands of sugar production and a work force that was composed disproportionately of young, unmarried men made the renegotiation of slave labor particularly contentious, and the violence that accompanied it especially savage. Few southern slaves were accustomed to working at the murderous pace sugar production demanded. In lower Louisiana, they learned at the end of the lash. "At the season's end, when cane is cut," noted one visitor to Louisiana in the 1830s, "nothing but the severest application of the lash can stimulate the human frame to endure it." "From the time of the commencement of sugar making to the close, the grinding and boiling does not cease day or night," recalled Northup.

"The whip was given to me with directions to use it upon anyone who was caught standing idle."[39]

The demands on slaves were felt in the quarter as well as in the field. While the slave population of the cotton South grew through natural increase, deaths in the sugar parishes outnumbered births. At mid-century, the fertility rate of slave women in St. Barnard and St. James parishes was only 60 percent of that of slave women in the cotton South. This demographic profile was more akin to the sugar islands of the Caribbean than to the mainland. With high mortality and low fertility, sugar planters sustained their workforce only by importation.[40]

Still, the slave masters did not have everything their own way. Whether growing cotton or sugar, slaves found advantages in the very circumstances that allowed planters to ratchet up the level of exploitation. They employed the primitive conditions of the new plantations, their knowledge of the process of production, and their sheer numbers to roll back the owners' early gains. Driven at times by violence (and violent resistance) and lubricated at other times by concessions (and counter offers), the reorganization of labor turned the new cotton and sugar plantations into sites of intense renegotiation of the terms of enslavement.

Like their forebears in seventeenth-century Virginia and Carolina, pioneer planters often found themselves working across a sawbuck from a slave. Laboring in the same fields, sleeping in the same tents, and eating out of the same pot flattened plantation hierarchies, and slaveholders' need for allies as well as workers eroded the differences between free and slave. The 1798 Kentucky law that allowed "all negroes, mulattoes, and Indians, bond or free, living on any frontier plantation . . . to keep and use guns and powder, shot and weapons, offensive and defensive," spoke precisely to those necessities. Consequently, a few slaves found new opportunities in the west. Millie Ann Smith's grandfather did nothing but hunt during his first two years on the Texas frontier. "He stay[ed] in the woods all the time, killing deer and wild hogs and turkeys and coons and the like for the white folks to eat," according to his granddaughter. When his master tried to put him to work, grandpa "used to run off." Truancy was easy enough in untamed wilderness, but some men escaped permanently, finding freedom in the new land.[41]

So did some women. Aspiring planters, often unmarried and pioneering in the west on their own, frequently found sexual partners among their slave women. For the most part these were casual couplings, born of loneliness and raw exploitation more than tender feelings. But in time some of these relationships outlived their tawdry beginnings and flowered into deep affection. Slave women became plantation mistresses in both meanings of that word. Pioneer conditions, particularly the shortage of marriageable white women, allowed black women to play the role of wife openly. Although few in number, such relationships became notorious. Their renown meant that planters who were not personally acquainted with white men and enslaved women living as husband and wife probably knew of such couples. The acceptance of these relationships encouraged a few frontier planters to act with a degree of openness that scandalized their seaboard counterparts. Richard Mentor Johnson, a pioneer Kentucky planter who served as vice president under Martin Van Buren, was only the most prominent such individual when he took his black wife and children to Washington in 1836. Like many men in this position, he educated his daughters and saw that they married white men.[42] From their place of privilege within slave society, a few people of African descent scaled the wall to freedom.

While there was little room for free people of color within the plantation region itself, some found places on its periphery. Fleeing the dangers of the countryside, they gravitated toward Mobile, Memphis, and New Orleans, where free colored communities had established safe and lucrative niches.[43] The men found employment in the service trades as barbers, draymen, and stable keepers, while free colored women worked as seamstresses, mantua makers, and peddlers—occupations that white men and women disdained but which allowed free people of color to enjoy a modest prosperity and a degree of economic security. During the nineteenth century the elite among these urban free people of color became some of the wealthiest, most skilled, and best educated black men and women in the United States. To the extent that they could camouflage themselves in the cosmopolitan ports lining the Gulf of Mexico and the South Atlantic, adopt the language and demeanor of white people, make themselves economically indispensable, find patrons among well-placed customers and business associates, and assure authorities that they posed no threat to the plantation regime, free people of color were able to expand their place as a middle caste.

Securing and maintaining that place required free people of color—especially those of the propertied classes—to disassociate themselves from plantation slaves, for even a hint of shared aspirations might provoke planters' fears of insurrection. While northern free blacks boldly assaulted the institution of slavery, southern free people of color dared not openly espouse abolitionism. Their precarious place in plantation society hinged on allying themselves with the planter class through their dress, language, deportment, and constant reassurances of loyalty. They remained trapped between the planters who feared and despised them and slaves with whom they dared not identify.

This social isolation led some free people of color to desperation and even self-destruction. But others celebrated their extraordinary achievements under the most difficult of circumstances. Attaining an unprecedented prosperity and creating their own churches, schools, literary associations, and fraternal organizations, they asserted—never publicly but among themselves—not merely their equality but their superiority to the free white and the enslaved black people around them. It was they, not white people, who should rule.

The fullest manifestation of this middle-caste and often mixed-race chauvinism emerged in New Orleans and Mobile, where bilingual and trilingual free people of color educated on both sides of the Atlantic created sophisticated cultures. Schooled in Paris and Port-au-Prince and informed by an interest in romantic poetry, spiritualism, freemasonry, and radical republicanism, they exulted in their distinctive status, character, and color. This sense of self-worth was not confined to the Gulf ports. In 1844 Michael Eggart, a light-skinned wheelwright, delivered the annual address to the Friendly Moralist Society, one of a number of racially exclusive benevolent associations in Charleston. Elaborating on the colored people's peculiar predicament of being caught between the "untainted prejudice of the white man" or "the deeper hate of our more sable brethren," Eggart urged "our union as A people" to take its proper place atop southern society.[44]

Few people of undiluted African descent could be counted in Michael Eggart's "union as A people." But plantation slaves, unable to escape the weight of the new labor regime, nonetheless brought their fullest range of weapons to bear in an ongoing struggle to improve their circumstances, perhaps reestablish their customary privileges, and even acquire new ones. Planters, dependent on black workers to wring profits from their cotton and sugar estates, often found themselves bending to their slaves' demands. The new order imposed by cotton and sugar, despite the taxing regimen and endless days, rested as much as the tobacco and rice regimes on negotiations between masters and slaves.

With labor everywhere in short supply and time still scarcer, slaves pressed their owners to respect the traditional understanding of the task or stint, turning the planters' urgent need to get a crop in the ground to their own advantage. In trespassing on their slaves' free Sunday or half-Saturday, planters found themselves in dangerous territory as they risked further alienating and demoralizing their workers. Rather than chance all by simply appropriating the slaves' free time, many planters enticed them to the field with payment in kind or cash.[45]

Slaves gained leverage from their control over production. In the sugar region, the timing of the harvest and the intricate processes necessary to turn raw cane into refined sugar required numerous skilled workers and managers. While cotton flattened the occupational hierarchies of seaboard plantations, sugar production expanded them, as the multitude of tasks and processes created a complex organizational edifice. Gangs—organized by age and sex—were assigned specific tasks, and artisans, many of whom had undergone extensive training, operated some of the most sophisticated industrial machinery in the United States. These mills burned thousands of cords of wood, sending slave lumbermen deep into the cypress swamps, where they generally worked far from the direct supervision of whites. In addition, the animals and wagons that delivered the cane to the mills and then carried the refined sugar to market needed tending. Finally, the very complexity of the plantation—its mixture of field and factory— meant that some slaves had to be given supervisory responsibilities, even when they worked under white overseers or stewards. While the cotton economy eviscerated slave artisanship, the sugar economy revivified it, allowing small numbers of slaves to gain skills and the prerogatives that customarily accompanied them.[46]

When slaveowners tried to dismantle long-established practices in order to extract more work from their laborers, slaves countered by trying to mobilize customs against their owners. In the cotton-producing region, the resistance to gang labor was especially intense among those who had labored by the task and who appreciated how tasking allowed them the time to tend their own gardens and provision grounds. Having inherited a plantation with a tradition of task labor, planter-politician James Henry Hammond encountered intense opposition when he tried to introduce gang labor. Only the greatest exertions enabled him to put the new order in place, and then not for long, as the slaves' commitment to their customary practice outlasted even the planter's most determined efforts. Eventually, he conceded some ground to his slaves. "Men of sense have discovered," Frederick Law Olmsted observed of the planters' style of management, " . . . [that] it was better to offer them rewards then to whip them; to encourage than drive them."[47]

The rewards took a variety of forms. Desperate to clear fields and initiate cotton production or get that first crop in the ground, planters paid for Sunday and evening work, time which traditionally belonged to slaves. Other masters permitted their slaves to keep gardens or provision grounds. The few coins slaves earned by their own labor—"overplus" from "overwork"—had great significance. They allowed slaves to supplement their meager diet and clothing and even enjoy small luxuries. "Den each fam'ly have some chickens and sell dem and de eggs and maybe go huntin' and sell de hides and git some money," remembered one former Alabama slave. "Den us buy what am Sunday clothes with dat money, sech as hats and pants and shoes and dresses." The slaves' cash attracted itinerant traders, Indians, and smallholders, who were eager to serve customers among the black population, slave or free. Connections with these white nonslaveholders enlarged the slaves' world. But perhaps most important, the masters' concessions acknowledged the slaves' claim to their own time and legitimated the independent productive activities that had been threatened during the early years of the cotton and sugar revolutions.[48]

Once slaveholders accepted the right of their slaves to keep barnyard fowl, maintain gardens and grounds, and market their own produce, there was no turning back. Before long, slaves had reestablished their own economy, enmeshed in the masters' economy but also apart from it. In the cotton region, they began to grow their own cotton, which they generally marketed through their owners. In the sugar region, they earned money by overwork, which was particularly plentiful during grinding season, by chopping wood to sell to the mills and by making staves for barrels. Moving beyond the boundaries of the plantation, slave lumbermen sold wood to steamboats, which began to navigate southern rivers during the third decade of the nineteenth century. Exploiting their familiarity with the waterways of the interior, many slave men and women traveled to the small ports that lined the rivers, where they hawked produce and purchased small items for resale on the plantation. When the towns were inaccessible, slaves found that peddlers were willing enough to come to them. Taking on the role of petty merchants, slaves entered into competition with their owners, some of whom established plantation stores to profit from the growth of the cash economy in the quarter. Slaves also established ties with white nonslaveholders, many of whom were delighted to purchase their surplus along with almost anything the slaves could steal from their owners. These exchanges spawned relationships—and friendships—that deeply concerned slaveowners.

To some extent, planters benefited from their slaves' economy, as it reduced plantation expenses. Corn and other foodstuffs purchased from slaves fed the plantation population; wood purchased from slaves powered the boilers and vacuum pans; and produce and game purchased from slaves enriched the masters' table. Small wonder some slaveholders welcomed their slaves' pledge of obedience in return for a new frock or a pair of shoes. But the planters' reliance on the slaves' independent productive activities legitimated the slaves' right to their own time and property—rights that were occasionally written into law.[49] No matter what benefits accrued to them, slave masters were chagrined to discover that they needed to bargain for the fealty which they assumed to be theirs by right.

Despite their enormous power, slaveholders found such compromises prudent. Many of the new plantations stood among some of the densest forests and swamps on the North American continent. Often they were located on rivers, giving slaves an easy exit. Their very locations invited truancy and maroonage. While permanent escape was a doubtful and perilous enterprise, desertion for a few days was easily accomplished, and flight during critical moments in the production cycle could be disastrous for the master. Appreciating their owners' vulnerability, slaves played upon the fear of truancy. Often the threat of flight was as effective as flight itself.

This was particularly true as slaves grew in number. New arrivals poured into the interior, and one of the region's distinguishing features—its black majority—emerged. In some places, planters and overseers were the only white persons on the plantation or even in the district. The cotton-producing county of Houston in central Georgia went from a white to a black majority between 1830 and 1840. The black majority grew still further during the following decade, when slaves comprised over 60 percent of Houston's population. As the cotton revolution pushed west, the pattern was repeated in Alabama, Mississippi, and finally Arkansas and Texas. Beginning in the 1830s, Chicot County, Arkansas, underwent the same color change. By 1850, four of five residents of Chicot were slaves, and the black majority was even larger in some of Louisiana's sugar parishes.[50] As the size of plantation units grew and the proportion of white households with slaves increased, nonslaveholders decamped. Warren County, Mississippi, typified this change in the southern interior: between 1810 and 1830, the average number of slaves held by planters there nearly doubled, and the percent of slaves living in units larger than ten grew from 58 to 77 percent.[51]

Racial imbalance in the cotton and sugar South put slaveholders on notice that they might easily be overwhelmed. The planters' omnipresent fear of Saint Domingue—which had echoed in Louisiana's St. John the Baptist Parish and would reverberate in Virginia's Southampton County —drove some masters to extraordinary acts of seemingly gratuitous violence, as they sought to overawe their slaves. While such brutal displays subdued some slaves, they incited others. Rather than increase the perils inherent in slavery, many slave masters returned to the bargaining table.

As masters and slaves confronted one another and redefined their mutual rights and responsibilities, each understood acquiescence to be conditional. As plantation society matured, the advantages slaves had gained from the primitive conditions of the frontier disappeared, and planters reclaimed—and, where possible, extended—the authority they believed to be theirs. Slaves, for their part, surrendered nothing easily. Instead, they too made new demands, continuing a contest of wills that dated back to their original enslavement.

Whether they grew cotton or sugar, slaves transported to a strange land struggled to recapture the life they had once known. Their lives were informed by a deep nostalgia for the world they had lost. Some tried to maintain ties with that world by collecting bits of information from the newly arrived, who might bring word from family and friends. In the letters that slaveowners wrote to their own families, some slaves were allowed to append small notes to loved ones back home, hoping the return mail would bring news of the health of an aged parent, the progress of a child, or the birth of a niece or nephew. "I wish to let you know that I think of you often and wish to see you very bad," Rose wrote from a caravan en route to Alabama by way of her mistress's letter to North Carolina. The mistress-amanuensis confirmed she had "a great many Messages from the Servants," although most were reported as little more than "all the negroes say howdy to you all white and black." Such flat renditions of the slaves' heartfelt sentiments encouraged those few slaves who could write "to take their pens in hand." Literate slaves maintained an independent correspondence, and their messages had more bite.

Pheobia and Cash tried to keep in touch with their kin even as they were transported from Georgia to Louisiana. "Pleas tell my daughter

Clairissa and Nancy a heap of how a doo." Then after reminding Clairissa that her "affectionate mother and Father sends a heap of Love to you and your Husband and my Grand Children Phebea. Mag. & Cloe. John. Judy. Sue," Pheobia and Cash could not help but observe "that what [food] we have got to t[h]row away now it would be anough to furnish your Plantation for one Season." Occasionally, some fortunate slaves returned home with their owner and had the opportunity to visit the old homestead. More commonly, wives and children were forced to follow their husbands and fathers west, a transfer that slaveholders rarely opposed, for they came to see advantages in family stability.[52]

Yet, whatever the advantages that accrued to slaveowners from domestic stability in the slave quarter, there were precious few family reunions for those forcibly conveyed to the southern interior. Fugitive bits of information carried by newly arrived immigrants, appended to a planter's correspondence or overheard at the master's table, only added to the uncertainty. Had a wife really remarried, was a brother in fact sold, had an aged parent died? The slaves' "grapevine telegraph" moved information at high speed but with dubious reliability. At best, transplanted slaves held onto a few priceless mementos of their bygone lives—a quilt stitched by their mother, a carving made by their father, a ring or comb, a few pots and pans. Even these small items were beyond most. At some point, the most optimistic resigned themselves to the reality they would never again see their families and friends.

But there were memories. Hawkins Wilson, sold from Virginia to Texas in 1843, treasured the memory of the biscuits his sister had prepared for him upon his departure. For more than twenty years, he maintained a mental genealogy of his extended family, compensating for his profound loss by rehearsing the smallest family connections. In 1867, when as a free man he took up the search for "his poor old mother" and "my own dearest relatives," Wilson could still recall the family he left behind: "My sister belonged to Peter Coleman in Caroline County and her name was Jane— Her husband's name was Charles and he belong to Buck Haskin and lived near John Wright's store in the same county—She had three children, Robert Charles and Julia, when I left—Sister Martha belonged to Dr. Jefferson, who lived two miles above Wright's store—Sister Matilda belonged to Mrs. Botts, in the same county—My dear uncle Jim had a wife at Jack Langley's and they all belonged to Jack Langley."[53] But, even as Hawkins Wilson sustained the memory of the world he had lost, he, like other exiled slaves, began to reconstruct his world anew.

Central to migrants' attempt to rebuild their lives was the reestablishment of the world of their parents. By the nineteenth century, Africa had become truly historic for most slaves; but the young men and women taken from the seaboard South knew enough of their fathers and mothers to try to duplicate their lives. It was the world of the Chesapeake and Carolinas—not Senegambia and Angola—they wanted to recreate in the blackbelt. Charles Ball, transported from Maryland to South Carolina, put the case directly, noting that his fellow slaves "pants for no heaven beyond the waves of the ocean . . . on the banks of the Niger, or the Gambia."[54]

The family—half remembered and often idealized—became the conduit for reproducing the lost world of eighteenth-century Virginia and the Carolinas. Almost upon arrival, transplanted slaves began to remake the families they had known. With their fathers and mothers gone, these young men and women selected substitute parents among the few elderly slaves who had been transported west. "Uncles" and "aunts" became revered figures on the pioneer plantations, for they kept alive the life that once was. While older slaves, many of whom had been forcibly separated from husbands or wives, were not quick to establish new families for fear that any new match might be broken again, young people married and soon became parents. The Second Middle Passage, like the first, dismantled families, but not the idea of family.[55]

Reconstructing family life amid the chaos of the cotton revolution was no easy matter. Under the best of circumstances, the slave family on the frontier was extraordinarily unstable because the frontier plantation was extraordinarily unstable. For every aspiring master who climbed into the planter class, dozens failed because of undercapitalization, unproductive land, insect infestation, bad weather, or sheer incompetence. Others, discouraged by low prices and disdainful of the primitive conditions, simply gave up and returned home. Those who succeeded often did so only after they had failed numerous times. Each failure or near-failure caused slaves to be sold, shattering families and scattering husbands and wives, parents and children. Success, moreover, was no guarantee of security for slaves. Disease and violence struck down some of the most successful planters. Not even longevity assured stability, as many successful planters looked west for still greater challenges. Whatever the source, the chronic volatility of the plantation took its toll on the domestic life of slaves.[56]

Despite these difficulties, the family became the center of slave life in the interior, as it was on the seaboard. From the slaves' perspective, the most important role they played was not that of field hand or mechanic but husband or wife, son or daughter—the precise opposite of their owners' calculation. As in Virginia and the Carolinas, the family became the locus of socialization, education, governance, and vocational training. Slave families guided courting patterns, marriage rituals, child-rearing practices, and the division of domestic labor in Alabama, Mississippi, and beyond. Sally Anne Chambers, who grew up in Louisiana, recalled how slaves turned to the business of family on Saturdays and Sundays. "De women do dey own washing den. De menfolks tend to de gardens round dey own house. Dey raise some cotton and sell it to massa and git li'l money dat way."[57]

As Sally Anne Chambers's memories reveal, the reconstructed slave family was more than a source of affection. It was a demanding institution that defined responsibilities and enforced obligations, even as it provided a source of succor. Parents taught their children that a careless word in the presence of the master or mistress could spell disaster. Children and the elderly, not yet or no longer laboring in the masters' fields, often worked in the slaves' gardens and grounds, as did new arrivals who might be placed in the household of an established family. Charles Ball, sold south from Maryland, was accepted into his new family but only when he agreed to contribute all of his overwork "earnings into the family stock."[58]

The "family stock" reveals how the slaves' economy undergirded the slave family in the southern interior, just as it had on the seaboard. As slaves gained access to gardens and grounds, overwork, or the sale of handicraft, they began trading independently and accumulating property. The material linkages of sellers and buyers—the bartering of goods and labor among themselves—began to knit slaves together into working groups that were often based on familial connections. Before long, systems of ownership and inheritance emerged, joining men and women together on a foundation of need as well as affection.

Extended kinship groups—sometimes located on one plantation, more commonly extended over several—became the central units of slave life, ordering society, articulating values, and delineating identity by defining the boundaries of trust. They also became the nexus for incorporating the never-ending stream of arrivals from the seaboard states into the new society, cushioning the horror of the Second Middle Passage, and socializing the deportees to the realities of life on the plantation frontier. Playing the role of midwives, the earlier arrivals transformed strangers into brothers and sisters, melding the polyglot immigrants into one.

In defining obligations and responsibilities, the family became the centerpole of slave life. The arrival of the first child provided transplanted slaves with the opportunity to link the world they had lost to the world that had been forced upon them. In naming their children for some loved one left behind, pioneer slaves restored the generational linkages for themselves and connected their children with grandparents they would never know. Some pioneer slaves reached back beyond their parents' generation, suggesting how slavery's long history on mainland North America could be collapsed by a single act.[59]

Along the same mental pathways that joined the charter and migration generations flowed other knowledge. Rituals carried from Africa might be as simple as the way a mother held a child to her breast or as complex as a cure for warts. Songs for celebrating marriage, ceremonies for breaking bread, and last rites for an honored elder survived in the minds of those forced from their seaboard homes, along with the unfulfilled promise of the Age of Revolution and evangelical awakenings. Still, the new order never quite duplicated the old. Even as transplanted slaves strained their memories to reconstruct what they had once known, slavery itself was being recast. The lush thicket of kin that deportees like Hawkins Wilson remembered had been obliterated by the Second Middle Passage. Although pioneer slaves worked assiduously to knit together a new family fabric, elevating elderly slaves into parents and deputizing friends as kin, of necessity they had to look beyond blood and marriage.

Kin emerged as well from a new religious sensibility, as young men and women whose families had been ravaged by the Second Middle Passage embraced one another as brothers and sisters in Christ. A cadre of black evangelicals, many of whom had been converted in the revivals of the late eighteenth century, became chief agents of the expansion of African-American Christianity. James Williams, a black driver who had been transferred from Virginia to the Alabama blackbelt, was just one of many believers who was "torn away from the care and discipline of their respective churches." Swept westward by the tide of the domestic slave trade, they "retained their love for the exercises of religion."

Still, the believers faced enormous obstacles in converting their fellow slaves. For more than two centuries, black people had resisted Christianity, often with the tacit acquiescence of their owners. During the seventeenth and eighteenth centuries, Christian missionaries who attempted to bring slaves into the fold confronted a hostile planter class, whose only interest in the slaves' spirituality was to denigrate it as idolatry. Westward-moving planters showed little sympathy with slaves who prayed when they might be working and even less patience with separate gatherings of converts, which they suspected to be revolutionary cabals. An 1822 Mississippi law barring black people from meeting without white supervision spoke directly to the planters' fears.

But the trauma of the Second Middle Passage and the cotton revolution sensitized transplanted slaves to the evangelicals' message. Young men and women forcibly displaced from their old homes were eager to find alternative sources of authority and comfort. Responding to the evangelical message, they found new meaning in the emotional deliverance of conversion and the baptismal rituals of the church. In turning their lives over to Christ, the deportees took control of their own destiny.[60]

White missionaries, some of them still committed to the evangelical egalitarianism of the eighteenth-century revivals, welcomed black believers into their churches. Slaves—sometimes carrying letters of separation from their home congregations—were present in the first evangelical services in Mississippi and Alabama. The earliest religious associations listed black churches, and black preachers—free and slave—won fame for the exercise of "their gift."

Established denominational lines informed much of slaves' Christianity. The large Protestant denominations—Baptist and Methodist, Anglican and Presbyterian—made the most substantial claims, although Catholicism had a powerful impact all along the Gulf Coast, especially in Louisiana and Florida. From this mélange, slaves selectively appropriated those ideas that best fit their own sacred universe and secular world. With little standing in the church of the master, these men and women fostered a new faith. For that reason, it was not the church of the master or even the church of the missionary that attracted black converts; they much preferred their own religious conclaves. These fugitive meetings were often held deep in the woods in brush tents called "arbors." Kept private by overturning a pot to muffle the sound of their prayers, these meetings promoted African-American spirituality and mixed black and white religious forms into a theological amalgam that white clerics found unrecognizable—what one planter-preacher called "a jumble of Protestantism, Romanism, and Fetishism."

Under the brush arbor, notions of secular and sacred life took on new meanings. The experience of spiritual rebirth and the conviction that Christ spoke directly to them armed slaves against their owners, assuring them that they too were God's children, perhaps even his chosen people. It infused daily life with the promise of the Great Jubilee and eternal life that offered a final escape from earthly captivity.[61] In the end, it would be they—not their owners—who would stand at God's side and enjoy the blessing of eternal salvation.

Reconstructed families and reformulated religion spawned a new leadership class to replace the old one that had been devastated by the Second Middle Passage. Some of these new leaders were anointed by slave masters, who elevated a few trusted individuals to prominent positions within the plantation hierarchy, employed them as drivers, foremen, and artisans, and occasionally taught them to read and write. Such men and women—by dint of their connections to the owner and the power they possessed to dole out rations, assign work, and inflict punishment—were often feared as well as admired, hated as much as loved. Most slaves achieved status within the black community by winning the respect of their fellow slaves, not their owners. Indeed, slave leaders generally secured their high standing by virtue of opposing their owners, not collaborating with them. Many were connected with the new religiosity in the quarter, as preachers, shamen, and conjurers—men and women who could join the natural and unnatural worlds together, whether through African folk rituals or biblical injunctions. Others were healers and midwives, and still others earned the respect of their peers in the field or workshop. A few secured a bit of book learning and were able to read the Bible. All were enmeshed in the expanding web of kinship and spirituality—connections of blood, marriage, and belief—that bound slaves together. While they may have exhibited some personal quality, such as courage, intelligence, honesty, or piety, that their compatriots found attractive, it was kinship—a sense of belonging to a common family, on this earth or in heaven hereafter—that carried them to the top of black society and provided the basis for solidarity.

Whether their social position rested on knowledge of the cosmos or the key to the corn crib, whether their authority derived from the Big House or the quarter, it was to these men and women—not their owners—that slaves turned first in moments of distress. And few crises shook slave society as deeply as the transfer from the seaboard to the interior. Annealed in the furnace of the Second Middle Passage and the cotton and sugar revolutions, a new generation of leaders struggled to express the collective aspirations of a people who were often divided by their multiple origins, diverse expectations, and increasingly differential wealth.

Nowhere was this new leadership more important than in adjudicating the rules of the new slave economy. Although the slaves produced little in the way of surplus, the surplus they did produce was no less important to them than wealth was to their owners. Without access to the law, the commerce among slaves—even more than among owners—rested upon mutual understandings backed by customary agreements. Naturally, some of those agreements failed; and when they did, slaves needed some mechanism to resolve their internal conflicts, if only to prevent their owners from becoming involved in the dispute—a practice that could be dangerous indeed. Here, the new leader class stepped up to its responsibilities.

The new leadership structure in the quarter revealed the complexity of intra- (and inter-) plantation politics and economies. Diverse origins and competing ambitions fractured plantations and neighborhoods as often as they created new solidarities. Differences among slaves fueled powerful and often deadly disputes—rivalries rooted in petty accumulations of wealth or the other small rewards of plantation life. Still other conflicts arose between older residents and new arrivals. Slaveholders became maestros at recognizing and manipulating these rivalries, seizing upon their slaves' diverse personalities, abilities, aspirations, and petty jealousies to promote one individual, family, or faction at the expense of others. Planters understood that small privileges distributed to slaves could reap large advantages for themselves.

But, if masters appreciated the strategy of divide and conquer, slaves also understood that, despite their internal differences, they had a common foe whose power knew few bounds and whose compunctions about using it had even fewer limitations. Fear from above, as well as common experience, compelled slaves to stand together, and as they did, the terrain of struggle between master and slave shifted once again.

The task of those who rose to leadership within the slave quarter, whether preachers or artisans, was made immeasurably more difficult by the increasing wealth and confidence of the planter class. Having successfully transferred the plantation regime from the seaboard and reestablished a slave society in the interior, planters consolidated their rule. Although cotton—not sugar—became the staple of choice of many small slaveholders and even some slaveless farmers, over time the most successful planters grew an ever larger portion of the total crop. Buying more and more of the best land, sometimes owning multiple estates spread across several states, extended plantation families—fathers who provided sons and sons-in-law with a start—created slaveholding conglomerates that controlled hundreds and sometimes thousands of slaves. The grandees' vast wealth allowed them to introduce new hybrid cotton seeds and strains of cane, new technologies, and new forms of organization that elevated productivity and increased profitability. In some places, the higher levels of capitalization and technical mastery of the grandees reduced white yeomen to landlessness and forced smallholders to move on or else enter the wage-earning class as managers or overseers. As a result, the richest plantation areas became increasingly black, with ever-larger estates managed from afar as the planters retreated to some local county seat, one of the region's ports, or occasionally some northern metropolis.[62]

Claiming the benefits of their new standing, the grandees—characterized in various places as "nabobs," "a feudal aristocracy," or simply "The Royal Family"—established their bona fides as a ruling class. They built great houses strategically located along broad rivers or high bluffs. They named their estates in the aristocratic manner—the Briars, Fairmont, Richmond—and made them markers on the landscape. Planters married among themselves, educated their sons in northern universities, and sent their wives and daughters on European tours, collecting the bric-a-brac of the continent to grace their mansions. Reaching out to their neighbors, they burnished their reputations for hospitality. The annual Christmas ball or the great July Fourth barbecue were private events with a public purpose. They confirmed the distance between the planters and their neighbors and allowed leadership to fall lightly and naturally on their shoulders, as governors, legislators, judges, and occasionally congressmen, senators, and presidents.[63]

Few could equal the wealth and power of the great planters, but even middling planters often left their rude cabins and built more commodious dwellings. If their houses rarely boasted whitewashed columns and decked porticos, they did at least have separate sleeping, dining, and cooking quarters. Slaves were no longer stowed away in backrooms or attics but in rows of cabins located at a respectable distance from the Big House, relieving planters of the egalitarian discomfort of living directly with field laborers. Occasionally, they too named their estates and attempted to imitate the practices of the nabobs, often constructing genealogies that affirmed their fine lineage. While such pretension did little to close the social distance between themselves and "The Royalty," at least it distinguished the successful middling planters from the white yeomen who still labored in the fields alongside their wives, children, and an occasional slave.[64]

The emergence of the planter class, like the earlier expansion of the plantation itself, did not take place at once. The cotton revolution moved west in the wake of frontier settlement. The sugar revolution, though confined to a small area, expanded steadily along the bayous of southern Louisiana. But the pattern was clear. What had once been Indian territory became nascent plantation country and then, perhaps a decade later, a mature plantation society. Everywhere, however, the gyrations of the staple economy sped the process, as the hard times that ruined marginal producers became just another opportunity for the grandees to enlarge their holdings. In 1830 one slave in three in Georgia's premier cotton-producing county of Houston resided in units of twenty or more, and the largest plantation contained fifty slaves; twenty years later—following the depression of the late 1830s—the proportion had doubled to two in three, and five plantations contained over one hundred slaves. In 1860 three of four slaves in Houston County lived on plantation-size units, and the largest estate counted 343 slaves. A similar consolidation took place in the sugar parishes, where during the 1850s the number of plantations declined while the production of sugar increased, with the largest plantation producing an increasing proportion of the crop. In 1860 planters with more than fifty slaves controlled over two-thirds of all slaves in the sugar region, owned nearly 70 percent of the improved lands, and produced 77 percent of the region's sugar.[65]

The consolidation of the plantation regime could not, however, be measured simply by the planters' wealth, the size of slaveholding units, or the demographic balance between slave and free or black and white. The diverse geography of a slave society that stretched halfway across the North American continent created a variety of social configurations. In the uplands, most prominently the hills of Appalachia and the Ozarks, substantial planters resided alongside a majority of smallholders, many of whom joined the slaveowning class only intermittently if at all. Slavery in the hill country took a different form, affecting both the planters' ideology and their relations with their slaves. But regional variations had to be balanced against the connections that bound planters together.[66] This was particularly true as the grandees multiplied their estates and elevated their kin into the slaveholding ranks, so that Tennessee planters owned estates in Mississippi and Georgia planters extended their holdings to Arkansas and eventually Texas.

The emergence of the grandees and the consolidation of slave society in the interior deeply affected all those touched by the plantation, perhaps none more than those few slave women who had gained an elevated position within the plantation. As slave society matured and white women joined "their" men, the black wife departed or disappeared from view. With their white families in residence, white men who continued to maintain relationships with black women erected labyrinthine façades to hide their wives of color and their children, lest they too be proscribed from respectable society. For some, the façade was an elaborate pretense and public denial. For others, it was literally a physical barrier from beyond which they disclaimed their forbidden relationship. In the 1830s, when Nathan Sayre constructed Pomegranate Hall—his mansion in the tiny county seat of Sparta, Georgia—he built a secret apartment for his free colored mistress, Susan Hunt, and their three children. For almost a quarter of a century, Hunt and Sayre—who grew increasingly prominent first as a state senator, aide to the governor, and finally as a judge on Georgia's Superior Court—raised their children in the hidden home behind Pomegranate's false walls, as Sayre publicly maintained a fictional bachelorhood. With relatives conspiring in the charade and neighbors turning a blind eye, the "secret" was complete. Still, in recognizing his black family, educating his children, and providing for their future, Sayre did much more than most white men who fathered children by black women.[67]

Alongside the disappearance of the black wife as an indicator of the planters' consolidation of power was the deteriorating status of free people of color. By mid-nineteenth century, the expanding slave regime had driven free people of color from the plantation region, so that they became mere curiosities in the areas of intensive staple production. In 1860

Marango County in the middle of Alabama's blackbelt counted one free black, and Issaquena County, Mississippi, and Chicot County, Arkansas, on the Mississippi River had not a single one. Free people of color who fled the countryside for the great ports felt the strain, as southern legislatures pounded them with new restrictions and proscriptions, requiring them to take white guardians and pay special head taxes.

Planters, whose new orthodoxy claimed that slavery was a positive good for the slave as well as the master, saw free people of color as a dangerous contradiction: if slavery was the appropriate condition for people of African descent, why would they want to be free? Would it not be best to return all black people to their natural condition as slaves? New laws limited and sometimes prohibited manumission and offered free people of color the opportunity to renounce their freedom. When few volunteered, some lawmakers urged their physical removal and, failing that, demanded their re-enslavement. Under this pressure, the growth of the free black population of the southern interior slowed, and their prosperity faltered. During the 1840s, the number of free people of color in New Orleans declined for the first time in the nineteenth century, dropping by more than one-third. Elsewhere in the interior, the free colored population barely sustained itself. The days when colored militiamen, resplendent in gold braid, their bayonets gleaming, accepted the accolades of grateful authorities lived on only in the memories of a few veterans of a bygone era.[68]

For those black people at the very center of slave society, the expansion of the plantation had an equally powerful effect. It allowed for a finer division of labor among slaves. The wealthiest planters assigned some slaves to fulltime work in the Big House, as cooks, maids, butlers, gardeners, and stable keepers. Housework, previously only a stage in the lives of some slaves, became a lifetime position. On some estates, the position of house servant became hereditary, as a few slave families became identified with service to the masters' family. By default, fieldwork also became a matter of inheritance, as those who tended the crops rarely escaped the field. But they too found their work reorganized, as the new divisions of labor touched all aspects of work on the estate.

Fulltime or seasonal absenteeism by planters, especially on the largest estates, meant that stewards and overseers governed a growing number of plantations. Many slaves never met their owner. Relations between masters and slaves became increasingly triangular, a circumstance that generally redounded to the slaves' disadvantage. Even when the grandees governed as absentees, they viewed their domains as small kingdoms—"imperium in imperio," in the words of a Tennessee master—and disliked violations of the sovereignty of their estates. "I never permit my servants to leave the plantation," declared an Alabama planter. "Neither do I permit other negroes to visit my place." Such slaveowners fretted about the extension of the slaves' economy beyond the boundaries of the plantation. Some prohibited inter-plantation trading, as "it was better that negroes never saw anybody off their own plantation and that they had no intercourse with other white men than their owner or overseer."

When slavemasters could not limit the slaves' economy, they tried to alter it to fit their own needs. During the pioneer period in upland Carolina, the slaves' economy focused around overwork, as masters found that paying for their labor was the easiest way to get slaves into the fields on Sundays and Saturdays. But as the cotton economy matured and the need for such labor slackened, slaveowners allowed their slaves to grow their own cotton. In agreeing to market the slaves' produce, they not only controlled the slaves' system of independent production but also kept slaves confined within the boundaries of the plantation. For like reasons, other planters limited visiting and discouraged "broad" marriages, as such relations presumed continual movement.

The planters' efforts to seal their plantations from outside influences failed utterly, in large measure because the requirements of production necessitated at least some slave mobility. Slaves developed an intricate system of internal communication, and news between plantations moved with lightning speed. Still, the planters' efforts to wall off their estates, combined with the near-total absence of interior towns and the growing size of slaveholding units, increased the density of the slave population and deepened its identification with the land.[69]

As slave families became connected to particular estates, they began to claim a sense of proprietorship over the plantation on which they and their children resided and on which their parents were buried. The strange world they had been forced to inhabit gradually became identified as "home." Increasingly, plantation slaves became provincials, linked to place, land, and kin. With the attachment to place, the slaves' world shrank. Their limited knowledge of the larger society stood in sharp contrast to the boundless vision of the charter generations. Though they were not peasants by the classic definition, the character of slave life in the interior endowed plantation slaves with many of the characteristics found in peasant societies.

It was not that plantation slaves were ignorant of the larger world. The grapevine telegraph operated with remarkable efficiency, not only in harvesting news of neighborhood events but also developments in the nation and world. Plantation slaves' understanding of national politics—pieced together from scraps of conversations picked up at their owners' table, Fourth of July bombast heard from the edges of the crowd, and the readings of a few literate slaves—might be crude, but it informed them that there were others in the world beyond their plantation who opposed slavery. At the very least, these men—Wilberforce, Garrison, Douglass, Brown, Lincoln—might serve as agents of emancipation. While slaves played the role of the innocent or the fool, they penetrated deeply into the slaveowners' world. But the slaves' primary concerns centered upon kin and neighbors, the men and women on whom they had to depend. Their deep knowledge of the landscape and its secrets, the rhythm of agricultural production, and the mysteries of cultivation and husbandry tied them to the land they worked and came to hold dear. If the crops they grew and the animals they tended did not enrich them or provide for the independence they craved, they appreciated that someday it might.

From the portico of the Big House, the planters assumed their mastery was complete. Some grandees denied what had been self-evident only a generation earlier—doubting, for example, that "white men had the physical ability to cultivate 'profitably' . . . bottom lands of the lower Mississippi and its tributaries."[70] But even as they prepared to enjoy their new wealth, they found their world under siege and slavery on the defensive. The long shadow of Toussaint's successful revolution in Saint Domingue and the looming specter of radical abolition depreciated a previous generation's apologies for slavery. After the discovery of Denmark Vesey's conspiracy and Nat Turner's deadly rampage through Southside Virginia, it was no longer possible to parry the condemnations of slavery by conceding it to be an evil and assenting to its demise in an undefined but infinitely distant future. If northern and international opinion viewed the old apologies with skepticism, the planters also worried about the loyalty of the growing number of white southerners with no direct material attachment to slavery.

No matter how loudly or often planters proclaimed white solidarity, gnawing doubts continued to surface. Debates over the taxation of slave property, the employment of slave artisans, and public expenditures for roads, schools, and other social services revealed disturbing fissures in the bonds that supposedly bound all white people together, as did the continuing presence of white men and women who traded, gambled, or slept with slaves. Differences in public policy reflected even more disturbing personal conflicts that manifested themselves in the disdain—often contempt—many smallholders and even propertyless men and women showed toward their presumed betters. While planters alternately sneered at the propertyless and patronized them as kin, they never doubted their power or fully trusted them. Much the same was true of their slaves. Indeed, the planters' increasing distress drew upon the growing disorder in the quarter and the slaves' persistent defiance as manifested in flight, sabotage, and even direct and deadly confrontation with their owners, all against a background of rumored conspiracies that, upon occasion, were no rumor.[71] Denmark Vesey might be dismissed as a free black schemer and Nat Turner condemned as a deranged visionary, but slaveholders never doubted there were more of their kind in the slave quarter.

At the confluence of these turbulent waters, planters began to remake what even they called their "peculiar institution." Slavery's reformers were hardly of one mind, and they moved in many directions. Some wanted the slaves "more gently worked"; others just the opposite. Some carried religion to the quarter, others advocated improvements in slaves' domestic life, diet, medical practice, housing, and sanitary habits. Whether the new reforms emanated from the pulpit, legislative chamber, judicial bench, physicians' office, or the planters themselves, and whether the amelioration of slavery was aimed at its northern opponents, potential southern critics, or increasingly restive slaves, all pointed to a more mannerly contest between master and slave. The watch word was "system," as slaveowners searched for ways to rationalize and order the plantation. Arrangements that "move[d] off like clock work" or established a "wholesome and well regulated system" would replace the violence that encumbered the master-slave relationship.[72]

The installation of bells and horns spoke to the new regimen. "While at work, they should be brisk," advised an 1851 treatise entitled "Management of Negroes": "I have no objection their whistling or singing some lively tune, but no drawling tunes are allowed in the field, for their motions are certain to keep time with the music."[73] But if the rhythm of a lively tune or the tick of the clock paced the new order, domesticity was its idiom. Slaveholders, like traditional elites the world over, had long articulated their dominance in the language of family, claiming to be benevolent patriarchs to legitimate their authority and sustain claims to absolute obedience. For more than two centuries, American planters had elaborated the paternal ideal by means of the monthly distribution of rations, the annual Christmas gifting, and their insistence upon the title of "master." But during the middle years of the nineteenth century, the paternalist idiom grew in significance as planters responded to the abolitionist assault.

Setting themselves in opposition to those who merely rented or employed labor, the great planters and their apologists cloaked themselves in the mantle of *pater familias* and asserted a parental interest in their slaves. Slaves, once seen as competitors who could not be trusted precisely because they shared with all men an unquenchable desire for liberty, became perpetual juveniles, whose childhood extended into dotage. The systematic application of the language of family to every aspect of the master-slave relationship elevated the importance of the domestic metaphor. From the new perspective, the plantation joined master and slave together in a collective enterprise that benefited all. Planters—particularly the great ones—and their apologists spoke grandly of "their people" and their "family, black and white," asserting the mutual affection between master and slave and bemoaning the heavy responsibilities of mastership.[74]

But the rhetoric of family could hardly disguise the brutal contest between master and slave, and the old struggle over the slaves' labor hardly ceased. If the language of the controversy adapted to a new era, the rules of engagement did not. Slaveholders never surrendered the lash as essential to their rule, and slaves answered by malingering, destroying tools, maiming animals, slowing the line, and taking to the woods. If anything, the struggle grew in intensity, as planters, eager to make their estates more productive, searched for ways to work their slaves longer and harder. Agricultural societies, farm journals, and newspapers dwelled upon such matters. Amid an endless stream of articles on calcareous manures, blooded stock, efficient gins, and new varieties of cotton and sugar, planters found —and gave—advice on how best to manage their slaves, with the language of family serving as the medium through which slavery could be defended before the world and justified to themselves.

According to the new dispensation, successful mastership was not confined to the field or the workshop. Instead, good masters followed their slaves to their cabins, where they intervened in the most intimate aspects of slave life, regulating sanitation, health, religion, marital relations, and child-rearing. Whereas the struggle between master and slave had once been largely confined to the organization of labor, the delineation of the task, and the definition of the stint, concerns as diverse as personal hygiene and deportment now fell into the planters' purview. No part of slave life was exempt, as slaves soon found themselves fending off their owners' attempts to name their children, sanitize their cabins, and regulate their diet.[75]

Slaves resented these intrusions and resisted them much as they did the slaveholders' appropriation of their labor. But the new contest naturally took different forms. When masters demanded they whitewash their cabins and groom their yards according to new notions of cleanliness, slaves found other ways to busy themselves. Although masters sent physicians to medicate their slaves, slaves continued to rely on their own healers. Mistresses' offers to assist in delivering children were rebuffed, as slave women preferred midwives from the quarter. Planters scowled at the rejection of their superior wisdom, condemned the slaves' ignorance, and damned their obstinacy as proof of their unfitness for freedom.

No negotiations between master and slave were more revealing of the new contest than matters touching upon the slaves' spiritual world. Slave masters who had barely tolerated the cadre of black evangelicals suddenly cultivated piety in the quarter. Discerning benefits in the conversion of their slaves, slaveowners welcomed to their plantations the Christian missionaries whom they had once condemned as insurrectionary provocateurs or, at best, ill-informed meddlers. Some planters, having themselves accepted Christ, acted out of a deep commitment to their faith. Others, stung by the antislavery charge that they denied their slaves access to the Gospel, moved to counter the abolitionist critique. Still others believed church membership was yet another way of bending slaves to their will and countering the influence of black preachers.

Whatever their motives, during the fourth decade of the nineteenth century, large numbers of planters took up the Cross. They supported the denominational missions to the still skeptical slaves, welcomed itinerants onto their estates, and paid them to tutor their slaves in the Bible, visit the sick, attend funerals, and even perform marriages. Some built plantation chapels for their slaves. A few led their "black family" in prayer, just as they did their white family. Operating against restrictive legislation passed in the wake of the Nat Turner rebellion of 1831, they even encouraged slaves to take to the pulpit, if not as preachers—which was illegal in many places—then as exhorters or deacons. For many masters, the paternalist burden became a Christian burden, and Christian responsibilities became the slaveholders' responsibilities.[76]

Slaves remained suspicious of the new concern for their spiritual well-being, but their responses varied. Those with no interest in their masters' new obsession saw yet another encroachment on their free Sundays, depriving them of time to work gardens and provision grounds, visit their family and friends, or simply rest. For them, the dubious privilege of spending yet more time with their owners was something less than appealing, and the gospel of "Servants, obey your masters" was an insult to their intelligence. Others, who had earlier been attracted to Christianity, welcomed their masters' conversion. They discovered in Christianity a new means to advance their people and themselves. These slaves found something compelling in the Christian narrative, with its promise of salvation and rebirth through Christ. But, as white missionaries soon learned, slaves had "formed religious opinions and notions, every way different than ours." Of those differences none was more central than the belief that salvation was not simply spiritual. "The idea of a revolution in the conditions of the whites and the blacks, is the corner-stone of the religion of the latter," declared Charles Ball. Slaves quickly appropriated the biblical Exodus as their own narrative, and began to shape a theology in which the emancipation of the Old Testament prefigured their own Jubilee. Charlie Davenport, a former Mississippi slave, recalled how the black preachers "exhort us dat us was the chillun o' Israel in de wilderness an' de Lawd done sont us to take dis lan' o' milk an' honey."[77] .

Away from their owners, slaves fused the natural and supernatural as they elaborated their own understanding of Christianity, an interpretation which asserted that the meek were indeed blessed and that the last would surely be first. While the bush arbor remained the venue of choice for many, increasingly some slaves found advantages in their owner's church. Church membership incorporated them into the larger community, affirming their equality in the sight of God. Much as the slaveholders might deny it in word and deed, the biracial fellowship made master and slave brothers and sisters in Christ, for all were captive sinners redeemed by grace, and all were bound together by a covenant before God.

At least in theory, the church subjected slaveowners to the oversight of their slaves. So while planters employed their control over the church to admonish their slaves against theft, sloth, drunkenness, and fornication, the same Gospel demanded that masters treat their slaves in accord with Christianity's Golden Rule. The church councils that censured the slaves' moral lapses occasionally condemned the slavemasters' failures as well. The biracial church gave slaves a forum to question the very essence of the slaveholders' power. Slaveowners squirmed uncomfortably when the church meetings debated the right of slave members to vote on ecclesiastical matters, or considered the logic of slave divorce, or pondered the authority of slave husbands over their wives and children. While biracial Christianity hardly resolved critical matters respecting the masters' authority and the slaves' subordination, it forced slaveowners to address those questions publicly in a manner that occasionally redounded to the slaves' benefit.[78]

Church membership empowered slaves in other ways as well. Although by practice as well as in law they were almost always denied a formal ministerial voice, slaves commonly served as deacons or exhorters. Much to the dismay of white churchmen, black deacons promoted themselves to the ministerial rank, exercising "their gift," preaching to their people, interpreting the Bible by their own lights, and resolving disputes and disciplining fellow slaves according to the standards of the slave community. In the process, they also set community standards, gaining themselves a place of authority they extended beyond the walls of the church.

The deacons used the language of Christianity to distinguish themselves from their white co-religionists. Differences between the slaves' enthusiastic worship and the decorous services of their owners facilitated this seizure of power, as the clamor emanating from the gallery provided the occasion for slaves to enlarge their independence and embody it in the form of separate services. Ned Chaney, who was born in Alabama, recalled that the "'leben o'clock service was fer de white people an' de three o'clock service was fer de colored people."[79]

Sometimes planters supported the creation of separate chapels, providing an abandoned shed or dilapidated outbuilding for that purpose. Occasionally, when the congregation outgrew its old building, white members built a new church for themselves and gave, or more often sold, the old structure to the slaves. The purchase—often with their savings from overwork and various petty enterprises—did not confer legal ownership, as slaves had no right to own property. But slave congregants believed the church was theirs, and planters—eager to counter the abolitionists' charge that they kept salvation from their slaves—rarely contradicted that presumption. Planters generally insisted on the right to police the services, and were required by law to do so, but the supervision was haphazard at best. Whereas the interest of most slaveowners in the slaves' salvation was secondary to the main business of the plantation, the slaves' interest was continual and intense. Before long, the slave church was functioning as an independent body. The struggle between master and slave moved once again to new terrain.

The church, like the family, became a place where slaves formulated their collective aspirations, mobilized their resources, and infused them with spiritual meaning to challenge the seemingly limitless power of their owners. In the absence of other civic platforms, the church became the slaves' press, labor association, and convention hall. If the challenge to slavery that emerged from its councils fell far short of success, the occasional victories sustained an oppositional culture that cheered slaves and alarmed slaveholders. Even as planters reached the pinnacle of their wealth and power, slaves who rebuilt their lives and communities in the interior of the South worshipped in their own way and waited for the opportunity to make a new life once again, one more of their own choosing. So too did those the Second Middle Passage left behind in the seaboard South.

THE SEABOARD SOUTH

The effects of the Second Middle Passage were not confined to the southern interior. While the exiles struggled with the task of creating a new economy for their owners and a new community for themselves, those left behind faced an equal challenge in resuscitating and extending the old ones. Soil exhaustion, competition from the west, and fluctuating world markets were all leaving their mark on the seaboard South. As planters, farmers, and mechanics tried to reestablish their former prosperity by turning to new commodities, new technologies, and new forms of organization, they were pressed to reconstruct their labor force, introducing new workers and employing old ones in novel ways. In the process, slaves found their lives altered, sometimes beyond recognition.

The recasting of slave life took a variety of forms, in large measure because the region was so diverse and because the boundaries of the region changed as states that once imported slaves began to export them. In some places, like Maryland and Virginia, the transformation of agriculture and artisanal production was well under way, having begun in the mid-eighteenth century. In other places, such as portions of Kentucky and Missouri, plantation economies remained vibrant and expansive with the introduction of new staples or new varieties of old ones. In still other places, like lowcountry Carolina and Georgia, the changes might be best characterized as agricultural adjustment.

Of the eighteenth-century's great staples, none survived better than rice. The post-revolutionary revival of rice cultivation and the replacement of indigo with short-staple cotton sustained the expansion of slavery between the Cape Fear River in North Carolina and the St. Johns River in Florida. During the nineteenth century, wealth became ever more concentrated in the hands of the largest planters; indeed, lowland planters had secured their status as the greatest of the southern grandees. In 1860 more than half of the South's largest planters grew rice. Some, like Nathaniel Heywood, who owned well over two thousand slaves, were wealthy beyond the imagination of most Americans. But despite the prosperity of individual planters, the lowcountry did not regain its standing as the richest region in America. Behind the façade of enormous personal wealth, competition from rice growers on the other side of the globe was pushing the lowcountry into an economic decline from which it never recovered.[80]

The planters' great wealth and the haunting specter of decline deeply affected lowcountry slaves. Many were sold from their ancestral homes to sustain the owners' prosperity, and the demands on those who remained grew ever more stringent. For some slaves, this required enlarging the rice fields and performing the hated mud work that accompanied the construction of new embankments. For others, it meant mastering new machinery that planters installed in hopes of increasing productivity. But since neither new fields nor new equipment restored the lowcountry's former preeminence, planters drove their slaves harder, reclaiming more and more of the riverine swamps and turning them into plantations, which they irrigated with tidal flows. The cost in lost lives and misery was horrendous. Nowhere in mainland North America—not even on the new sugar plantations of southern Louisiana—did slaves suffer greater mortality.[81]

Slaves balked at these new impositions. When masters disavowed customary practices that allowed slaves a modicum of independence, slaves held tightly to the long-established terms of labor. For more than a century task labor had insulated slaves from the harshest aspects of life in the rice swamps and had safeguarded their access to the gardens and provision grounds that provided the basis for their independent economic activities. During the nineteenth century, lowcountry slaves repelled attempts to introduce gang labor, and in some places extended tasking into cotton production.

But while slaves maintained the old work regime, the task itself became a source of contention, as planters redefined the task to equal a full working day—some ten to twelve hours by the planters' estimate and doubtless more by the slaves. Slaves found themselves spending more time in their owners' fields and less time working for themselves. One planter was so successful in expanding the size of the task that even his overseer complained that the task had grown too large for slaves to reasonably complete. When they could not redefine the task to their liking, planters reduced the slaves' allowance of food and clothing, so that the slaves' independent productive activities did not create a surplus but merely assured subsistence. Slaves who failed to meet their quotas faced hunger, the lash, or, perhaps more terrifying still, a trip to the "workhouse." During the nineteenth century, absentee masters turned over the discipline of their most intractable slaves to specialists in intimidation and torture located in the workhouses of Charleston, Savannah, and other rice ports.[82]

As in the lowcountry, the character of slavery in the Upper South altered dramatically during the nineteenth century. The switch from tobacco monoculture to mixed farming, already well advanced at the end of the revolutionary era, continued apace. Small grain production, cattle raising, dairying, and truck farming became the dominant forms of agricultural enterprise in the older portions of the region. Towns and cities, identified with mixed farming and small-scale manufacture, grew rapidly. Unlike the plantation interior—where the thriving ports of New Orleans, Mobile, and Memphis were surrounded by a plantation hinterland—crossroads villages dotted the Upper South, leading to larger towns and then to substantial cities. These towns and cities were as much centers of production as centers of commerce. In some, the majority of the population—both slave and free—labored in workshops or factories producing flour, tobacco, iron, and a host of other goods.

But contrary to the predictions of eighteenth-century abolitionists, the advent of mixed agriculture and manufacture did not topple the institution of slavery. Grain farmers and industrialists became some of the largest slaveholders in the region. Moreover, tobacco did not disappear from the roster of agricultural production. In the new states of the Upper South—Kentucky and Missouri—it enjoyed a modest revival. In the 1840s tobacco prices spiked and the planters invested heavily in it, along with hemp, a new staple which, like tobacco, mixed easily with other forms of agricultural production.

While the new cotton and sugar planters of the interior divided workers into disciplined gangs and demanded a lockstep regimen, the organization of mixed agriculture and manufacture in the Upper South bespoke flexibility and versatility. Slaves generally worked singly or in squads, often alongside their owner and other free men and women, black and white, especially during planting and harvest. Plowing one day, gardening another, working the orchards the next, repairing plantation machinery when necessary, slaves confounded the fine division of labor upon which the plantation rested, making gang labor—and sometimes even slave labor—superfluous. The Shenandoah Valley exhibited many of the regional trends that could be found throughout the slave-exporting states. Although plantation-size units dotted the valley, farms and small slaveholdings became far more numerous. As the size of slave units in the cotton and sugar South were expanding, they were contracting in the Shenandoah. Indeed, in most places, the majority of agricultural units worked no slaves at all.[83]

The declining profitability of slave labor in the Upper South, along with the soaring wealth promised by plantation production in the southern interior, profoundly altered the coastal region's demography. In 1800 nearly three-quarters of American slaves resided between the Delaware and Savannah rivers. By 1820 that proportion dropped to less than two-thirds, and by 1840 it fell again, so that no more than half of America's slaves lived in what had once been slavery's heartland. In 1860 the majority of the slave population—over 60 percent—resided outside the seaboard slave states, and portions of the border states had devolved from slave societies to societies with slaves. During each decade of the nineteenth century, 10 percent or more of slaves in the exporting region were sold or taken to the interior. In the states contiguous with the North—Delaware, Maryland, and the northernmost counties of Virginia, Kentucky, and Missouri—the decrease in the slave population was not simply proportional but absolute, as the real number of slaves declined, sometimes sharply.

The transformation of the seaboard South into a slave-exporting region, like the westward march of the cotton revolution, did not take place all at once. Slaveholders and traders began removing slaves from Delaware, Maryland, and Virginia even before the century began. As the Second Middle Passage gathered force in the 1820s, North Carolina, Kentucky, and South Carolina—states that had once imported large numbers of slaves—were also shipping the descendants of the plantation generation west. Delaware and Maryland's share of the trade declined but did not end. Attempts by the older slave states to prevent—sometimes by criminal sanction—the export of slaves failed, as the superior profitability of cotton and sugar drove the forcible removal inexorably forward. With slavery expanding across Arkansas and Texas during the 1850s, Tennessee, Georgia, parts of Alabama, and even Missouri joined the list of exporters.[84]

The growth of slavery slowed in the seaboard South. Virginia's slave population, which had increased by nearly 20 percent in the last decade of the eighteenth century, was barely sustaining itself by 1850, at a growth rate of less than 4 percent. North Carolina and South Carolina followed a similar course. Moreover, as the new states themselves became slave exporters, they repeated the pattern. Kentucky's slave population, which

doubled during the first decade of the nineteenth century, declined thereafter and grew by less than 7 percent between 1850 and 1860. Some states
lost slave population. There were fewer slaves in Delaware and Maryland
in 1860 than at the beginning of the century, with free blacks outnumber-
ing slaves.

The Second Middle Passage did not simply remove slaves; it altered the
population that remained. Because slave traders and westward-bound
planters sought out young men and women, the seaboard South became
an aging society, generally weighted toward women. In 1820 slaves over
age 45 comprised 11 percent of the slave population of Virginia, while they
made up less than 7 percent of the slave population of Alabama. A comparison between Greene County in Alabama's blackbelt, where only four
slaves in a hundred had reached the age of 45, and Surry County in Virginia's tidewater, where 45-year-old slaves were four times as numerous,
exposes the stark contrast between the age structure of the slave-importing
states of the interior and that of the exporting states of the seaboard.[85]

The seaboard South was also a disproportionately female society, which
fit well with its function as the nursery of the workforce for the southern interior. Although abolitionists (and, subsequently, historians) found
charges of the forced breeding of slaves difficult to substantiate, the slaveholders' appreciation of the value of the slaves' increase cannot be questioned.[86] For some seaboard slaveowners, slave children were their most
profitable "crop."

As the coffles of slaves trudged from the seaboard South by the thousands, slave spouses came to understand the fragility of the marriage
bond, and slave parents came to realize that their teenaged children could
disappear, never to be seen again. Sales to the interior shattered approximately one slave marriage in three and separated one fifth of all children
under fourteen from one or both of their parents.[87] The trauma of loss
weighed as heavily on those left behind as on those traded away, for few
slave families escaped the catastrophic effects of the massive deportation.
If a husband or wife, son or daughter, brother or sister did not disappear
into the interior, then a niece or nephew or some neighbor's child did.

Like a recurrent epidemic, the threat of deportation hung over the slave quarter, feared but also expected. The dreaded event was predictable on estates where planters regularly culled their work force or balanced their accounts by selling "surplus" men and women. But separations could also come suddenly, heightening the pain; no slave could tell when they or a loved one might be tapped for sale. Viney Baker, a former Virginia slave, remembered, "One night I lay down on de straw mattress wid my mammy, an' de nex' mo'nin I woke up an' she wuz gone." Baker later learned that "a speculator comed dar de night before an' wanted ter buy a 'omen." They took her mother, she lamented, "widout wakin' me up."[88]

Fear of sale gnawed at the heart of slave life. "The Negroes here dread nothing on earth so much as this," declared an observer of the transfer of slaves from Maryland to Georgia. "They regard the south with perfect horror, and to be sent there is considered as the worst punishment that could be inflicted on them." Even the youngest children appreciated the ominous implications of sale. Taken from her mother in North Carolina and sold with ten other children, seven-year-old Laura Clark sensed her fate: she "never seed her no mo' in dis life." Although given candy to keep her quiet, she just "roll over on de groun' jes' acryin'."[89]

The character of slavery in the Upper South exacerbated the effects of the Second Middle Passage. The prevalence of small units in the Upper South meant that few husbands and wives resided on the same estate. Kinship ties extended across the landscape, linked together by visiting and continuous consultation. While young children generally lived with their mothers, older children might be hired, so that the ownership of a slave family might be vested in numerous slaveholders. Even the largest slaveowners rarely maintained a single large estate. Instead, they divided their holdings among various farms or quarters, townhouses, and industrial enterprises. The migration of a single planter, the dissolution of one estate, or even the sale of a lone slave rippled through the slave population and disrupted dozens of families in a multitude of quarters.[90]

The seeming capriciousness of the process by which slaves were selected for sale put every black man and woman on guard. A master's death, a financial squeeze, or some unfathomable personal pique could spell disaster. "Mamma used to cry," Sarah Grant recalled, "when she had to go back to work because she was always scared some of us kids would be sold while she was away." To ward off such an eventuality, some slaves tried to hide in plain sight. When the itinerant trader arrived, they "didn' dare look up, jes' work right on."[91] Others sought sanctuary in God. "The night before the sale they would all pray in their cabins," remembered a former Tennessee slave. "You could hear the hum of voices in all the cabins down the row." Yet other slaves made it known they would not go quietly. Many took to the woods, while others mustered their small savings from overwork and the like and tried to purchase themselves or a loved one. Few slaves had the necessary cash, so men and women slated for sale scrambled to find a local purchaser rather than risk being sold to a trader.

Maria Perkins alerted her husband Richard to the fact that their son, Albert, had been sold and that she would be placed on the market. "I want you to tell dr Hamelton and your master if either will buy me . . . I don't want a trader to get me . . . I am quite heart sick." While it became the custom in some places to allow slaves to find a new owner, the practice was not always respected. Richmond's First Baptist Church excommunicated one slaveholding member for denying his slave the opportunity and shipping him off to New Orleans instead. In such circumstances, slaves— seeing nothing to lose—boldly confronted their master or mistress. A Virginia slave told his new owner that he might be sold but he would not stay sold. "Lewis says he will not live with me, but will runaway if I attempt to keep him," declared the astounded slaveowner.[92]

Occasionally, the slaves' threats and supplications had the desired effect. When his owner put his "brother on the block and sold him off," a Virginia slave remembered that he "cried and cried till master's brother told me to hush crying and he would get him tomorrow." Some slaves went further. When faced with the possibility of separation from her infant child, one slave mother "took the baby by its feet . . . And with the baby's head swinging downward, she vowed to smash its brains out before she'd leave it." The master relented. Yet, such reprieves were rarely permanent, for death and financial reverses played havoc with the lives of slaveowners—and with them the lives of their slaves.[93]

The slaves' daring confrontations pushed hard against the limits of acceptable protest, and slaveholders often answered in kind. Negotiations over sale between slave and master grew tense, and none were more portentous. Slaveholders, who understood the slaves' fears, elicited promises of faithful service and pledges of future loyalty. More than a few used the threat "to put a slave in their pocket"—meaning to put cash in their pocket in exchange for the slave—as a way of extracting additional drafts of labor. For slaveowners, sale became not only a source of wealth and a means to rationalize the workforce but also the owners' most powerful weapon in their struggle with the slave. Through sale and threat of sale, planters could strip the quarter of its most effective leaders and intimidate those who remained.

But slaves, pushed to the wall, had weapons of their own. While they might begin the negotiation by recalling old loyalties, slaves—and their owners—knew that implicit in their supplications were hazards that went beyond the threat of flight. The Denmark Vesey conspiracy and the Nat Turner rebellion did not occur in response to the raw exploitation of the southern interior but in response to the depressing futility of the slave-exporting seaboard. Although planters rarely mused on the sources of slave rebellions—except to blame inherent African savagery and meddling outsiders—few could fail to appreciate the coincidence between these threats to order and the massive forced deportation.

Perhaps because the moment of sale exposed the very essence of human bondage, slavemasters also disliked it. Fearful that a sale would upset the precarious detente that governed the plantation and turn slaves into fugitives or worse, slaveholders hid their intentions and sought to extract their slaves as quietly as possible. James Green's owner nonchalantly asked his mother if "you will allow Jim to walk down the street with me?" "We walks down the street where the houses grows close together and pretty soon comes the slave market," Green recalled. He never saw his mother again. Nothing more was said; no chance for last-minute exchanges were given.[94]

Against their owners' duplicity, slaves continued to search for some way to shape their own destiny. Unable to prevent their own sale or that of a husband, wife, or child, they maneuvered to have the entire family sold together or, failing that, to find a local purchaser rather than a distant one. Slaves put up for sale championed their spouses or children to their potential buyers, boasting of their value and fidelity to slave traders while none too subtly hinting to their owners that their worth would decrease if they were separated from their loved ones.[95]

When at last it became clear that nothing could be done to prevent removal, slaves set about making preparations for their departure. Those who had accumulated property—in household items, furniture, and barnyard animals—sold them to provide a small cushion of cash to carry to their new home. Often slaveholders would buy their slaves' goods, but sale also became the occasion for masters to expropriate that to which slaves had no legal right. To prevent such loses, some deportees quickly passed their property onto kin and friends.

While some slaves prepared to transfer their material possessions, others sought to settle their intangible accounts. Friends and relatives had to be notified so they could say their last goodbyes. "With much regret" and hopes that "if we Shall not meet in this world I hope to meet in heaven," Abrean Scriven informed his wife that he had been sold from Georgia to New Orleans and requested that she give his "love to my father & mother and tell them good Bye for me." That done, the disconsolate Scriven declared, "My pen cannot Express the griffe I feel." Slave parents looked for someone who might accept the role of adoptive parent. Laura Clark recalled that her mother turned to a friend, Julie Powell, who was sold alongside Laura. "Moma said to old julie, 'Take keer of my baby chile . . . and iffen I never sees her no mo' raise her for God.'" Through the tears, there might be a series of ritual exchanges, along with last-minute words of advice. Mementos that would represent the hopes of a lifetime had to be presented to the deportees. Taking a bag of biscuits from his sister, Hawkins Wilson left a lock of his hair and the promise never to forget.[96]

News of a sale cast a pall over the slave quarter. "Tomorrow the negroes are to get off," observed a Virginia slaveowner as she dispatched her slaves to Kentucky, "and I expect there will be great crying and morning, children Leaving there mothers, mothers there children, and women there husbands." Since the loss affected entire neighborhoods, hundreds might turn out to say a final goodbye. Viewing the departure from a nearby wharf, a South Carolina mistress could not help but be moved to tears by "the wail from those on shore echoed by those on board!" The trauma of separation broke some men and women. Charles Ball, who was a child when he and his family were sold from Maryland, observed that his father "never recovered from the effect[s] of the schock." Once of "a gay, social temper," he became "gloomy and morose." His sullen demeanor disturbed his new owner, who threatened to sell him again. At that, Ball's father fled and was never heard of again.[97]

While Ball's father escaped to parts unknown, many more slaves whose progeny had been systematically stripped away lived an isolated existence. Their lamentable condition touched the entire slave community. The plight of Frederick Douglass's grandmother, living alone in a ramshackle cabin on the fag end of the Lloyd estate, every one of her children and most of her grandchildren having been sold South, deeply affected the young Douglass.[98] The sorrow that pervaded slave spirituals owed much to the dismemberment of slave families in the wake of the Second Middle Passage. Songs of motherless children and bereaved parents filled the slaves' musical repertoire. In the 1930s Emma Howard recalled "one of de saddest songs we sungen durin' slavery days."

> Mammy, is Ol' Massa gwin' er sell us tomorrow?
> Yes, my chile.
> What he gwin'er sell us?
> Way down South in Georgia.

"It always did make me cry," Howard reflected.[99]

For those who were left behind, the land to which their loved ones had been transported was unknown but not unknowable. Indeed, slaves in the exporting states strained to learn of the deportees' destination. The great fear was that it might be Louisiana, whose reputation "as a place of slaughter" had filtered back to the exporting states. The hope was that they might join with others who had been shipped west. While those tramping west learned about the extent of slave society through their own experience, those left behind also gained a sense of the expansive nature of the slave regime through rumors that echoed back east. But this knowledge did little to mitigate their anger, for sale starkly revealed the fundamental injustice of the slave regime and the conflicting interests of master and slave. Interviewed almost a century after emancipation, William Hamilton declared, "'Twas something Ise never fo'gits. Ever' time Ise thinks 'bout it, my blood heats."[100]

Seaboard planters also fretted about the massive migration, but their anxiety pointed them in different directions. In lowland South Carolina and Georgia, the exodus of laborers affirmed the planters' commitment to slavery. Whatever difficulties and distress rice producers faced during the nineteenth century, doubts about slavery were not among them. Low-country planters joined the grandees of cotton and sugar to celebrate chattel bondage and took the lead in shoring up its defenses. But they worried about the steady leaching of slaves from the Upper South, and with good reason. Upper South slaveholders, seeing their slaves steadily disappear to the plantation interior, accepted as inevitable the decline of chattel bondage. Their acknowledgment of slavery's eventual demise measured the distance between the plantation interior and the mixed economies of the periphery. Whereas the great planters of the interior wanted more slaves, with some even urging the reopening of the African trade and demanding the re-enslavement of free people of color, slavemasters in the Upper South prepared for the day when black people would be legally free.

Few slaveholders converted to abolitionists in the face of this realization. Rather, it steeled their determination to maintain slavery for as long as they could, not through a celebration of chattel bondage but through practical measures that would extend the institution's life. Save for a few ideologues, slaveowners in the Upper South invested little time in elaborate defenses and showed even less interest in intruding into the lives of their slaves, either to name children or to sanitize quarters. Reformist ideologies—notions of "our family, black and white"—had little meaning when every day slaves were sold from the region like bales of cotton. Instead, planters in the Upper South began to accommodate themselves to the realities of their changing labor force. Rather than import Africans,

they pocketed the profits from selling African Americans. Rather than ex-
pel or re-enslave free blacks, they extracted their labor for a pittance. Instead of reinvigorating slavery, Upper South slaveholders looked for practical ways to prolong the life of a dying institution, as so much of their
prosperity depended upon it. They found three strategies: renting slaves,
allowing slaves to hire themselves, and selling slaves their freedom.

Slave rentals served a variety of purposes. Hired slaves met the seasonal
and task-specific requirements of a system of mixed agriculture and manufacture. It allowed slaveholders to squeeze additional income from their
property, and—by giving white nonslaveholders access to slave labor—it
tied them to the slave regime at a time when their commitment appeared
to be flagging. The availability of hired slaves also spurred the development of a variety of new enterprises. In the countryside, coal mines, iron
forges, and saltworks as well as turnpikes, canals, and railroads all relied
on hired slaves, as a new class of entrepreneurs found profitable employment for the slave population. During the 1840s and 1850s hired slaves replaced white wage earners in some industries, most famously in Richmond's sprawling Tredagar Iron Works, where a strike by white iron
molders became an excuse to create a largely enslaved work force.

By the middle of the nineteenth century, slave hiring had become a distinguishing feature of chattel bondage in the Upper South. Slaveowners
rented their slaves for every conceivable purpose and in every conceivable
arrangement, by the day, week, month, year, or job. Cities became mag-
nets for slave hirelings, employing vast numbers. In Baltimore and Richmond, Frederick and Lynchburg, and dozens of similar places, small armies of hired slaves labored in the flour mills and tobacco factories,
worked the warehouses and docks, and drove the wagons and drays. But
the countryside also was deeply touched by the demand for hired slaves.
In 1860 over one-third of the slaves in Loudoun County, an agricultural
center in Virginia's piedmont, were hired, and there is every indication
that Loudoun typified the mixed-agriculture South. By mid-century few
slaves in the Upper South escaped being hired at one time or another, and
some lived apart from their owners for most of their lives.[101]

Hiring posed special dangers for slaves. Trying to maximize profits, slaveowners shuttled their slaves from job to job and from countryside to city and back, sometimes placing them with other slaveowners, sometimes with nonslaveowners, and sometimes with corporate enterprises in which ownership was distant, if visible at all. As a general rule, hirers had less interest in the slaves' well-being than their owners, and abuse was common as they too strove to maximize their profits. Even in the best of circumstances, hiring added uncertainty to slave life, since slaves rarely knew to whom and where they would be rented.[102]

But hiring offered slaves numerous opportunities to improve their circumstances and edge their way toward independence. Especially in the region's growing cities, hiring allowed slaves to practice a variety of trades, many of them skilled. It mobilized slaves and sent them in all directions, giving them a broad knowledge of the countryside and its inhabitants. Many found themselves working alongside wage workers, white as well as black. In the region's cities, many of their co-workers and neighbors were immigrants unfamiliar with the niceties of American racial etiquette. Some were outright hostile to slavery. These combinations of white wage workers and hired slaves gave black men and women yet another view of freedom. As their knowledge grew, so did their confidence.[103]

Although the rental of slaves was, by law, a transaction between the slaveowner and a potential employer, slaves actively entered into the bargaining. Playing buyer against seller, slaves maneuvered to get the best deal for themselves, rejecting some hirers and approving others. Even then, according to one critic of slave hiring, slaveowners were "compelled to persuade, exhort, and even pay their own negroes to go where they had been hired." While owners might ignore the slaves' preference, they did so at their peril, as an abusive hirer might damage their property and an unhappy hireling might flee, depriving owners of income and, ultimately, their property. For just those reasons, hirers often "electioneered" with slaves, purchasing their consent with promises of good treatment, independence, and even cash.[104]

While the threat of sale forced slaves to negotiate on a narrow terrain of the masters' choosing, hiring often enlarged that ground and gave slaves an advantage. A few slaves seized control of the hiring process and, in practice if not in law, became contractors of their own labor; in the words of one disenchanted commentator, the slave could "choose his own master." Once their work was complete, these slaves were on their own. With no master inquiring into their deportment, regulating their diet, and meddling in their religious life and leisure activities, hired slaves rid themselves of slavery's most annoying intrusions. Some used control over the hiring process to reunite their families. "I hope you will grant me the privilege of hiring my own time," wrote a North Carolina slave to his owner in 1835, "I wish to live in Raleigh, so that I can be with my wife."[105] Bending the system of hiring to their own purposes required complicated and often prolonged negotiations, since at least two other parties were involved. Not every slave was up to it. But most slaves had long bargained over their labor, deportment, and spirituality and were no strangers to wheeling and dealing to make things go their way.

Hiring—as much as any other feature of slavery—distinguished black life in the Upper South from the plantation interior. Although the cotton and sugar planters also hired slaves, and slave hiring was as common in Lower South cities as in those of the Upper South, the differences in scale were substantial. While the expansion of cotton and sugar production tethered slaves to their home plantations, the opposite often transpired in the Upper South.[106] Rather than being confined to the great estates, mobile slaves traversed the countryside. Their ability to travel openly, sometimes live independently, and converse with whom they pleased compromised the sovereignty of the master and gave black people—especially black men—a clear view of life outside of slavery. Slaves, given the right "to choose a master," complained an angry slaveowner, will soon "refuse to accept one at all." Indeed, more than a few hired slaves simply seized their freedom, so that it was difficult to distinguish runaways as hired slaves from hired slaves as runaways.[107]

That was precisely what worried many whites, slaveholders and non-slaveholders alike. Allowing slaves to sell themselves for a period of time smacked of freedom, even if slaves kept only a tiny fraction of the proceeds and their owners profited all the more. Critics never ceased reiterating that slave hire, and particularly self-hire, subverted the master-slave relationship, and accelerated—rather than delayed—slavery's demise. They worried that it alienated white wage workers by subjecting them to competition from slaves. But the profitability of slave rental for the owner and its practicality for the hirer trumped the critics, whose pleas rarely carried much weight except in moments of crisis. Slave hiring in the Upper South increased steadily during the nineteenth century. As it did, the door to freedom cracked wider.

With freedom itself at issue and slaves desperate to escape bondage, some slaveowners saw yet another way to turn a profit, discipline black workers, and extend slavery's life. Negotiations over freedom became particularly common in the border states of Delaware, Maryland, northern parts of Virginia, Kentucky, and Missouri, where slaves could literally walk to freedom in the North—or, following Frederick Douglass's lead, board a railroad car in Baltimore as a slave and step off it in Philadelphia as a free man. Faced with a sullen and refractory slave who might bolt to the free states if threatened with the lash or with sale, slaveholders conceded the possibility of freedom. But it was usually freedom deferred—a deal in which hard work and good behavior in the present were traded for the promise of liberty at some future date. Slaves were quick to grab their owners' offers; indeed, they usually took the initiative in proposing such arrangements. Term slavery, previously identified with urban life, expanded into the countryside, as rural masters exchanged eventual freedom for a few years of "good service." On the northern periphery, slave societies reverted to societies with slaves.

As they did, the line between slavery and freedom attenuated. The number of black people whose ambiguous status fit into the category of neither free nor slave increased. Some of these had been manumitted but, as a condition of freedom, had remained illegally in states that required their departure. Others had been purchased by friends and relatives and given de facto freedom where formal manumission was difficult, expensive, or illegal. Amid these statusless men and women, fugitive slaves camouflaged themselves and remained at large.[108]

At the very time free people of color were being squeezed from the interior, the number of free blacks were increasing in the slave-exporting states. At mid-century, the census counted almost 75,000 free blacks in Maryland, over 50,000 in Virginia, nearly 30,000 in North Carolina, and another 10,000 in Kentucky, and these numbers were just a fraction of the black people who had broken with slavery as understood by black-belt planters.[109] The large number of free blacks, hired and self-hired slaves, and hired slaves in the process of purchasing their freedom—some of whom were living independently of their owners—and runaway slaves at large blurred the line between slavery and freedom. The slaves' mobility added to a general sense that chattel bondage was unraveling. From the perspective of the southern interior, the exporting region was no longer the slave states but "free negro states."

The halting death of slavery in the border states gave black people only small cause for celebration, because slaveholders hastily erected barriers between their former slaves and full freedom. The exhilaration that accompanied the massive post-revolutionary manumission faded as individuals exited slavery one by one and entered a freedom circumscribed by state laws, local ordinances, and customary practice. During the 1840s and 1850s Delaware and Maryland enacted new regulations—many of them precursors to postbellum black codes—requiring free blacks to sign yearly contracts and giving slave hirers the rights of a master. Elsewhere, the regulation of free black life was not nearly as systematic, but a farrago of vagrancy laws, head taxes, and apprenticeship regulations constrained the rights of free people of color. The enforcement of these laws—although desultory—weighed heavily on free people, allowing employers, many of them slaveholders or former slaveholders, to extort labor in ever-more creative ways. Often these entailed the forced apprenticing of black children as a means of gaining access to the labor of their parents. Some planters and farmers sold a few otherwise worthless acres to free blacks with the understanding that their labor remained available, particularly during critical periods in the agricultural cycle. Villages of so-called cottagers sprang up in various portions of the border states, just as they had in post-revolutionary Pennsylvania.[110]

The ubiquity of hiring and the presence of free blacks gave slave life in the exporting region a different shape than in the plantation interior. Regional differences were reflected in patterns of leadership, family life, and religious practices. Leaders emerged from within seaboard society to help shape negotiations with whites over a multitude of contentious issues, among them the threat of sale to the South, the terms of hire, and the conditions of freedom. These leaders often came from widely traveled jobbing slave artisans and property-owning free blacks, whose dealings with a variety of white men and women in the larger world, as well as with other slaves and free blacks, gained them a broad reputation in the neighborhood. The negotiations—unlike those in the interior—took place in a slave society that reached back into the seventeenth century. While the roots of black leadership in the interior were shallow, those in the exporting states ran deep. By the nineteenth century, leading men and women drew upon longstanding precedents as they confronted the owners in matters as various as food and shelter, work and leisure, and domestic and religious life.

The Second Middle Passage remade slave family life in the Upper South no less emphatically than it did in the southern interior. The shrinking size of agricultural units in the exporting region, the growing sexual imbalance of the slave population, with its high proportion of women, and the expansion of hiring made it increasingly difficult for slaves to find partners on the same estate and for parents and their children to share a residence. The physical separation of family members compromised marriages and thwarted attempts to establish stable households, forcing slaves and free blacks to adopt a variety of domestic arrangements. Slave family life ranged from "broad" spouses, single parenting, or multigenerational households to co-residential nuclear families, with the extended family becoming the most prominent form. Since men, far more than women, were allowed to travel and since both slaveholders and slaves agreed that women could best nurture children, most families took the form of resident women and children and absent men.

Slave women found themselves not only working in their masters' fields but also tending the family's garden plot or provision grounds, as well as performing the domestic tasks of their own household. The gradual feminization of the slave population nudged women into new positions of domestic authority, making men adjuncts to the day-to-day business of family life. While slave men frequently provided critical support to the family, the structure of slave society meant that they played a diminished role in the daily education of their children and were rarely present when their wives needed them the most. Increasingly, mothers alone had to prepare their children for a life different from their own and had to finish these grim lessons before children reached their mid-teens, when they were almost certain to be hired out, sold locally, or deported to the interior. Last-minute words of advice to departing children might be reassuring, but it made more sense to begin long before the slave trader or hirer appeared.

Caught between the threat of sale and the hope of freedom, black families in the Upper South spread domestic responsibilities from parents to a larger kin group whose connections reached beyond the individual farm, plantation, or workshop into the larger neighborhood or community, some of whose members were free but most of whom were slave. Domestic life became especially complicated for black families that included both slave and free members. The enslavement of one family member often held the entire family hostage to slaveholders, who might force the free spouse to apprentice himself or herself in exchange for visitation rights or the promise of future freedom. Violation of the terms of indenture or apprenticeship might lead to extended service, allowing slaveholders to squeeze yet additional labor from slaves and the free members of their families. If such subterfuges failed, masters could always threaten to sell loved ones south, an event so common that black people dared not ignore it.[111]

Like every other aspect of slave life, the development of the black church followed a different course in the exporting states than in the interior. The institutional head start born of the post-revolutionary awakenings gave African-American religion a powerful presence in the seaboard states, particularly in the Upper South. Independent black churches created during the eighteenth century survived into the nineteenth. In some places black people—slave as well as free—continued to enjoy all the rights of church membership, voting on ecclesiastical matters and attending local association meetings and synods into the 1820s. But overall, the rights of black church members steadily attenuated in the new century and then disappeared entirely in the wake of Nat Turner's rebellion in 1831. State after state placed new regulations on black meetings, barring black men and women from preaching or even assembling without white supervision. White churches dismantled boards of black deacons and stripped black congregants of their few remaining rights. Under these conditions, black membership in biracial churches fell dramatically.

But as the fears of insurrection dissipated over the next decade, individual congregations began to relax their strictures, ignoring state laws and even their own regulations. Black deacons resumed their customary role as preachers and black congregants once again regulated their own affairs, asserting their claim to Jesus' message. Independent or quasi-independent black churches revived or appeared in the region's towns and cities. Although by law these churches operated under white supervision, in practice black deacons, exhorters, and sometimes ministers enjoyed independence. In local associational meetings or regional synods, some blacks pushed for greater control over their religious life, demanding official sanction for their de facto activities. In border areas, the northern-based African Methodist Episcopal Church (AME) had made inroads, infiltrating the region with circuit riders and missionaries.

Where independent black churches did not exist, black men and women made up a substantial minority of the membership in biracial congregations, and in some places constituted a majority. Their numbers alone forced these biracial institutions to license black men as preachers and exhorters, some of whom regularly attended regional meetings. With its roots in the eighteenth century, African-American Christianity was well advanced in the slave-exporting states on the eve of the cotton revolution.[112]

Yet slaves did not uniformly embrace Christianity, and slaveholders' opposition to the Christianization of slaves remained substantial, particularly when black churches had northern connections. Citing the danger of just that relationship, planters barred the establishment of black churches and even dismantled African churches. The presence of an AME minister in Charleston was reason enough for slaveholders and their accomplices to disassemble—literally, board by board—an established black Methodist church in 1817. Similar concerns prevented the organization of an independent church in Richmond until the 1840s, despite the efforts of the city's leading free people of color. In addition, many slaves remained indifferent toward the Gospel even after slaveholders warmed to the notion of conversion. Their skepticism about the religion of the owners remained a powerful source of opposition to Christianity well into the nineteenth century. In 1831 John Hartwell Cocke, a Virginia planter deeply committed to the spiritual lives of his slaves, queried them on their acceptance of Christ. There was every reason for his slaves to supply Cocke with the answer he so desperately wished to hear, but instead they disappointed him in a most pointed manner.[113]

Still, the number of slaves in the seaboard South who were connected to Christian churches increased steadily during the nineteenth century. For some, the church balcony offered a convenient place to socialize and enjoy a few minutes to themselves. More than one white minister complained that during Sunday services "the usual African resort is a loud, comfortable snoring nap." But for other slaves and free people of color, conversion represented a deep commitment to a new faith and its promise of a world turned upside down.

The growing presence of black men and women initiated a familiar struggle between white churchmen and black deacons, and with increasing frequency the deacons claimed victory. This was especially true in urban churches, whose leadership was drawn from the propertied free black population, but even slave deacons in rural congregations reasserted their authority. In 1845 one church in the Virginia countryside replaced the entire board of deacons when it discovered that black churchmen had "so transcended the power vested in them as to take the whole discipline of the coloured members into their own hands." It would not be the last time such action would be necessary. Although by custom and in some places by law the ministry remained in the hands of a white man, black deacons controlled the day-to-day operations.[114]

Under the deacons' direction, the church became the institutional hub of the black community, performing many of the services denied slaves and free persons of color. In Richmond's First African Church, the Committee on Debt became a small claims court, and other committees regulated sexuality by sanctioning marriages and punishing adultery. Like the First African, other black churches sponsored schools and benevolent societies. "Who has not heard of the 'burial society' among the negroes of Richmond?" piped that city's leading newspaper in 1853. Indeed, according to the press, everyone in Richmond knew about it, as well as a host of other associations formed by black men and women for religious, educational, and benevolent purposes. In a world made turbulent and insecure by the Second Middle Passage, such institutions offered a shelter strong enough to sustain its members and flexible enough to address the realities of sale. Churches, schools, and associations—with their charters, regular meetings, and membership rosters—provided passports to community leadership, sites for debating the events of the day, and a means to mobilize slaves and free people of color.[115]

But if reordering of slave society in the Upper South eased some of the burdens of bondage, the steady sale south only increased the anxieties of slaves and free people of color. As the region's most famous fugitive later explained, "If a slave has a bad master his ambition is to get a better, when he gets a better, he aspires to have the best; and when he gets the best, he aspires to be his own master."[116] Frederick Douglass, whose planning for his own freedom began when he gained permission to hire himself in Baltimore, understood how the changes taking place in the Upper South only intensified slaves' desire for freedom and expanded their ability to achieve it. The massive torrent of the Second Middle Passage, which every year washed thousands of slaves southward, also spawned a small tributary that carried hundreds north.

THE NORTH

New arrivals in the northern states found a society undergoing a fundamental transformation, as the gradual emancipation laws enacted in the wake of the American Revolution did their work. In some places, piecemeal abolition was accelerated by decisions to halt the gradualist process and preemptively end slavery. New York did so in 1817, when the state legislature—at the governor's urging—ordered a final and complete emancipation on July 4, 1827. But as New York was putting a dying institution out of its misery, other jurisdictions were trying to revive it. Chattel bondage gained new life on the western frontier, as slaveholders attempted to transfer slavery into the territories that would be carved out of the Northwest Territory—Ohio, Indiana, Illinois, Michigan, Wisconsin, and parts of Minnesota. They made the greatest progress in Illinois, where only the heroic effort of Governor Edward Coles, a protégé of Thomas Jefferson, prevented the expansion of slavery north of the Ohio River.

Even that defeat could not put slavery down. The Northwest Ordinance's exclusion of slavery did not emancipate slaves already in place, and in 1820 there were still nearly one thousand in Illinois, where the institution lingered until a state constitutional provision abolished it in 1848. Tobacco planters in southern Ohio regularly hired Kentucky slaves to work their crop. Meanwhile, some white farmers and merchants simply flouted the law, employing a variety of subterfuges—long-term indentureships and apprenticeships being the most prominent—to keep black people in a servitude that often resembled slavery in everything but name.[117]

Perhaps more important, white northerners introduced new constraints on black life. Limitations on liberty marched lock-step with liberation from bondage. Various northern states prohibited free blacks from sitting on juries, testifying in court, carrying guns, attending public schools, and traveling freely. Other new proscriptions threatened to turn the state itself into a surrogate master. As part of the national government, white northerners joined white southerners in excluding black people from the rights that became identified with American citizenship. In 1792 the first Congress refused to naturalize Africans and denied black men the right to serve in the national militia or carry the mail, one of the few sources of employment controlled by the federal government. Northern state legislators needed no encouragement from their southern counterparts to extend proscriptions on free blacks. During the 1820s and 1830s, when state constitutional conventions expanded democracy for white men by eliminating property qualifications for voting and holding office, northern lawmakers simultaneously stripped black men of the suffrage.[118]

Where legislative enactments dared not tread, informal practice—newly established but anointed with the force of custom—served the same proscriptive function. By general consent, white employers barred free blacks from trades they had practiced openly as slaves, driving them deep into poverty. Unable to gain employment except as day laborers and domestics, black people then found themselves ridiculed for their lack of ambition and irregular work habits. Respectable white men and women shunned them, denying people of color entry to public places and excluding them from churches, schools, and fraternal orders. Older communities "warned out" free blacks, and newer ones barred their entry. When black men and women refused to leave or continued to immigrate, they were assaulted, physically as well as verbally. Their continued presence spurred a movement to colonize or "repatriate" people of African descent, with Africa being the chosen destination. In liquidating slavery, white northerners tried to rid themselves of black people as well.[119]

When colonization failed, white people set black people apart socially and ideologically. The belief that people of African descent were somehow different, if not in origins then certainly by experience and perhaps by nature, gained force during the first half of the nineteenth century. White northerners voiced ideas rarely heard prior to the Revolution. Many, perhaps most, accepted the notion that slavery had permanently disabled black people and barred them from full participation in American society. By the 1830s and 1840s, some white northerners pressed beyond the notion that distinctions between black and white rested on the legacy of bondage and instead maintained that racial differences had a physical or even providential basis. A few argued that such distinctions could be measured by the size of crania, slope of face angles, and width of noses. In the popular press and in everyday life, black people found themselves depicted in animalistic images.[120] For some white northerners, placing black people outside the pale of humanity made universal white equality possible. Black subordination provided the foundation upon which notions of white equality were constructed.[121]

The systematic proscription of free people of color compromised the North's claim to be a free society. Rather than "free states," the post-emancipation North might better be described as a region whose transition from a society with slaves was still incomplete. The protracted evolution from slavery to freedom was affirmed by the extraordinarily slow growth of abolitionist sentiment, which was not fully articulated until the 1830s, and by the continued role that white northerners played in supporting southern slavery through membership in the Democratic Party. With the silent complicity—if not the active concurrence—of white northerners, the federal government became the agent of slavery's expansion during the nineteenth century and its surest source of security in a world that was turning against chattel bondage. Certainly without the acquiescence of the North's white majority, there would have been no delay in closing the slave trade, no enactment of a federal fugitive slave law, no expansion of slavery into the territories, and no new slave states. Until the final break with slavery on January 1, 1863, the North was a part of a slaveholding republic.

The North's prolonged devolution from a society with slaves and the constriction of African-American freedom meant that slavery was no mere memory in the free states. Well into the mid-nineteenth century and after, there were many black men and women who had personally endured slavery and many more who lived slavery through the experience of their parents, neighbors, and friends.[122] Because they were embedded in a slaveholding nation, black communities in the North assumed many of the characteristics of maroon enclaves. Although they lacked the territorial integrity that was one of the distinguishing marks of maroon life elsewhere in the Americas, black northerners—like other maroons—lived apart from most white people. In both countryside and city, black people huddled in the least desirable areas, residing on isolated scraps of rural land no one else seemed to want and in the poorest and least attractive urban neighborhoods. Most worked at marginal jobs, excluded not only from the skilled trades but also from manufacture—the sector of the northern society that was expanding most rapidly and was most fully identified with wage labor. Their position grew more precarious still as an influx of European immigrants ousted them from employment at the bottom tier of northern society. Since black men rarely enjoyed the suffrage, their role in the political system was that of supplicants, pressing the government through petitions and protests. "We are slaves in the midst of freedom," declared Martin Delany in 1852.[123]

Like maroon enclaves, black northern communities developed an internal coherence in ideology, leadership, and institutions that stood in opposition to the plantation society from which these communities drew many of their members. The fugitive nature of black life in the North was reinforced by the fact that many black northerners were in fact fugitives, sometimes from the slave states, sometimes from slavery, and sometimes from both—as the north-flowing tributary of the Second Middle Passage grew larger. Restrictive legislation enacted in many southern states to stem the growth of the free black population required that newly manumitted slaves leave the state upon receipt of freedom. Those who failed to emigrate could be forcibly deported, if not re-enslaved.

The exodus of southern free people of color was augmented by a growing number of runaway slaves, for whom compromised freedom in the North was far superior to captivity in the South. As a result, black southerners—many of them former slaves—composed a large share of the North's black population. At mid-century, almost 30 percent of the free black people in Pennsylvania had been born in the slave South, as had 20 percent of black New Yorkers. What was true of the North generally was even more true of the urban North. Half of the black people in Philadelphia and Pittsburgh derived from the slave states, as did more than one fifth of the black population of Boston, Brooklyn, and Providence. In cities bordering directly on the slave states, the proportion was higher still. Over 70 percent of Cincinnati's black population had been born in the slave South. In all, of the quarter million black people residing in the North in 1860, one third, and perhaps as many as one half, had their origins in the slave states.[124]

Black southerners not only constituted a substantial portion of the northern black population but also made up an even more substantial portion of those who were economically successful and politically active.

By any measure—wealth, skill, or literacy—immigrants from the South stood atop black society in the North. These men and women—many of them light-skinned—also made up a disproportionate share of participants in the state and national conventions at the center of black activism in the North. In the person of men like Henry Bibb, William Wells Brown, Frederick Douglass, and Samuel Ringgold Ward, they became some of the most articulate representatives of northern black life. Having experienced slavery first hand, they were especially active in the movement against slavery.[125] By their prominence as well as their numbers, southern-born former slaves and free people of color shaped black life in the North.

The continual influx of southern fugitives, refugees, and deportees to the North constantly renewed the memory of slavery. Those free people of color who had abandoned profitable businesses and severed ties with family and friends in the South shared the sting of exile. But even black people native to the North with long pedigrees in freedom knew of someone—a parent, friend, even husband or wife—who had their origins in bondage. Slavery was ubiquitous—its marks need not be discussed to be understood. A back disfigured by the lash, an ankle bruised by a shackle, a body seared by a branding iron were all silent reminders that slavery's history was none too distant. "Our backs are yet scarred by the lash. And our souls are yet dark under the pall of slavery," declared a representative to the National Convention of Colored People in 1848. The assembled delegates needed little reminder.[126]

The long shadow of slavery trailed black northerners and united them with those who remained enslaved. For some people of color, it was fear of recapture and for others it was fear of kidnapping—both were omnipresent realities as the westward expansion of slavery inflated the price of black men and women. Knowledge that a black man or woman might bring several hundred dollars in the slave marts of Richmond and even more in New Orleans was simply too much temptation for some ill-disposed men and women to resist. The violent apprehension of a fugitive or alleged fugitive, one who perhaps had long enjoyed freedom, was an event witnessed and experienced by many black northerners. Even Richard Allen, perhaps the most prominent black man in post-revolutionary Philadelphia, came near to being enslaved. Like Allen, few forgot their brush with kidnappers. Warnings of the dangers of seizure were a part of every black child's education, reinforced by reminders from the pulpit of every church. The insecurity that so pervaded black life was heightened by the contempt white men and women demonstrated for the liberty of former slaves. Although white northerners denounced man-stealing and even legislated against it, they rarely enforced their own laws, and some were deeply implicated in the crime.[127]

The omnipresent fear of re-enslavement strengthened the notion that the free states were but precarious enclaves in which the freedom of black men and women—like that of maroons—was always at risk. Although legal freedom gave black communities in the North a different shape than that of the maroon village, in both situations black people resided in a nether world between slavery and freedom. The willingness of white northerners to act as the agents for southern slaveholders—opposing abolition and defending the colorline, along with the exclusion of black people from civil society in the North—encouraged black people to think of themselves as fugitives.

On this precarious terrain of northern freedom, black people created their own society. Central to the black communities of the North was an independent family life, which emerged slowly from the dependency of slavery. By the 1830s the vast majority of northern black people had established households apart from former owners and employers. But the African-American family stretched beyond the boundaries of the household and reached deep into black society, incorporating nonresident relatives, friends, and associates through an expansive definition of kinship. In patterns of migration, neighborhood alliances, mutual assistance associations, and even street life, it often seemed that all black people were related, if not by blood then by choice.

As formidable as it was, the African-American family was afflicted by all manner of adversity. Death stalked black people in the North. The mortality rate of black men and women was substantially higher than that of whites, turning wives into widows, husbands into widowers, and children into orphans at a fearsome rate. Those who survived faced deep poverty, which further destabilized domestic life. To find regular employment, black men and women frequently had to separate from each other and from their children, with men often taking to sea and women accepting positions as live-in servants. The proportion of northern black families headed by two parents declined steadily during the antebellum years. Still, despite these many obstacles, most black children lived in households with both a mother and a father. Indeed, the commitment to two-head households ran so deep that "aunts" and "uncles" in the community regularly adopted children who lost their birth parents. The flexibility of the African-American family and its ability to absorb a variety of unattached individuals reflected both the difficult circumstances of black life and the commitment to maintaining kinship ties.[128]

The family was but one of the institutions that joined northern black people together. Of the others, none was more significant than the Christian church. Building upon the efforts of a small cadre of men and women who had been converted in the religious awakenings in the last decades of the eighteenth century, African-American Christianity spread rapidly throughout the free states, even as it remained confined to a few urban enclaves in the South. By the first decade of the nineteenth century, African churches of nearly every denomination could be found in the North, fusing a variety of seemingly incompatible religious traditions— African spirituality, enthusiastic evangelicalism, formalistic Anglicanism, and Quaker pietism. The most important were African Baptist and Methodist churches, especially the African Methodist Episcopal Church, which under Philadelphia's Richard Allen organized as an independent denomination in 1817.[129]

By mid-century, Christian churches—with their distinctive sermons, music, and liturgy—had become the center of the black community, "the Alpha and Omega of all things," according to one prominent black leader.[130] Radiating out from the churches were a variety of other associations. These included schools, libraries, and debating clubs, as well as fraternal and benevolent societies, trade associations, and political alliances, many of them founded in the post-revolutionary struggle for freedom. Alongside these organizations were independent newspapers, theaters, clubs, and conventions, all reflecting the distinct cultures that emerged from the experience of black people in the free states.

Fissures in this complex institutional structure exposed the diversity of northern black life, despite its many sources of solidarity. Perhaps the sharpest lines divided black northerners into an aspiring bourgeoisie eager to demonstrate their respectability through language, dress, decorum, and education and a raucous working class known more for its swinging gait, tavern life, loud music, and open sexuality. Such differences, visible in the years immediately following emancipation, grew during the nineteenth century, although the material basis of these distinctions remained small. The respectables surrounded themselves with books, built commodious churches, and promoted self-improvement to affirm their fitness—and that of "their people"—for full citizenship. "It is for us to convince the world by uniform propriety of conduct, industry, and economy, that we are worthy of esteem and patronage," observed one leading respectable. Through ties of shared religion (both pietistic and evangelical) and politics (almost always Federalist, later Whig, and then Republican), they sought alliances with white men and women whose lifestyle they admired and imitated. Meanwhile the laboring poor—marginalized by their impoverishment—grew more estranged from and resentful of those who presumed to speak for them.

Social divisions within black society bred intense suspicions and animosities. The aspiring gentlemen and ladies feared the black poor would confirm the worst racial stereotypes, and the poor remained profoundly distrustful of those who acted like white people. Regional origins (southern and northern) expanded the social distance between the respectables and the poor, since many of the most successful people of color had their beginnings in the slave states.[131] Somatic differences—the so-called complexional distinction—exacerbated those of region and class, since the respectables tended to be lighter in color than their working-class neighbors.[132]

Ideological differences cut across these social distinctions. Members of each camp—both the nascent bourgeoisie and laboring poor—shared an aspiration for equality, an elastic concept that stretched in all directions but meant, at the very least, full participation in American society. But they differed sharply as to how equality might best be achieved. Some turned inward to the black community and, viewing white men and women as irreconcilably hostile, maintained that black people could look only to themselves. Others, believing such independence either impossible or undesirable, worked to integrate the black community into the larger northern society, becoming among the most eloquent spokespersons for the nation's founding ideals. These dual, overlapping, and sometimes contradictory positions sparked seemingly endless debate among black northerners, and various positions shifted over time, with new permutations falling in and out of popular favor. On one hand, increasing racial proscriptions, disfranchisement, shrinking economic opportunity, and growing violence pulled black northerners inward toward a celebration of blackness and their common African origins. On the other hand, the growth of the antislavery movement and the abolitionist assault on racial proscription encouraged black northerners to identify with the national ideal and press for integration into northern society. The debate was never resolved, in large measure because neither strategy substantially diminished the ostracism, impoverishment, and political impotence that characterized black life in the North.[133]

But the intense internal debate refined a tradition of political activism that dated at least from the Revolution. Building upon the few but fundamental civil liberties they enjoyed—the right to hold property, to collect a wage, to establish an independent family life, to assemble as they wished and speak as they pleased—black men and women elaborated their political culture in the nineteenth century. Black northerners supported newspapers that created a knowledgeable public and lectures that spawned a tradition of eloquent oratory. They held rallies and organized conventions that mobilized thousands and produced an articulate, informed, and often charismatic leadership class. In 1829 Samuel Cornish—co-founder of *Freedom's Journal*, the first black newspaper—charged the agents of his new journal, *The Rights of All*, with "travelling from one extremity of our country to the other, forming associations, communicating with our people and the public generally, on all subjects of interest, collecting monies, and delivering stated lectures on industry, frugality, enterprise, etc."[134]

By mid-century, African-American civic life extended across the Atlantic. Traveling as abolitionist emissaries, Christian missionaries, African colonizers, and, most commonly, salt-water sailors, African Americans re-entered the Atlantic and restored the cosmopolitan world of the charter generations. Yet the experience they carried to Europe, Africa, and the Caribbean was radically different from the experience their ancestors had brought to the mainland more than a century earlier. No longer multilingual cultural brokers, they represented a distinctly North American perspective in language, religion, commerce, and politics. As agents of an African-American diaspora, they began to transform the Atlantic from west to east as their forebears had once transformed it from east to west. Broadcasting abolitionist sentiments, evangelical Christianity, and republican ideology, they also hoped to profit from the expansion of commercial capitalism even as they sought a refuge for their people. The renewal of transatlantic ties to Africa as well as to other diasporic communities in Europe and the Americas reinvigorated African-American intellectual life.[135]

Whether they remained within the bounds of mainland North America or traveled the Atlantic, black men and women assaulted the fettered freedom that confined them to poverty and social marginality in the North. But however they felt about the society in which they dwelled, they knew exactly where they stood with respect to the plantation South, for their hatred of slavery was open and deep. At every opportunity, they denounced slaveholders as the essence of evil and the social order of the plantation as an affront to the ideal of American nationality; they challenged the idea of the happy slave and the benevolent master.[136] Planters returned their enmity in kind. For them, the mere existence of free black people undermined the ideology and practice of slavery. Pointing to the dismal poverty of black northerners—and adducing from that their sloth and depravity—the planter-congressmen James Henry Hammond concluded that "such miserable and degraded wretches are the blessed fruits of Abolition."[137]

The war between black northerners and slaveowning southerners did not stop with words. Slaveholders raided the black communities of the North much as they would other maroon enclaves, recapturing fugitive slaves and seizing free people to sell into bondage. Black northerners protected themselves by organizing vigilance committees and "wide-awake" societies. But they were not content merely to defend their own person. Led by the exiled southerners among them, they turned their formidable protest tradition against slavery, drawing on their own experience as slaves to lambast the slaveowning enemy.

Their rhetorical assaults were just the beginning. Before long, they attacked the plantation directly, establishing freedom trails to provide directions, safe houses, and protection for those who fled the South. Not waiting for runaways to come to them, increasingly they sought out slaves who were willing to risk all for liberation. A few intrepid black northerners famously went south to recruit would-be fugitives and lead them to freedom. These efforts coalesced in an informal network of like-minded men and women. During the middle years of the nineteenth century, agents of the Underground Railroad reached deeper and deeper into the slave states, and the network of co-conspirators thickened. So-called conductors were aided by new means of transportation, from which the Underground Railroad took its name. Whereas escape had previously been limited to those on the periphery of the South, by the 1830s steamboats and railroads provided many more slaves with a channel to freedom.

The successful—and often spectacular—long-distance flights of Henry "Box" Brown (who shipped himself North in a crate), Ellen and William Craft (her near-white color allowed the pair to disguise themselves as a mistress and servant), and others demonstrated that freedom was within the reach of the most distant plantation. With every escape, slaveholders discovered some new route by which slaves had exited bondage and added to the list of those who had aided them. The willingness of a growing number of men and women to protect fugitives with their lives made attempts to retake runaways an increasingly dangerous endeavor.[138]

Driving the exodus was the determination of refugees, deportees, and successful fugitives to widen the migratory stream that had carried them north, thus securing the freedom of families and friends still in bondage.

While some tried to bargain with slaveowners and buy the freedom of loved ones, others—perhaps despairing of such a possibility—returned to the slave South to guide their families to freedom. In the late 1850s, Dangerfield Newby, who had recently fled Virginia for Ohio, raised $740 in a failed effort to purchase his enslaved wife and children. Newby's frustration left him desperate to extricate his family. But he was only one of many black expatriates prepared to challenge slavery on its home base.

Slaveowners denied Newby and parried the thrust of others who tried to free the slaves. They insulated the slave states by banning antislavery literature, prohibiting discussion of abolition, and intimidating white opponents of slavery with raw violence and exiling those whom they could not intimidate. To prevent the spread of antislavery texts, southern lawmakers barred teaching slaves and even free blacks to read and write. Everywhere slaveowners blocked the exits from slavery by mobilizing slave patrols, enforcing pass laws, prohibiting the return of free black migrants, and denying the entry of black sailors, even for an overnight stay. Former slaves captured while trying to retrieve their families or friends not only saw them sold away but were themselves re-enslaved or worse, as vigilantes hunted down abolitionist emissaries. But slaveholders were not content with such defensive measures. They demanded and—with the passage of the Fugitive Slave Act of 1850 and the Dred Scott decision of 1857—received legal cover for their incursions into the North, announcing that no black person was beyond the reach of the plantation regime.

The threat of enslavement shocked and terrified black northerners, sending many into exile. But it steeled others for the battle to come. Before long they opened their own assault on slavery. In 1859 Dangerfield Newby joined John Brown in attacking Harpers Ferry, a small Virginia town at the confluence of the Shenandoah and the Potomac rivers. Newby died early in the raid, but the contents of his pocket revealed the cause that led him to join John Brown's rag-tag army. A crumpled letter from his wife related her fear that sale would eventually destroy their "bright hops of the futer."[139] In the aftermath of the raid, she and their children were sold South, the migratory tides carrying them not to the small tributary that flowed north toward freedom but to the mighty torrent that rushed toward slavery's new heartland.

Although black northerners' political mobilization was far in advance of their southern counterparts, a shared opposition to slavery produced a common understanding of freedom. As slaves and former slaves, black people had been denied proprietorship of their labor and its product. Their energy and creativity had been usurped to support owners and make them rich. Black people felt confident their labor would do the same for them. With control of their own labor, they presumed, came rights they had long been denied or enjoyed only at their owner's sufferance. Freedom would mean dominion over their own person, denying anyone the ability arbitrarily to discipline, sell, and transport them against their will. As a free people, they would be at liberty to assemble, marry, educate their children, and provide for their parents, as their lives would no longer be held hostage to an owner's whims. Like other free people, they could bear arms to defend themselves and organize churches, schools, and other associations to articulate their interests.

Freedom was more than the negation of slavery. Black people had drunk deeply from the republican culture that surrounded them for more than a century. Perhaps no Americans more fully understood the rights of citizens than those who had been forced to protest their exclusion. Black northerners had as much practice at such remonstrances as anybody. Black southerners—free and slave—had been denied that form of expression, but they learned their rights well enough from scraps of dinnertime conversations and the bombast of Fourth of July orations that echoed the words of Jefferson's Declaration. Perhaps, with the Jubilee, there would also be some cosmic rebalancing of the scale of justice. What had been stolen would be returned to its rightful owners and, as the Bible had promised, the last would be first and the meek would inherit the earth. Perhaps too they would even be given the delicious pleasure of balancing those scales themselves and taking what had been theirs, although getting revenge for past injustice mattered less than simply getting free.

Hopes for such Jubilee had survived since the first ship left Africa. They had been nurtured by members of the charter generations who sought their rights in colonial courts and legislative chambers. They had been sustained by the newly arrived Africans of the plantation generations who disappeared over the horizon paddling small canoes to the east. They had been given concrete form by the churches, schools, and benevolent societies created by the revolutionary generations. Their hopes had been carried south where the migration generation gave them divine sanction in the story of Exodus. But, as the nineteenth century passed its midpoint, the possibility of freedom gained greater salience.

Rumors of the demise of slavery elsewhere in the world and the upswell of abolitionist strength in the North entered the slave quarter in fragments of conversations, newspaper accounts, and—perhaps most significantly—their owners' increasingly exaggerated and vitriolic public denunciation of antislavery fanatics and "Black Republicans." Traveling in the deep South in the 1850s, Frederick Law Olmsted became convinced that "knowledge of abolition agitation [had been] carried among the slaves to the most remote districts." By the 1850s, few slaves did not know of the struggle between slave and free states or appreciate how that conflict might affect their future. According to one planter, slaves followed the election of 1860 almost as closely as their owners, having "very generally got the idea of being emancipated when 'Lincoln' comes in."[140]

As the rumors gained force, slaves sensed a shift in the balance of power. For more than three centuries, they had negotiated with masters from a position of inferiority. The new possibilities were as ominous to slaveowners as they were auspicious to slaves.

EPILOGUE

FREEDOM GENERATIONS

IN THE SPRING of 1861, with sectional divisions flaring in open warfare, the balance of power between slave and slaveowner abruptly tilted in the slaves' favor. After nearly three centuries of negotiating from a position of weakness, black people found their enemy distracted and divided. They quickly seized the moment. Some slaves pressed for better food and clothing, larger gardens, an end to corporal punishment, the removal of overseers, and less work in their owners' fields and more time with their families. Others, seeing the revolutionary possibilities of the moment, ignored the boundaries that had long confined negotiations between master and slave to matters of material comfort and degrees of independence. They demanded freedom and, as their opportunities arose, they took it. Wartime changes—many shaped by events beyond their control, but some of the slaves' own making—transformed men and women born in slavery into the freedom generation.

But the destruction of slavery was neither easy nor direct. Rather than surrender to the slaves' new demands, slaveholding planters and their allies answered threats with fresh constraints. As planters prepared to defend slavery on the field of battle, black people faced greater restrictions and still harsher punishments. But slaves believed they had new allies in the "black Republicans" their owners denounced and in the person of Abraham Lincoln, whom their owners demonized.[1] Presuming that the enemy of their enemy must be their friend, slaves dismissed the official pronouncements of President Lincoln, his cabinet officers, and his generals that the conflict between the North and South was a war for national union in which black people had no place. Instead, they offered their loyalty, their labor, and their lives to the federal cause, eventually transforming the war for union into a war for freedom. Before war's end, Lincoln gained the title of "Great Emancipator," and black men and women began celebrating the long awaited Jubilee.

Joining the slaves' struggle were free people of color, North and South. Black northerners signed on quickly, often standing in the vanguard. Highly politicized, tightly organized, these charter members of the antislavery movement saw the war as an occasion to press the case for full citizenship and universal equality. Free black southerners, particularly the free people of color in the port cities, initially hesitated in making common cause with slaves. Protective of their special status and fearful they would be stripped of their property, deported, or enslaved, some pledged themselves to the Confederacy. But as wartime events linked their own elevation and the slaves' freedom, free people of color exchanged their Confederate gray for Union blue. The Native Guard became the Corps Afrique.

For slaves and free people of color, the destruction of slavery was only the first step toward securing freedom and citizenship. As they shed their shackles, black men and women remade their lives. Retracing the events of the Age of Revolution, former slaves took new names, found new residences, reconstituted their families, and transformed their own labor into material independence. Institutions that had been clandestine—churches, schools, and burial associations—functioned openly, and leaders who had previously muffled their voices spoke freely or, at least, more freely than in times past. A new world was dawning, and with it previously unimaginable possibilities. For while the post–Civil War reconstruction of African-American life may have replicated the changes that had accompanied the

arrival of freedom in the late eighteenth century, unlike in the earlier partial emancipations of the revolutionary era, freedom no longer co-exited
with slavery. The speed of the general emancipation that accompanied the
Civil War, its growing velocity, and its ever-widening scope made for a social revolution of mammoth proportions. Within less than a decade from
the war's beginning, slaves were transformed to a free people, serving as
soldiers in the world's most powerful army and as citizens of the republic.
Black men took their place in the nation's executive offices, legislative
halls, and judicial chambers. The last was not first, but no longer last.

But the long shadow of slavery loomed over the new figure of universal
freedom. Old aspirations emerged and mixed with new hopes, enabling
freedpeople to envision a world turned upside down. The possibilities of
freedom in the New World glimpsed by the charter generation in the seventeenth and eighteenth centuries again hove into view. They were tempered by the remembrance of the plantation regime, which had crushed
that promise, and of the hopes rekindled in the Age of Revolutions, which
had seen so many people of African descent escape servitude to an imperfect freedom and so many more condemned to an even more burdensome
bondage.

Such memories forced black people to draw upon their past. As they
did, the diversity of the ideologies African Americans had formed during
the nearly three centuries of captivity became manifest. Some ideas derived from the North, where black men and women marooned in the free
states took the central tenet of the revolutionary age and expanded it into
a powerful claim to a full place in American society. Their persistent pleas
that the American republic realize its first principle gained new urgency as
the nation was tested in civil war. Other ideas derived not from the activ-
ist tradition of the literate, liberated free people of color but from the
rough experience of the enslaved, most of whom had been denied access
to the written word. Their ideologies, though less polished, were no less
eloquent. They spoke to the desire of peoples who had worked the fields
of the South for nearly three centuries for landed independence and a
place where they might support themselves by their own labor, rebuild
their families, and enlarge their kin networks. They also reflected the de-

sire of black men and women who had been shuttled from place to place, hired to farmers and mechanics—sometimes seasonally, sometimes annually, and sometimes by the job—for a modicum of stability, for a home where they could enter the marketplace and sell their labor on their own terms.

These diverse experiences of generations of free people of color and slaves shaped the freedom generations' aspiration to become, in the words of one former slave, "a People."[2] The origins of that new people was as much a product of centuries of captivity as it was of the moment of emancipation, as former slaves drew upon their experience in slavery to create their new life in freedom.

REVOLUTION AND THE FUTURE

Even before the fighting began, black people sensed the possibilities of revolutionary change. In the North, free men of color organized volunteer militias to serve in a war they believed would bring the final end of slavery.[3] As befitted their condition, slaves in the South and West were more circumspect, in part because slaveholders—ever fearful of insurrection—enacted new, harsh regulations and enforced old ones with renewed enthusiasm. Bombarded with the slaveholders' warnings that the Yankees intended to despoil their homes and sell them to Cuba, slaves reasserted their devotion to their owners or, more commonly, kept their own counsel. "Are they stolidly stupid or wiser than we," fretted one slave mistress, fearful that her silent slaves were merely "biding their time." But not even the most impassive façades could disguise the fact that slaves were, as one white Alabaman observed, "very Hiley Hope up that they soon would be free."[4]

News of Lincoln's election, public discussion of southern secession, and evidence of Confederate mobilization caused some black men and women to act decisively. In March 1861, a month before the first shots at Fort Sumter, eight fugitive slaves presented themselves at Fort Pickens, a federal installation on the coast of Florida, "entertaining the idea"—in the words of the fort's commander—that federal forces "were placed here to protect them and grant them their freedom." The commander dismissed the claim, took them into custody, and turned them over to local officers "to be returned to their owners." But the ideas that stirred these men and women were much alive, even on the most isolated estates. Deep in the plantation interior far from tramping armies, slaves had gotten "the great impression" that there would be "a great upheaval of some kind."[5]

The dislocations that accompanied military mobilization set yet others in motion. For some, it was the new demands placed upon them, for the Confederate war effort required that slaves not only feed themselves and their owners but also build fortifications, drive wagons, chop wood, clean camps, and hundreds of other chores required for the defense of the new slaveholding republic. Thousands of slave men accompanied their masters to the warfront or were offered to Confederate quartermasters as part of their owners' contribution to the war effort. Thousands more slaves found themselves impressed into Confederate service, something that neither they nor their owners welcomed. To protect their slaves from impressment and to avoid the flight that often followed, many masters sequestered or—in the language of the day, "refugeed"—their slaves to some distant place that was, they believed, beyond the reach of both invading Yankees and intrusive Confederates. For slaves, such unwanted transfers evoked memories of the slave trade and forced the dissolution of families and friendships once again. Slaves wanted no part in yet another forced migration, and some fled at the rumor that they would be carried to Texas or an even more distant place. Others jumped train en route to their war-time homes or simply refused to move. Rather than lose the value of their property, some masters put their slaves on the auction block. The possibility of imminent sale, like refugeeing and impressment, became the occasion for slaves to recalculate the advantages of remaining on their old estate and the dangers that flight entailed.[6]

The unsettled circumstances that accompanied the arrival of federal troops on the periphery of the South in 1861 and 1862 deeply disturbed slaves and made them willing to take unprecedented risks. To be sure, runaways chanced harsh retribution, punitive sale, perhaps even death if recaptured, for many Confederate loyalists defined flight as treason. But the slaves' familiarity with the countryside, gleaned from their antebellum movement from job to job and from farm to town to city, gave them confidence they could find their way to federal encampments. With conditions on the plantations and farms deteriorating and the Union army within reach, some—mostly unattached young men—began to test their owners' assertions about Yankee abolitionism.

Most of the first fugitives met bitter disappointment, as they discovered that a few northern soldiers measured up to their owners' direct warnings. Eager to reassure wavering slaveholders, particularly in the border slave states, and to encourage unionism in the Confederacy, federal officers reiterated the Lincoln administration's determination not to tamper with slavery. But occasionally fugitive slaves found a safe harbor in federal encampments, some of which were garrisoned by abolitionists determined to put their principles into practice. More often, however, federal soldiers cared little about either slavery or the slaves themselves but gladly provided the safety of their encampments in exchange for the slaves' knowledge of the countryside and willingness to do the dirty work of the war as cooks, hostlers, and laundresses.

If exchanging information, labor, and food for protection was cheap and easy for invading northern soldiers, it was a bargain slaveholders deemed far too costly. They demanded and, with the aid of federal authorities, generally were granted the return of their wayward property. But the recapture of runaways also exacted a high price. Watching frightened men and women who had done nothing but assist them being dragged back to bondage and certain punishment offended federal soldiers. It transformed many into practical abolitionists. The process accelerated when these same slaves were put to work on Confederate fortifications. To Union soldiers, it was foolish in the extreme to decline the fugitives' assistance while the enemy was making full use of slave labor. They became increasingly reluctant to execute federal policy. Some simply refused to return fugitives and assaulted slaveholders who dared to claim the runaways, hounding them out of Union bivouacks in a hail of epithets and bric-a-brac.

In time, the logic of federal soldiers of the lowest ranks ascended the chain of command, finding a voice in General Benjamin F. Butler's question to Secretary of War Simon Cameron: shall the rebels "be allowed the use of this property against the United States, and we not be allowed to use them in aid of the United States"? As was his wont, Butler answered his own query, accepting fugitive slaves as "contraband of war" and placing black men and women to work in the Union cause. Cameron ratified Butler's action, and Congress affirmed it with the passage of the First Confiscation Act in August 1861, making all property used in support of the rebellion "subject to prize and capture."[7]

As the war entered its second year, slaves found the Confiscation Act a weak hook on which to hang their hopes for freedom, especially in the hands of hostile federal commanders. But they nonetheless continued to press their case, fleeing to federal lines in larger and larger numbers. When federal armies moved from the border slave states deeper into the South where most slaveholders were perceived as implacable foes, slaves found it increasingly easy to gain shelter within Union lines. Thousands fled to the Yankees, leaving slaveowners—employing the familiar animalistic analogies—to sputter about "the stampede."

Flight also became easier because the federal war effort had come to depend on the labor of former slaves. By the summer of 1862, tens of thousands of black men and women, almost all of them former slaves, constructed fortifications, drove wagons, chopped wood, cooked food, prepared camps, and nursed the sick and wounded for the federal army and navy. In July, recognizing the Union's dependence on black labor, Congress enacted the Second Confiscation Act and the Militia Act, authorizing the president to hire—for money wages—persons of African descent to suppress the rebellion and granting freedom to slaves so employed and to their immediate families. Within days of Congress's action, Lincoln issued an executive order instructing federal forces to "employ as laborers . . . so many persons of African descent as can be advantageously used for military and naval purposes." Then, trumping Congress, on July 22, Lincoln informed his cabinet of his intention to issue a proclamation of general emancipation. At the cabinet's recommendation, Lincoln withheld his public announcement until the occasion of a Union victory. The battle of Antietam, while hardly a stirring triumph, sufficed, and Lincoln acted. On September 22, 1862, President Lincoln promulgated the preliminary emancipation proclamation, serving notice that on January first he would declare all slaves in the states still in rebellion "thenceforth, and forever free."[8]

Under the congressional and presidential edicts issued in the summer of 1862, thousands more black men and women entered into Union lines and secured their freedom. Increasingly they arrived not singly but in family groups, often comprising several generations. Once inside federal lines, many organized themselves in quasi-military style and, led by family elders, returned to their old neighborhoods to retrieve yet other relatives and friends from slavery.[9] During the summer of 1862, the trickle of fugitives turned into a flood.

Trying to prevent the massive influx from overwhelming federal resources, Union officials established "contraband camps" for the former slaves. The army chaplains and missionaries who supervised the hastily constructed enclaves greeted the newly arrived slaves with guarantees that they no longer would be punished by the lash, that men and women who worked for the army would be paid wages, that their families would not be subject to sale, and that they could worship as they pleased. Freedpeople welcomed the retirement of the lash, assurances that they would no longer stand helpless while a spouse was abused or a child battered, and promises that their spirituality would not be insulted by a doctrine of obedience to earthly masters. But when the camp superintendents plied them with axioms about the relationship of cleanliness and godliness, godliness and chastity, chastity and property accumulation, and all to regular labor, they found that freedpeople had their own ideas.

Camp life exuded the freedpeople's "spirit of liberty" and with it their belief that work should not be coerced but compensated and that simple justice gave them equity in the land they had worked as slaves. Although often disorderly and disease ridden, the camps provided black men and women with "a feeling that they are no longer slaves, but hired laborers; and that they demanded to be treated as such." It created "a new sense of independence" that could not be ignored. When it was ignored, according to one federal officer, there was "trouble, and the negroes band together, and lay down their own rules."[10] The "rules" which governed the quarter in slavery now guided black people in freedom.

In search of that "new sense of independence," many former slaves left the camps. Taking up positions in the no-man's land between Union and Confederate lines, some returned to their old plantations after their owners had fled or squatted on abandoned estates. Although they expropriated comforts aplenty—often liberating furniture from the Big House and provisions from their masters' cellars—they faced new dangers. Confederate soldiers raided these estates with regularity and took great pleasure in returning black men and women to bondage. Nonetheless, the precarious independence afforded by the abandoned plantations allowed black men and women the opportunity to reorganize production to their own liking and rebuild their families. They grew crops that would feed themselves and their loved ones and bypassed those that had made their owners rich.

Some contracted with agents of the U.S. Treasury Department, who had been given responsibility to supervise such estates. Slave squatters welcomed the protection that accrued to plantations under federal control but frequently found the agents' obsession with cotton as irksome as that of their old owners. The conflicts that ensued escalated when the Treasury Department rented many of the abandoned plantations to northern entrepreneurs. These "new masters" adopted many of the methods of the old, as they too wished to maximize staple production. But, as freedpeople made clear, their desire to be free of planter control extended to all, whatever their origins.[11]

Nothing spoke more loudly of the freedpeople's aspirations than the schoolhouses that appeared "like mushrooms after a storm" among newly liberated slaves. Slaves and sometimes free blacks had been denied—by custom and often by law—the right to a formal education, and they believed access to the word to be an essential element of freedom as well as a practical means of self-advancement. Literacy would enable them to crack the secret code white men had used to enslave them. Newly freed slaves flocked to schools established by northern missionaries, who testified to the enthusiasm for education among former slaves. When denied school-

ing, freedpeople petitioned federal agents and missionaries for its establishment so they might "become a People capable of self support." And
when schools were not forthcoming—and sometimes even when they
were—freedpeople pooled their scant resources to hire teachers, build
schoolhouses, and establish libraries. Aspirations long pent up in slavery
burst into the open.[12]

Like the camps and the abandoned plantations, military service offered
former slaves an opportunity to realize their own idea of freedom. Although a few irregular black units had been established in South Carolina,
Louisiana, and Kansas prior to the Emancipation Proclamation, the vast
majority of black men in federal service shouldered shovels, drove teams,
and built fortifications, affirming the belief of most white northerners that
soldiering was white man's work. When Lincoln's proclamation offered
the possibility that black men might be regularly enlisted in the federal
army, northern black leaders fanned out over the free states to enlist them,
boldly asserting—in Frederick Douglass's words—that once "the black
man gets upon his person the brass letters, U.S. . . . he has earned the
right to citizenship in the United States."[13]

Black men needed little encouragement. Free or slave, they ached for
the opportunity to strike a blow at slavery and even scores with the master
class. During the first months of 1863, black northerners had their chance,
and they rushed to enlist in regiments established by the governors of
Massachusetts, Connecticut, and Rhode Island. By late spring, the New
England regiments had taken to the field and slaves had their opportunity
to enlist. In April the abolitionist general Edward A. Wild began recruiting his "African Brigade" from the largely slave population of tidewater
North Carolina and Virginia. Former slave men seized the moment,
dropped the façade that had often masked their contest with their owners, and rushed to a direct confrontation. Thereafter, most of the black
enlistees were former slaves.

In May, the federal government created the Bureau of Colored Troops,
and federal recruitment officers moved into the lower Mississippi Valley
where the bulk of the slave population resided. By year's end they had enlisted thirty regiments of black soldiers, and that was but the beginning.

Over 200,000 black men—most of them former slaves—served as soldiers and sailors in the federal army and navy during the Civil War. That number amounted to about one fifth of the black men of military age in the United States, and a much higher proportion in the North and parts of the South under Union control.[14]

Military service became the surest solvent of slavery. As federal troops advanced into the Mississippi Valley, Union officers transformed captured plantations into recruiting stations. In one sweeping motion, they freed slaves, transported women and children to contraband camps, and enlisted men. Although the number of black recruits was smaller in the border states, the proportion of black men who enlisted was larger, and military service proved particularly important in the destruction of slavery, as it extended the commitment to freedom to areas of the South untouched by the liberating provisions of the Emancipation Proclamation. But everywhere black men relished the opportunity to be liberators of their people. Once enlisted, they insisted their families be freed whether or not they were entitled to freedom by various wartime edicts, a stipulation Congress affirmed in March 1865. Before long, it seemed that all black people were related.[15]

Military service was not only a door by which black people exited slavery but also a portal to citizenship. Fighting and dying for the Union advanced black soldiers' claims and those of all African Americans to full membership in American society. Their sense of entitlement to the rights of citizens grew with military service. "We cam out to be true union soldiers the Grandsons of Mother Africa Never to Flinch from Duty," and thus black men in uniform fully expected to be treated as other Americans. Victory over those who had previously dominated their lives bred a sense of pride which touched the entire black community. While black people reveled in the battlefield derring-do of "their men" at Fort Wagner, Port Hudson, and Milliken's Bend, soldiering also provided practical lessons in the rights of citizenship and how to secure them. Promised all the rights and privileges of American soldiers, black men—free as well as slave—found they were paid less than white soldiers, denied commissions as officers, and forced to dig while others fought. Black soldiers and their families viewed these discriminatory and exclusionary policies as breaches of faith and launched massive protests. The campaign for equal pay was particularly significant in this regard, as it mobilized newly emancipated slaves as well as free blacks. The sense of empowerment that derived from political as well as military mobilization—and the eventual success of both—contributed to the conviction that, at last, history was on their side.[16]

The army was literally a school for freedom in other ways as well, for, like the contraband camps, nearly every regimental encampment had its own school. In the words of one chaplain, the "cartridge box and spelling book are attached to the same belt." But the process of educating soldiers for citizenship also proceeded outside the regimental classroom. As slaves, black people had been governed by a single all-powerful white man. While powerful, imperious white men aplenty could be found in the federal officers corps, none could claim singular and personal sovereignty over soldiers. Instead, like all soldiers, black men under arms were governed by detailed rules that regulated every aspect of military service. Military law forbade officers from tyrannizing their subordinates, distinguishing "lawful orders" and punishments from personal and arbitrary ones. Understanding the code of military conduct could be an enormous advantage for soldiers, just as understanding the law was for citizens. In learning to navigate the maze of regulations that governed military life and the countless procedures to implement those regulations, former slaves took their place as citizens of the republic and understood that superiors and subordinates alike answered to a higher law. For slave-men-turned-soldiers, military service provided a way station between chattel bondage and citizenship.[17]

As black soldiers confronted their former masters directly on the field of battle, black men and women far from the warfront opened their own assault on slavery. Unable to flee to Union lines because of distance or circumstance, slaves on the farms and plantations of the southern interior nonetheless undermined the old order, employing the traditional weapons of opposition with unprecedented success. As news of the failure of southern armies filtered back from the war after 1862—carried by refugeed slaves, servants of furloughed Confederate soldiers, or the ubiquitous "grapevine telegraph"—slaveowners found that slaves shirked their duties and became increasingly intractable workers. Although they collected their rations as usual, slaves disappeared when needed in the fields. Increased truancy and the slaves' sullen and sometimes violent resistance to customary discipline reduced Confederate agricultural and industrial productivity and threw the plantation into turmoil. Often slaves simply tended their garden plots and provision grounds, "working," according to one planter, "only as they see fit." Women seemed especially determined to break with the old regime. "The females," he observed, "have quit entirely or nearly so."[18]

The ongoing contest between master and slave took on new moment, as the processes by which slaveowners had escalated demands on their slaves were suddenly thrown into reverse. Long-established understandings—the definition of the stint, the character of the task, the pace of work, and length of the workday—unraveled as slaves demanded a reconsideration. When these matters appeared settled, others came to the fore, as slaves pressed for the removal of overseers and the cessation of corporal punishment. With the young white men who had previously disciplined slaves serving the Confederacy on some distant battlefield, the white residents who remained on the estates—disproportionately women and elderly men—discovered that slaves challenged the very essence of servitude, demanding compensation for their labor. Trying to maintain the tattered remnants of their authority, exasperated slaveowners reluctantly yielded, put aside the lash, and even promised a great present at year's end. But token concessions and the language of paternalism no longer carried much weight in the quarter.

As the Union army grew closer, slaves enlarged their demands and became more aggressive in pursuing them. The old order crumbled amid the slaveowners' complaints of "demoralization," a charge that might mean anything from the refusal of slaves to go to the field to the failure to tip a hat. Planters who prided themselves in their knowledge of the "negro character" discovered the shallowness of their understanding, as the men and women who had appeared to be most devoted to their owners were among the first to throw down their tools and leave the plantation. Having gone through a long series of negotiations with his slaves, one Tennessee planter concluded that the institution of slavery was "worthless" and simply abandoned his estate. Others, trying to salvage what they could, entered into share agreements, allowing their slaves a portion of the crop in return for remaining at work.

Such strategic retreats were often the better part of valor. Where planters refused to recognize the new balance of power, slaves broke tools, burned barns, raided larders, and turned the system of terror that had long been employed against them onto their owners. After the manager of the Magnolia plantation in southern Louisiana dismissed the slaves' claim for wages, the slaves erected a gallows within the shadow of the Big House. Learning that they intended "hang their master [so] that they will be free," the managers paid and fled.[19]

Slavery collapsed under the pounding of federal troops from the outside and the subversion of plantation-bound black men and women from the inside. By war's end, the old order was in disarray, even in areas where the Union army was not present to enforce emancipation. The freedom generation had earned its name. Ties of kinship, common experience, and shared aspirations had created powerful bonds of solidarity that allowed black men and women to act in concert. Through their long history in bondage, with constant negotiation and renegotiation of the terms of servitude, they constructed the shared understanding—if not the institutional structure—that enabled them to seize their freedom when the moment arrived. Whether in flight from their owners, soldiering in the Union army, protesting unequal pay, or demanding compensation for their labor, black people drew upon their collective experience in negotiating with their old masters to address their new liberators. The revolution of emancipation had begun.

REVOLUTION AND THE PAST

The revolution was as much about the past as it was about the future. While the radical new circumstances that accompanied wartime emancipation presaged change, the new society that black people created in freedom bore the markings of the old. Former slaves and free people of color gladly jettisoned the practices that had been forced upon them by their owners and happily dismissed conventions that defined their relationship to white people. But there was much of their old lives that they wanted to preserve and, if possible, enlarge. Rather than create something new, former slaves and free people of color openly practiced that which had previously been forbidden. As they did, clandestine relationships emerged from the shadows and freedpeople grafted their vision of free society formed in slave times onto the new circumstances. Rather than disappear, the old ways gained new life with emancipation, as time after time black men and women called upon their experience in slavery to help them construct their lives in freedom. For black people, the new society that emerged from slavery bore the marks of the generations of captivity.

What one officer of the Freedmen's Bureau, the federal agency established to oversee the transition from slavery to freedom, called "a small matter" revealed how freedpeople stitched attire suitable for free men and women out of the garments they once wore as slaves. Writing from up-country South Carolina, he noted that "it had been the custom, heretofore, for the negro to take the surname of the master." With the collapse of slavery, many "refused to do this, but instead have selected the surnames of other planters in the vicinity, and some quite remote." He surmised that the renaming represented "the feeling on the part of the negro and a determination to change their employers." Some years later, a former slave provided a fuller explication, recalling "us'n changed our names, so effen the white folks get together and change their minds and don't let us be free any more, then they have a hard time finding us."[20]

Indeed for many freedpeople the naming or renaming process was as much about reclaiming what they and their forebears had made in slavery as creating something new in freedom. Following an ancient tradition, some identified themselves with trades or skills, taking surnames—or "titles," as black people called them—like Barber, Cooper, Carpenter, Smith, or Taylor. Others ennobled themselves with the name King or Prince. While still others called themselves Black or Brown—markers of the obvious—others took the name White, perhaps presuming that the privileges of color would follow the name. Place names also came into vogue among former slaves, as some adopted the names of great cities like Paris or London. Boston, the center of the abolitionist movement, became a special favorite. So too did patriotic names. Franklins, Jeffersons, and Jacksons flourished among the ex-slaves. No one thought it unusual to have a black George Washington addressing an Abraham Lincoln. As freedom enlarged the slaves' world, the cosmopolitanism that marked the names of members of the charter generation reappeared.

Freedom allowed yet other former slaves to display a long-concealed appellation. Freedpeople employed names openly that had previously been spoken only among themselves. Many of these titles had long, furtive histories. Digging deep into their own past, freedpeople had used these ancient titles to connect themselves to their ancestors and reestablish lineages shattered by enslavement. Freedom was as much about restoring that which had been suppressed and publicly denied as about inventing something new.[21]

The same spirit that pushed former slaves to take a new name sent them in search of a new residence. As slaves, black people—especially in the southern interior—had been tied to their owners and bound to particular plantations. They could travel only with special permission documented by passes or, for free blacks, freedom papers. The ability to move at liberty and to live in a place of their own choosing was one of the rights freedpeople identified most closely with their new status. Many took special pleasure in leaving their erstwhile owners, especially abusive ones. Planters complained bitterly about the former slaves' abandonment, seeing such departures as not-so-subtle condemnations of their mastership. They viewed the freedpeople's comings and goings as evidence of the anarchy that accompanied freedom. Indeed, the extraordinary numbers of black men and women who took to the road alarmed Union officials as well. In the immediate aftermath of slavery's demise, federal officers put some places off limits to black people and instituted pass systems as stringent as any that existed during slavery.

But the freedpeople's movement was anything but anarchic. While their

bundles of bedding and stacks of household implements suggested vaga-
bondage, black people generally knew exactly where they were going.
Looking for a fresh start, many desired to escape the memories of slavery
and those who knew them only in servitude. Others searched for new opportunities. The chance for higher wages sent some westward; the lure of
a richer social life drew others cityward. Some went north, as the region
had long been identified with freedom. But some black northerners migrated south, as changes that accompanied the war made the South—with
its large black population—the new land of opportunity. The geographic
inversion was another signal of the changes in African-American life
set loose by emancipation, adding importance to the generations of captivity.[22]

But just as black people recovered their old names rather than manufacture new ones, many former slaves returned to their old residences and
neighborhoods rather than search for new homes. Massive wartime dislocations and refugeeing had separated thousands of black men and women
from the web of kinship in which they had long been enmeshed and from
the landscape they had come to love. By far the most common impetus to
post-war movement was the desire to reunite families and reconstruct
communities. Freedpeople filled newspaper columns with notices for family members, and every Sunday ministers read aloud pleas for information
about this child, that mother, or this father who had been deported to
parts unknown. Some former slaves traveled half a continent on the mere
possibility they might embrace a spouse or child who had been sold away
years before. Upon finding their loved ones or news of their loved ones'
fate, they turned toward home.

The effort to rebuild families also dated back into slavery. Martin Lee,
who had been sold from his first wife and other relatives in Georgia in
slave times, subsequently purchased his freedom and that of his mother
and his second wife. Emancipation enabled him to extend his efforts to
even more distant kin—not only his children and grandchildren but also
siblings, nieces, and nephews. In late 1866 Lee traveled from Alabama to
Georgia and "Got My Daughter and dear Children," but his "Sisters Son"
eluded him. When he found out that his nephew had been bound to a

former owner under the state's apprenticeship laws, he began the process all over again, appealing to the local Freedmen's Bureau agent and offering cash in return for the boy's release.[23]

Testing their new freedom roiled relations between freedpeople and the men and women who had known them only as slaves. Former masters did not accept the new circumstances easily, interpreting the freedpeople's actions as ingratitude or insolence. White nonslaveholders were similarly outraged as the distance between themselves and former slaves shriveled to nothing more than their white skin. Emancipation challenged habits of thought that had been centuries in the making, and it seemed that some would never forget. If newly freed slaves gloried at not having to tip their hat to every white man or yield the sidewalk to every white woman, white people lamented the demise of these rituals of superiority. Many smoldered silently at slights of commission or omission, but others exploded in violence. A simple breach of sidewalk etiquette—the failure to yield the wall or employ the right intonation—might detonate deadly confrontations. The violence that accompanied emancipation led both black and white to withdraw into separate worlds.

For black people, such separation provided the occasion to rediscover their special history and reclaim their unique heritage. The independence of the slave quarter—its distinctive language, music, beliefs, and patterns of leadership—blossomed with the emergence of black schools, fraternal associations, benevolent societies, and, most importantly, churches. These institutions enjoyed a fragile, often furtive existence prior to the war or, in the case of the biracial churches, confined black people to a subordinate role that only generously could be classified as second-class citizenship.

But the massive exodus from the biracial churches trod along a familiar path. Like so many other institutions of freedom, the black churches followed a trail that had been hewed during slavery, sometimes inheriting the buildings and almost always the leadership, denominational affiliations, and theologies formed prior to the war. Like the names freedpeople took and the families they reconstructed, the churches black people created were often those of the old order, purged of the constraints of slavery. Indeed, missionaries who tried to alter the established patterns of worship found black people "were not anxious to see innovations introduced in religious worship."[24] The brush arbor had come in from the cold.

Nothing so demonstrated the continuity between the old and new religious orders—as well as the changes that accompanied freedom—than disputes over the ownership of church property. During the years prior to the war, as slaves and free people of color struggled to control their own religious life, they purchased the buildings in which they worshipped, often from white congregations who abandoned them as too small, too old, or too unworthy of the congregation's aspirations. Although black congregants paid cash for these discarded structures, the deeds were generally held by white trustees, as slaves had no legal right to property. With freedom, most trustees quietly transferred ownership to the black members. But some resisted. In a dispute that typified many others, in 1865 the leaders of the Colored Methodist Church of Portsmouth, Virginia, reported that "the Color people themselves paid nearly $5000" for the building in which they worshipped. With freedom, black congregants seceded from the Methodist Church South, elected their own trustees, and replaced the former minister, a white man who professed "affection for their race" but who had declared "That it was no more sin to sell a 'Nigger' baby from its Mother than it was to sell a calf from a cow." White trustees objected and refused to relinquish the deed to the church, which they held since "by the laws of state of Virginia white men only can act as trustees of colored churches." The controversy was lengthy, eventually finding its way from the local Freedom's Bureau office to the national headquarters, where it remained unresolved in 1866.[25]

Separation on Sunday morning thus did not come easily, but separation in the workplace proved far more difficult if not impossible. From the first, black people claimed the right to the land they had worked, in some places for centuries. Traveling in the South prior to the war, Frederick Law Olmsted discovered that the "agrarian notion . . . formed a fixed point of the negro system of ethics: that the result of labour must of right belong to the labourer." The treason of former owners and wartime confiscations of Confederate property—indeed, the creation of the Freedmen's Bureau (its full name was the Bureau of Refugees, Freedmen, and

Abandoned Lands)—encouraged former slaves to believe that the federal government would expropriate their owners' property and give them access to land. The idea of "forty acres and a mule" gained enormous force among former slaves, fueling anticipation that land would soon be theirs. By the end of 1865, even explicit denials by President Andrew Johnson and the highest ranking officers of the army and Freedmen's Bureau failed to dissuade former slaves.[26]

In the years that followed, freedpeople developed a variety of schemes to gain access to land of their own. In some places they pooled their resources, creating buying co-ops to purchase land. Elsewhere they traded labor for land. They also continued to call upon the federal government to do what they considered justice in this critical matter. Writing from Elizabeth City, North Carolina, in December 1867, freedpeople requested the passage of a law enabling them to purchase small farms, on reasonable terms, "taken from Rebel Estates or Public Lands," adding that the proceeds from the sales "should be appropriated to establish Common Schools for this State in order that our *Children may learn to read, understand and obey the Laws of theirs Country.*"[27]

But as the evidence mounted that the promise would not be kept and land and other productive resources would not pass from their former owners to them, freedpeople reentered negotiations with their former owners over the terms on which they would work. To be sure, freedom changed the terrain of those negotiations, but the issues remained the same. The nature of the stint, the definition of the task, and the pace of labor remained as central to the struggle between black employees and white employers as they did among black slaves and white masters.

Even when the new circumstances of freedom created new issues, they mixed with old, familiar disputes. While freedpeople insisted upon compensation and the rights accorded other free men and women, the nature of that compensation and how those rights would be defined were deeply embedded in understandings inherited from slavery. Would compensation include rations, clothing, and shelter? When would wood lots and provision grounds be available? Who would bear responsibility for the elderly, the disabled, the very young, and others unable to work? Men and women who had once negotiated the ever-changing terms of slavery began to negotiate the ever-changing terms of freedom. Often those negotiations followed along lines established during slavery. For example, black men and women who had been hired or hired themselves as slaves in the Upper South continued the familiar negotiation with employers, although now in their own name. Likewise, freedpeople in the lowcountry built upon precedents drawn from the experience of task work, while those who operated the cane factories spoke of wages.

Such negotiations revealed the vast differences between former master and former slave. Freedpeople drew upon a work ethic honed by years of bondage. "We have [been] laboring for White people [all] of our lives [and] know nothing else but," an Alabama freedmen informed the Freedmen's Bureau in 1865. "We wish to make our liveing Honestly not for philfor and steal but to live upright in the fear of the lord." But many former masters doubted that black people would work without compulsion or would respond to the incentives of wage labor. Only grudgingly did many promise to do well by former slaves at year's end, and others would not concede compensation beyond food, clothing, and quarters "as heretofore." Freedpeople, for their part, assumed that their labor would be compensated—what else could freedom mean?—and that not only would they determine the price of their labor but they would set the conditions under which they would work. Such radically different expectations made the renegotiations of the terms of labor particularly difficult. Moreover, when former slaves and former slaveholders finally began to negotiate the terms of labor under the new regime, the issues that divided them only grew in complexity. Should remuneration be weekly, monthly, or annually, and should it be paid to individual workers or heads of household? What of the labor of women and children, the ability of freedpeople to forage their animals, and the all-important right to quit? Addressing these and many other matters, freedpeople often drew upon their experience as slaves and the negotiations with owners over precisely these questions of who worked, where, and how.[28]

Among the new weapons freedpeople brought to the struggle was a public voice. As slaves, black men and women were legally an extension of their masters' will, with no independent standing or avenue to register their opinions beyond supplications. But with the destruction of the masters' sovereignty, freedpeople gained a new place in society. No longer confined to the politics of personal domination, they demanded the right to testify in court, sit on juries, prove their accounts at law, vote, and even stand for office. Their claims, moreover, rested upon their service as laborers and soldiers who—in the face of the slaveowners' treachery—secured the survival of the nation. The moral power of those claims created the possibility of alliances with others who shared their allegiance to the Union. Grateful federal officials and an appreciative northern electorate stood high among these, but others had also opposed planter rule, among them white nonslaveholders and even some loyal slaveowners.

Black northerners, with their tradition of political activism, scored the first gains, as demands from black and white abolitionists bent the color-line toward equality. Various northern states repealed the black codes that barred entry of black immigrants, denied black men the right to serve on juries, and barred their testimony in court. In 1865 Massachusetts passed the first law requiring equal treatment of black men and women in public accommodations. With emancipation an accomplished fact and with tens of thousands of black men serving in the federal army and navy, pressure for black suffrage increased, although opposition remained intense.[29]

Black southerners were just a step behind their northern brethren in demanding their rights as citizens. In January 1865, even before the formal cessation of hostilities, the "colored citizens" of Nashville petitioned a convention of Tennessee unionists, claiming that their loyalty to the federal government and service in the war earned them suffrage. "The Government has asked the colored man to fight for its preservation and gladly he has done it," declared the petitioners. "It can afford to trust him with the vote as it trusted him with the bayonet." Before long, black people all over the former slave states echoed those demands in meetings, rallies, and conventions at which the freedpeople asserted their rights as Americans established by the Declaration and the Constitution, often joining the two documents as if they were one. "We think that the Constution of thease united States Sezs, that all its Cituzens Shall [possess] Life, Liberty and the Persutes of happyness," declared the "Color Citizens" of Apalachicola, Florida, in January 1866. "But We fear that we will Never get Justice in this Country, unless it is given by the U.S."[30]

Notions of justice—what was right and how the right was to be adjudicated—were central to the former slaves' idea of freedom, for they stood in stark contradiction to the arbitrary character of life in slavery. No longer subject to the whim of a master, black men and women demanded equal treatment. "We have come out Like men & we Expected to be Treeated as men," declared a group of black soldiers, "but we have bin Treeated more Like Dogs then men." No longer would black people be reduced to animals. "They dont grant us to have any testimony in court . . . or government but to Be ruled like mules and oxens some thing unto Slavery," a Georgia freedmen wrote to President Andrew Johnson. "If we have no testimony in court how will we Ever Become a people of tyhe united States with the full rights and protections of the government and of the national Council." Freedpeople answered that question by calling for a color-blind justice. When such equality was not forthcoming they returned to the Declaration of Independence, observing that "this is not the pursuit of happiness." Again and again, they drew upon their understanding of the right from the wrong of slavery. "These rebels wont give us Justice No. How they abuse us. and use us like Slaves. We are free and will Die will be treated."[31]

Yet even on the radically altered political terrain of freedom much remained the same. Leadership within the freedpeople's own ranks drew upon familiar sources. Men and women who had secured elevated positions during slave times maintained their place atop black society. Many of these had long enjoyed freedom, and their education, property, experience, and connections with whites assured an elevated place within African-American society. Among the most important of these were black northerners, some of whom came south as Union soldiers, Christian missionaries, and school teachers. They arrived carrying their tradition of political activism, their hatred of slavery, and a strong desire to create an egalitarian society. But along with their idealism and practical knowledge often came very different notions of the meaning of freedom and the best ways to attain it.[32]

The formerly free and the formerly slave were just two among many who claimed to know the true interests of black people. The urban and the rural, the skilled and the unskilled, the literate and the illiterate, the propertied and the impoverished each believed that their own experience best represented the experience of former slaves and former free people of color. Differences soon manifested themselves not only on the specific questions of land, labor, civil rights, and social equality but also in strikingly different political style and social sensibilities. Diverse commitments and beliefs scattered black men and women across the post-war political landscape. Once freedom was secured, there was hardly anything they agreed upon. If freedom was slavery's negation, then freedom had many meanings because slavery had many meanings.[33]

Soon after the war ended, events on the Sea Islands off the coast of South Carolina revealed how the terrain of freedom was defined as much by generations spent in captivity as by moments spent in freedom. In the summer of 1865, speaking to an audience of former lowcountry slaves, Major Martin Delany, a militant black abolitionist whose commission made him the highest-ranking black officer in the Union army, articulated a vision of the post-emancipation world familiar to black northerners but utterly strange to former plantation slaves. Speaking in the language of self-improvement and social advancement, he urged the former slaves to "cultivate Rice and Cotton." "1 Acre will grow a crop of cotton of 90—now a land with 10 Acres will bring $900 every year," he calculated as he painted a portrait of former slaves grown rich on the profits of staple production. Keep your "fields in good order and well tilled and planted," Delany assured them, and the wealth of their former owners would be theirs.

The concern for order in the fields and the profits of staple production were hardly foremost for the Committee on Behalf of the People, which emerged several months later in the political revolution that accompanied freedom on the Sea Islands. Rather than calculating the profitability of

cotton and rice, the committee made the case for landed independence—
the "promised Homesteads"—in terms of "getting land enough to lay our
Fathers bones upon." That striking figure spoke to the desire of plantation
slaves to secure not just any land but *their* land, meaning specifically the
land that they and their forebears had worked and in the process made
part of themselves. It was not the hope of social mobility and a vision of
opulence that animated the former slaves for whom the committee spoke.
Rather, the committee articulated the freedpeople's desire to secure a competency and live on their own surrounded by their families. Delany's
speech was greeted warmly by the former slaves who strained to see a
black man wearing an officer's stripes, but his vision of freedom was foreign to men and women who had spent their lives in slavery.[34]

The different meanings that an urban free person of color and rural former slaves attributed to land were only one manifestation of the political
differences among black people as they gained the vote and took their
places in legislative, judicial, and occasionally executive offices. Whether
they pressed for civil rights or mechanic lien laws, access to land or to
public accommodations, their actions reflected the generations of captivity as well as the revolutionary changes that accompanied emancipation.
The freedom generation could no more escape its past than previous generations of black men and women. Like those who came before them,
they too had no desire to deny their history, only to transform it in the
spirit of the revolutionary possibilities presented by emancipation. Their
successes—and failures—would resonate into the twenty-first century.

Table 1. Slave Population of the American Colonies and the United States, 1680–1860 (% of total population)

Region and colony/state	1680[a]	1700[a]	1720[a]	1750[a]	1770[a]	1790[n]	1810[p]	1820	1840	1860
NORTH	1,895 (2)	5,206 (4)	14,081 (5)	30,172 (5)	47,735 (4)	40,420 (2)	27,081 (2)	19,108 (<1)	1,113 (<1)	64 (<1)
New Hampshire	75 (4)	130 (3)	170 (2)	550 (2)	654 (1)	158 (<1)	0	0	1 (<1)	0
Vermont	—	—	—	—	25 (<1)	16 (<1)	0	0	0	0
Massachusetts	170 (<1)	800 (1)	2,150 (2)	4,075 (2)	4,754 (2)	0	0	0	0	0
Connecticut	50 (<1)	450 (2)	1,093 (2)	3,010 (3)	5,698 (3)	2,764 (1)	310 (<1)	97 (<1)	17 (<1)	0
Rhode Island	175 (6)	300 (5)	543 (5)	3,347 (10)	3,761 (6)	948 (1)	108 (<1)	48 (<1)	5 (<1)	0
New York	1,200 (12)	2,256 (12)	5,740 (16)	11,014 (14)	19,062[f] (12)	21,324 (6)	15,017 (<1)	10,088 (1)	4 (<1)	0
New Jersey	200 (6)	840 (6)	2,385 (6)	5,354 (7)	8,220 (7)	11,423 (6)	10,851 (4)	7,557 (3)	674 (<1)	18 (<1)
Pennsylvania	25 (4)	430 (2)	2,000 (8)	2,822[f] (2)	5,561[f] (2)	3,787 (1)	795 (<1)	211 (<1)	64 (<1)	0
Ohio	—	—	—	—	—	—	0	0	3 (<1)	0
Indiana	—	—	—	—	—	—	—	190 (<1)	3 (<1)	0
Illinois	—	—	—	—	—	—	—	917 (2)	331 (<1)	0
Maine	—	—	—	—	—	—	—	—	0	0
Michigan	—	—	—	—	—	—	—	—	0	0

Minnesota	—	—	—	—	—	—	—	—	0
Iowa	—	—	—	—	—	—	—	—	0
Wisconsin	—	—	—	—	—	—	—	— 11 (<1)	0
Kansas	—	—	—	—	—	—	—	—	2 (<1)
Oregon	—	—	—	—	—	—	—	—	0
California	—	—	—	—	—	—	—	—	0
Nebraska	—	—	—	—	—	—	—	—	15
Colorado	—	—	—	—	—	—	—	—	0
Dakota	—	—	—	—	—	—	—	—	0
Nevada	—	—	—	—	—	—	—	—	0
New Mexico	—	—	—	—	—	—	—	—	0
Utah	—	—	—	—	—	—	—	—	29 (<1)
Washington	—	—	—	—	—	—	—	—	0
CHESAPEAKE/ UPPER SOUTH	4,876 (7)	20,752 (20)	42,749 (24)	171,846 (36)	322,854 (37)	520,969 (33)	810,423 (34)	965,514 (30)	1,215,497 (27)	1,530,229 (22)
Delaware	55 (5)	135 (5)	700 (12)	1,496 (5)	1,836 (5)	8,887 (15)	4,177 (6)	4,509 (6)	2,605 (3)	1,798 (2)
Maryland	1,611 (9)	3,227 (11)	12,499 (19)	43,450 (31)	63,818 (32)	103,036 (32)	111,502 (30)	107,397 (26)	89,737 (19)	87,189 (13)
Virginia	3,000 (7)	16,390[b] (28)	26,550[b] (30)	107,100[g] (46)	187,600[b] (42)	292,627 (39)	392,518 (40)	425,153 (40)	449,087 (36)	490,865 (31)
North Carolina	210 (4)	1,000[c] (4)	3,000[c] (14)	19,800 (27)	69,600 (35)	100,572 (26)	168,824 (30)	205,017 (32)	245,817 (33)	331,059 (33)
Kentucky	—	—	—	—	—	12,430 (16)	80,561 (20)	126,732 (22)	182,258 (23)	225,483 (20)

Region and colony/state	1680[a]	1700[a]	1720[a]	1750[a]	1770[a]	1790[n]	1810[p]	1820	1840	1860
Missouri	—	—	—	—	—	—	3,011 (14)	10,222 (15)	58,240 (15)	114,931 (10)
Tennessee	—	—	—	—	—	3,417 (10)	44,528 (18)	80,107 (19)	183,059 (22)	275,719 (25)
District of Columbia	—	—	—	—	—	—	5,395 (23)	6,377 (19)	4,694 (11)	3,185 (4)
LOWCOUNTRY/ LOWER SOUTH	200 (17)	3,000 (36)	11,828 (60)	39,900 (57)	92,178 (58)	136,932 (41)	303,234 (46)	408,129 (48)	633,699 (47)	926,349 (49)
South Carolina	200 (17)	3,000[d] (44)	11,828[d] (64)	39,000 (61)	75,178 (61)	107,094 (43)	196,365 (47)	258,475 (51)	327,038 (55)	402,406 (57)
Georgia	—	—	—	600[h] (20)	15,000[h] (45)	29,264 (35)	105,218 (42)	149,654 (44)	280,944 (41)	462,198 (44)
East Florida	—	—	—	300[j] (13)	2,000[k] (67)	574[o] (26)	1,651[o] (54)	—	—	—
Florida	—	—	—	—	—	—	—	?	25,717 (47)	61,745 (44)
LOWER MISSISSIPPI VALLEY/ DEEP SOUTH	—	—	1,385 (36)	4,730 (60)	7,100	18,700 (52)	51,748 (47)	145,394 (39)	637,130 (45)	1,497,118 (43)
Louisiana	—	—	1,385[c] (36)	4,730[j] (60)	5,600[l]	18,700[l] (52)	34,660 (50)	69,064 (45)	168,452 (48)	331,726 (47)
West Florida	—	—	?	?	1,500[m] (27)	?	?	—	—	—
Alabama	—	—	—	—	—	—	—	41,879 (33)	253,532 (43)	435,080 (45)

Mississippi	—	—	—	—	?	17,088 (42)	32,814 (43)	195,211 (52)	436,631 (55)	
Arkansas	—	—	—	—	—	—	1,617 (11)	19,935 (20)	111,115 (26)	
Texas	—	—	—	—	—	—	—	—	182,566 (30)	
MAINLAND	6,971	28,958	70,043	246,648	469,867[m]	717,021	1,192,486	1,538,145	2,487,439	3,953,760

a. Unless otherwise indicated, populations are drawn from U.S. Bureau of the Census, *Historical Statistics of the United States, Colonial Times to 1970,* 2 vols. (Washington, DC, 1975), 2: 1168.

b. Douglas B. Chambers, "'He Is an African but Speaks Plain': Historical Creolization in Eighteenth-Century Virginia," in Alusine Jalloh and Stephen E. Maizlish, eds., *Africa and the African Diaspora* (College Station, TX, 1996), 110.

c. Marvin L. Michael Kay and Lorin Lee Cary, *Slavery in Colonial North Carolina: 1748–1775* (Chapel Hill, 1995), 307 n13 (1700) and 19 (1720).

d. Peter H. Wood, *Black Majority: Negroes in Colonial South Carolina from 1670 through the Stono Rebellion* (New York, 1974), 152.

e. 1726: Daniel H. Usner, Jr., *Indians, Settlers, and Slaves in a Frontier Exchange Economy: The Lower Mississippi Valley before 1783* (Chapel Hill, 1992), 49.

f. Gary B. Nash and Jean R. Soderlund, *Freedom by Degrees: Emancipation in Pennsylvania and Its Aftermath* (New York, 1991). 7.

g. Allan Kulikoff, "A 'Prolifick' People: Black Population Growth in the Chesapeake Colonies, 1700–1790," *Southern Studies,* 16 (1977). 45.

h. Betty Wood, *Slavery in Colonial Georgia, 1730–1775* (Athens, GA, 1984), 89.

i. Peter H. Wood, Gregory A. Waselkov, and M. Thomas Hatley, eds., *Powhatan's Mantle: Indians in the Colonial Southeast* (Lincoln, NE, 1989), 38.

j. Gwendolyn Midlo Hall, *Africans in Colonial Louisiana: The Development of Afro-Creole Culture in the Eighteenth Century* (Baton Rouge, 1992), 177.

k. 1775: J. Leitch Wright, Jr., "Blacks in British East Florida," *Florida Historical Quarterly* 54 (1976), 427.

l. 1776, 1788: Paul F. Lachance, "The Politics of Fear: French Louisiana and the Slave Trade, 1786–1809," *Plantation Society* 2 (1979), 196.

m. 1774: Usner, *Indians, Settlers, and Slaves,* 112.

n. Unless otherwise indicated, 1790 populations are drawn from *Return of the Whole Number of Persons within the Several Districts of the United States* (Philadelphia, 1791).

o. Jane L. Landers, "Traditions of African American Freedom and Community in Spanish Colonial Florida," in David R. Colburn and Jane L. Landers, eds., *The African American Heritage of Florida* (Gainesville, FL, 1995), 37 n11.

p. Unless otherwise indicated, 1810 populations are drawn from *Aggregate Amount of Persons within the United States in the Year 1810* (Washington, DC, 1811). 1820–1840 populations are drawn from *Population of the United States in 1860* (Washington, DC, 1864), 598–604.

Table 2. Free Black Population of United States, 1790–1820

Region and state	1790[a]			1810[b]			1820[c]		
	Free black population	Total black population	Free blacks as % of black population	Free black population	Total black population	Free blacks as % of black population	Free black population	Total black population	Free blacks as % of black population
NORTH	27,109	67,479	40	78,181	105,691	74	99,281	118,389	84
New Hampshire	630	788	80	970	970	100	786	786	100
Vermont	255	272	94	750	750	100	903	903	100
Massachusetts	5,463	5,463	100	6,737	6,737	100	6,740	6,740	100
Connecticut	2,801	5,560	50	6,453	6,763	95	7,844	7,941	99
Rhode Island	3,469	4,421	79	3,609	3,717	97	3,554	3,602	99
New York	4,654	25,978	18	25,333	40,350	63	29,279	39,367	74
New Jersey	2,762	14,185	20	7,843	18,694	42	12,460	20,017	62
Pennsylvania	6,537	10,274	64	22,492	23,287	97	30,202	30,413	99
Ohio	—	—	—	1,899	1,899	100	4,723	4,723	100
Indiana	—	—	—	393	630	62	1,230	1,420	87
Illinois	—	—	—	613	781	79	457	1,374	33
Maine	538	538	100	969	969	100	929	929	100
Michigan	—	—	—	120	144	83	174	174	100
CHESAPEAKE/ UPPER SOUTH	30,158	551,327	6	94,085	904,608	10	114,070	1,079,584	11
Delaware	3,899	12,786	30	13,136	17,313	76	12,958	17,467	74
Maryland	8,043	111,079	7	33,927	145,429	23	39,730	147,127	27
Virginia	12,766	306,193	4	30,570	423,088	7	36,889	462,042	8
North Carolina	4,975	105,547	5	10,266	179,090	6	14,612	219,629	7

Kentucky	114	11,944	1	1,713	82,274	2	2,759	129,491	2
Missouri	—	—	—	607	3,618	17	347	10,569	3
Tennessee	361	3,778	10	1,317	45,852	3	2,727	82,834	3
District of Columbia	—	—	—	2,549	7,944	32	4,048	10,425	39
LOWCOUNTRY / LOWER SOUTH	2,199	139,131	2	6,355	309,589	2	8,589	416,727	2
South Carolina	1,801	108,895	2	4,554	200,919	2	6,826	265,301	3
Georgia	398	29,662	1	1,801	107,019	2	1,763	151,417	1
East Florida	?	574	?	?	1,651	?	—	—	—
LOWER MISSISSIPPI VALLEY	?	18,700	?	7,825	59,573	13	11,564	156,938	7
Louisiana	?	18,700	?	7,585	42,245	18	10,476	79,540	13
West Florida	?	?	?	?	?	?	—	—	—
Mississippi	?	?	?	240	17,328	1	458	33,272	1
Alabama	—	—	—	—	—	—	571	42,450	1
Arkansas	—	—	—	—	—	—	59	1,676	4
MAINLAND	59,466	776,637	8	186,446	1,379,461	14	233,504	1,771,638	13

a. 1790 populations are drawn from *Return of the Whole Number of Persons within the Several Districts of the United States* (Philadelphia, 1791).

b. 1810 populations are drawn from *Aggregate Amount of Persons within the United States in the Year 1810* (Washington, DC, 1811).

c. 1820 populations are drawn from *Population of the United States in 1860* (Washington, DC, 1864), 598–602.

Table 3. Free Black Population of United States, 1840–1860[a]

Region and state	1840			1860		
	Free black population	Total black population	Free blacks as % of black population	Free black population	Total black population	Free blacks as % of black population
NORTH	170,728	171,857	99	226,152	226,216	99
New Hampshire	537	538	99	494	494	100
Vermont	730	730	100	709	709	100
Massachusetts	8,669	8,669	100	9,602	9,602	100
Connecticut	8,105	8,122	99	8,627	8,627	100
Rhode Island	3,238	3,243	99	3,952	3,952	100
New York	50,027	50,031	99	49,005	49,005	100
New Jersey	21,044	21,718	97	25,318	25,336	99
Pennsylvania	47,854	47,918	99	56,949	56,949	100
Ohio	17,342	17,345	99	36,673	36,673	100
Indiana	7,165	7,168	99	11,428	11,428	100
Illinois	3,598	3,929	92	7,628	7,628	100
Maine	1,355	1,355	100	1,327	1,327	100
Michigan	707	707	100	6,799	6,799	100
Minnesota	—	—	—	259	259	100
Iowa	172	188	91	1,069	1,069	100
Wisconsin	185	196	94	1,171	1,171	100
Kansas	—	—	—	625	627	99
Oregon	—	—	—	128	128	100
California	—	—	—	4,086	4,086	100
Nebraska	—	—	—	67	82	82
Colorado	—	—	—	46	46	100
Dakota	—	—	—	0	0	—
Nevada	—	—	—	45	45	100
New Mexico	—	—	—	85	85	100
Utah	—	—	—	30	59	51
Washington	—	—	—	30	30	100

CHESAPEAKE / UPPER SOUTH	174,957	1,390,454	13	224,963	1,755,192	13
Delaware	16,919	19,524	87	19,829	21,627	92
Maryland	62,678	152,415	41	83,942	171,131	49
Virginia	49,852	498,939	10	58,042	548,907	11
North Carolina	22,732	268,549	8	30,463	361,522	8
Kentucky	7,317	189,575	4	10,684	236,167	5
Missouri	1,574	59,814	3	3,572	118,503	3
Tennessee	5,524	188,583	3	7,300	283,019	3
District of Columbia	8,361	13,055	64	11,131	14,316	78
LOWCOUNTRY / LOWER SOUTH	11,846	645,545	2	14,346	940,695	2
South Carolina	8,276	335,314	2	9,914	412,320	2
Georgia	2,753	283,697	1	3,500	465,698	<1
Florida	817	26,534	3	932	62,677	1
LOWER MISSISSIPPI VALLEY / DEEP SOUTH	29,372	666,502	4	22,609	1,519,727	1
Louisiana	25,502	193,954	13	18,647	350,373	5
Alabama	2,039	255,571	<1	2,690	437,770	<1
Mississippi	1,366	196,577	<1	773	437,404	<1
Arkansas	465	20,400	2	144	111,259	<1
Texas	—	—	–	355	182,921	<1
MAINLAND	386,303	2,873,758	13	488,070	4,441,830	11

a. 1840–1860 populations are drawn from *Population of the United States in 1860* (Washington, DC, 1864), 603–604.

ABBREVIATIONS

AH	*Agricultural History*
AHQ	*Alabama Historical Quarterly*
AHR	*American Historical Review*
AJLH	*American Journal of Legal History*
AR	*Alabama Review*
Catterall, ed., *Judicial Cases*	Helen Catterall, ed., *Judicial Cases Concerning American Slavery and the Negro*, 5 vols. (New York, 1926–1937)
CWH	*Civil War History*
Donnan, ed., *Slave Trade*	Elizabeth Donnan, ed., *Documents Illustrative of the Slave Trade to America*, 4 vols. (Washington, DC, 1930–1935)
EEH	*Explorations in Economic History*
FCHQ	*Filson Club Historical Quarterly*
FHQ	*Florida Historical Quarterly*
Freedom	Ira Berlin et al., eds., *Freedom: A Documentary History of Emancipation, 1861–1867* (Cambridge, UK, 1982–)
GHQ	*Georgia Historical Quarterly*

Gray, *So. Ag.*	Lewis Cecil Gray, *History of Agriculture in the Southern United States*, 2 vols. (Washington, DC, 1935)
HA	*History in Africa*
HAHR	*Hispanic American Historical Review*
HArch	*Historical Archeology*
HJ	*Historical Journal*
HJM	*Historical Journal of Massachusetts*
HMPEC	*Historical Magazine of the Protestant Episcopal Church*
IRSH	*International Review of Social History*
JAAHGS	*Journal of the Afro-American Historical and Genealogical Society*
JAH	*Journal of African History*
JAmH	*Journal of American History*
JEH	*Journal of Economic History*
JER	*Journal of the Early Republic*
JIH	*Journal of Interdisciplinary History*
JLS	*Journal of Legal Studies*
JNH	*Journal of Negro History*
JSH	*Journal of Social History*
JSL	Josiah Smith Letterbooks, Southern History Collection, University of North Carolina, Chapel Hill
JSoH	*Journal of Southern History*
JUH	*Journal of Urban History*
LC	Library of Congress, Washington, DC
LH	*Louisiana History*
LHist	*Labor History*
LHQ	*Louisiana Historical Quarterly*
LHR	*Law and History Review*
LP	Legislative Petition, Virginia State Library, Richmond
LS	*Louisiana Studies*
MHM	*Maryland Historical Magazine*
MHW	*Military History of the Southwest*

MVHR	*Mississippi Valley Historical Review*
NA	National Archives, Washington, DC
NGSQ	*National Geneological Society Quarterly*
NJH	*New Jersey History*
NY Documents	E. B. O'Callaghan, ed., *Documents Relative to the Colonial History of the State of New-York,* 15 vols. (Albany, 1853–1887)
NYGBR	*New York Genealogical and Biographical Register*
NYH	*New York History*
NYHQ	*New-York Historical Society Quarterly*
NY Manuscripts	E. B. O'Callaghan, ed., *Calendar of Historical Manuscripts in the Office of the Secretary of State, Albany, N.Y.* (Albany, 1865)
PAH	*Perspectives in American History*
PAPS	*Proceedings of the American Philosophical Society*
PH	*Pennsylvania History*
PMHB	*Pennsylvania Magazine of History and Biography*
PS	*Plantation Societies*
PSQ	*Political Science Quarterly*
RKHS	*Register of the Kentucky Historical Society*
Runaway Advertisements	Lathan A. Windley, comp., *Runaway Slaves Advertisements: A Documentary History from the 1730s to 1790,* 4 vols. (Westport, CN, 1983)
S&A	*Slavery and Abolition*
SCHM	*South Carolina Historical and Genealogical Magazine*
SCHS	South Carolina Historical Society, Charleston
SS	*Southern Studies*
SSH	*Social Science History*
T&C	*Technology and Culture*
THQ	*Tennessee Historical Quarterly*

VaHS   Virginia Historical Society, Richmond
VBHS   Virginia Baptist Historical Society,
        Richmond
VMHB   *Virginia Magazine of History and Biography*
WMQ   *William and Mary Quarterly,* 3rd series

NOTES

PROLOGUE: SLAVERY AND FREEDOM

1. *Freedom*, ser. 3, vol. 2:331–338.

2. Thomas Jefferson, *Notes on the State of Virginia* (New York, 1964), query xviii.

3. Claude Meillassoux, *Anthropologie de l'esclavage: le ventre de fer et argent* (Paris, 1986), translated as *The Anthropology of Slavery: The Womb of Iron and Gold*, trans. Alide Dasnois (Chicago, 1991), 99–100; Orlando Patterson, *Slavery and Social Death: A Comparative Study* (Cambridge, MA, 1982), 5–6; M. I. Finley, *Ancient Slavery and Modern Ideology* (New York, 1980), 74–75; Stanley M. Elkins, *Slavery: A Problem in American Institutional and Intellectual Life* (Chicago, 1959).

4. Keith Hopkins, *Conquerors and Slaves: Sociological Studies in Roman History*, 2 vols. (Cambridge, UK, 1978), 1:99; Moses I. Finley, "Slavery," *International Encyclopedia of the Social Sciences* (New York, 1968); Finley, *Ancient Slavery and Modern Ideology*, 79–80.

5. Anne Grant, *Memoirs of an American Lady* (New York, 1809), 26–29.

6. Frank Tannenbaum, *Slave and Citizen: The Negro in the Americas* (New York, 1946), 117.

7. Although they differ in their emphases, two particularly clear statements are

Richard S. Dunn, *Sugar and Slaves: The Rise of the Planter Class in the English West Indies, 1624–1713* (Chapel Hill, 1972), and Richard B. Sheridan, *Sugar and Slavery: An Economic History of the British West Indies, 1623–1775* (Baltimore, 1973).

8. Edmund S. Morgan, *American Slavery, American Freedom: The Ordeal of Colonial Virginia* (New York, 1975), ch. 13.

9. Russian serf masters mused that the bones of their serfs were black. Peter Kolchin, *Unfree Labor: American Slavery and Russian Serfdom* (Cambridge, MA, 1987), 170.

10. David Brion Davis, *The Problem of Slavery in the Age of Revolution, 1770–1823* (Ithaca, NY, 1975); Robin Blackburn, *The Overthrow of Colonial Slavery* (London, 1988); David Barry Gaspar and David Patrick Geggus, eds., *A Turbulent Time: The French Revolution and the Greater Caribbean* (Bloomington, IN, 1997).

11. *Freedom;* Eric Foner, *Nothing but Freedom: Emancipation and Its Legacy* (Baton Rouge, 1983); Thomas C. Holt, *The Problem of Freedom: Race, Labor and Politics in Jamaica and Britain, 1832–1938* (Baltimore, 1992); Frank McGlynn and Seymour Drescher, eds., *The Meaning of Freedom: Economics, Politics, and Culture after Slavery* (Pittsburgh, 1992); Frederick Cooper, Thomas C. Holt, and Rebecca J. Scott, *Beyond Slavery: Explorations of Race, Labor, and Citizenship in Postemancipation Societies* (Chapel Hill, 2000).

12. Michael A. Gomez, *Exchanging Our Country Marks: The Transformation of African Identities in the Colonial and Antebellum South* (Chapel Hill, 1998); Philip D. Morgan, *Slave Counterpoint: Black Culture in the Eighteenth-Century Chesapeake and Lowcountry* (Chapel Hill, 1998); Joanne Pope Melish, *Disowning Slavery: Gradual Emancipation and "Race" in New England, 1780–1860* (Ithaca, 1998); Robert Olwell, *Masters, Slaves, and Subjects: The Culture of Power in the South Carolina Low Country, 1740–1790* (Ithaca, 1998); Douglas R. Egerton, *He Shall Go Out Free: The Lives of Denmark Vesey* (Madison, 1999); Graham Russell Hodges, *Root and Branch: African Americans in New York and East Jersey, 1613–1863* (Chapel Hill, 1999); Thomas N. Ingersoll, *Mammon and Manon in Early New Orleans: The First Slave Society in the Deep South, 1718–1819* (Knoxville, 1999); Jane Landers, *Black Society in Spanish Florida* (Urbana, IL, 1999); Theresa A. Singleton, ed., *"I, Too, Am American": Archeological Studies of African-American Life* (Charlottesville, 1999); David Eltis, *The Rise of African Slavery in the Americas* (Cambridge, UK, 2000) along with Eltis, Stephen D. Behrendt, David Richardson, and Herbert S. Klein, *The Transatlantic Slave*

Trade: A Database on CD-ROM (Cambridge, UK, 1999); Peter Linebaugh and Marcus Rediker, *The Many-Headed Hydra: Sailors, Slaves, Commoners, and the Hidden History of the Revolutionary Atlantic* (Boston, 2000); Judith A. Carney, *Black Rice: The African Origins of Rice Cultivation in the Americas* (Cambridge, MA, 2001); Kenneth Morgan, *Slavery and Servitude in Colonial North America: A Short History* (New York, 2001); Linda M. Heywood, ed., *Central Africa and Cultural Transformation in the American Diaspora* (Cambridge, UK, 2002); Alan Gallay, *The Indian Slave Trade: The Rise of the English Empire in the American South, 1670–1717* (New Haven, 2002).

13. Kenneth M. Stampp, *The Peculiar Institution: Slavery in the Ante-Bellum South* (New York, 1956); Eugene D. Genovese, *Roll, Jordan, Roll: The World the Slaves Made* (New York, 1974); Elizabeth Fox-Genovese, *Within the Plantation Household: Black and White Women of the Old South* (Chapel Hill, 1988).

14. Philip D. Curtin, *The Rise and Fall of the Plantation Complex: Essays in Atlantic History* (Cambridge, UK, 1990).

15. Genovese, *Roll, Jordon, Roll;* Elizabeth Fox-Genovese and Eugene D. Genovese, *Fruits of Merchant Capital: Slavery and Bourgeois Property in the Rise and Expansion of Capitalism* (New York, 1983).

16. Don E. Fehrenbacher, *The Slaveholding Republic: An Account of the United States Government's Relations to Slavery,* ed. Ward M. McAfee (Oxford, 2001).

1. CHARTER GENERATIONS

1. "Creole" derives from the Portuguese *crioulo,* meaning a person of African descent born in the New World. It has been extended to native-born free people of many national origins (including both Europeans and Africans) and of diverse social standing. It has also been applied to people of partly European but mixed racial and national origins in various European colonies and to Africans who entered Europe. In the United States, creole has also been specifically applied to people of mixed but usually non-African origins in Louisiana. Staying within the bounds of the broadest definition of creole and the literal definition of African American, I use both terms to refer to black people of native American birth; John A. Holm, *Pidgins and Creoles: Theory and Structure,* 2 vols. (Cambridge, UK, 1988–1989), 1:9. On the complex and often contradictory usage in a single place see Gwendolyn Midlo Hall, *Africans in Colonial Louisiana: The Development of Afro-Creole Culture in the Eighteenth Century* (Baton Rouge, 1992), 157–159, and Joseph G. Tregle, Jr., "On that Word 'Creole' Again: A Note," *LH,* 23 (1982), 193–198. This section draws upon "From Cre-

oles to African: Atlantic Creoles and the Origins of African-American Society in Mainland North America." These notes provide only essential references to this chapter; for the full citations see *WMQ*, 53 (1996), 251–288.

2. Peter Linebaugh and Marcus Rediker, *The Many-Headed Hydra: Sailors, Slaves, Commoners, and the Hidden History of the Revolutionary Atlantic* (Boston, 2000). From the perspective of the making of African American culture, see John Thornton, *Africa and Africans in the Making of the Atlantic World, 1400–1800* (Cambridge, UK, 1998), and the larger Atlantic perspective, see Paul Gilroy, *The Black Atlantic: Modernity and Double Consciousness* (Cambridge, MA, 1993).

3. A. C. de C. M. Saunders, *A Social History of Black Slaves and Freedmen in Portugal, 1441–1555* (Cambridge, UK, 1982), 11–12, 145, 197 n52, 215 n73; G. R. Crone, ed., *The Voyages of Cadamosto and Other Documents on West Africa in the Second Half of the Fifteenth Century* (1937, rpt. New York, 1967), 55, 61; P. E. H. Hair, "The Use of African Languages in Afro-European Contacts in Guinea, 1440–1560," *Sierra Leone Language Review*, 5 (1966), 7–17; George E. Brooks, *Landlords and Strangers: Ecology, Society, and Trade in West Africa, 1000–1630* (Boulder, CO, 1993), ch. 7; Kwame Yeboa Daaku, *Trade and Politics on the Gold Coast, 1600–1720: A Study of the African Reaction to European Trade* (Oxford, 1970), ch. 5, esp. 96–97. For the near-seamless, reciprocal relationship between the Portuguese and the Kongolese courts in the sixteenth century see John K. Thornton, "Early Kongo-Portuguese Relations, 1483–1575: A New Interpretation," *HA*, 8 (1981), 183–204.

4. For an overview see Thornton, *Africa and Africans*, ch. 2, esp. 59–62. See also Daaku, *Gold Coast*, ch. 2; Brooks, *Landlords and Strangers*, chs. 7–8; Philip D. Curtin, *Economic Change in Precolonial Africa: Senegambia in the Era of the Slave Trade* (Madison, WI, 1975), ch. 3; Ray A. Kea, *Settlements, Trade, and Polities in the Seventeenth-Century Gold Coast* (Baltimore, 1982); John Vogt, *Portuguese Rule on the Gold Coast, 1469–1682* (Athens, GA, 1979). *Lançados* from a contraction of *lançados em terra* (to put on shore); Curtin, *Economic Change in Precolonial Africa*, 95. As the influence of the Atlantic economy spread to the interior, Atlantic creoles appeared in the hinterland, generally in the centers of trade along the rivers that reached into the African interior.

5. Kea, *Settlements, Trade, and Polities*, ch. 1, esp. 38; Vogt, *Portuguese Rule on the Gold Coast*; Harvey M. Feinberg, *Africans and Europeans in West Africa: Elminans and Dutchmen on the Gold Coast during the Eighteenth Century*, American Philosophical Society, *Transactions*, 79, no. 7 (Philadelphia, 1989).

For mortality see Curtin, "Epidemiology and the Slave Trade," *PSQ,* 83 (1968), 190–216.

6. Kea, *Settlements, Trade, and Polities,* ch. 1, esp. 38–50, 133–134; Vogt, *Portuguese Rule on the Gold Coast;* Feinberg, *Africans and Europeans in West Africa.*

7. Brooks, *Landlords and Strangers,* chs. 7–9, and Brooks, "Luso-African Commerce and Settlement in the Gambia and Guinea-Bissau Region," *Boston University African Studies Center Working Papers* (1980); Daaku, *Gold Coast,* chs. 5–6; Curtin, *Economic Change,* 95–100, 113–121. For the development of a similar population in Angola see Joseph C. Miller, *Way of Death: Merchant Capitalism and the Angolan Slave Trade, 1730–1830* (Madison, WI, 1988), esp. chs. 8–9; Miller, "Central Africa during the Era of the Slave Trade, c. 1490–1850," in Heywood, ed., *Central Africans in the American Diaspora,* 24–29.

8. Daaku, *Gold Coast,* chs. 4–5; Brooks, *Landlords and Strangers,* chs. 7–9, esp. 188–196; Curtin, *Economic Change,* 95–100. See also Miller's compelling description of Angola's Luso-Africans in the eighteenth and nineteenth centuries that suggests something of their earlier history, in *Way of Death,* 246–250. Brooks notes the term *tangosmãos* passed from use at the end of the seventeenth century, in "Luso-African Commerce and Settlement in the Gambia and Guinea-Bissau," 3.

9. Speaking of the Afro-French in Senegambia in the eighteenth century, Curtin emphasizes the cultural transformation in making this new people, noting that "the important characteristic of this community was cultural mixture, not racial mixture, and the most effective of the traders from France were those who could cross the cultural line between Europe and Africa in their commercial relations," in *Economic Change,* 117. Peter Mark in his study of seventeenth-century Luso-African architecture describes the Luso-Africans "physically indistinguishable from other local African populations." "Constructing Identity: Sixteenth- and Seventeenth-Century Architecture in the Gambia-Geba Region and the Articulation of Luso-African Ethnicity," *HA,* 22 (1995), 317.

10. Holm, *Pidgins and Creoles;* Thornton, *Africa and Africans,* 213–218; Saunders, *Black Slaves and Freedmen in Portugal,* 98–102 (see the special word—*ladinhos*—for blacks who could speak "good" Portuguese, p. 101); Brooks, *Landlords and Strangers,* 136–137; C. Jourdan, "Pidgins and Creoles: The Blurring of Categories," *Annual Review of Anthropology,* 20 (1991), 186–210. The architecture of the Atlantic creole villages was also called "à la portugaise." Mark, "Constructing Identity," 307–327. More generally, see Peter Burke and Roy Porter, eds., *The Social History of Language* (Cambridge, UK, 1987);

Mervyn C. Alleyne, *Comparative Afro-American: An Historical-Comparative Study of English-Based Afro-American Dialects of the New World* (Ann Arbor, MI, 1980).

11. Robin Law and Kristin Mann, "West Africa in the Atlantic Community: The Case of the Slave Coast," *WMQ*, 56 (1999), 307–334. Daaku, *Gold Coast*, chs. 3–4; Feinberg, *Africans and Europeans*, ch. 6; Kea, *Settlements, Trade, and Polities*, esp. pt. 2; Curtin, *Economic Change*, 92–93.

12. John K. Thornton, *The Kongolese Saint Anthony: Dona Beatriz Kimpa Vita and the Antonian Movement, 1684–1706* (Cambridge, UK, 1998); Vogt, *Portuguese Rule on the Gold Coast*, 54–58; Daaku, *Gold Coast*, 99–101; Thornton, "The Development of an African Catholic Church in the Kingdom of Kongo, 1491–1750," *JAH*, 25 (1984), 147–167; Anne Hilton, *The Kingdom of Kongo* (London, 1985), 32–49, 154–161, 179, 198; Wyatt MacGaffey, *Religion and Society in Central Africa: The BaKongo of Lower Zaire* (Chicago, 1986), 191–216; and MacGaffey, "Dialogues of the Deaf," 249–267. Pacing the cultural intermixture of Africa and Europe was the simultaneous introduction of European and American plants and animals, which compounded and legitimated many of the cultural changes; Alfred W. Crosby, *Ecological Imperialism: The Biological Expansion of Europe, 900–1900* (Cambridge, UK, 1986).

13. Feinberg, *Africans and Europeans*, 65, 82–83; Kea, *Settlements, Trade, and Polities*, 197–202, 289–290.

14. Charles Verlinden, *The Beginnings of Modern Colonization: Eleven Essays with an Introduction* (Ithaca, 1970), 39–40; Saunders, *Black Slaves and Freedmen in Portugal*, ch. 1; Ruth Pike, "Sevillian Society in the Sixteenth Century: Slaves and Freedmen," *HAHR*, 47 (1967), 344–359, and Pike, *Aristocrats and Traders: Sevillian Society in the Sixteenth Century* (Ithaca, 1972), 29, 170–192; P. E. H. Hair, "Black African Slaves at Valencia, 1482–1516," *HA*, 7 (1980), 119–131; Thornton, *Africa and Africans*, 96–97; James H. Sweet, "The Iberian Roots of American Racist Thought," *WMQ*, 54 (1997), 162–164; A. J. R. Russell-Wood, "Iberian Expansion and the Issue of Black Slavery: Changing Portuguese Attitudes, 1440–1770," *AHR*, 83 (1978), 20. For European Atlantic creoles, see Sue Peabody, *"There Are No Slaves in France": The Political Culture of Race and Slavery in the Ancien Regime* (New York, 1996); Peter Fryer, *Staying Power: A History of Black People in Britain* (London, 1984), 9–11; Jane Landers, *Black Society in Spanish Florida* (Urbana, IL, 1999), 7–12.

15. Peter C. W. Gutkind, "Trade and Labor in Early Precolonial African History: The Canoemen of Southern Ghana," in Catherine Coquery-Vidrovitch and

Paul E. Lovejoy, eds., *The Workers of African Trade* (Beverly Hills, 1985), 27–28, 36; Kea, *Settlements, Trade, and Polities,* 243; Curtin, *Economic Change,* 302–308.

16. The northern colonies of North America often received "refuse" slaves. For complaints and appreciations, see Joyce D. Goodfriend, "Burghers and Blacks: The Evolution of a Slave Society at New Amsterdam," *NYH,* 59 (1978), 139; Lorenzo J. Greene, *The Negro in Colonial New England, 1620–1776* (New York, 1942), 35; William D. Pierson, *Black Yankees: The Development of an Afro-American Subculture in Eighteenth-Century New England* (Amherst, MA, 1988), 4–5; Edgar J. McManus, *Black Bondage in the North* (Syracuse, 1973), 18–25; James G. Lydon, "New York and the Slave Trade, 1700 to 1774," *WMQ,* 35 (1978), 275–279, 381–390; Darold D. Wax, "Negro Imports into Pennsylvania, 1720–1766," *PH,* 32 (1965), 254–287, and Wax, "Preferences for Slaves in Colonial America," *JNH,* 58 (1973), 374–376, 379–387.

17. J. Fred Rippy, "The Negro and the Spanish Pioneer in the New World," *JNH,* 6 (1921), 183–189; Leo Wiener, *Africa and the Discovery of America,* 3 vols. (Philadelphia, 1920–1922); Saunders, *Black Slaves and Freedmen in Portugal,* 29; for sailors see 11, 71–72, 145, and Hall, *Africans in Colonial Louisiana,* 128. A sale of six slaves in Mexico in 1554 included one born in the Azores, another born in Portugal, another born in Africa, and the latter's daughter born in Mexico; Colin A. Palmer, *Slaves of the White God: Blacks in Mexico, 1570–1650* (Cambridge, MA, 1976), 31–32; "Abstracts of French and Spanish Documents Concerning the Early History of Louisiana," *LHQ,* 1 (1917), 111.

18. Saunders, *Black Slaves and Freedmen in Portugal,* 152–155; Russell-Wood, "Black and Mulatto Brotherhoods in Colonial Brazil," *HAHR,* 54 (1974), 567–602, and Russell-Wood, *The Black Man in Slavery and Freedom in Colonial Brazil* (New York, 1982), ch. 8, esp. 134, 153–154, 159–160. See also Pike, *Aristocrats and Traders,* 177–179. In the sixteenth century, some 7 percent (2,580) of Portugal's black population was free; Saunders, *Black Slaves and Freedmen in Portugal,* 59.

19. Hodges, *Root and Branch,* 6–7; Simon Hart, *The Prehistory of the New Netherland Company, Amsterdam Notarial Records of the First Dutch Voyages to the Hudson* (Amsterdam, 1959), 23–26, 74–75, quotations on 80–82; Thomas J. Condon, *New York Beginnings: The Commercial Origins of New Netherland* (New York, 1968), ch. 1, esp. 30; Oliver A. Rink, *Holland on the Hudson: An Economic and Social History of Dutch New York* (Ithaca, 1986), 34, 42; Van Cleaf Bachman, *Peltries or Plantations: The Economic Policies of the Dutch West India Company in New Netherland, 1623–1639* (Baltimore, 1969), 6–7.

20. C. R. Boxer, *The Dutch in Brazil, 1624–1654* (Oxford, 1957); Boxer, *Four Centuries of Portuguese Expansion, 1415–1825; A Succinct Survey* (Berkeley, CA, 1961), 48–51; P. C. Emmer, "The Dutch and the Making of the Second Atlantic System," in Barbara L. Solow, ed., *Slavery and the Rise of the Atlantic System* (Cambridge, MA, 1991), 75–96, esp. 83–84; Johannes Menne Postma, *The Dutch in the Atlantic Slave Trade* (Cambridge, UK, 1990), chs. 2–3, 8; Thornton, *Africa and Africans*, 64–65, 69–77; Cornelius C. Goslinga, *The Dutch in the Caribbean and on the Wild Coast, 1580–1680* (Gainesville, FL, 1971).

21. McManus, *Black Bondage in the North*, 18–25, and McManus, *A History of Negro Slavery in New York* (Syracuse, 1966), 35–39; Lydon, "New York and the Slave Trade," 381–394; Wax, "Negro Imports into Pennsylvania," 254–287; Wax, "Africans on the Delaware: The Pennsylvania Slave Trade, 1759–1765," *PH*, 50 (1983), 38–49; Wax, "Preferences for Slaves in Colonial America," 374–376, 379–387; Sharon V. Salinger, *"To Serve Well and Faithfully": Labor and Indentured Servants in Pennsylvania, 1682–1800* (Cambridge, UK, 1987), 75–78; quotes in Goodfriend, "Burghers and Blacks," 139; in Cecil Headlam, ed., *Calendar of State Papers, Colonial Series*, 40 vols. (Vaduz, 1964), 1:110; also in Greene, *Negro in New England*, 35; in A. J. F. Van Laer, ed., *Correspondence of Jeremias Van Rensselaer, 1651–1674* (Albany, 1932), 167–168 and 175. See a 1714 New York law favoring the importation of African over West Indian slaves because of the large number of "refuse" and criminal slaves, *Journal of the Legislative Council of the Colony of New-York, 1619–1743*, 2 vols. (Albany, 1861), 1:433–434.

22. An abstract of the black population between 1630 and 1644 by name can be found in Robert J. Swan, "The Black Population of New Netherland: As Extracted from the Records of Baptisms and Marriages of the Dutch Reformed Church (New York City), 1630–1644," *JAAHGS*, 14 (1995), 82–98. A few names suggest the subtle transformation of identity as the creoles crossed the Atlantic. For example, Anthony Jansen of Salee or Van Vaes, a dark-skinned man who claimed Moroccan birth, became "Anthony the Turk," perhaps because the Turks were not only considered fierce—as Anthony's litigious history indicates he surely was—but, also importantly, alien and brown in pigment. Leo Herskowitz, "The Troublesome Turk: An Illustration of Judicial Process in New Amsterdam," *NYH*, 46 (1965), 299–310.

23. Nothing evidenced the creoles' easy integration into the mainland society better than the number who survived into old age. There are no systematic demographic studies of people of African descent during the first years of settlement, and perhaps, because the numbers are so small, there can be none. Nev-

ertheless, "old" or "aged" slaves are encountered again and again, sometimes in descriptions of fugitives, sometimes in the deeds that manumit—that is, discard—superannuated slaves. Before the end of the seventeenth century, numbers of black people lived long enough to see their grandchildren. Berthold Fernow, ed., *The Records of New Amsterdam from 1653 to 1674 Anno Domini*, 7 vols. (Baltimore, 1976), 5:337, cited in Joyce D. Goodfriend, *Before the Melting Pot: Society and Culture in Colonial New York City, 1664–1730* (Princeton, 1992), 252 n25.

24. Suzanne Miers and Igor Kopytoff, eds., *Slavery in Africa: Historical and Anthropological Perspectives* (Madison, WI, 1977); Paul E. Lovejoy, *Transformations in Slavery: A History of Slavery in Africa* (Cambridge, UK, 1983); Patrick Manning, *Slavery and African Life: Occidental, Oriental, and African Slave Trades* (Cambridge, UK, 1990); Thornton, *Africa and Africans in the Making of the Atlantic World*, ch. 3; Claude Meillassoux, *The Anthropology of Slavery: The Womb of Iron and Gold* (Chicago, 1991); Martin A. Klein, "Introduction: Modern European Expansion and Traditional Servitude in Africa and Asia," in Klein, ed., *Breaking the Chains: Slavery, Bondage, and Emancipation in Modern Africa and Asia* (Madison, WI, 1993), 3–26; Toyin Falola and Lovejoy, "Pawnship in Historical Perspective," in Falola and Lovejoy, eds., *Pawnship in Africa: Debt Bondage in Historical Perspective* (Boulder, CO, 1994), 1–26. A dated but still useful critical review of the subject is Frederick Cooper, "The Problem of Slavery in African Studies," *JAH*, 20 (1979), 103–125.

25. Goodfriend, *Before the Melting Pot*, 10, ch. 6; E. van den Boogaart, "The Servant Migration to New Netherland, 1624–1664," in P. C. Emmer, ed., *Colonialism and Migration: Indentured Labour Before and After Slavery* (Dordrecht, 1986), 58; *NY Documents*, 1:154.

26. Goodfriend, *Before the Melting Pot*, ch. 6; Goodfriend, "Burghers and Blacks," 125–144; Goodfriend, "Black Families in New Netherland," *JAAHGS*, 5 (1984), 94–107; Morton Wagman, "Corporate Slavery in New Netherland," *JNH*, 65 (1980), 34–42; McManus, *Slavery in New York*, 2–22; Michael Kammen, *Colonial New York: A History* (New York, 1975), 58–60; van den Boogaart, "Servant Migration to New Netherland," 56–59, 65–71; Vivienne L. Kruger, "Born to Run: The Slave Family in Early New York, 1626 to 1827" (Ph.D. diss., Columbia University, 1985), ch. 2, esp. 46–48, ch. 6, esp. 270–277; Rink, *Holland on the Hudson*, 161 n33. Between 1639 and 1652, marriages recorded in the New Amsterdam Church represented 28 percent of the marriages recorded in that period—also note one interracial marriage. For baptisms see "Reformed Dutch

Church, New York, Baptisms, 1639–1800," New York Genealogical and Biographical Society, *Collections,* 2 vols. (New York, 1901), 1:10–27, 2:10–38; for the 1635 petition see I. N. Phelps Stokes, *The Iconography of Manhattan Island, 1498–1909,* 6 vols. (New York, 1967), 4:82; and No. 14, Notulen W1635, 1626 (19–11–1635), inv. 1.05.01. 01 (Oude), Algemeen Rijksarchief, The Hague. A petition by "five blacks from New Netherland who had come here [Amsterdam]" was referred back to officials in New Netherland. Marcel van der Linden of the International Institute of Social History in Amsterdam kindly located and translated this notation in the records of the Dutch West India Company.

27. Petition for freedom, in *NY Manuscripts,* 269. White residents of New Amsterdam protested the enslavement of the children of half-free slaves, holding that no one born of a free person should be a slave. The Dutch West India Company rejected the claim; *NY Documents,* 1:302, 343; O'Callaghan, ed., O'Callaghan, comp., *Laws and Ordinances of New Netherland, 1638–1674,* 4 vols. (Albany, 1868), 4:36–37. For the Dutch West India Company "setting them free and at liberty, on the same footing as other free people here in New Netherland," although children remained property of the company, see van den Boogaart, "Servant Migration to New Netherlands," 69–70.

28. For black men paying tribute to purchase their families, see *NY Manuscripts,* 45, 87, 105; *NY Documents,* 1:343; Goodfriend, "Burghers and Blacks," 125–144, and "Black Families in New Netherlands," 94–107; McManus, *Slavery in New York,* 2–22; Wagman, "Corporate Slavery in New Netherland," 38–39; quotation in Gerald Francis DeJong, "The Dutch Reformed Church and Negro Slavery in Colonial America," *Church History,* 40 (1971), 430; Kruger, "Born to Run," ch. 1, esp. 90–92; Henry B. Hoff, "Frans Abramse Van Salee and His Descendants: A Colonial Black Family in New York and New Jersey," *NYGBR* 121 (1990), 65–71, 157–161.

29. Goodfriend estimates that 75 of New Amsterdam's 375 blacks were free in 1664, in *Before the Melting Pot,* 61.

30. Kruger, "Born to Run," 52–55, 591–600, tells the story of the creation of a small class of black landowners via gifts from the Dutch West India Company and direct purchase by the blacks themselves. Quote on p. 592. Also Goodfriend, *Before the Melting Pot,* 115–117; Peter R. Chrisoph, "The Freedmen of New Amsterdam," *JAAHGS,* 5 (1984), 116–117; Stokes, *Iconography of Manhattan Island,* 2:302; 4:70–78; 100, 104–106, 120–148, 265–266; Gehring, ed., *New York Historical Manuscripts;* van den Boogaart, "The Servant Migration to New Netherland, 1624–1664," 69–71. For the employment of a white

housekeeper by a free black artisan, see *ibid.*, 69; Fernow, ed., *Minutes of the Orphanmasters Court,* 2:46; Roi Ottley and William J. Weatherby, eds., *The Negro in New York: An Informal Social History, 1626–1940* (New York, 1967), 12.

31. *NY Manuscripts,* 87, 105, 269 (for manumission, dubbed "half slaves"), 222 (adoption), 269 (land grants). See also Goodfriend, *Before the Melting Pot,* ch. 6; and Fernow, ed., *Records of New Amsterdam,* 3:42, 5, 172, 337–340, 7, 11 (for actions in court); Goodfriend, "Burghers and Blacks," 125–144, and "Black Families in New Netherlands," 94–107; van den Boogaart, "Servant Migration to New Netherlands," 56–59, 65–71; McManus, *Slavery in New York,* 2–22; DeJong, "Dutch Reformed Church and Negro Slavery," 430; Kruger, "Born to Run," 46–48, 270–278; Hoff, "Frans Abramse Van Salee and His Descendants"; Kammen, *Colonial New York,* 58–60. For blacks using Dutch courts early on see Rink, *Holland on the Hudson,* 160–161—for example, in 1638, Anthony Portuguese sued Anthony Jansen for damages done by his hog; soon after, one Pedro Negretto claimed back wages. For adoption of a black child by a free black family see Kenneth Scott and Kenn Stryker-Rodda, eds., *The Register of Salomon Lachaire, Notary Public of New Amsterdam, 1661–1662* (Baltimore, 1978), 22–23; *NY Manuscripts,* 222, 256; Kruger, "Born to Run," 44–51.

32. Anthony Johnson's primacy and "unmatched achievement" have made him and his family the most studied members of the charter generation in the Chesapeake. The best account of the Johnsons is in J. Douglas Deal, *Race and Class in Colonial Virginia: Indians, Englishmen, and Africans on the Eastern Shore of Virginia during the Seventeenth Century* (New York, 1993), 217–250. Also useful are T. H. Breen and Stephen Innes, *"Myne Owne Ground": Race and Freedom on Virginia's Eastern Shore, 1640–1676* (New York, 1980), ch. 1; Ross M. Kimmel, "Free Blacks in Seventeenth-Century Maryland," *MHM,* 71 (1976), 22–25; Alden T. Vaughan, "Blacks in Virginia: A Note on the First Decade," *WMQ,* 29 (1972), 475–476; James H. Brewer, "Negro Property Owners in Seventeenth-Century Virginia," *WMQ,* 12 (1955), 576–578; Susie M. Ames, *Studies of the Virginia Eastern Shore in the Seventeenth Century* (Richmond, 1940), 102–105; John H. Russell, *The Free Negro in Virginia, 1619–1865* (Baltimore, 1913), and Russell, "Colored Freemen as Slave Owners in Virginia," *JNH,* 1 (1916), 234–237. Evidence of the baptism of the Johnsons' children comes indirectly from the 1660s, when John Johnson replied to a challenge of his right to testify by producing evidence of baptism. He may, however, have been baptized as an adult. Breen and Innes, *"Myne Owne Ground,"* 17.

33. Deal, *Race and Class in Colonial Virginia,* 218–222. Breen and Innes, *"Myne Owne Ground,"* 8–11, makes a convincing case for Johnson's connections with

the Bennetts, although the evidence is circumstantial. Also see, *ibid.*, 12–15. On Mary Johnson, see Kathleen M. Brown, *Good Wives, Nasty Wenches, and Anxious Patriarchs: Gender, Race, and Power in Colonial Virginia* (Chapel Hill, 1996), 107–109, 112–113.

34. Morgan, *American Slavery, American Freedom*, 108–179, 215–249, 108–179, 215–249; Wesley Frank Craven, *White, Red, and Black: The Seventeenth-Century Virginian* (Charlottesville, VA, 1971), 75–99.

35. Deal, *Race and Class*, 187–188; Breen and Innes, *"Myne Owne Ground,"* 68–69; Edmund S. Morgan, "Slavery and Freedom: The American Paradox," *JAmH*, 59 (1972), 18 n39; Allan Kulikoff, "A 'Prolifick' People: Black Population Growth in the Chesapeake Colonies, 1700–1790," *SS*, 16 (1977), 392–393.

36. Paul Heinegg, *Free African Americans of Maryland and Delaware: From the Colonial Period to 1810* (Baltimore, 2000).

37. Breen and Innes, *"Myne Owne Ground,"* 75–87; Deal, *Race and Class*, 163–405.

38. A. J. R. Johnson, with Hilary Russell, Barbara Schmeisser, David Starter, and Ruth Whitehead, "Mathieu Da Costa and Early Canada: Possibilities and Problems," unpublished essay courtesy of Hilary Russell.

39. Glenn R. Conrad, comp. and trans., *The First Families of Louisiana*, 2 vols. (Baton Rouge, 1970), 1:117; Daniel H. Usner, Jr., *Indians, Settlers, and Slaves in a Frontier Exchange Economy: The Lower Mississippi Valley Before 1783* (Chapel Hill, 1992), 47; Usner, "From African Captivity to American Slavery: The Introduction of Black Laborers to Colonial Louisiana," *LH*, 20 (1979), 36–38; Thomas N. Ingersoll, "Free Blacks in a Slave Society: New Orleans, 1718–1812," *WMQ*, 48 (1991), 175–176; Henry P. Dart, ed., "Records of the Superior Council of Louisiana," *LHQ*, 4 (1921), 236; Hall, *Africans in Colonial Louisiana*, 128–132.

40. The Bambaras had complex relations with the French. Although many Bambaras—usually captives of the tribe whom the French also deemed Bambaras (although they often were not)—became entrapped in the international slave trade and were sold to the New World, others worked for the French as domestics, boatmen, clerks, and interpreters in the coastal forts and slave factories. Their proud military tradition—honed in a long history of warfare against Mandingas and other Islamic peoples—made them ideal soldiers as well as slave catchers. Along the coast of Africa, "Bambara" became a generic word for soldier; Hall, *Africans in Colonial Louisiana*, 42, and Curtin, *Economic Change in Precolonial Africa*, 115, 143, 149, 178–181, 191–192; see the review of Hall in *Africa*, 64 (1994), 168–171.

41. The first census of the French settlement of the lower Mississippi Valley comes

from Biloxi in 1699. It lists 5 naval officers, 5 petty officers, 4 sailors, 19 Canadians, 10 laborers, 6 cabin boys, and 20 soldiers; Hall, *Africans in Colonial Louisiana,* 3, and esp. ch. 5. Usner makes the point in comparing the use of black sailors on the Mississippi and the Senegal, in "From African Captivity to American Slavery," 25–47, esp. 36, and more generally in *Indians, Settlers, and Slaves.* See also James T. McGowan, "Planters without Slaves: Origins of a New World Labor System," *SS,* 16 (1977), 5–20; John G. Clark, *New Orleans, 1718–1812: An Economic History* (Baton Rouge, 1970), ch. 2; Thomas N. Ingersoll, *Mammon and Manon in Early New Orleans: The First Slave Society in the Deep South, 1718–1819* (Knoxville, 1999), chs. 2–3.

42. *Ibid.,* 106–112; du Pratz, *Histoire de la Louisiane,* 3:305–317; Usner, "From African Captivity to American Slavery," 37, 42.

43. Under the *Code Noir,* manumitted slaves had "the same rights, privileges, and immunities which [were] enjoyed by free-born persons," but they could lose their freedom for harboring a fugitive slave and a variety of other crimes. Thomas N. Ingersoll, "Slave Codes and Judicial Practice in New Orleans, 1718–1807," *LHR,* 13 (1995), 28–36, 38–39; Carl A. Brasseaux, "The Administration of the Slave Regulations in French Louisiana, 1724–1766," *LH,* 21 (1980), 141–142, 151–153; Donald E. Everett, "Free Persons of Color in Colonial Louisiana," *LH,* 7 (1966), 23–27. An abstract of the *Code Noir* is published in Charles Gayarré, *History of Louisiana,* 4 vols. (New York, 1854), 1: 531–540.

44. J. G. Dunlop, "William Dunlop's Mission to St. Augustine in 1688," *SCHM,* 34 (1933), 24; Jane Landers, "Spanish Sanctuary: Fugitives in Florida, 1687–1790," *FHQ,* 62 (1984), 296–302; John J. TePaske, "The Fugitive Slave: Intercolonial Rivalry and Spanish Slave Policy, 1687–1764," in Samuel Proctor, ed., *Eighteenth-Century Florida and Its Borderlands* (Gainesville, FL, 1975), 2–12. Quote in Landers, "Gracia Real de Santa Teresa de Mose: A Free Black Town in Spanish Colonial Florida," *AHR,* 95 (1990), 13–14.

45. Landers, "Spanish Sanctuary," 296–302; Landers, "Mose," 14; Landers, "Traditions of African American Freedom and Community in Spanish Colonial Florida," in David R. Colburn and Jane G. Landers, eds., *The African American Heritage of Florida* (Gainesville, FL, 1995), 22–23; TePaske, "The Fugitive Slave," 2–12; Theodore G. Corbett, "Migration to a Spanish Imperial Frontier in the Seventeenth and Eighteenth Centuries: St. Augustine," *HAHR,* 54 (1974), 428–430.

46. Landers, "Spanish Sanctuary," 296–302, and "Mose," 13–15; TePaske, "The Fugitive Slave," 2–12; I. A. Wright, comp., "Dispatches of Spanish Officials Bearing on the Free Negro Settlement of Gracia Real de Santa Teresa de Mose,

Florida," *JNH,* 9 (1924), 144–193, quote on 150; Zora Neale Hurston, "Letters of Zora Neale Hurston on the Mose Settlement and the Negro Colony in Florida," *JNH,* 12 (1927), 664–667; John D. Duncan, "Servitude and Slavery in Colonial South Carolina, 1670–1776" (Ph.D. diss., Emory University, 1971), ch. 17, quote on 664; Dunlop, "William Dunlop's Mission," 1–30. Several of the slaves who rejected freedom and Catholicism in St. Augustine and returned to South Carolina were rewarded with freedom, creating a competition between English and Spanish colonies that redounded to the slaves' advantage. See Duncan, "Servitude and Slavery in Colonial South Carolina," 381–383. For the African conversion of South Carolina slaves, see John K. Thornton, "On the Trail of Voodoo: African Christianity in Africa and the Americas," *Americas,* 44 (1988), 268.

47. Landers, "Mose," 13–15; Peter H. Wood, *Black Majority: Negroes in Colonial South Carolina from 1670 through the Stono Rebellion* (New York, 1974), 304–305.

48. Wood, *Black Majority,* 239–298, 304–307, 310.

49. For the pre-transfer conversion of slaves from central Africa to Christianity, see John K. Thornton, "The Development of an African Church in the Kingdom of Kongo, 1491–1750," *JAH,* 25 (1984), 147–167, and Thornton, "Religion and Ceremonial Life in the Kongo and Mbundu Areas, 1500–1700," in Heywood, *Central Africans and the American Diaspora,* 71–90; Hilton, *Kingdom of Kongo,* ch. 2, 154–161, 179–198; MacGaffey, *Religion and Society in Central Africa,* 191–216; Thornton, "African Dimensions of the Stono Rebellion," *AHR,* 96 (1991), 1101–1111, quote on 1102. Thornton makes a powerful case for the Kongoloses origins of the Stono rebels, in their military organization and in the nature of their resistance. In 1710 an Anglican missionary in Goose Creek Parish, South Carolina, observed that the black slaves had been "born and baptized among the Portuguese." Frank J. Klingberg, ed., *Carolina Chronicle: The Papers of Commissary Gideon Johnston, 1707–1716* (Berkeley, CA, 1946), 69.

50. Wright, "Dispatches of Spanish Officials," 173–174; Landers, "Mose," 17; "The Mose Site," *Escribino,* 10 (1973), 52. In 1749 slave conspirators plotting rebellion in St. Thomas Parish, South Carolina, planned to escape to Florida after setting fire to Charles Town. Philip D. Morgan and George D. Terry, "Slavery in Microcosm: A Conspiracy Scare in Colonial South Carolina," *SS,* 21 (1982), 122.

51. Wood, *Black Majority,* chs. 11–12; Edward A. Pearson, "'A Countryside Full of Flames': A Reconsideration of the Stono Rebellion and Slave Rebelliousness in the Early Eighteenth-Century South Carolina Lowcountry," *S&A,* 17 (1996),

22–50; Mark M. Smith, "Remembering Mary, Shaping Revolt: Reconsidering the Stono Rebellion," *JSoH*, 67 (2001), 513–535; Larry W. Kruger and Robert Hall, "Fort Mose: A Black Fort in Spanish Florida," *Griot*, 6 (1987), 42.

52. Thornton, "African Dimensions of the Stono Rebellion," 1107; Landers, "Mose," 27.

53. Landers, "Mose," 15–17.

54. Landers, "Mose," 17–18; "Mose Site," 53; quote in Wright, "Dispatches of Spanish Officials Bearing on Mose," 146–149. Menéndez commanded Mose until 1740, when another English assault, in response to the Stono rebellion, forced a Spanish retreat and the evacuation of Mose's black population to St. Augustine.

55. Landers, "Mose," 15–21, quote on 20.

56. *Ibid.*

57. Landers, "Mose," 21–22, quote on 22.

58. Landers, "Mose," 23–24.

59. John R. Dunkle, "Population Changes as an Element in the Historical Geography of St. Augustine," *FHQ*, 37 (1958), 5; Landers, "Traditions of African American Freedom," 22–23; Landers, "Mose," 24–28, quote on 21; Kruger and Hall, "Fort Mose," 41–42.

60. Theodore J. Corbett, "Population Structure in Hispanic St. Augustine, 1619–1763," *FHQ*, 54 (1976), 268; Corbett, "Migration to a Spanish Imperial Frontier," 430; "Mose Site," 52–55.

61. Corbett, "Migration to a Spanish Imperial Frontier," 420; Wilbur H. Siebert, "The Departure of the Spaniards and Other Groups from East Florida, 1763–1764," *FHQ*, 19 (1940), 146; Robert L. Gold, "The Settlement of the East Florida Spaniards in Cuba, 1763–1766," *FHQ*, 42 (1964), 216–217; Landers, "Mose," 23–30, quote on 21; Landers, "Acquisition and Loss on a Spanish Frontier: The Free Black Homesteaders of Florida, 1784–1821," *S&A* 17 (1996), 88.

2. PLANTATION GENERATIONS

1. For insights into discussion of slave naming patterns in the Americas, see Trevor G. Bernard, "Slave Naming Patterns: Onomastics and the Taxonomy of Race in Eighteenth-Century Jamaica," *JIH* (2001), 325–346; Jerome S. Handler and JoAnn Jacoby, "Slave Names and Naming in Barbados, 1650–1830," *WMQ*, 53 (1996), 692–697; Cheryll Ann Cody, "There Was No 'Absalom' on

the Ball Plantations: Slave Naming Practices in the South Carolina Low Country, 1720–1865," *AHR*, 9 (1987), 572–573.

2. On the rise of the planter class in the Chesapeake, see Morgan, *American Slavery, American Freedom*, ch. 15; Allan Kulikoff, *Tobacco and Slaves: The Development of Southern Cultures in the Chesapeake, 1680–1800* (Chapel Hill, 1986), pt. 2, esp. ch. 7. John J. McCusker and Russell R. Menard, *The Economy of British America, 1607–1789* (Chapel Hill, 1985), ch. 6, provide an informed overview of the Chesapeake economy.

3. William Waller Hening, comp., *The Statutes at Large: Being a Collection of All the Laws of Virginia*, 13 vols. (Richmond, 1819–23), 2:283, 404, 440, quote on 346; Morgan, *American Slavery, American Freedom*, 330.

4. Kulikoff, *Tobacco and Slaves*, 37–42, 65, 319–320; Kulikoff, "A 'Prolifick' People," 391–396, 403–405; and Kulikoff, "The Origins of Afro-American Society in Tidewater Maryland and Virginia, 1700 to 1790," *WMQ*, 35 (1978), 229–231; Russell R. Menard, "The Maryland Slave Population, 1658 to 1730: A Demographic Profile of Blacks in Four Counties," *WMQ*, 32 (1975), 30–32; Menard, "From Servants to Slaves," 359–371, 381–382; Craven, *White, Red, and Black*, 86–103; quote in Marion Tinling, ed., *The Correspondence of the Three William Byrds of Westover, Virginia, 1684–1776*, 3 vols. (Charlottesville, 1977), 2:487.

5. Kulikoff, *Tobacco and Slaves*, 319–324; Menard, "From Servants to Slaves," 366–369; Walter Minchinton, Celia King, and Peter Waite, *Virginia Slave Trade Statistics, 1698–1775* (Richmond, 1984); Craven, *White, Red, and Black*, 86–87; Susan Westbury, "Analyzing a Regional Slave Trade: The West Indies and Virginia, 1668–1775," *S&A*, 7 (1986), 241–256. Herbert S. Klein maintains that West Indian re-exports remained the majority into the first two decades of the eighteenth century, see "Slaves and Shipping in Eighteenth-Century Virginia," *JIH*, 3 (1975), 384–385.

6. Menard, "Maryland Slave Population," 49–53; Kulikoff, "A 'Prolifick' People," 393–396; Darold D. Wax, "Black Immigrants: The Slave Trade in Colonial Maryland," *MHM*, 73 (1978), 30–35; Klein, "Slaves and Shipping in Eighteenth-Century Virginia," 383–412; Donald M. Sweig, "The Importation of African Slaves to the Potomac River, 1732–1772," *WMQ*, 42 (1985), 507–524.

7. Thornton, *Africa and Africans*, ch. 11; Kulikoff, *Tobacco and Slaves*, ch. 8; Sylvia R. Frey, *Water from the Rock: Black Resistance in a Revolutionary Age* (Princeton, 1991), ch. 1, esp. 28–44; Eric Klingelhoffer, "Aspects of Early Afro-American Material Culture: Artifacts from the Slave Quarters at Garrison

Plantation," *HArch*, 21 (1987), 112–119; quote in John C. Van Horne, ed., *Religious Philanthropy and Colonial Slavery: The American Correspondence of the Associates of Dr. Bray, 1717–1777* (Urbana, IL, 1985), 99–101.

8. Kulikoff, *Tobacco and Slaves*, 320–321, 325–27; Kulikoff, "A 'Prolifick' People," 392–406; Menard, "The Maryland Slave Population," 30–35, 38–49; and Craven, *White, Red, and Black*, 98–101; Darrett B. Rutman and Anita H. Rutman, "'More True and Perfect Lists': The Reconstruction of Censuses for Middlesex County, Virginia, 1668–1704," *VMHB*, 88 (1980), 55, and Darrett B. Rutman, Charles Wetherman, and Anita H. Rutman, "Rhythms of Life: Black and White Seasonality in the Early Chesapeake," *JIH*, 11 (1980), 36–38.

9. Quoted in Lorena Walsh, "A 'Place in Time' Regained: A Fuller History of Colonial Chesapeake Slavery through Group Biography," in Larry E. Hudson, Jr., ed., *Working toward Freedom: Slave Society and Domestic Economy in the American South* (Rochester, NY, 1994), 14; Lorena S. Walsh, *From Calabar to Carter's Grove: A History of a Virginia Slave Community* (Charlottesville, 1997), 34; for the names of Carter's slaves, see Inventory, Estate of Robert Carter, Esq., Carter papers in the Alderman Library, University of Virginia, Charlottesville. The naming of Chesapeake slaves is discussed in Kulikoff, *Tobacco and Slaves*, 325–326; Mechal Sobel, *The World They Made Together: Black and White Values in Eighteenth-Century Virginia* (Princeton, 1987), ch. 11. A "new Negro," declared a visitor to Maryland in 1747 with the finality gained by long experience, "must be broke." Kulikoff, *Tobacco and Slaves*, 325.

10. Gerald W. Mullin, *Flight and Rebellion: Slave Resistance in Eighteenth-Century Virginia* (New York, 1972), chs. 1–3; Kulikoff, *Tobacco and Slaves*, esp. 319–334; Menard, "The Maryland Slave Population," 29–54; Lois Green Carr and Lorena S. Walsh, "Economic Diversification and Labor Organization in the Chesapeake, 1650–1820," in Stephen Innes, ed., *Work and Labor in Early America* (Chapel Hill, 1988), 144–188. Before 1740, most Chesapeake slaves lived in units of less than ten slaves, and the quarters to which the newly arrived Africans were assigned were generally smaller than the average. Kulikoff, *Tobacco and Slaves*, 320, 331.

11. Hening, comp., *Statutes at Large*, 2: 292–293, 481; 3: 447–462; 4: 126–134; "Management of Slaves, 1672," *VMHB*, 7 (1900), 314.

12. Deal, *Race and Class in Colonial Virginia*, 331–332. New laws also prevented slaves from gathering together outside of their owner's estate for more than four hours. Hening, comp., *Statutes at Large*, 2:492–493. For the powerful force of social and verbal isolation, see Paul Edwards, ed., *The Life of Olaudah Equiano or Gustavus Vassa: The African* (New York, 1969), 54.

13. Mullin, *Flight and Rebellion,* 9–10; Philip D. Morgan and Michael L. Nicholls, "Slaves in Piedmont Virginia, 1720–1790," *WMQ,* 46 (1989), 211–212; Winthrop D. Jordan, "Planter and Slave Identity Formation: Some Problems in the Comparative Approach," in Vera Rubin and Arthur Tuden, eds., *Comparative Perspectives on Slavery in New World Plantation Societies, Annals of New York Academy of Sciences,* 292 (1977), 38–39.

14. Mullin, *Flight and Rebellion,* 14–16; Kulikoff, *Tobacco and Slaves,* 319–322; Kulikoff, "Origins of Afro-American Society," 230–235; Wax, "Black Immigrants," 30–45; Walsh, *From Calabar to Carter's Grove,* ch. 2; David Hackett Fischer and James C. Kelly, *Away, I'm Bound Away: Virginia and the Westward Movement* (Richmond, 1993), 30–33, quote on 31. For the collapse of African nationality into the term "New Negro," see Michael Mullin, *Africa in America: Slave Acculturation and Resistance in the American South and the British Caribbean, 1736–1831* (Urbana, IL, 1992), 3, quote on 24. For another perspective which sees the cultural preeminence of Igbo peoples in the Chesapeake, particularly in the second quarter of the eighteenth century, see Douglas B. Chambers, "'He is an African But Speaks Plain': Historical Creolization in Eighteenth-Century Virginia," in Alusine Jalloh and Stephen Maizlish, eds., *Africa and the African Diaspora* (College Station, TX, 1996), 100–133, and "'My Own Nation': Igbo Exiles in the Diaspora," *S&A,* 18 (1997), 73–97; Heywood, ed., *Central Africans in the American Diaspora,* esp. chs. 1–3.

15. A. Leon Higginbotham, Jr., *In the Matter of Color: Race and the American Legal Process, The Colonial Period* (New York, 1978), 22–30; Marvin L. Michael Kay and Lorin Lee Cary, *Slavery in North Carolina: 1748–1775* (Chapel Hill, 1995), chs. 2–3; Philip J. Schwarz, *Twice Condemned: Slaves and the Criminal Laws of Virginia, 1705–1865* (Baton Rouge, 1988), 13–26, 72–82, see p. 82 for increasingly severe penalties for slave criminals. Donna J. Spindel, *Crime and Society in North Carolina, 1663–1776* (Baton Rouge, 1989), 13–26, 54–55, 60–62, 65–66, 72–82, 133–137; Morgan, *American Slavery, American Freedom,* 311–315; Brown, *Good Wives,* 350–355; Darrett B. Rutman and Anita H. Rutman, *A Place in Time: Middlesex County, Virginia, 1650–1750* (New York, 1984), 170–177, esp. 173. For Byrd (who also used the "bit"), see Louis B. Wright and Marion Tinling, eds., *The Secret Diary of William Byrd of Westover, 1709–1712* (Richmond, 1941), 112, 117; and for Carter, see Lancaster County, Virginia, Order Book #5, 1702–1713, 185; Robert Carter to Robert Jones, 10 Oct. 1727, Carter Papers, University of Virginia Library, Charlottesville (both citations courtesy of Emory Evans); Schwarz, *Twice Condemned,* 80–81.

16. Hening, comp., *Statutes at Large,* 2:270, 299–300, 481–482; 3:86–87, 447–462;

4:132. See the difference between an early non-racial law respecting the punishment of servants. *Ibid.*, 1: 538. Thomas D. Morris, *Southern Slavery and the Law, 1619–1860* (Chapel Hill, 1996), 163–169. As slaves became more subject to violent punishment, they lost much of the traditional protections afforded the accused under English law. Hening, comp., *Statutes at Large,* 3:102–103, 269–270, 4:127.

17. Carr and Walsh, "Economic Diversification and Labor Organization," 157–161; Walsh, *From Calabar to Carter's Grove,* 85–86, 93–94.

18. Quote in Philip V. Fithian, *Journal and Letters of Philip Vickers Fithian, 1773–1774: A Plantation Tutor of the Old Dominion,* ed. Hunter D. Farish (Williamsburg, 1943), 73, 98, and Edmund S. Morgan, *Virginians at Home: Family Life in the Eighteenth Century* (Charlottesville, 1963), 53–54; Dell Upton, "White and Black Landscapes in Eighteenth-Century Virginia," in Robert Blair St. George, ed., *Material Life in America* (Boston, 1988), 362–368; Terrence W. Epperson, "Race and the Disciplines of the Plantation," *HArch,* 24 (1990), 29–36. Also see the occupational structure of George Washington's Mount Vernon estate, Donald Jackson and Dorothy Twohig, eds., *The Diaries of George Washington,* 4 vols. (Charlottesville, 1978), 4:277–283. The fullest view of the operation of an eighteenth-century Chesapeake plantation-town can be gained in Jack P. Greene, ed., *The Diary of Colonel Landon Carter of Sabine Hall, 1752–1778,* 2 vols. (Charlottesville, 1965), and its architecture can be glimmered in Thomas T. Waterman, *The Mansions of Virginia, 1706–1776* (Chapel Hill, 1946), also Brown, *Good Wives,* ch. 8; Rhys Isaac, *The Transformation of Virginia, 1740–1790* (Chapel Hill, 1982), chs. 1–2.

19. Isaac, *The Transformation of Virginia;* quote in Mullin, *Flight and Rebellion,* vii.

20. The close supervision of slaves by resident planters can be viewed in the operation of Landon Carter's vast estate. See, for example, Greene, ed., *Diary of Colonel Landon Carter,* 1:422, 497, 502; Kulikoff, *Tobacco and Slaves,* 337–339, 382–386; Walsh, "Slaves and Tobacco in the Chesapeake," 172, 176–180; Lorena S. Walsh, "Plantation Management in the Chesapeake, 1620–1820," *JEH,* 49 (1989), 393–396, esp. 394 n2. "Black slaves, not white servants, made most of the largest individual crops recorded, and most of these efficient workers were Africans, not creoles." Lorena S. Walsh, "Slave Life, Slave Society, and Tobacco Production in the Tidewater Chesapeake, 1620–1820," in Ira Berlin and Philip D. Morgan, eds., *Cultivation and Culture: Labor and the Shaping of Slave Life in the Americas* (Charlottesville, 1993), 176; Philip D. Morgan, "Task and Gang Systems: The Organization of Labor on New World Plantations," in Innes, ed., *Work and Labor in Early America,* 198–201, 203–204.

21. Hening, comp., *Statutes at Large,* 3: 102–103; Mullin, *Flight and Rebellion,* 118–119 and Mullin, *Africa in America,* 138–139, 149–150; Greene, ed., *Diary of Colonel Landon Carter,* 1:390, 396. Thomas Jefferson's slaves worked their own gardens and provision grounds, but when they planted tobacco, Jefferson was quick to object. Thomas Jefferson, *Thomas Jefferson's Farm Book,* ed. Edwin M. Betts (New York, 1953), 268–269; Mary Beth Norton, *Liberty's Daughters: The Revolutionary Experience of American Women, 1750–1800* (New York, 1980), 32. For the implication of the restrictions on slave propertyholding on slave family life and particularly on the role of slave men as "providers," see Brown, *Good Wives,* 183–184.

22. Philip D. Morgan "Slave Life in Piedmont Virginia," in Lois Green Carr, Philip D. Morgan, and Jean B. Russo, eds., *Colonial Chesapeake Society* (Chapel Hill, 1988), 468–469; Walsh, "Slaves and Tobacco in the Chesapeake," 176–177, 180; Mullin, *Africa in America,* 149–154 and Mullin, *Flight and Rebellion.*

23. W. N. Sainsbury et al., eds., *Calendar of State Papers, Colonial Series, America and West Indies,* 40 vols. (London, 1860–1969), 25:83; 33:192, 297–298; 36:333–336, 414–415; 37:277; 38:41; H. R. McIlwaine et al., ed., *Executive Journals of the Council of Colonial Virginia,* 6 vols. (Richmond, 1925–1954), 3:234–236, 242–243, 574–575; quote on 3:574; 4:20, 29, 31, 228 (courtesy of Emory Evans).

24. See, for example, Olaudah Equiano's resistance to having his name changed. Edwards, ed., *The Life of Olaudah Equiano,* 56–57. Quote in "Eighteenth-Century Maryland as Portrayed in the 'Itinerant Observations' of Edward Kimber," *MHM,* 51 (1956), 327–328.

25. Mullin, *Flight and Rebellion,* 39–45; Sobel, *The World They Made Together,* 95; Kulikoff, *Tobacco and Slaves,* 328–329, 352; Mullin, *Africa in America,* 39, 44–45; Michael Mullin, ed., *American Negro Slavery: A Documentary History* (New York, 1976), 83. Once winter set in, planters found runaway slaves returning of their own accord. See Robert Carter to Robert Jones, 10 Oct. 1729, Carter Letterbooks, University of Virginia; Walsh, "Slaves and Tobacco," 176–179; Kay and Cary, *Slavery in North Carolina,* 122.

26. The story of runaways is best told by the slaveholders who chased them. A systematic, but still incomplete, collection of advertisements for fugitive slaves is *Runaway Slave Advertisements.*

27. Quote in Emory G. Evans, ed., "A Question of Complexion: Documents Concerning the Negro and the Franchise in Eighteenth-Century Virginia," *VMHB,* 71 (1963), 414; Winthrop D. Jordan, *White over Black: American Attitudes toward the Negro, 1550–1812* (Chapel Hill, 1968), 122–126; Ira Berlin, *Slaves*

Without Masters: The Free Negro in the Antebellum South (New York, 1974), 6–9; Douglas Deal, "A Constricted World: Free Blacks on Virginia's Eastern Shore, 1680–1750," in Carr, Morgan, and Russo, eds., *Colonial Chesapeake Society,* 276–279; Michael L. Nicholls, "Passing Through This Troublesome World: Free Blacks in the Early Southside," *VMHB,* 92 (1984), 51–53; Brown, *Good Wives,* chs. 4, 7; Kay and Cary, *Slavery in North Carolina,* 66–68.

28. Hening, comp., *Statutes at Large,* 2:481, 490, 492–493, 3: 86–88, 102, 172, 238, 250, 269, 298, 453–454. In 1723 manumission became the prerogative of the governor and the Council in Virginia. *Ibid.,* 4:132. In 1752 Maryland banned testamentary manumission. William Hand Browne et al., eds., *Archives of Maryland* (Baltimore, 1884–1972), 50:76.

29. Virginia Easley DeMarce provides an excellent overview; "'Verry Slitly Mixt': Tri-Racial Isolate Families of the Upper South—A Genealogical Study," *NGSQ,* 80 (1992), 5–35.

30. A 1755 Maryland census, the only known pre-Revolutionary enumeration of free black people in the region, counted slightly more than 1,800 free persons of African descent, about 4 percent of Maryland's black population and less than 2 percent of its free population. *Gentlemen's Magazine and Historical Chronicle,* 34 (1764), 261. Although no other Chesapeake colony took a similar census, there is no evidence that any contained a larger proportion of black free people than Maryland. Petition from Petersburg, 11 Dec. 1805, Legislative Petitions, Virginia State Library, Richmond; *Proceedings and Debates of the Convention of North-Carolina Called to Amend the Constitution of the State* (Raleigh, 1835), 351.

31. Morgan, "Slave Life in Piedmont Virginia," 461–464, quote on 462; Nicholls, "Passing Through This Troublesome World," 55–58. Brown, *Good Wives,* 411–416.

32. Peter H. Wood, "'More Like a Negro Country': Demographic Patterns in Colonial South Carolina, 1700–1740," in Stanley L. Engerman and Eugene D. Genovese, eds., *Race and Slavery in the Western Hemisphere: Quantitative Studies* (Princeton, 1975), 131–145, quote on p. 132 and Wood, *Black Majority,* 3–91; Peter A. Coclanis, *The Shadow of a Dream: Economic Life and Death in the South Carolina Low Country: 1670–1920* (New York, 1988), 164–165; Daniel C. Littlefield, *Rice and Slaves: Ethnicity and the Slave Trade in Colonial South Carolina* (Baton Rouge, 1981); Russell R. Menard, "Slave Demography in the Lowcountry, 1670–1740: From Frontier Society to Plantation," *SCHM,* 96 (1995), 291–302; Philip D. Morgan, ed., "Profile of a Mid-Eighteenth Century South Carolina Parish: The Tax Return of Saint James' Goose Creek," *SCHM,*

81 (1980), 51–65; *Historical Statistics,* 2: 1168. For the development of slavery and a plantation order in colonial Georgia, see Darold D. Wax, "'New Negroes Are Always in Demand': The Slave Trade in Eighteenth-Century Georgia," *GHQ,* 68 (1984), 193–200; Betty Wood, *Slavery in Colonial Georgia, 1730–1775,* (Athens, GA, 1984), 91–98 and Wood, "Some Aspects of Female Resistance to Chattel Slavery in Low Country Georgia, 1763–1815," *HJ,* 30 (1987), quote on 604. For the growth of rice culture in East Florida and the growth of the black population in Florida under British rule between 1763 and 1784, see J. Leitch Wright, Jr., "Blacks in British East Florida," *FHQ,* 54 (1976), 426–442, and Daniel F. Schafer, "'Yellow Silk Ferret Tied Round Their Wrists': African Americans in British East Florida, 1763–1784," in Colburn and Landers, eds., *African American Heritage of Florida,* 71–99, quote on 76; also Donnan, *Slave Trade,* 4:382.

33. William R. Snell, "Indian Slavery in Colonial South Carolina, 1671–1795" (Ph.D. diss., University of Alabama, 1972); Wood, "The Changing Population of the Colonial South," in Peter H. Wood, Gregory A. Waselkov, and M. Thomas Hatley, eds., *Powhatan's Mantle: Indians in the Colonial Southeast* (Lincoln, NE, 1989), 47; Alan Gallay, *The Indian Slave Trade: The Rise of the English Empire in the American South* (New Haven, 2002).

34. Littlefield, *Rice and Slaves,* ch. 2; W. Robert Higgins, "Charleston: Terminus and Entrepôt of the Colonial Slave Trade," in Martin L. Kilson and Robert I. Rotberg, eds., *The African Diaspora* (Cambridge, MA, 1976), 115; Wood, "'More Like a Negro Country,'" 144; Russell R. Menard, "The Africanization of the Lowcountry Labor Force, 1670–1730," in Winthrop D. Jordan and Sheila L. Skemp, eds., *Race and Family in the Colonial South* (Jackson, 1987), 93–94. With the beginning of slavery in Georgia in the 1750s, many of the slaves entering that colony came from South Carolina. By the 1760s, however, Georgia planters also imported their slaves directly from Africa and most slaves were "African born." Harold E. Davis, *The Fledgling Province: Social and Cultural Life in Colonial Georgia, 1733–1776* (Chapel Hill, 1976), 131.

35. Littlefield, *Rice and Slaves,* 8–11; "'More like a Negro Country,'" 149–154; Coclanis, *Shadow of a Dream,* 60, 243–244 n44; Higgins, "Charleston: Terminus and Entrepôt," 118–127; Wax, "Preferences for Slaves in Colonial America," 388–399; Wood, *Slavery in Colonial Georgia,* 103. Philip D. Curtin, *The Atlantic Slave Trade: A Census* (Madison, WI, 1969), 143, 156–157; Philip M. Hamer, ed., *The Papers of Henry Laurens,* 15 vols. (Columbia, SC, 1968–), 1:275, 294–295, 331; 2:179–182, 186, 230, 357, 400–402, 423, 437; 4:192–193. On the age and sex preferences of South Carolina planters, see Donnan, *Slave*

Trade, 4:329; *Laurens Papers,* 1:295 (quote), 2:186, 204, 230, 278, 315, 348, 357, 400–402. By the 1720s, the sex ratio of South Carolina slaves was normally 120 or more, and it continued to increase during the next decade. Wood, *Black Majority,* 153, 160, 164–165; Littlefield, *Race and Slaves,* 58–59. Developments in Georgia followed the pattern established in South Carolina, Wood, *Slavery in Colonial Georgia,* 108.

36. The continual arrival of Africans into the lowcountry and the purchase of slaves in large groups enabled slaves not only to maintain a generalized knowledge of Africa but specific nationalities and ethnicities. In 1737 a South Carolina planter attempting to find a fugitive reminded his fellows that "as there is abundance of Negroes in this Province of that Nation, he may chance to be habour'd among some of them." *Runaway Advertisements,* 3:29 (Charles Town *South Carolina Gazette* [Timothy], 6–13 July 1737). If slaveholders sensed the significance of tribal solidarities, slaves valued them even more. Africans ran away in tribal groups often enough in the lowcountry to make masters wary of national or ethnic solidarities. *Runaway Advertisements,* 3:23 (out of the same cargo, 11 Sept. 1736); 3:341–342 (31 Oct. 1774). Runaways harbored slaves of their own nation; Littlefield, *Rice and Slaves,* 126. Solidarities derived from Africa also appear to have influenced marriage patterns and other forms of social action; *Runaway Advertisements,* 3:7 (Charles Town *South-Carolina Gazette,* 9–16 June 1733), quote on 3:467–468 (Charles Town *South-Carolina and American General Gazette,* 17–24 Feb. 1775). For Oswald, see Alexander Peter Kup, *A History of Sierra Leone 1400–1787* (Cambridge, UK, 1961), 190–191; *Laurens Papers,* 4:585; 5:370; Schafer "'Yellow Silk Ferret Tied Round Their Wrists,'" 79–85.

37. Coclanis, *Shadow of a Dream,* 98; Morgan, "A Mid-Eighteenth Century South Carolina Parish," 51–65; Russell R. Menard, "Slavery, Economic Growth, and Revolutionary Ideology in the South Carolina Lowcountry," in Ronald Hoffman et al., eds., *The Economy of Early America: The Revolutionary Period, 1763–1790* (Charlottesville, 1988), 262–265. The units in which Georgia slaves resided were considerably smaller than those in South Carolina but were growing rapidly. Wood, *Slavery in Colonial Georgia,* 104–108. For the Cape Fear area, see Kay and Cary, *Slavery in North Carolina,* 23–24.

38. *Historical Statistics,* 2:1192–1193; McCusker and Menard, *The Economy of British America,* 175–179; Coclanis, *Shadow of a Dream,* ch. 3; R. C. Nash, "South Carolina and the Atlantic Economy in the Late Seventeenth and Eighteenth Centuries," *EHR,* 45 (1992), 680; Wood, *Black Majority,* 55–62; Gray, *So. Ag.,* 1: 277–290; Converse D. Clowse, *Economic Beginnings in Colonial South*

Carolina, 1670–1730, 122–132; Julia Floyd Smith, *Slavery and Rice Culture in Low Country Georgia, 1750–1860* (Knoxville, 1985), 15–29; Russell R. Menard argues that the lowcountry was transformed from a society with slaves to a slave society prior to the rice revolution. "Africanization of the Lowcountry Labor Force," 92.

39. For an excellent contemporary description of the process of rice cultivation and its changing technology, see William Butler, "Observations on the Culture of Rice, 1786," SCHS, Joseph W. Barnwell, ed., "Diary of Timothy Ford, 1785–1786," *SCHM*, 13 (1912), 182–184; Gray, *So. Ag*, 1:281–297; Sam B. Hilliard, "Antebellum Tidewater Rice Culture in South Carolina and Georgia," in James R. Gibson, ed., *European Settlement and Development in North America: Essays on Geographical Change in Honour and Memory of Andrew Hill Clark* (Toronto, 1978), 109–110. Quote in Evangeline Walker Andrews and Charles M. Andrews, eds., *Journal of a Lady of Quality* (New Haven, 1934), 194.

40. Gray, *So. Ag.*, 1:290–97; McCusker and Menard, *Economy of British America*, 185–187; Joyce E. Chaplin, *An Anxious Pursuit: Agricultural Innovation and Modernity in the Lower South, 1730–1815* (Chapel Hill, 1993), 190–208; Nash, "Atlantic Economy," 679–680; Menard, "Slavery, Economic Growth, and Revolutionary Ideology," 254–255, 257 (table 1); David L. Coon, "Eliza Lucas Pinckney and the Reintroduction of Indigo Culture in South Carolina," *JSoH*, 42 (1976), 61–76; G. Terry Sharrer, "The Indigo Bonanza in South Carolina, 1740–90," *T&C*, 12 (1971), 449–452, and Sharrer, "Indigo in Carolina, 1671–1796," *SCHM*, 72 (1971), 94–103; David H. Rembert, Jr., "The Indigo of Commerce in Colonial North America," *Economic Botany*, 33 (1979), 128–134.

41. Wood, "'More Like a Negro Country,'" 153–164; Coclanis, *Shadow of a Dream*, 39–47; Menard, "Slave Demography in the Lowcountry," 294–301; Morgan, *Slave Counterpoint*, 58–101. But by the 1750s, there were large numbers of native-born slaves in South Carolina; see Governor James Glen, writing in 1751: Many slaves "are natives of Carolina, who have no notion of liberty, nor no longing after any other country." H. Roy Merrens, ed., *The Colonial South Carolina Scene: Contemporary Views, 1697–1774* (Columbia, SC, 1977), 183. As the black population began to increase naturally, slaveholders began to demonstrate concern for their slaves' family life. *Laurens Papers*, 4:595–596, 625; 5:370; Coclanis, *Shadow of a Dream*, 43–45; McCusker and Menard, *Economy of British America*, 181; quotes in Littlefield, *Rice and Slaves*, 67–68, and Menard, "Slavery, Economic Growth, and Revolutionary Ideology," 261.

42. Philip Morgan, "Three Planters and Their Slaves: Perspectives on Slavery in

Virginia, South Carolina, and Jamaica, 1750–1790," in Jordan and Skemp, eds., *Race and Family in the Colonial South,* 65.

43. Frank J. Klingberg, ed., *The Carolina Chronicle of Dr. Francis Le Jau, 1706–1717* (Berkeley, 1956), 54–55, 121–122, 129–130, quotes on 55, 108; quote in George F. Jones, ed., "John Martin Boltzius's Trip to Charleston, October 1742," *SCHM,* 82 (1981), 93; Morgan, "Three Planters and Their Slaves," 63–65.

44. Thomas J. Cooper and David J. McCord, comps., *The Statutes at Large of South Carolina,* 10 vols. (Columbia, SC, 1837–1841), 7:346–347, 410–411; Morris, *Southern Slavery and the Law,* 164–165, 169–170.

45. Wood, *Black Majority,* ch. 12; Edward A. Pearson, "'A Countryside Full of Flames,'" 22–50.

46. Van Horne, *Religious Philanthropy and Colonial Slavery,* 112, 116; Klingberg, ed., *Carolina Chronicle of Dr. Francis Le Jau,* 69–70, 74.

47. Theresa A. Singleton, "The Archeology of Afro-American Slavery in Coastal Georgia: A Regional Perception of Slave Household and Community Patterns" (Ph.D. diss., University of Florida, 1980); Thomas R. Wheaton and Patrick H. Garrow, "Acculturation and the Archeological Record in the Carolina Lowcountry"; Lynne G. Lewis, "The Planter Class: The Archeological Record at Drayton Hall"; Kenneth E. Lewis, "Plantation Layout and Function in the South Carolina Lowcountry"; and Steven L. Jones, "The African-American Tradition in Vernacular Architecture," all in Theresa A. Singleton, ed., *The Archeology of Slavery and Plantation Life* (San Diego, 1985), 35–65, 121–140, 199–200, 239–259; quotes in Morgan and Terry, "Slavery in Microcosm," 128; Daniel L. Schafer, "Plantation Development in British East Florida: A Case Study of the Earl of Egmont," *FHQ,* 63 (1984), 176–177; Margaret Washington Creel, *"A Peculiar People": Slave Religion and Community-Culture among the Gullahs* (New York, 1988).

48. George C. Rogers, Jr., *Charleston in the Age of the Pinckneys* (Norman, OK, 1969); Coclanis, *Shadow of a Dream,* 5–11; Carl Bridenbaugh, *Myths and Realities: Societies of the Colonial South* (Baton Rouge, 1952), 59–60, 76–94; Frederick P. Bowes, *The Culture of Early Charleston* (Chapel Hill, 1942). For Charles Town's population, see Coclanis, *Shadow of a Dream,* 114, 18 n14; R. C. Nash, "Urbanization in the Colonial South, Charleston, South Carolina as a Case Study," *JUH,* 19 (1992), 3–29. South Carolina's wealth is variously calculated by Alice Hanson Jones, *Wealth of a Nation To Be: The American Colonies on the Eve of the American Revolution* (New York, 1980).

49. Olwell, *Masters, Slaves, and Subjects;* McCusker and Menard, *Economy of British America,* 183–184; Morgan, "Three Planters and Their Slaves," 37–42, 54–

68. For the interplay of quasi-absenteeism and planter ideology in the nineteenth century, see William W. Freehling, *Prelude to Civil War: The Nullification Controversy in South Carolina, 1813–1836* (New York, 1966), 65–70; Michael P. Johnson, "Planters and Patriarchy: Charleston, 1800–1860," *JSoH*, 46 (1980), 45–72. The development of a unique style of plantation architecture provides a measure of the growing confidence of the planter class; see Samuel Gaillard Stoney, *Plantations of the Carolina Low Country* (Charleston, 1938) and Mills Lane, *Architecture of the Old South: South Carolina* (Savannah, 1984).

50. William L. Van Deburg, *The Slave Drivers: Black Agricultural Labor* (Westport, CT, 1979), provides basic information on this understudied figure.

51. Morgan, "Task and Gang Systems," 191–192; Morgan, "Work and Culture: The Task System and the World of Lowcountry Blacks, 1700–1880," *WMQ*, 39 (1982), 563–599.

52. Betty Wood, *Women's Work, Men's Work: The Informal Slave Economies of Lowcountry Georgia* (Athens, GA, 1995), 105–107; Morgan, "Charleston," 190, 200–205, and Morgan, "Colonial South Carolina Runaways: Their Significance for Slave Culture," *S&A*, 6 (1985), 63; Carl Bridenbaugh, *Colonial Craftsmen* (New York, 1950), 139–141, and Bridenbaugh, *Cities in Revolt: Urban Life in America, 1743–1776* (New York, 1964), 88–89, 244, 274, 285–286; Richard B. Morris, *Government and Labor in Early America* (New York, 1946), 183–185; Wood, *Slavery in Georgia*, 131–132, 143–145; Peter H. Wood, "'Taking Care of Business' in Revolutionary South Carolina: Republicanism and the Slave Society," in Jeffrey J. Crow and Larry E. Tise, eds., *The Southern Experience in the American Revolution* (Chapel Hill, 1978), 273; quote in Barnwell, ed., "Diary of Timothy Ford," 142. The rise of the slave artisanry can be traced in the struggle between white tradesmen and slaveholders over the employment of skilled slaves, a struggle complicated by the fact that many white tradesmen *were* slaveholders. Wood, *Women's Work, Men's Work*, chs. 5 and 7. Quote in Morris, *Government and Labor in Early America*, 184, generally 182–188. Quote in *Runaway Advertisements*, 4:59 (Savannah *Georgia Gazette*, 16 Nov. 1774). "Presentments of the Charles Town Grand Jury, 1733–1734," *SCHM*, 25 (1924), 193; Wood, *Black Majority*, 209 n48; Wood, *Women's Work, Men's Work*, 82–83, 101–121; Morgan, "Charleston," 191–194; Wood, *Slavery in Colonial Georgia*, chs. 8–9; quote in Peter H. Wood, "'Taking Care of Business,'" 273. Morris, *Government and Labor in Early America*, quote on 185. Cooper and McCord, comps., *South Carolina Statutes at Large*, 2:22–23; 3:395–399, 456–461; 7:343, 345–347, 356–368, 385–397, 412–413; Donald R. Lennon and Ida Brooks Kellam, eds., *The Wilmington Town Book, 1743–1778* (Raleigh, 1973), 165–169,

204–205, 210–211, 219–221, 225–229, 234, 238, for the various regulations governing the slaves' living out and hiring out. For slaves pocketing their earnings, see *Laurens Papers,* 10:201.

53. The handful of black men and women who gained legal freedom were closely allied with the planter class, often as the product of a sexual liaison. Robert Olwell, "Becoming Free: Manumission and the Genesis of a Free Black Community in South Carolina, 1740–90," *S&A,* 17 (1996), 1–19; Wood, *Black Majority,* 100–103; Weir, *Colonial South Carolina,* 199–200; Coclanis, *Shadow of a Dream,* 256 n123, 115; Morgan, "Charleston," 188, 193–194; Marina Wikramanayake, *A World in Shadow: The Free Black in Antebellum South Carolina* (Columbia, SC, 1973), ch. 1.

54. Charles Town *South-Carolina Gazette,* 24 May 1773, quote in Duncan, "Servitude and Slavery," quote on 234, also see 233–237; Klaus G. Loewald et al., eds., "Johann Martin Bolzius Answers a Questionnaire on Carolina and Georgia," *WMQ,* 14 (1957), quote on 236; Cooper and McCord, comps., *Statutes at Large of South Carolina,* 7:396–412; Wood, *Women's Work, Men's Work,* ch. 6.

55. Quotes in Charles Town *South-Carolina Gazette* in Robert M. Weir, *Colonial South Carolina: A History* (Millwood, NY, 1983), 190, and Charles Town *South-Carolina and American General Gazette,* 6 January 1775; Mark Anthony De Wolfe Howe, ed., "Journal of Josiah Quincy, Junior," *Massachusetts Historical Society Proceedings,* 49 (1915–1916), 424–481; Charles S. Henry, comp., *A Digest of All the Ordinances of Savannah* (Savannah, 1854), 95–97; Alexander Edwards, comp., *Ordinances of the City Council of Charleston* (Charleston, 1802), 65–68; Cooper and McCord, comps., *Statutes at Large of South Carolina,* 7:363, 380–381, 393; Lennon and Kellam, eds., *Wilmington Town Book,* xxx-xxxi, 165–168, 204–205; Duncan, "Servitude and Slavery," 467–469, 481–484; Leila Sellers, *Charleston Business on the Eve of the American Revolution* (Chapel Hill, 1934), 99–102, 106–108.

56. Wood, *Women's Work, Men's Work,* 70–79, 135–137, and Wood, *Slavery in Colonial Georgia,* 85, 114–115, 159–162; Morgan, "Charleston," 206–208, 222–229; Lennon and Kellam, eds., *Wilmington Town Book,* 168–169, 187, 205–214, 234, 238; Alan D. Watson, "Impulse toward Independence: Resistance and Rebellion among North Carolina Slaves, 1750–1775," *JNH,* 63 (1978), 319. When Flora ran off to Savannah in 1774, her owner "supposed" her "to be haboured under the Bluff by sailors." *Runaway Advertisements,* 4:53 (Savannah *Georgia Gazette,* 13 July 1774). For laws against trading with slaves, see Cooper and McCord, comps., *South Carolina Statutes at Large,* 3:163, 7:353, 367.

57. Harvey H. Jackson, "Hugh Bryan and the Evangelical Movement in Colonial

South Carolina," *WMQ*, 43 (1986), 594–614; Allan Gallay, "The Origins of the Slaveholders' Paternalism: George Whitefield, the Bryan Family, and the Great Awakening in the South," *JSoH*, 53 (1987), 369–394; Charles S. Bolton, *Southern Anglicanism: The Church of England in Colonial South Carolina* (Westport, CT, 1982), 118; James B. Lawrence, "Religious Education of the Negro in the Colony of Georgia," *GHQ*, 14 (1930), 41, 47–51.

58. Jordan, *White over Black*, 144–150, 167–178, and Jordan, "American Chiaroscuro: The Status and Definition of Mulattoes in the British Colonies," *WMQ*, 19 (1962), 186–200, quote on 187; Wood, *Black Majority*, 100–103; Coclanis, *Shadow of a Dream*, 256 n123. A sample of manumissions taken from the South Carolina records between 1729 and 1776 indicates that two-thirds of the slaves freed were female and one-third of the slaves freed were mulattoes at a time when the slave population of South Carolina was disproportionately male and black. Duncan, "Servitude and Slavery," 395–398; Olwell, "Becoming Free," 5–7.

59. Gary B. Nash, *Forging Freedom: The Formation of Philadelphia's Black Community, 1720–1840* (Cambridge, MA, 1988), 10; van den Boogaart, "Servant Migration," 58; Graham Russell Hodges, *Slavery and Freedom in the Rural North: African Americans in Monmouth County, New Jersey, 1665–1865* (Madison, WI, 1996), 11–14; Robert V. Wells, *The Population of the British Colonies in America before 1776* (Princeton, 1975), 112.

60. van den Boogaart, "Servant Migration," 65–71; U.S. Bureau of the Census, *A Century of Population Growth* (Washington, DC, 1909), 150–151, 156–157; Gary B. Nash, *The Urban Crucible: Social Change, Political Consciousness, and the Origins of the American Revolution* (Cambridge, MA, 1979), 13–15, 106–111, 320–321; Nash, "Slaves and Slaveowners in Colonial Philadelphia," *WMQ*, 30 (1973), 223–256; Gary B. Nash and Jean R. Soderlund, *Freedom by Degrees: Emancipation in Pennsylvania and Its Aftermath* (New York, 1991), 14–16; Soderlund, *Quakers and Slavery: A Divided Spirit* (Princeton, 1985), 58, 64; Thomas J. Archdeacon, *New York City, 1664–1710: Conquest and Change* (Ithaca, 1976), 46–47; Greene, *Negro in Colonial New England*, 78, 81–82, 84–88, 92–93; David E. Van Deventer, *The Emergence of Provincial New Hampshire, 1623–1741* (Baltimore, 1976), 113–114; Lynne Withey, *Urban Growth in Colonial Rhode Island: Newport and Providence in the Eighteenth Century* (Albany, NY, 1984), 71; Elaine Forman Crane, *A Dependent People: Newport, Rhode Island, in the Revolutionary War* (New York, 1985), 49–52; Bruce C. Daniels, *Dissent and Conformity on Narragansett Bay: The Colonial Rhode Island Town* (Middletown, CT, 1983), 57–59; Jackson Turner Main, *Society and*

Economy in Colonial Connecticut (Princeton, 1985), 82, 181, 269, 283–284, 294–295, 305, esp. 366. Quote in Carl Bridenbaugh, *Cities in the Wilderness: The First Century of Urban Life in America, 1625–1742* (New York, 1938), 49.

61. Morris, *Government and Labor in Early America*, 182–184; Nash and Soderlund, *Freedom by Degrees*, 16–22; Soderlund, *Quakers and Slavery*, 58–59, 64; Nash, *Forging Freedom*, 11; Nash, *Urban Crucible*, 107–109, 320–321; Nash, "Slaves and Slaveowners," 248–252 and table 8; Archdeacon, *New York City, 1664–1710*, 89–90, esp. 89 n16; Kammen, *Colonial New York*, 182; Greene, *Negro in Colonial New England*, 111–119; Bridenbaugh, *Cities in Revolt*, 88, 285–286; Shane White, *Somewhat More Independent: The End of Slavery in New York City, 1770–1810* (Athens, GA, 1991), 12. For the success of white cartmen in excluding black competitors, see Graham Russell Hodges, *New York City Cartmen, 1667–1850* (New York, 1986), 25–26, 152–159. Quote in Patrick M'Robert, "Tour through Part of the North Provinces of America," ed. Carl Bridenbaugh, *PMHB*, 59 (1935), 142.

62. Peter O. Wacker and Paul G. E. Clemens, *Land Use in Early New Jersey: A Historical Geography* (Newark, 1995), 100–101; Hodges, *Slavery and Freedom in the Rural North*, ch. 2, esp. 45–46.

63. Nash, *Forging Freedom*, 9–11; Nash, "Slaves and Slaveowners in Colonial Philadelphia," 226–232; Soderlund, "Black Importation and Migration into Southeastern Pennsylvania, 1682–1810," *PAPS*, 133 (1989), 146; Salinger, *"To Serve Well and Faithfully,"* 140; James B. Lydon, "New York and the Slave Trade, 1700–1774," *WMQ*, 35; Hodges, *Slavery and Freedom in the Rural North*, 8–9; Lydon, "New York and the Slave Trade," 387–388; Darold D. Wax, "Quaker Merchants and the Slave Trade in Colonial Pennsylvania," *PMHB*, 86 (1962), 145; Wax, "Africans on the Delaware," 38–49, and "Negro Imports into Pennsylvania," 256–257, 280–287.

64. See, for example, Philadelphia *Pennsylvania Gazette*, 17 June 1734 and 21 Feb. 1776 in Billy G. Smith and Richard Wojtowicz, eds., *Blacks Who Stole Themselves: Advertisements for Runaways in the Pennsylvania Gazette, 1728–1790* (Philadelphia, 1989), 18, 128; *Philadelphia Journal*, 27 May 1762; Kruger, "Born to Run," 68.

65. Susan E. Klepp, *Philadelphia in Transition: A Demographic History of the City and Its Occupational Groups, 1720–1830* (New York, 1989), 233, and Klepp, "Seasoning and Society: Racial Differences in Mortality in Eighteenth-Century Philadelphia," *WMQ*, 51 (1994), 474, 477–506; Nash and Soderlund, *Freedom by Degrees*, 15, 24–25; Nash, *Forging Freedom*, 33–34; White, *Somewhat More Independent*, 88–92; Kruger, "Born to Run," 424–431; John B. Blake,

Public Health in the Town of Boston, 1630–1822 (Cambridge, MA, 1959), chs. 5–6; William D. Piersen, *Black Yankees: The Development of an Afro-American Subculture in Eighteenth-Century New England* (Amherst, MA, 1988), 19–21; Crane, *A Dependent People,* 80. The majority of slaveholders in Boston, Philadelphia, and New York owned only one or two slaves, a tiny fraction of a percent owned more than nine, Gary Nash, "Forging Freedom: The Emancipation Experience in the Northern Seaport Cities, 1775–1820," in Ira Berlin and Ronald Hoffman, eds., *Slavery and Freedom in the Age of the American Revolution* (Charlottesville, 1983), 27–30, esp. tables 6–7; White, *Somewhat More Independent,* 88–92; Hodges, *Slavery and Freedom in the Rural North,* 15–18.

66. Although focused on colonial New York, the fullest discussion of the slave family in the North is Kruger, "Born to Run," esp. ch. 4. Also McManus, *Slavery in the North;* Nash, *Forging Freedom,* 11–16, 33; Nash and Soderlund, *Freedom by Degrees,* 25; Klepp, "Seasoning and Society," 475–477; Main, *Colonial Connecticut,* 178–179; Goodfriend, *Before the Melting Pot,* 118. Quote in Kruger, "Born to Run," 329. Between 1767 and 1775, fewer than 100 black children were born and survived in Philadelphia, while, at the same time, some 679 slaves and free blacks died in the city.

67. McManus, *Black Bondage in the North,* 38; Bridenbaugh, *Cities in Revolt,* 88, 285–286, and *Cities in the Wilderness,* 163, 200–201; Nash, "Slaves and Slaveowners in Colonial Pennsylvania," 243–244; Archdeacon, *New York City,* 89–90; Nash and Soderlund, *Freedom by Degrees,* 27–29; *A Century of Population Growth,* 170–180; McManus, *New York Slavery,* 44–45, and *Black Bondage in the North,* 37–39; Crane, *A Dependent People,* 77; Main, *Colonial Connecticut,* 177–179; Wells, *Population of the British Colonies,* 116–123; Nash and Soderlund, *Freedom by Degrees,* 32.

68. Kruger, "Born to Run," 169–176, ch. 7, esp. 321–338; Klepp, *Philadelphia in Transition,* 475–476; Nash and Soderlund, *Freedom by Degrees,* 23–26; Soderlund, "Black Importation," 147–148. Franklin quoted in Nash and Soderlund, *Freedom by Degrees,* xii.

69. Charles Z. Lincoln, William H. Johnson, and A. Judd Northrop, comps., *The Colonial Laws of New York from the Year 1664 to the Revolution,* 5 vols. (Albany, NY, 1894–1896), 2:679–681; Bernard Bush, comp., *Laws of the Royal Colony of New Jersey, 1703–1756,* New Jersey Archives, 3rd ser., 5 vols. (Trenton, NJ, 1977–1986), 2:28–29.

70. Lincoln, Johnson, and Northrop, comps., *Colonial Laws of New York,* 1:764–765; Bush, comp., *Laws of New Jersey,* 2:130–137; James T. Mitchell and Henry Flanders, comps., *The Statutes at Large of Pennsylvania from 1682 to 1801,* 17

vols. (Harrisburg, 1896–1915), 4:59–64; J. H. Trumball and C. J. Hoadly, eds., *The Public Records of Connecticut,* 15 vols. (Hartford, 1850–1890), 4:375–376, 408; 5:233; John R. Bartlett, ed., *Records of the Colony of Rhode Island and Providence Plantations,* 10 vols. (Providence, 1857), 2:251–253; Zilversmit, *First Emancipation,* 16–19; Goodfriend, *Before the Melting Pot,* 116–117; Nash and Soderlund, *Freedom by Degrees,* 61–62.

71. Hodges, *Root and Branch,* 79. "Throughout the pre-Revolutionary period," write Gary B. Nash and Jean R. Soderlund in their study of Pennsylvania, "manumissions were rare." Nash and Soderlund tell of the excruciatingly slow exodus of black people from bondage in one of the few places where the issue of slavery's legitimacy had been raised. Nash and Soderlund, *Freedom by Degrees,* ch. 2, quote on 57. Nash, *Forging Freedom,* 32–37. Of the 437 slaves freed by their masters in a sample of testamentary declarations from 1669 to 1829 only nineteen were freed between 1669 and 1717 and only 103 were freed between 1717 and 1771, Kruger, "Born to Run," ch. 10, esp. 593–597. Also see White, *Somewhat More Independent,* 153; Hodges, *Slavery and Freedom in the Rural North,* 61–62. Census takers failed to differentiate between free and slave blacks in the northern colonies. The statement by one historian of New York slavery that "free blacks before the first federal census in 1790 were generally either not enumerated by census takers or were mistakenly counted as slaves," appears to be true for other northern colonies. Kruger, "Born to Run," 601. See also Greene, *Negro in New England,* 97; Goodfriend, *Before the Melting Pot,* 13, 115–117; Shane White, "'We Dwell in Safety and Pursue Our Honest Callings': Free Blacks in New York City, 1783–1810," *JAmH,* 75 (1988), 448. The best assessment of the size of the North's free black population prior to the Revolution has been made by Jean Soderlund from the manumission records in Philadelphia. Soderlund estimates that in 1767 there were 57 free blacks in Philadelphia or about 4 percent of the city's black population and 2.5 percent of the city's entire population. The free black population increased rapidly in the years that followed, with the beginning of Quaker manumissions, but still in 1775, on the eve of the Revolution, Soderlund calculates there were 114 free blacks in Philadelphia, who composed 14 percent of a greatly reduced black population and 0.04 percent of a greatly expanded white population. Free blacks made up an even smaller percentage of the population, black and total, in the countryside. Soderlund, "Black Importation," 148, 151. The Quakers' decision to rid themselves of slavery created a small spurt of manumissions in the years prior to the Revolution. See Nash and Soderlund, *Freedom By Degrees,* ch. 2 and 74–88; Nash, *Forging Freedom,* 32–36; Kruger, "Born

to Run," 52–56, 608–614; John Cox, Jr., *Quakerism in the City of New York* (New York, 1930), 59–60; Hodges, *Slavery and Freedom in the Rural North,* 62–63.

72. Greene, *Negro in New England,* ch. 11; Piersen, *Black Yankees,* 46–48; Mitchell and Flanders, comps., *The Statutes at Large of Pennsylvania,* 4:49–64; Lincoln, Johnson, and Northrup, comps., *Colonial Laws of New York,* 1:761–767; Hodges, *Slavery and Freedom in the Rural North,* 23; Kruger, "Born to Run," ch. 10; Zilversmit, *First Emancipation,* 16–19.

73. John Hepburn, "The American Defense of the Christian Golden Rule," in Roger Bruns, ed., *Am I Not a Man and a Brother: The Antislavery Crusade of Revolutionary America, 1688–1788* (New York, 1977), 19. The point is made more fully in Klepp, "Seasoning and Society," 487. The number of free people of African descent with surnames declined after the Dutch were ousted from New Netherland. See Kruger, "Born to Run," 61 n22.

74. Linebaugh and Rediker, *The Many-Headed Hydra,* 174–210; Thomas J. Davis, *A Rumor of Revolt: The "Great Negro Plot" in Colonial New York* (New York, 1985); Daniel Horsmanden, *The New York Conspiracy,* ed. by Thomas J. Davis (Boston, 1971); Goodfriend, *Before the Melting Pot,* 122–127; Kenneth Scott, "The Slave Insurrection in New York in 1712," *NYHQ,* 45 (1961), 43–74.

75. James Oliver Horton and Lois E. Horton, *In Hope of Liberty: Culture, Community and Protest among Northern Free Blacks, 1700–1860* (New York, 1997), 16–17, 78–79; Hodges, *Slavery and Freedom in the Rural North,* 66–69; John Van Horne, "Impediments to the Christianization and Education of Blacks in Colonial America," *HMPEC,* 50 (1981), 260; Lawrence W. Towner, "'A Fondness for Freedom': Servant Protest in Puritan Society," *WMQ,* 19 (1962), 201–219; Franklin B. Dexter, ed., *The Literary Diary of Ezra Stiles,* 3 vols. (New York, 1901), 1:247–248, 294, 355, 415, quote on 213–214; Van Horne, ed., *Religious Philanthropy and Colonial Slavery,* 193–194, 220–221, 239–240, 247–248, 271–272, 315, 326. From among the slaves who attended SPG schools and registered their marriages at the Anglican churches, a small cadre of leaders began to emerge. In Newport, John Quamino, who had "tasted the Grace of the Lord Jesus" and wished "that his Relations and Countrymen in Africa might come to the knowledge of and taste the same blessed thing," led his fellow slaves in prayer in the home of a pious Newport Congregationist. Quamino and another African-born slave, Bristol Yamma, were later sent to Princeton to study.

76. Quoted in the Philadelphia *Pennsylvania Gazette,* 22 June 1769, in Smith and Wojtowicz, eds., *Blacks Who Stole Themselves,* 92.

77. Piersen, *Black Yankees,* ch. 9. For resistance tied to African ways, see Robert C.

Twombly, "Black Resistance to Slavery in Massachusetts," in William L. O'Neill, ed., *Insights and Parallels: Problems and Issues of American Social History* (Minneapolis, 1973), 26–32, and, for various association names, see Dorothy Porter, ed., *Early Negro Writing, 1760–1837* (Boston, 1971). Also James Deetz, *In Small Things Forgotten: The Archaeology of Early American Life* (Garden City, 1977), 140–142; Vernon G. Baker, "Archeological Visibility of Afro-American Culture: An Example from Black Lucy's Garden, Andover, Massachusetts," in Robert Schuyler, ed., *Archaeological Perspectives on Ethnicity in America* (Farmingdale, NY, 1980), 34–35.

78. Quotes in Piersen, *Black Yankees,* 121; White, *Somewhat More Independent,* 97.

79. James Thomas McGowan, "Creation of a Slave Society: Louisiana Plantations in the Eighteenth Century" (Ph.D. Diss., University of Rochester, 1976), 116–132, quote on 127; Hall, *Africans in Colonial Louisiana,* 9–10, 175–177, 182–186, table 8, quote on 175; Thomas N. Ingersoll, "The Slave Trade and the Ethnic Diversity of Louisiana's Slave Community," *LH,* 37 (1996), 138; Acosta Rodriguez, *La Problacion de la Luisiana Espanola (1763–1803)* (Madrid, 1979), 110. On enforcement of the *Code Noir's* provisions respecting the sanctity of the family, see Carl A. Brasseaux, "The Administration of the Slave Regulations in French Louisiana, 1724–1766," *LH,* 21 (1980), 141–142, 147–148.

80. Hall, *Africans in Colonial Louisiana,* 250–251; Jacob M. Price, *France and the Chesapeake: A History of the French Tobacco Monopoly, 1674–1791,* 2 vols. (Ann Arbor, 1973), I: ch. 13, esp. 357; Clark, *New Orleans, 1718–1812,* 56; Brian E. Coutts, "Boom and Bust: The Rise and Fall of the Tobacco Industry in Spanish Louisiana, 1770–1790," *Americas,* 42 (1986), 289–309.

81. J. Zitomersky, "Urbanization in French Colonial Louisiana (1706–1766)," *Annales, de demographie historique* (1974), 263–278; Usner, *Indians, Settlers, & Slaves,* 48–54.

82. Laura L. Porteus, trans., "The Documents in Loppinot's Case, 1774," *LHQ,* 12 (1929), 82.

83. Henry P. Dart, ed., "Cabildo Archives," *LHQ,* 3 (1920), 89–91; Hall, *Africans in Colonial Louisiana,* ch. 7, esp. 160–163, 181–190, 202–203; Gerard L. St. Martin, ed. and trans., "A Slave Trial in Colonial Natchitoches," *LH,* 28 (1987), 63–89, esp. 66–68, 71–74.

84. Quote in Porteus, trans., "Loppinot's Case," 106. Opponents of the slaves' free Sunday admitted this "abuse is tolerated because from time immemorial, with the general consent of the masters and connivance of the Superiors, slaves have labored without interruption in the presence of, and with the knowledge and consent of Magistrates." *Ibid.,* 106–107; Francisco Bouligny quoted in Alcée

Fortier, *A History of Louisiana*, 3 vols. (New York, 1904), 2:35–36; Hall, *Africans in Colonial Louisiana*, 176–177.

85. McGowan, "Creation of a Slave Society," 136–145, 152–155, 181–193, 206; Jean-Français-Benjamin de Montigny, "History of Louisiana," in Benjamin F. French, ed., *Historical Collections of Louisiana*, 5 vols. (New York, 1846–1853), 5:119–122, quote on 120–121; Porteus, trans., "Loppinot's Case," 56, 71, 109; Francisco Bouligny quoted in Fortier, *A History of Louisiana*, 2:36; Hall, *Africans in Colonial Louisiana*, 305–306. On the laws enjoining slaves trading independently, Brasseaux, "Administration of Slave Regulations," 145–146, 156.

86. Usner, *Indians, Settlers, & Slaves*, 40, ch. 5, esp. 165–168, 201, 215; St. Martin, ed., "Slave Trial," 65–67; quote in French, ed., *Historical Collections of Louisiana*, 5: 120–121; Porteus, ed. and trans., "Loppinot's Case," 79, 106.

87. Jerah Johnson, "New Orleans's Congo Square: Urban Setting for Early Afro-American Culture Formation," *LH*, 32 (1991), 117–133; Henry P. Dart, "Cabarets of New Orleans in the French Colonial Period," *LHQ*, 19 (1936), 578–583; Emily Clark and Virginia Meacham Gould, "The Feminine Face of Afro-Catholicism in New Orleans, 1727–1852," *WMQ*, 59 (2002), 409–448. The best description of Congo Square is one drawn by Benjamin Latrobe in the early nineteenth century. See, Edward C. Carter, II, John C. Van Horne, and Lee W. Formwalt, eds., *The Journals of Benjamin Henry Latrobe, 1799–1820*, 3 vols. (New Haven, 1980), 3:185, 203–204. For a summary view drawn from the accounts of nineteenth-century travelers, see David C. Estes, "Traditional Dances and Processions of Blacks as Witnessed by Antebellum Travelers," *Louisiana Folklore Miscellany*, 6 (1990), 1–14.

88. For the restrictive nature of French regulation of manumission, see Hans W. Baade, "The Law of Slavery in Spanish Luisiana, 1769–1803," in Edward F. Haas, ed., *Louisiana's Legal Heritage* (New Orleans, 1983), 49–50, 60; Everett, "Free Persons of Color in Colonial Louisiana," 22–23; Ingersoll, "Slave Codes and Judicial Practice," 34–35, 38–39, and Ingersoll, "Free Blacks in a Slave Society," 177. The appropriate sections of the *Code Noir* can be found in Gayarré, *History of Louisiana*, 1:539.

89. Hans W. Baade, "The Law of Slavery in Spanish Luisiana, 1769–1803," in Edward F. Haas, ed., *Louisiana's Legal Heritage* (New Orleans, 1983), 46–60; Everett, "Free People of Color in Colonial Louisiana," 29–33; Kimberly S. Hanger, "Avenues to Freedom to New Orleans' Black Population, 1769–1779," *LH*, 31 (1990), 244–245. Prior to 1769, fewer than 60—about one a year—gratuitous slaveholder-sponsored manumissions were registered in French Louisiana. Ingersoll, "Slave Codes and Judicial Practice," 39. In the absence of a sim-

ilar growth in the free colored population in West Florida—where, in 1767, the British enacted a slave code that severely limited manumission—testifies to the importance of Spanish governance and the laws and customs regulating manumission. Robin F. A. Fabel, *The Economy of British West Florida, 1763–1783* (Tuscaloosa, 1988), 23–25.

90. Hanger, "Avenues to Freedom," 243–245, 249–252, and Hanger, *Bounded Lives, Bounded Places: Free Black Society in Colonial New Orleans, 1769–1803* (Durham, NC, 1997), 26–33; Everett, "Free Persons of Color in Colonial Louisiana," 45–47; Ingersoll, "Free Blacks in a Slave Society," 186–188; McGowan, "Creation of a Slave Society," 201–205; Hall, *Africans in Colonial Louisiana,* 258–260, 266–274.

91. Hanger, "Avenues to Freedom," 246–254, and Hanger, "'The Fortunes of Women in America': Spanish New Orleans's Free Women of African Descent and Their Relations with Slave Women," in Patricia Morton, ed., *Discovering the Women in Slavery: Emancipating Perspectives on the American Past* (Athens, GA, 1996), 156–159; Ingersoll, "Free Blacks in a Slave Society," 186.

92. Baade, "Law of Slavery in Spanish Luisiana," 48–63, 67–70; Herbert S. Klein, *Slavery in the Americas: A Comparative Study of Virginia and Cuba* (Chicago, 1967), 57–65, 196–200; Leslie B. Rout, Jr., *The African Experience in Spanish America, 1502 to the Present Day* (Cambridge, UK, 1976), 87–93; Everett, "Free Persons of Color in Colonial Louisiana," 43–45; Ingersoll, "Free Blacks in a Slave Society," 180–180, 183–184; Hanger, "Avenues of Freedom," 240–245, 262–263; Hanger, "Origins of New Orleans's Free Creoles of Color," in James H. Dormon, ed., *Creoles of Color of the Gulf South* (Knoxville, 1996), 6–7, 17–23; Hanger, *Bounded Lives, Bounded Places,* 42–51.

93. Baade, "Law of Slavery in Spanish Luisiana," 67–70; Ingersoll, "Free Blacks in a Slave Society," 183–186; Everett, "Free Persons of Color in Colonial Louisiana," 45–46. Slaveowners contested one-fifth of all purchases of freedom. Hanger, *Bounded Lives, Bounded Places,* 25–26.

94. Hanger, "Avenues to Freedom," 244–247.

95. *Ibid.,* 243–245, 248, 252, 258–263.

96. *Ibid.,"* 239; McGowan, "Creation of a Slave Society," 196; Hall, *Africans in Colonial Louisiana,* 239–240, 258–259.

97. Hanger, "Avenues to Freedom," 239.

3. REVOLUTIONARY GENERATIONS

1. Benjamin Quarles, *The Negro in the American Revolution* (Chapel Hill, 1961); Frey, *Water from the Rock;* Jordan, *White over Black,* 269–314; Berlin and Hoffman, eds., *Slavery and Freedom.*

2. Quotation in Philip Foner, ed., *The Complete Writings of Thomas Paine*, 2 vols. (New York, 1945), 2:15–19; Jordan, *White over Black*, 291–294.

3. Isaac, *The Transformation of Virginia;* James D. Essig, *The Bonds of Wickedness: American Evangelicals against Slavery, 1770–1808* (Philadelphia, 1982); Christine Leigh Heyrman, *Southern Cross: The Beginnings of the Bible Belt* (New York, 1997); Donald G. Mathews, *Slavery and Methodism: A Chapter in American Morality, 1780–1845* (Princeton, 1965), chs. 1–3.

4. Blackburn, *The Overthrow of Colonial Slavery*, 163–264; C. L. R. James, *Black Jacobins: Toussaint L'Ouverture and the San Domingo Revolution* (New York, 1938); David Patrick Geggus, "Slavery, War, and Revolution in the Greater Caribbean, 1789–1815," in Gaspar and Geggus, eds., *A Turbulent Time*, 1–50. For a deft summary of how events in France shaped the demise of slavery in Saint Domingue, see Carolyn E. Fick, "The French Revolution in Saint Domingue: A Triumph or a Failure?" in *ibid.*, 51–75.

5. James, *Black Jacobins;* Carolyn E. Fick, *The Making of Haiti: The Saint Domingue Revolution from Below* (Knoxville, 1990); Gaspar and Geggus, eds., *A Turbulent Time;* Julius S. Scott, "The Common Wind: Currents of Afro-American Communication in the Era of the Haitian Revolution" (Ph.D. diss., Duke University, 1986), ch. 5.

6. Zilversmit, *First Emancipation*, chs. 5–8; William O'Brien, "Did the Jennison Case Outlaw Slavery in Massachusetts?" *WMQ*, 17 (1960), 219–241; John D. Cushing, "The Cushing Court and the Abolition of Slavery in Massachusetts: More Notes on the 'Quock Walker Case,'" *AJLH*, 5 (1961), 118–144; Arthur Zilversmit, "Quok Walker, Mumbet, and the Abolition of Slavery in Massachusetts," *WMQ*, 25 (1968), 614–624; Elaine MacEacheren, "Emancipation of Slavery in Massachusetts: A Reexamination, 1770–1790," *JNH*, 55 (1970), 289–306; Melish, *Disowning Slavery*, chs. 2–3.

7. Zilversmit, *First Emancipation*, chs. 5–6; Larry R. Gerlach, ed., *New Jersey in the American Revolution, 1763–1783: A Documentary History* (Trenton, 1975), 147–150.

8. Quarles, *Negro in the American Revolution*, ch. 10; Hodges, *Slavery and Freedom in the Rural North*, 109 n27. For refugeeing, see Trenton *New Jersey Gazette*, 5 June 1780; Chatham *New Jersey Journal*, 13 June 1780; Philadelphia *Pennsylvania Post*, 23 June 1780.

9. Quotations on Nash, *Forging Freedom*, 64–65.

10. Bruns, ed., *Am I Not a Man and a Brother*, quotation on 428–429; Herbert Aptheker, ed., *A Documentary History of the Negro People in the United States*, 2 vols. (New York, 1951), 1:9–12; Nash, *Forging Freedom*, 62–65; Nash and Soderlund, *Freedom by Degrees*, 112–113, 133.

11. Nash and Soderlund, *Freedom by Degrees*, chs. 6–7, 173–183, and esp. 194–195; Nash, *Forging Freedom*, 76–78; Kruger, "Born to Run," 158, table 8; White, *Somewhat More Independent*, 46; White, "'We Dwell in Safety and Pursue Our Honest Callings': Free Blacks in New York City, 1783–1860," *JAmH*, 75 (1988), 451–452.

12. Gary B. Nash, "Forging Freedom," in Berlin and Hoffman, eds., *Slavery and Freedom*, 20–27; Nash, *Forging Freedom*, 79–88; White, *Somewhat More Independent*, 192–194; Kruger, "Born to Run," 437–447. Also Quarles, *Negro in the American Revolution*, 51–52; Nash and Soderland, *Freedom by Degrees*, 90; Pierson, *Black Yankees*, 34–35. Some 90 percent of 580 manumitted slaves drawn from a sample of 2,000 whose names were listed in New York's manumission records between 1701 and 1831 had names different from their manumitters. Kruger, "Born to Run," 444–445.

13. "Book of Negroes," National Archives, RG 360; Graham R. Hodges, *The Black Loyalist Directory: African Americans in Exile in the Age of Revolution* (New York, 1996); Ellen G. Wilson, *The Loyal Blacks* (New York, 1976), ch. 3; Hodges, *Slavery and Freedom in the Rural North*, 101–103; Eldon Jones, "The British Withdrawal from the South, 1781–1785," in W. Robert Higgins, ed., *The Revolutionary War in the South: Power, Conflict, and Leadership* (Durham, 1979), 268–285; Ira Berlin, "The Structure of the Free Negro Caste in the Antebellum United States," *JSH*, 9 (1975), 300; Nash, *Forging Freedom*, 136–140, 142–144; Nash, "Forging Freedom," 8–11. Prior to the American Revolution there was little identification between the North and freedom among fugitive slaves. In 1767 a fugitive from Savannah was noted to be headed to some Caribbean island as he "has formerly attempted to get off for the West Indies." *Runaway Slave Advertisements*, 4:24 (Savannah *Georgia Gazette*, 16 Sept. 1767). A year later, Billie, who escaped from the Neabsco Iron-Works in northern Virginia, was thought to be "bound for Charles-Town, or to some place in Carolina, where he expects to be free." Smith and Wojtowicz, comps., *Blacks Who Stole Themselves*, 89. Even during the Revolution, numerous slaves ran southward; see for example, the case of Nat, who fled from southern Maryland to South Carolina. Lorena S. Walsh, "Rural African Americans in the Constitutional Era in Maryland," *MHM*, 84 (1989), 334, 336.

14. John Baur, "International Repercussions of the Haitian Revolution," *Americas*, 26 (1970), 394–418; Alfred N. Hunt, *Haiti's Influence on Antebellum America: Slumbering Volcano in the Caribbean* (Baton Rouge, 1988), ch. 3; Gabriel Debien and René Le Gardeur, "The Saint-Domingue Refugees in Louisiana, 1792–1804," in Carl A. Brasseaux and Glenn R. Conrad, eds., *The Road to Louisiana: The Saint-Domingue Refugees, 1792–1809*, trans. David Cheramie

(Lafayette, LA, 1992), 113–117; Horton and Horton, *In Hope of Liberty*, 109–110; White, *Somewhat More Independent*, 31–32, 155–156; White, "'We Dwell in Safety,'" 450; Nash, *Forging Freedom*, 140–144, 174–176. In Philadelphia, slaveholders freed their slaves under Pennsylvania law but quickly turned around and bound them into long-term indentures. During the 1790s French immigrant slaveholders indentured nearly 500 slaves in Philadelphia. Nash and Soderlund, *Freedom by Degrees*, 180–181. White, *Somewhat More Independent*, 153–156, quotation on 154.

15. Nash, *Forging Freedom*, 138, 142–143; Kruger, "Born to Run," 131.

16. During the colonial period, the balance in favor of men was always greater in the countryside than in the city, but even cities had sex ratios favoring men in the eighteenth century. In 1746 in New York City, for example, the sex ratio of black men and women was 127. Kruger, "Born to Run," 305, 370–371 n11; Nash, "Forging Freedom," 11–12. That changed dramatically by the time of the Revolution and even more dramatically following the Revolution. *Ibid.*, 11–15, esp. table 3; also *Returns of the Whole Number of Persons within the Several Districts of the United States* (Washington, DC, 1801); *Census for 1820* (Washington, DC, 1821). The meaning of the census enumerations, however, has been contested. Gary Nash argues that official records exaggerated the female majority. Many men were away at sea when census takers called. Men in disproportionate numbers avoided being counted. Nash, *Forging Freedom*, 135–136. Also see W. Jeffrey Bolster, *Black Jacks: African American Seamen in the Age of the Sail* (Cambridge, MA, 1997), 2–6, 159–165; Kruger, "Born to Run," 312, table 3, 908.

17. Salinger, "Artisans, Journeymen, and the Transformation of Labor," 66–68; Nash and Soderlund, *Freedom by Degrees*, 118–120, 138–140; White, *Somewhat More Independent*, 33–36.

18. Nash, *Forging Freedom*, 74–75, 146, 149, 152–153; White, *Somewhat More Independent*, 156–158, 163–164; White, "'We Dwell in Safety,'" 453–454, 457–459; Leon F. Litwack, *North of Slavery: The Negro in the Free States* (Chicago, 1961), 154.

19. Nash, *Forging Freedom*, 144–146; Howard B. Rock, ed., *The New York City Artisan, 1789–1825* (Albany, NY, 1989), 39–40; Paul A. Gilje and Howard B. Rock, "Sweep O! Sweep O! African-American Chimney Sweeps and Citizenship in the New Nation," *WMQ*, 51 (1994), 507–532.

20. Nash, *Forging Freedom*, 149–152; White, *Somewhat More Independent*, 158–166; Julie Winch, *Philadelphia's Black Elite: Activism, Accommodation, and the Struggle for Autonomy, 1787–1848* (Philadelphia, 1988), 17–147.

21. William H. Robinson, ed., *The Proceedings of the Free African Union Society*

and the African Benevolent Newport, Rhode Island, 1780–1824 (Providence, 1976), x–xi, and also list of births and deaths of free blacks; White, *Somewhat More Independent,* 166–171; Nash, "Forging Freedom," 31–33, and Nash, *Forging Freedom,* 75–76, 158–160. One of the first matters of business of Philadelphia's Free African Society, founded in 1787, was to establish "a regular mode of procedure with respect to . . . marriages." William Douglass, *Annals of the First African Church in the United States of America* (Philadelphia, 1862), 34–42; Nash, *Forging Freedom,* 74–75, 158–160, 298–299 n1. For the small size of black households in Newport, see Crane, *A Dependent People,* 82; and for the lag in the formation of independent black households in the countryside, see Kruger, "Born to Run," 897.

22. Within these neighborhoods, black people occupied the meanest quarters. Although they shared the same streets and courtyards with working-class white families, black people lived disproportionately in cellar rooms and attic apartments. Overcrowding—along with the absence of sanitation and potable water—bred disease, assuring that the high rates of morbidity and mortality that dogged black people in slavery would remain a part of black life in freedom. Unable to bear enough children who survived infancy to reproduce itself, the urban black population depended on new arrivals from the countryside to sustain its numbers. Nash, *Forging Freedom,* 40–43, 136, 163–171, 213–214; Nash, "Forging Freedom," 40–43; Emma J. Lapansky, "South Street Philadelphia, 1762–1854: A Haven for those Low in the World" (Ph.D. diss., University of Pennsylvania, 1975); Norman J. Johnson, "The Caste and Class of the Urban Form of Historic Philadelphia," *Journal of the American Institute of Planners,* 32 (1966), 334–349.

23. Quotation in Nash, *Forging Freedom,* 64–65, also see 180–183. Also see James Forten, *A Series of Letters by a Man of Color* (Philadelphia, 1913), rpt. in Aptheker, ed., *Documentary History of the Negro People.* Some black men continued to vote, usually supporting the Federalist Party, whose members were prominent in the manumission societies. Ottley and Weatherby, eds., *Negro in New York,* 53–56; Daniel Perlman, "Organizations of the Free Negro in New York City, 1800–1860," *JNH,* 56 (1971), 181–197; Herman Bloch, "The New York Negro's Battle for Political Rights, 1777–1865," *IRSH,* 11 (1964), 65–80; Robert J. Cottrol, *The Afro-Yankees: Providence's Black Community in the Antebellum Era* (Westport, CT, 1982).

24. Winch, *Philadelphia's Black Elite,* 6–7, 19, 22–24; Litwack, *North of Slavery,* 18–19, 25; Shane White, "'It was a Proud Day': African Americans, Festivals, and Parades in the North, 1741–1834," *JAmH,* 81 (1994), 13–50.

25. The Newport Free African Society in 1787 corresponded with the white colonizationist William Thornton respecting its "earnest desire of returning to Affrica and settling there" and proposed sending a delegation to see if land could be purchased with an eye toward settlement. But see the correspondence from black Bostonians and Philadelphians indicating their opposition even to these initial explorations. Robinson, ed., *Free African Union Society*, 16–18, 29.

26. Nash, *Forging Freedom*, 97–98, 103, 115–116, quotation on 98; "Minutes of the Free African Society," in Douglass, *Annals of the First African Church*, 17–19; Robinson, ed., *Free African Union Society*.

27. Quarles, *The Negro in the American Revolution*, ch. 2; Sylvia R. Frey, "Between Slavery and Freedom: Virginia Blacks in the American Revolution," *JSoH*, 49 (1983), 376–378, 387–388, 394–397.

28. Philip D. Morgan and Michael Nicholls, "Runaway Slaves in Eighteenth-Century Virginia," paper delivered at the Organization of American Historians meeting, 1990, 4 n4, esp. table 1 (courtesy of the authors); Allan Kulikoff, "Uprooted Peoples: Black Migrants in the Age of the American Revolution, 1790–1820," in Berlin and Hoffman, eds., *Slavery and Freedom*, 144.

29. *Historical Statistics*, 2:756.

30. Jean B. Lee, *The Price of Nationhood: The American Revolution in Charles County* (New York, 1994), 253; Lorena S. Walsh, "Work and Resistance in the New Republic: The Case of the Chesapeake, 1770–1820," in Mary Turner, ed., *From Chattel Slaves to Wage Slaves: The Dynamics of Labour Bargaining in the Americas* (Kingston, 1995), 97; John C. Fitzpatrick, ed., *The Writings of George Washington, 1745–1799*, 39 vols. (Washington, DC, 1931–44), 37:256–268, quotation on 338; Jackson and Twohig, eds., *Diaries of Washington*, 4:227–283.

31. Donald L. Robinson, *Slavery in the Structure of American Politics, 1765–1820* (New York, 1971), 82–83; *Md. Law*, 1783, c. 23; Hening, comp., *Statutes at Large*, II:24–25; Richard Dunn, "Black Society in the Chesapeake," in Berlin and Hoffman, eds., *Slavery and Freedom*, 52. Most Chesapeake slaves were taken not only to Kentucky but also to lowcountry South Carolina and Georgia. From 1780 to 1810, between 75,000 (Kulikoff) and 115,000 (Tadman) exited the region. Kulikoff, "Uprooted Peoples," 148; Michael Tadman, *Speculators and Slaves: Masters, Traders, Slaves in the Old South* (Madison, 1989), 12; Fischer and Kelly, *Away, I'm Bound Away*, 97–98.

32. Dunn, "Black Society in the Chesapeake," 62–66; Kulikoff, "Uprooted Peoples," 148–151; Lee, *The Price of Nationhood*, 252–253; Tadman, *Speculators and Slaves*, 12; Walsh, *From Calabar to Carter's Grove*, ch. 6; Ellen Eslinger, "The Shape of Slavery on the Kentucky Frontier, 1775–1800," *RKHS*, 92 (1994), 1–

23; Anita S. Goodstein, "Black History on the Nashville Frontier, 1780–1810," *THQ*, 38 (1979), 401–420; quotation in Merton L. Dillon, *Benjamin Lundy and the Struggle for Negro Freedom* (Urbana, IL, 1966), 6; Todd H. Barnett, "Virginians Moving West: The Early Evolution of Slavery in the Blue Grass," *FCHQ*, 73 (1999), 221–248.

33. Carr and Walsh, "Economic Diversification and Labor Organization," 147–148, 182; Walsh, "Plantation Management," 393–400; Walsh, "Rural African Americans," 337–338; Walsh, "Slave Life, Slave Society, and Tobacco Production," 170–173, 179–186, 190; Paul G. E. Clements, *The Atlantic Economy and Colonial Maryland's Eastern Shore: From Tobacco to Grain* (Ithaca, 1980); David Klingman, "The Significance of Grain in the Development of the Tobacco Colonies," *JEH*, 29 (1969), 268–278; Carville Earle and Ronald Hoffman, "Staple Crops and Urban Development in the Eighteenth-Century South," *PAH*, 10 (1976), 7–78; Harold B. Gill, Jr., "Wheat Culture in Colonial Virginia," *AH*, 52 (1978), 380–393.

34. The linkages are elaborated fully in Earle and Hoffman, "Staple Crops and Economic Development," 26–51. Also see Walsh, "Slaves and Tobacco in the Chesapeake," 184–185.

35. Kulikoff, *Tobacco and Slaves*, 342–344, 404–406; Walsh, "Rural African Americans," 330–332; Walsh, "Slave Life, Slave Society, and Tobacco Production," 193–194, 197–199; Dunn, "Black Society in the Chesapeake," 77–78; Kulikoff, "Uprooted Peoples," 153–166; Lee, *Price of Nationhood*, 252–253. For the near ubiquity of slave hire, see Sarah S. Hughes, "Slaves for Hire: The Allocation of Black Labor in Elizabeth City County, Virginia, 1782 to 1810," *WMQ*, 35 (1978), 260–286.

36. See Fitzpatrick, ed., *Writings of Washington*, 5:3, 355–356, for the use of a mixed labor force of free and slave.

37. Walsh, "Plantation Management," 404–406; Walsh, "Slaves and Tobacco in the Chesapeake," 185–199, for what Walsh calls the Chesapeake's "second system of agriculture," 185; Morgan, "Task and Gang Systems," 200.

38. Quotation in W. W. Abbot, ed., *The Papers of George Washington: Presidential Series*, 6 vols. (Charlottesville, 1987–), 1:223; Jackson and Twohig, eds., *Diaries of Washington*, 5:9–10.

39. Quotations in Walsh, "Slave Life, Slave Society, and Tobacco Production," 188–189, 196–197. William Strickland, *Journal of a Tour in the United States of America, 1794–1795*, ed. J. E. Strickland (New York, 1971), 33–34.

40. Kulikoff, *Tobacco and Slaves*, 337–343, 394, 397–406; Dunn, "Black Society in the Chesapeake," 67–68; Carr and Walsh, "Economic Diversification and La-

bor Organization," 176–178; Bayly E. Marks, "Skilled Blacks in Antebellum St. Mary's County, Maryland," *JSoH*, 53 (1987), 545–552; Fitzpatrick, ed., *Writings of Washington*, 31:465; see, for example, *Runaway Advertisements*, 2:26 (Annapolis *Maryland Gazette*, 11 Nov. 1756).

41. Quotation in Walsh, "Work and Resistance in the New Republic," 113, and in Fitzpatrick, ed., *Writings of Washington*, 32:65–66; Petition from Charlotte County, 20 Dec. 1810, LP; William Tatham, *An Historical and Practical Essay on the Culture and Commerce of Tobacco* (London, 1800), rpt. in G. Melvin Herdon, *William Tatham and the Cultivation of Tobacco* (Coral Gables, FL, 1969), 102–105. The continued importance of the slaves' economy as well as its limitations is revealed by the dispute at Mount Vernon when Washington changed the slaves' allowance from unsifted to sifted meal. Slaves, who used the hulls of the unsifted meal to feed their fowl, objected strenuously and forced Washington to reconsider. Fitzpatrick ed., *Writings of Washington*, 32:437–438, 474–475.

42. Ronald L. Lewis, *Coal, Iron, and Slaves: Industrial Slavery in Maryland and Virginia, 1715–1865* (Westport, CT, 1979), and Lewis, "The Use and Extent of Slave Labor in the Chesapeake Iron Industry: The Colonial Era," *LHist*, 17 (1977), 388–405; Charles B. Dew, "David Ross and the Oxford Iron Works: A Study of Industrial Slavery in the Early Nineteenth-Century South," *WMQ*, 31 (1974), 189–224.

43. Morgan, "Task and Gang Systems," 213; Walsh, "Work and Resistance in the New Republic," 102–103; Jackson and Twohig, eds., *Diaries of Washington*, 5:145.

44. Kulikoff, *Tobacco and Slaves*, 399–401; Carr and Walsh, "Economic Diversification and Labor Organization," 161, 176–183; Walsh, "Slave Life, Slave Society, and Tobacco Production," 186; Carole Shammas, "Black Women's Work and the Evolution of Plantation Society in Virginia," *LHist*, 26 (1985), 5–28; Mary Beth Norton, "'What an Alarming Crisis Is This': Southern Women in the American Revolution," in Jeffrey J. Crow and Larry E. Tise, eds., *The Southern Experience in the American Revolution* (Chapel Hill, 1978), 203–234; Mary Beth Norton, Herbert Gutman, and Ira Berlin, "Afro-American Family in the Age of Revolution," in Berlin and Hoffman, eds., *Slavery and Freedom*, 181–182; Dew, "David Ross and the Oxford Iron Works," 212–213; Kulikoff, *Tobacco and Slaves*, 373.

45. Quotation in Richard Parkinson, *A Tour in America in 1798, 1799, and 1800*, 2 vols. (London, 1805), 2:448; Greene, ed., *Diary of Colonel Landon Carter*, 2:648; Walsh, "Rural African Americans," 335; Norton, *Liberty's Daughters: The*

Revolutionary Experience of American Women, 1750–1800 (Boston, 1980), 29–33; Brenda E. Stevenson, *Life in Black and White: Family and Community in the Slave South* (New York, 1996); Herbert G. Gutman, *The Black Family in Slavery and Freedom, 1750–1825* (New York, 1976), 158–159. For Jefferson's opposition to "broad" wives, see Jefferson, *Farm Book,* ed. Betts, 450.

46. Sylvia R. Frey, "'Shaking the Dry Bones': The Dialectic of Conversion," in Ted Ownby, ed., *Black and White: Cultural Interaction in the Antebellum South* (Jackson, MS, 1993), 23–44; Frey, "'The Year of Jubilee Is Come': Black Christianity in the Plantation South in Post-Revolution America," in Ronald Hoffman and Peter J. Albert, eds., *Religion in a Revolutionary Age* (Charlottesville, 1994), 94–124; Russell E. Rickey, "From Quarterly to Camp Meeting: A Reconsideration of Early American Methodism," *Methodist History,* 23 (1985), 199–213, esp. 205–206; Frey, *Water from the Rock,* ch. 8. Heyrman observes that black women outnumbered black men in the early Baptist and Methodist churches three to two. *Southern Cross,* 217–218.

47. Elmer T. Clark et al., eds., *The Journal and Letters of Francis Asbury,* 3 vols. (Nashville, 1958), 1:403, 593; 3:15. Quotations in *Runaway Advertisements,* 1:269–270 (Williamsburg *Virginia Gazette* [Purdie], 1 May 1778); 421 (Richmond *Virginia Gazette and General Advertizer* [Davis], 27 Oct. 1790); 2:401 (*Maryland Journal and Baltimore Advertiser,* 8 Jan. 1790). For an estimate of African American membership in the Baptist, Methodist, and Presbyterian churches in 1810, see Heyrman, *Southern Cross,* 5, 23, 46, 218–220, 262–263.

48. Carville Earle and Ronald Hoffman, "The Urban South: The First Two Centuries," in Blaine A. Brownell and David R. Goldfield, eds., *The City in Southern History: The Growth of Urban Civilization in the South* (Port Washington, NY, 1977), 23–51; Marianne B. Sheldon, "Black-White Relations in Richmond, Virginia, 1782–1820," *JSoH,* 45 (1979), 26–44; Christopher Phillips, *Freedom's Port: The African American Community in Baltimore, 1790–1860* (Urbana, IL, 1997), 10–16, 57–59; G. Terry Sharrer, "Flour Milling in the Growth of Baltimore, 1750–1830," *MHM,* 71 (1976), 322–333; Earle and Hoffman, "Staple Crops and Urban Development," 7–78; Walsh, "Slave Life, Slave Society, and Tobacco Production," 191.

49. Walsh, "Slave Life, Slave Society, and Tobacco Production," 191–192, 354 n43; James Sidbury, "Slave Artisans in Richmond, Virginia, 1780–1810," 50, 56–60; Tina Sheller, "Freemen, Servants, and Slaves: Artisans and Craft Structure of Revolutionary Baltimore Town," 24–32, both in Howard B. Rock, Paul A. Gilje, and Robert Asher, eds., *American Artisans: Crafting Social Identity, 1750–1850* (Baltimore, 1995); Tommy L. Bogger, *Free Blacks in Norfolk, 1790–1860:*

The Darker Side of Freedom (Charlottesville, 1997), 20–21; T. Stephen Whitman, *The Price of Freedom: Slavery and Manumission in Baltimore and Early National Maryland* (Lexington, KY, 1997), 12–19; Phillips, *Freedom's Port*, 16, 18–19, 22–24, 32; Loren Schweninger, "The Underside of Slavery: The Internal Economy, Self-Hire, and Quasi-Freedom in Virginia, 1780–1865," *S&A*, 12 (1991), 2–3; Michael L. Nicholls, "Recreating White Virginia," in Lois Green Carr, ed., *The Chesapeake and Beyond* (Crownsville, MD, 1992), 28–29; Sheldon, "Richmond Black-White Relations," 29.

50. *Gentlemen's Magazine and Historical Chronicle*, 34 (1764), 261; Petition from Petersburg, 11 Dec. 1805, LP; *Proceedings and Debates of the Convention of North-Carolina Called to Amend the Constitution of the State* (Raleigh, 1835), 351; Berlin, *Slaves without Masters*, 45–49, 48 n47.

51. Whitman, *The Price of Freedom*, 93; Phillips, *Freedom's Port*, 54–55, 91–92. The manumission of men and women in roughly equal numbers and the movement toward numerical sexual equality was counter to patterns of manumission throughout the hemisphere. Herbert S. Klein, *African Slavery in Latin America and the Caribbean* (New York, 1986), 156–157. The phenomena may have been confined to Maryland. See Suzanne Lebsock, *Free Women of Petersburg: Status and Culture in a Southern Town, 1784–1860* (New York, 1984), 95–96, 281–83 n18–25; Bogger, *Free Blacks in Norfolk*, 21, for the traditional numerical dominance of women in at least one Virginia city.

52. Whitman, *The Price of Freedom*, 95; Phillips, *Freedom's Port*, 62–63.

53. Whitman, *The Price of Freedom*, 11–12, 24–27; Phillips, *Freedom's Port*, ch. 2.

54. Berlin, *Slaves without Masters*, ch. 4.

55. *Ibid.*, 51–52; Phillips, *Freedom's Port*, 88–92.

56. Quotation in Petition from Petersburg, 11 Dec. 1805, LP; Berlin, *Slaves without Masters*, 54–55; Dunn, "Black Society in the Chesapeake," 75–77; Lebsock, *Free Women of Petersburg*, 7; Michael L. Nicholls, "Recreating White Virginia," 27–28; Harry M. Ward and Harold E. Greer, Jr., *Richmond during the Revolution, 1775–1783* (Charlottesville, 1977), 8.

57. Phillips, *Freedom's Port*, 60, 91–101; Walsh, *From Calabar to Carter's Grove*, 217–218.

58. Phillips, *Freedom's Port*, 73–81, 108–109, 121; Bogger, *Free Blacks in Norfolk*, ch. 3.

59. Phillips, *Freedom's Port*, 32, 83–84, quotation on 83.

60. Thad W. Tate, *The Negro in Eighteenth-Century Williamsburg* (Charlottesville, 1965), ch. 4; Bogger, *Free Blacks in Norfolk*, 145–148; Lebsock, *Free Women of*

Petersburg, 9; Sidbury, "Slave Artisans in Richmond," 57; Phillips, *Freedom's Port,* ch. 5.

61. Ronald Hoffman, "The 'Disaffected' in the Revolutionary South," in Alfred F. Young, ed., *The American Revolution: Explorations in the History of American Radicalism* (DeKalb, IL, 1976), 273–316; John Shy, "The American Revolution: The Military Conflict Considered as a Revolutionary War," in Stephen G. Kurtz and James H. Hutson, eds., *Essays on the American Revolution* (Chapel Hill, 1973), 121–156, and Shy, "British Strategy for Pacifying the Southern Colonies, 1778–1781," in Crow and Tise, eds., *Southern Experience,* 155–173; John S. Pancake, *This Destructive War: The British Campaign in the Carolinas, 1780–1782* (University, AL, 1985). For the backcountry, see Rachel N. Klein, *Unification of a Slave State: The Rise of the Planter Class in the South Carolina Backcountry, 1760–1808* (Chapel Hill, 1990), ch. 3. In addition, pirates and privateers raided the coast, carrying off numerous slaves. Schafer, "'Yellow Silk Ferret Tied Round Their Wrists,'" 94.

62. Josiah Smith to James Poyas, quotation in 18 May 1775, also 16 June 1775, JSL; quotation in *Runaway Advertisements,* 3:345 (Charlestown *South-Carolina Gazette* [Timothy], 7 Nov. 1775).

63. Frey, *Water from the Rock,* 57–60; *Laurens Papers,* 10:320–322, quotation on 10:162–163; Robert M. Weir, *Colonial South Carolina: A History* (Millwood, NY, 1983), 200–203; Morgan, "Charleston," 213–214; Wood, "'Taking Care of Business,'" 284–287, quotation on 292 n49; Robert A. Olwell, "'Domestick Enemies': Slavery and Political Independence in South Carolina, May 1775–March 1776," *JSoH,* 55 (1989), 33–35, 38–39n.

64. Quotation in Frey, *Water from the Rock,* 65–66; Jeffrey J. Crow, "Slave Rebelliousness and Social Conflict in North Carolina, 1775 to 1802," *WMQ,* 37 (1980), 86–88; Betty Wood, "Some Aspects of Female Resistance to Chattel Slavery in Low Country Georgia, 1763–1815," *HJ,* 30 (1987), 612; quotation in George Smith McCowen, Jr., *The British Occupation of Charleston, 1780–1782* (Columbia, SC, 1972), 44. For the new tone of runaway advertisements see, for example, *Runaway Advertisements:* 3:529, 571 (Charleston *South-Carolina and American General Gazette,* 16 Apr. 1778, 4 Nov. 1780); 4:83–84 (Savannah *Royal Georgia Gazette,* 18 Jan. 1781).

65. Thomas Pinckney to Eliza Pinckney, 17 May 1779, Pinckney Family Papers, SCHS; *Runaway Advertisements,* 3:569 (Charleston *South-Carolina and American General Gazette,* 6 Sept. 1780, 21 Oct. 1780); 3:580 (Charleston *Royal Gazette,* 16–19 May 1781); 3:584 (Charleston *Royal Gazette,* 11–14 July 1781); 4:79 (Savannah *Royal Georgia Gazette,* 7 Sept. 1780); Frey, *Water From the Rock,* 92–

95; Josiah Smith to George Applely, 2 Dec. 1780, JSL. For the Indian connection, see Michael Mullin, "British Caribbean and North American Slaves in an Era of War and Revolution, 1775–1807," in Crow and Tise, eds., *Southern Experience*, 261.

66. Josiah Smith to [unknown], 15 Mar. 1781, JSL; Frey, *Water from the Rock*, 117–118; Morgan, "Black Society in the Lowcountry," 111–113; McCowen, *British Occupation of Charleston*, 33–34; Frey, *Water from the Rock*, 82–86. Still slaves were able to supply the market in Charleston and other rice ports through their gardening and marketing.

67. Eliza Pinckney to Thomas Pinckney, 17 May 1779, Pinckney Family Papers, SCHS; Eliza Pinckney to [unknown], 25 Sept. 1780, Pinckney Family Papers, LC; Josiah Smith to [unknown], 2 Dec. 1780, 15 Mar. 1781, JSL; Norton, *Liberty's Daughters*, 207–212; quotation in Morgan, "Black Society in the Lowcountry," 109–110; Jerome J. Nedelhaft, *The Disorders of War: The Revolution in South Carolina* (Orono, ME, 1981), 64; quotation in Joyce E. Chaplin, "Creating a Cotton South in Georgia and South Carolina, 1760–1815," *JSoH*, 57 (1991), 181–182; Chaplin, *Anxious Pursuit*, 234–235.

68. Gray, *So. Ag.*, 1:593–594; Frey, *Water from the Rock*, 208–209; G. Terry Sharrer, "The Indigo Bonanza in South Carolina, 1740–90," *T&C*, 12 (1971), 455; Chaplin, "Creating a Cotton South," 178–179, 181–183, and Chaplin, *Anxious Pursuit*, 157–158. On gardens, see Rouchefoucault Liancourt, *Travels through the United States of North America . . . in the Years 1795, 1796, and 1797*, 2 vols. (London, 1799), 1:599.

69. Chaplin, *Anxious Pursuit*, 208–220; Chaplin, "Creating a Cotton South," 182–186.

70. "Miscellaneous Papers of James Jackson," *GHQ*, 37 (1953), 78; Kenneth Coleman, *The American Revolution in Georgia, 1763–1789* (Athens, GA, 1958), 145–146; Frey, *Water from the Rock*, 106, 174–180; Morgan, "Black Society in the Lowcountry," 111; J. Leitch Wright, Jr., *Florida in the American Revolution* (Gainesville, FL, 1975), ch. 10; Landers, "Traditions of African American Freedom," 25–26; Nadelhaft, *Disorders of War*, 156; quotation in Max Farrand, ed., *The Records of the Federal Convention of 1787*, 5 vols. (New Haven, 1911), 2:371. Also Chaplin, *Anxious Pursuit*, 119.

71. "Letters of Joseph Clay Merchant of Savannah, 1776–1793," *Georgia Historical Society Collections*, 8 (1913), 167–175, quotation on 211; Klein, *Unification of a Slave State*, 114–115; Nadelhaft, *Disorders of War*, 145–157; Frey, *Water from the Rock*, 206–210, quotation on 208; Joyce E. Chaplin, "Tidal Rice Cultivation and the Problem of Slavery in South Carolina and Georgia, 1760–1815,"

WMQ, 49 (1992), 38–39; Chaplin, *Anxious Pursuit,* 236–238; Gray, *So. Ag.,* 1:277–290, 2:595–596; Coclanis, *Shadow of a Dream,* 133–134.

72. Quotation in Morgan, "Black Society in the Lowcountry," 109, 120. The ability to secede en masse continued to be a major weapon in the slaves' hands. In 1786 a Georgia planter reported that "all my working Negroes left me last night," he supposed because of "the short prospect of provision." Chaplin, *Anxious Pursuit,* 268–270, and Chaplin, "Tidal Rice Cultivation," 54.

73. Morgan, "Black Society in the Lowcountry," 138–140, esp. 139n; Nadelhaft, *Disorders of War,* 132; Quarles, *Negro in the American Revolution,* 174–175; Frey, *Water from the Rock,* 226–228, quotation on 227; Mullin, "British Caribbean and North American Slaves," 240–241. As measured by the number of advertisements placed in the Savannah *Georgia Gazette,* the number of runaways increased substantially after the war. Wood, "Female Resistance," 613–615. Wartime banditry also continued, see Robert M. Weir, "'The Violent Spirit': The Reestablishment of Order, and the Continuity of Leadership in Post-revolutionary South Carolina," in Ronald Hoffman et al., eds., *An Uncivil War: The Southern Backcountry during the American Revolution* (Charlottesville, 1985), 70–98; Klein, *Unification of a Slave State,* 116–118.

74. Klein, *Unification of a Slave State,* ch. 7; Hunt, *Haiti's Influence on Antebellum America,* ch. 3; Frances S. Childs, *French Refugee Life in the United States, 1790–1800* (Baltimore, 1940); Davis, *The Problem of Slavery in the Age of Revolution,* 113–163.

75. Morgan, "Black Society in the Lowcountry," 138–139. For the postwar consolidation of planter authority, see Klein, *Unification of a Slave State,* chs. 4–5, and for suppression of bandits, pp. 114–118; Nadelhaft, *Disorders of War,* 132; Loren Schweninger, "Slave Independence and Enterprise in South Carolina, 1780–1865," *SCHM,* 93 (1992), 116–117; Frey, *Water from the Rock,* 211, 227–228; William Dusinberre, *Them Dark Days: Slavery in the American Rice Swamps* (New York, 1996), 255. Planters also used other, more subtle incentives to create a new social order, see Chaplin, "Slavery and the Principle of Humanity: A Modern Idea in the Early Lower South," *JSH,* 24 (1990), 309–310.

76. Coclanis, *The Shadow of a Dream,* ch. 4; Chaplin, *Anxious Pursuit,* ch. 7. On the switch from inland to tidal rice production, see Gray, *So. Ag.,* 1:279–328, 2:721; Chaplin, "Tidal Rice Cultivation and the Problem of Slavery," 29–61; Morgan, "Lowcountry," 98–107; Johann David Schoepf, *Travels in the Confederation, 1783–1784,* ed. and trans. Alfred J. Morrison, 2 vols. (Philadelphia, 1911), 2:181–182, 221.

77. Landers, "Rebellion and Royalism in Spanish Florida: The French Revolution

on Spain's Northern Frontier," in Gaspar and Geggus, eds., *A Turbulent Time*, 156–177; Landers, "Acquisition and Loss on a Spanish Frontier: The Free Black Homesteaders of Florida, 1784–1821," *S&A*, 17 (1996), 85–102; Landers, *Black Society in Spanish Florida*, ch. 10; Susan R. Parker, "Men without God or King: Rural Planters of East Florida, 1784–1790," *FHQ*, 69 (1990), 135–155.

78. Gray, *So. Ag.*, 2:609; Chaplin, *Anxious Pursuit*, 208–226, 291–319; also John Hebron Moore, "Cotton Breeding in the Old South," *AH*, 30 (1956), 96–97. For sea island cotton see Charles F. Kovacik and Robert E. Mason, "Changes in the South Carolina Sea Island Cotton Industry," *Southeastern Geographer*, 25 (1985), 77–104; Frey, *Water from the Rock*, 212–213, 220–222.

79. "Letters of Joseph Clay," *Collections of the Georgia Historical Society Collections*, 8 (1913), 187, 194–195; Morgan, "Black Society in the Lowcountry," 84–89, 132; Frey, *Water from the Rock*, 180–185, 211–213; Schafer, "'Yellow Silk Ferret Tied Round Their Wrists,'" 97; *Runaway Advertisements*, 4:104–105, 111 (Savannah *Gazette of the State of Georgia*, 7 May 1783, 22 Jan. 1784); 3:403 (Charleston *State Gazette of South-Carolina*, [Timothy] 22 Jan. 1787). Similarly, in 1787, a North Carolina slaveholder tried to recover a fugitive purportedly at large since February 1781, who was reported to have been sent from Wilmington to Charleston by the British, "where he sometimes passed for a freeman, and hired himself as such." Some slaveholders attempted to recover slaves who had taken refuge with the Indians; see Theodora J. Thompson and Rosa S. Lumpkin, eds., *Journal of the House of Representatives, 1783–1784* (Columbia, SC, 1977), 530. Finally, slaveholders opened negotiations with slaves who had taken refuge in Florida; one slave told his master's envoy that he might return "willingly . . . but not at present." Morgan, "Black Society in the Lowcountry," 110.

80. Morgan, "Black Society in the Lowcountry," 84–86, quotation in n3; Robert William Fogel and Stanley L. Engerman, "Philanthropy at Bargain Prices: Notes on the Economics of Gradual Emancipation," *JLS*, 3 (1974), 381–383; Chaplin, "Creating a Cotton South," 186–187; Chaplin, *Anxious Pursuit*, 290–291; G. Melvin Herndon, "Samuel Edward Butler of Virginia Goes to Georgia, 1784," *GHQ*, 52 (1968), 115–131; Kulikoff, "Uprooted Peoples," 149.

81. Morgan, "Black Society in the Lowcountry," 84–92, 132; Patrick S. Brady, "The Slave Trade and Sectionalism in South Carolina, 1787–1808," *JSoH*, 38 (1972), 612–614; Kulikoff, "Uprooted Peoples," 149–151; Chaplin, *Anxious Pursuit*, 320–322.

82. Morgan, "Black Society in the Lowcountry," 83–85, 93–96. "The best tidal swamp was worth at least twice as much as inland swamp—up to four times as

much if improved." Chaplin, "Tidal Rice Cultivation," 36–46; Chaplin, *Anxious Pursuit*, 237–280, indicates that the enormous capital investment in tidal rice production squeezed out smaller planters and barred the entry of newcomers; Klein, *Unification of a Slave State*, 21–26, 151–153, 247–268; Frey, *Water from the Rock*, 213–215; Gray, *So. Ag.*, 1:438, 444–446.

83. Morgan, "Black Society in the Lowcountry," 105–108, 118–120; Chaplin, "Tidal Rice Cultivation and the Problem of Slavery," 55–56; Chaplin, *Anxious Pursuit*, ch. 7, esp. 231, 266–270, 326–367; Dusinberre, *Them Dark Days*, 274–275. The drivers' authority also grew because of an increase in absenteeism among owners, who increasingly withdrew to Charleston and also spent more time living abroad. Luigi Castiglioni, an Italian nobleman who visited the lowcountry after the war, believed most planters were "raised in England" and lived "for the most part in Charleston, visiting their lands two or three times a year." Luigi Castiglioni, *Viaggio: Travels in the United States of North America, 1785–1787*, ed. and trans. Antonio Pace (Syracuse, NY, 1983), 164; Morgan, "Work and Culture," 575; Wood, *Women's Work, Men's Work*, 16–17; Mullin, "British Caribbean and North American Slaves," 249; Chaplin, "Tidal Rice Cultivation and the Problem of Slavery," 56–57. Quotation in Richard K. Murdock, ed., "Letters and Papers of Dr. Daniel Turner: A Rhode Islander in South Georgia," *GHQ*, 54 (1970), 102.

84. Morgan, "Black Society in the Lowcountry," 105–106. For the resistance of former lowcountry slaves to the gang labor system preferred by upcountry planters, see Chaplin, *Anxious Pursuit*, 122–123, 324–325, 327.

85. Morgan, "Black Society in the Lowcountry," 97–108; Ira Berlin, "The Slaves' Changing World," in James O. Horton and Lois E. Horton, eds., *A History of the African American People* (New York, 1995), 42–59.

86. Petition of James Brock(?) et al., nd, Petition Collection, South Carolina General Assembly Papers, South Carolina Department of Archives and History, Columbia; Morgan, "Black Society in the Lowcountry," 122–124; Morgan, "Charleston," 194–195; Loren Schweninger, "Slave Independence and Enterprise in South Carolina, 1780–1865," *SCHM*, 93 (1992), 105–107, quotation on 105.

87. Morgan, "Black Society in the Lowcountry," 92, 129–131; Chaplin, *Anxious Pursuit*, 321.

88. Morgan, "Black Society in the Lowcountry," 132.

89. Chaplin, "Tidal Rice Cultivation," 57–59; Chaplin, *Anxious Pursuit*, 270–273. On the slaves' sacred space, see Margaret Washington Creel, "Gullah Attitudes toward Life and Death," in Joseph E. Holloway, ed., *Africanisms in American*

Culture (Bloomington, 1990), 69–97; Creel, *"A Peculiar People,"* 179; Morgan, "Black Society in the Lowcountry," 124–129.

90. Schweninger, "Slave Independence and Enterprise," 114; Morgan, "Black Society in the Lowcountry," 123–124; Wood, *Women's Work, Men's Work,* chs. 4–5, 7 (for population of Savannah, see 211–212 n6). See especially the struggle to regulate the sale of badges for slaves. *Ibid.,* 94–96; John Lambert, *Travels through Lower Canada and the United States of North America* (London, 1810), 2:403; Schopf, *Travels in the Confederation,* 2:201–202; *Laurens Papers,* 10:201; Whittington B. Johnson, *Black Savannah, 1788–1864* (Fayetteville, AR, 1996), 91, 93–94, 96.

91. Morgan, "Lowcountry," 115–117, 122; Wikramanayake, *A World in Shadow,* ch. 2; Olwell, "Becoming Free"; Wood, *Women's Work, Men's Work,* 122–125; *Runaway Advertisements,* 3:410–411 (Charleston *State Gazette of South-Carolina,* [Timothy] 5 Apr. 1790). The imperfect record of South Carolina manumission during the eighteenth century yields some 379 examples of slaves gaining their freedom. Of those, some 199 or 53 percent were recorded after 1775. Olwell, "Becoming Free," 5; Wikramanayake, *A World in Shadow,* ch. 1; Coclanis, *Shadow of a Dream,* 115.

92. Olwell, "Becoming Free," 5–7; Morgan, "Black Society in the Lowcountry," 116, 122; Duncan, "Servitude and Slavery in Colonial South Carolina," 398. The number of slaves purchasing their freedom also increased sharply following the Revolution. Olwell, "Becoming Free," 10–11.

93. Successful fugitives seemed to share many of the characteristics of manumittees. In the words of one slaveholder, they were creoles who were "tolerably free from the common Negro dialect." *Runaway Advertisements* (Charleston *State Gazette of South Carolina* [Timothy], 18 Feb. 1790), 3:410.

94. Michael P. Johnson and James L. Roark, *Black Masters: A Free Family of Color in the Old South* (New York, 1984), 3–4.

95. Morgan, "Charleston," 205–206; Loren Schweninger, *Black Property Owners in the South, 1790–1915* (Urbana, IL, 1990), 20–21.

96. E. Horace Fitchett, "The Origin and Growth of the Free Negro Population of Charleston, South Carolina," *JNH,* 26 (1941), 421–437; Fitchett, "The Traditions of the Free Negro in Charleston, South Carolina," *JNH,* 25 (1940), 148.

97. See, for example, "Eighteenth Century Petition of South Carolina Negroes," *JNH,* 31 (1946), 98–99.

98. Rouchefoucault Liancourt, *Travels through the United States,* 602; Larry Koger, *Black Slaveowners: Free Black Slave Masters in South Carolina, 1790–1860* (Jefferson, NC, 1985), 13–14; Schweninger, *Black Property Owners in the South,* 23;

Johnson, *Black Savannah*, 79–81. On passing, see Koger, *Black Slaveowners*, 14–16.

99. *Rules and Regulations of the Brown Fellowship Society, Established at Charleston, South Carolina, November 1, 1790* (Charleston, 1844); Fitchett, "The Traditions of the Free Negro," 139–152, quotation on 144; Robert L. Harris, Jr., "Charleston's Free Afro-American Elite: The Brown Fellowship Society and the Humane Brotherhood," *SCHM*, 82 (1981), 289–310. In 1803 its members joined together to form the Minor's Moralist Society to support and educate indigent and orphaned colored children.

100. D. Clayton James, *Antebellum Natchez* (Baton Rouge, 1968), 17–18; Wright, *Florida in the American Revolution*, 10–12, 14, 22–23, 46. As a result of refugeeing, the wartime population of West Florida doubled and that of East Florida quintupled. *Ibid.*, 21.

101. Hall, *Africans in Colonial Louisiana*, ch. 7; Usner, *Indians, Settlers, and Slaves*, 136–138; Gilbert C. Din, "Cimarrones and the San Malo Band in Spanish Louisiana," *LH*, 21 (1980), 240–245; Ingersoll, *Mammon and Manon*, ch. 8, esp. 231.

102. Hanger, "A Privilege and Honor to Serve: The Free Black Militia of Spanish New Orleans," *MHW*, 21 (1991), 59–79, and Hanger, *Bounded Lives, Bounded Places*, ch. 4; Roland C. McConnell, *Negro Troops of Antebellum Louisiana: A History of the Battalion of Free Men of Color* (Baton Rouge, 1968), ch. 2; Jack D. L. Holmes, *Honor and Fidelity: The Louisiana Infantry Regiment and the Louisiana Militia Companies, 1766–1821* (Birmingham, 1965); Harold E. Sterkx, *Free Negro in Ante-Bellum Louisiana* (Rutherford, NJ, 1972), 73–79. Although free colored militiamen served under officers of their own color, black and brown, both pardo and moreno units had white "advisors."

103. Hanger, "Origins," 7–9, esp. table 1; Ingersoll, *Mammon and Manon*, ch. 8.

104. McGowan, "Creation of a Slave Society," ch. 4; Ingersoll, "Free Blacks in a Slave Society," 183, 186–187; Hanger, "Origins," 8–9; Hanger, "Avenues to Freedom," 247, 257; Hanger, *Bounded Lives, Bounded Places*, 12, 26–33; Sterkx, *Free Negro in Ante-Bellum Louisiana*, 36–51; Paul F. Lachance, "The Formation of a Three-Caste Society: Evidence from Wills in Antebellum New Orleans," *SSH*, 18 (1994), 234; Thomas M. Fiehrer, "The African Presence in Colonial Louisiana: An Essay on the Continuity of Caribbean Culture," in Robert R. McDonald, John R. Kemp, and Edward F. Haas, eds., *Louisiana's Black Heritage* (New Orleans, 1979), 23–24.

105. Carl A. Brasseaux and Glenn R. Conrad, eds., *The Road to Louisiana: The Saint-Domingue Refugees, 1792–1809*, trans. David Cheramie (Lafayette, LA,

1992); Hunt, *Haiti's Influence on Antebellum America,* ch. 3; Dunbar Rowland, ed., *Official Letter Books of W. C. C. Claiborne, 1801-1816,* 6 vols. (Jackson, MS, 1917), 4:381-382, 391-393, 409; 5:1-3, 30-31. For the population of New Orleans: Hanger, "Avenues to Freedom," 239, and Hanger, "Origins," 2; Lachance, "The Formation of a Three-Caste Society," 234; McGowan, "Creation of a Slave Society," 196-197; for Mobile: Lawrence Kinnaird, *Spain in the Mississippi Valley, 1765-1794,* 3 vols. (Washington, DC, 1946-1949), 2:196; for Pensacola: William Coker and Douglas Inglis, *The Spanish Census of Pensacola, 1784-1820: A Genealogical Guide to Spanish Pensacola* (Pensacola, 1980); Duvon C. Corbitt, "The Last Spanish Census of Pensacola, 1820," *FHQ,* 24 (1945), 30-32; Pablo Tornero Tinajero, "Estudio de la poblacion de Pensacola (1784-1820)," *Annurio de Estudios Americans,* 34 (1977), 537-561.

106. For New Orleans: McGowan, "Creation of a Slave Society," 196-203; Kinnaird, *Spain in the Mississippi Valley,* 2:196; *New Orleans in 1805, A Directory and Census* (New Orleans, 1936); and a summary table in Hanger, "Avenues to Freedom," 239; for Mobile: Kinnaird, *Spain in the Mississippi Valley,* 2:196; Virginia Meacham Gould, "The Free Creoles of Color of the Antebellum Gulf Ports of Mobile and Pensacola: A Struggle for the Middle Ground," in Dormon, ed., *Creoles of Color,* 33-35; for Pensacola: *ibid.;* Jack D. L. Holmes, "The Role of Blacks in Spanish Alabama: The Mobile District, 1780-1813," *AHQ,* 37 (1975), 8; Coker and Inglis, *The Spanish Census of Pensacola;* Corbitt, "The Last Spanish Census of Pensacola," 30-32; Tinajero, "Estudio de la poblacion de Pensacola," 537-561.

107. Carl A. Brasseaux and Glenn R. Conrad, "Introduction," in Brasseaux and Conrad, eds., *Road to Louisiana,* xiii; Paul Lachance, "The 1809 Immigration of Saint-Domingue Refugees to New Orleans: Reception, Integration, and Impact," in *ibid.,* 247-248; Lachance, "The Formation of a Three-Caste Society," 226, 234. In 1820 the sex ratio for white people in New Orleans was 246, and 44 for free colored people. See *ibid.,* 224.

108. Ingersoll, "Free Blacks in a Slave Society," 189, 198-199; Carl A. Brasseaux, "Creoles of Color in Louisiana's Bayou Country, 1766-1877," in Dormon, ed., *Creoles of Color,* 69-71; Roulhac Toledano and Mary Louise Christovich, eds., *New Orleans Architecture,* 7 vols. (Gretna, LA, 1980), 6: ch. 16.

109. Hanger, *Bounded Lives, Bounded Places,* ch. 2, esp. 58-59; Berquin-Duvallon, *Vue de la colonie espagnole du Mississippi,* quoted in Paul Alliot, "Historical and Political Reflections on Louisiana," in James A. Robertson, ed., *Louisiana under the Rule of Spain, France, and the United States, 1785-1807,* 2 vols. (Cleveland, 1911), 1:219; Lachance, "The Foreign French," in Arnold J. Hirsch and

Joseph Logsdon, eds., *Creole New Orleans: Race and Americanization* (Baton Rouge, 1992), 124.

110. Kimberly S. Hanger, "Household and Community Structure among the Free Population of Spanish New Orleans, 1778," *LH*, 30 (1989), 72–74; Hanger, "'The Fortunes of Women in America,'" 159–165; and Hanger, *Bounded Lives, Bounded Places*, 69–87.

111. Caroline M. Burson, *The Stewardship of Don Estaban Miro, 1782–1792* (New Orleans, 1942), 124–143; Clark, *New Orleans*, 183–186; Usner, *Indians, Settlers, and Slaves*, 108–111; Carl A. Brasseaux, *The Founding of New Acadia: The Beginnings of Acadian Life in Louisiana, 1765–1803* (Baton Rouge, 1987); Andrew S. Walsh and Robert V. Wells, "Population Dynamics in the Eighteenth-Century Mississippi River Valley: Acadians in Louisiana," *JSH*, 11 (1978), 521–545; Gilbert C. Din, "Early Spanish Colonization Efforts in Louisiana," *LS*, 11 (1972), 31–49, and "Spain's Immigration Policy and Efforts in Louisiana during the American Revolution," *ibid.*, 14 (1975), 241–275; Fabel, *Economy of British West Florida*, 6–21; J. Burton Starr, *Tories, Dons, and Rebels: The American Revolution in British West Florida* (Gainesville, FL, 1976), 33–34; Clinton N. Howard, *British Development of West Florida, 1763–1769* (Berkeley, 1947), 50–101; Hall, *Africans in Colonial Louisiana*, 277–278; Lachance, "The Politics of Fear: French Louisiana and the Slave Trade, 1789–1809," *PS*, 1 (1979), 196; Thomas M. Fiehrer, "The African Presence in Colonial Louisiana: An Essay on the Continuity of Caribbean Culture," in McDonald, Kemp, and Haas, eds., *Louisiana's Black Heritage*, 11; Robert L. Paquette, "Revolutionary Saint Domingue in the Making of Territorial Louisiana," in Gaspar and Geggus, eds., *A Turbulent Time*, 222 n25.

112. Ingersoll, "Slave Codes and Judicial Practice," 47–60; Baade, "Law of Slavery in Spanish Luisiana," 63–66, 70–74; Gilbert C. Din and John E. Harkins, *The New Orleans Cabildo: Colonial Louisiana's First City Government, 1769–1803* (Baton Rouge, 1996), 160–162; McGowan, "Creation of a Slave Society," 242–243; James D. Padgett, ed., "A Decree for Louisiana, Issued by the Baron de Carondelet, June 1, 1795," *LHQ*, 20 (1937), 590–605; quotation in Ronald R. Morazan, "Letters, Petitions, and Decrees of the Cabildo of New Orleans, 1800–1803: Edited and Translated," 2 vols. (Ph.D. diss., Louisiana State University, 1972), 1:179–180, 185.

113. Hall, *Africans in Colonial Louisiana*, 213–236; Din, "Cimarrones," 244–262; Din and Harkins, *New Orleans Cabildo*, 156–159, 162–163, 166–169; McConnell, *Negro Troops*, 22–23; Burson, *Stewardship of Don Estaban Miró*,

214–220; Gayarré, *History of Louisiana,* 3:57–66; Usner, *Indians, Settlers, and Slaves,* 140–141; McGowan, "Creation of a Slave Society," 233–242.

114. Hall, *Africans in Colonial Louisiana,* chs. 8–9, esp. 285–286; Ingersoll, "The Slave Trade and Ethnic Diversity," 151; Lachance, "The Politics of Fear," 167, 180, 182, 196–197; James, *Antebellum Natchez,* 45; Fabel, *Economy of British West Florida,* ch. 2; Catterall, ed., *Judicial Cases,* 4:524–525.

115. Clark, *New Orleans,* chs. 10–11, esp. 183–192; Burson, *Stewardship of Don Estaban Miró,* 74; Jack D. L. Holmes, "Indigo in Colonial Louisiana and the Floridas," *LH,* 8 (1967), 335–340; Jack D. L. Holmes, *Gayoso: The Life of a Spanish Governor in the Mississippi Valley, 1789–1799* (Baton Rouge, 1965), 91–98; James, *Antebellum Natchez,* 48–51; Coutts, "Boom and Busts," 305–309.

116. René J. Gardeur, Jr., "The Origins of the Sugar Industry in Louisiana," in *Green Fields: Two Hundred Years of Louisiana Sugar* (Lafayette, LA, 1980), 1–28; Clark, *New Orleans,* 202–203, 217–220; J. Carlyle Sitterson, *Sugar Country: The Cane Sugar Industry in the South, 1753–1950* (Lexington, KY, 1953), 11–12; Arthur P. Whitaker, *The Mississippi Question, 1795–1803* (New York, 1934), 131–132; Lachance, "Politics of Fear," 170 n26, 192; Lachance, "The 1809 Immigration of Saint-Domingue Refugees," 271. For the problems of growing sugar with a six-month growing cycle, see Alliot, "Historical and Political Reflections on Louisiana," in Robertson, ed., *Louisiana,* 1:61–63; James Pitot, *Observations on the Colony of Louisiana from 1796 to 1802,* trans. Henry C. Pitot (Baton Rouge, 1979), 73–76, 115–116.

117. Clark, *New Orleans,* 202–203, 217–220; James, *Antebellum Natchez,* 48–52; John Hebron Moore, *The Emergence of the Cotton Kingdom of the Old Southwest* (Baton Rouge, 1988), 1–17; Holmes, *Gayoso,* 96–101; Fortier, *A History of Louisiana,* 2:29–30; Andrew Ellicott, *The Journal of Andrew Ellicott* (Chicago, 1962 [1803]), 133.

118. Ronald L. F. Davis, *The Black Experience in Natchez, 1720–1880* (Natchez, MS, 1993), 44–50; Samuel Wilson, Jr., "Architecture of Early Sugar Plantations," in *Green Fields,* 51–82; Morton Rothstein, "The Natchez Nabobs: Kinship and Friendship in an Economic Elite," in Hans Trefousse, ed., *Essays in Honor of Arthur C. Cole* (New York, 1977), 97–112; quotation in Lachance, "Politics of Fear," 162. When the new American governor arrived in Louisiana in 1804, he found "but one sentiment throughout the Province—*they must import more Slaves, or the Country was ruin'd forever.*" Clarence E. Carter, ed., *Territorial Papers of the United States,* 18 vols. (Washington, DC, 1934–), 9:340.

119. Lachance, "The Politics of Fear," 186–197; Clark, *New Orleans,* 222–225; Ingersoll, "The Slave Trade and Ethnic Diversity," 133; Ingersoll, *Mammon and*

Manon, ch. 7, esp. 184–186; Brady, "The Slave Trade and Sectionalism in South Carolina," 616.

120. Hall, *Africans in Colonial Louisiana,* ch. 9 and 252 (Hall maintains that most of the new arrivals were, like the previous influx, from Senegambia, 288); Kulikoff, "Uprooted Peoples," 149, 162–163; Davis, *The Black Experience in Natchez,* 10–13, 16, esp. table 1; Ingersoll, *Mammon and Manon,* ch. 7; Ingersoll, "The Slave Trade and Ethnic Diversity," 154–155; James, *Antebellum Natchez,* 41–43, 45–46, esp. 46; Fabel, *Economy of British West Florida,* 37–38; Margaret Fisher Dalrymple, ed., *The Merchant of Manchac: The Letterbooks of John Fitzpatrick, 1768–1790* (Baton Rouge, 1978), 425–431.

121. Davis, *The Black Experience in Natchez,* 10–12, 15; Kulikoff, "Uprooted Peoples," 154, 162–163, esp. n35; Hall, *Africans in Colonial Louisiana,* 295–301, 363–364; Ingersoll, *Mammon and Manon,* chs. 6–7; McGowan, "Creation of a Slave Society," 271 n24.

122. LaChance, "Politics of Fear," 173; McGowan, "Creation of a Slave Society," 245–252; C. C. Robin, *Voyage to Louisiana, 1803–1805,* trans. Stuart O. Landry (New Orleans, 1966), 238. For the trials of one newly imported African, see Terry Alford, *Prince among Slaves* (New York, 1977), ch. 3.

123. Hall, *Africans in Louisiana,* 253–256, ch. 10; Burson, *Stewardship of Don Estaban Miró,* 121–122; LaChance, "Politics of Fear," 170–171; Din and Harkins, *New Orleans Cabildo,* 169; Holmes, "The Abortive Slave Revolt at Pointe Coupee, Louisiana, 1975," *LH,* 11 (1970), 341–362; Ulysses S. Ricard, Jr., "The Pointe Coupée Slave Conspiracy of 1791," in Patricia Galloway and Philip Boucher, eds., *Proceedings of the Fifteenth Meeting of the French Colonial Historical Society* (1992); McGowan, "Creation of a Slave Society," ch. 8; Sterkx, *Free Negro in Ante-Bellum Louisiana,* 91–93; McConnell, *Negro Troops,* 27–28; Carter, ed., *Territorial Papers,* 9:575–576; James H. Dormon, "The Persistent Specter: Slave Rebellion in Territorial Louisiana," *LH,* 28 (1977), 389–393; Juan Jose Andreu Ocariz, *Movimientos Rebeldes de los Esclavaos Negros el Dominino Español en Luisiana* (Zaragoza, 1977), 75–86, 97–106, 117–177; Hanger, "Conflicting Loyalties," esp. 12–13 n21; Debien and Le Gardeur, "Saint-Domingue Refugees in Louisiana," 175–183; Scott, "The Common Wind," 234–235, 265–274.

124. Berquin-Duvallon, *Vue de la colonie espagnole du Mississippi,* quoted in Alliot, "Historical and Political Reflections on Louisiana," 1:118–122; Carter, Van Horne, and Formwalt, eds., *Journals of Benjamin Henry Latrobe,* 3:171–172, 291, quotation on 201. Viewed from the perspective of the nineteenth century, slaves in the lower Mississippi Valley maintained an active internal economy.

Roderick A. McDonald, "Independent Economic Production by Slaves on An-
tebellum Louisiana Sugar Plantations," in Berlin and Morgan, eds., *Cultivation
and Culture*, 273–302; McDonald, *The Economy and Material Culture of Slaves:
Goods and Chattels on the Sugar Plantation of Jamaica and Louisiana* (Baton
Rouge, 1993), chs. 2, 4; Virginia Meachum Gould, "'If I Can't Have My
Rights, I Can Have My Pleasures, and If They Won't Give Me Wages, I Can
Take Them': Gender and Slave Labor in Antebellum New Orleans," in Mor-
ton, ed., *Discovering the Women in Slavery*, 188–190.

125. McDonald, *The Economy and Material Culture of Slaves*, 12–14, 60–61; Mc-
Donald, "Independent Economic Production by Slaves," 277–278, 284–285;
Berquin-Duvallon, *Vue de la colonie espagnole du Mississippi;* Perrin du Lac,
Voyage, quoted in Robertson, ed., *Louisiana,* 1:181–184.

126. Berquin-Duvallon, *Vue de la colonie espagnole du Mississippi,* quoted in Alliot,
"Historical and Political Reflections on Louisiana," 1:121; Daniel H. Usner, Jr.,
"Indian-Black Relations in Colonial and Antebellum Louisiana," in Stephan
Palmié, ed., *Slave Cultures and the Cultures of Slavery* (Knoxville, 1995), 155–156;
Usner, "American Indians on the Cotton Frontier: Changing Economic Rela-
tions with Citizens and Slaves in the Mississippi Territory," *JAmH,* 72 (1985),
306–312, quotations on 311.

127. Randy J. Sparks, "Religion in Amite County, Mississippi," in John B. Boles,
ed., *Masters and Slaves in the House of the Lord: Race and Religion in the American South, 1740–1870* (Lexington, KY, 1988), 59–60.

128. Ernest R. Liljegren, "Jacobinism in Spanish Louisiana, 1792–1797," *LHQ,* 22
(1939), 47–97; Kimberly Hanger, "Conflicting Loyalties: The French Revolution and People of Color in Spanish New Orleans," *LH,* 34 (1993), 5–33.

129. No one has sorted through all of the various conspiracies, rumors of conspiracies, and actual acts of rebellion during the 1790s. Until that is done, the nature of the threat to Spanish rule or the slave society cannot be gauged with
any accuracy. However, these threats were taken with the utmost seriousness
by Spanish authorities and the largely French planter class, and, on the basis of
official adjudication, hundreds of men and women were jailed, imprisoned,
deported, lashed, and hung.

130. Hall, *Africans in Colonial Louisiana,* 317–319, ch. 11; Holmes, "Slave Revolt at
Pointe Coupée," 341–362; McGowan, "Creation of a Slave Society," ch. 8;
Ocariz, *Movimientos Rebeldes de los Esclavaos Negros,* 117–177.

131. Berlin, *Slaves without Masters,* 117–120; Carter, ed., *Territorial Papers,* 9:174–
175; Rowland, ed., *Claiborne Letter Books,* 2:217–219.

132. Berlin, *Slaves without Masters,* 120–121; Caryn Cossé Bell, *Revolution, Romanti-*

cism, and the Afro-Creole Protest Tradition in Louisiana, 1718–1868 (Baton Rouge, 1997), 33–36; quotation in Lachance, "1809 Immigration of Saint-Domingue Refugees," 121; Jane Lucas de Grummond, *Renato Beluche: Smuggler, Privateer, and Patriot: 1780–1860* (Baton Rouge, 1983), ch. 5; Stanley Faye, "Privateers of Guadeloupe and their Establishment in Barataria," *LHQ,* 23 (1940), 431–434.

133. Martin, comp., *Orleans Law,* 1:620, 640–642, 648, 656, 660; 2:104, 326–332; Berlin, *Slaves without Masters,* 122–123; Ingersoll, "Free Blacks in New Orleans," 196–198; Ingersoll, "Slave Codes and Judicial Practice," 60–61; Baade, "Law of Slavery in Spanish Luisiana," 71–74.

134. Dormon, "The Persistent Specter," 393–404.

4. Migration Generations

1. D. W. Meinig, *The Shaping of America: A Geographical Perspective on 500 Years of History,* 3 vols. (New Haven, 1983–), 2:3–32; Reginald Horsman, *The Frontier in the Formative Years, 1783–1815* (New York, 1970), ch. 1; James E. Lewis, *The American Union and the Problem of Neighborhood: The United States and the Collapse of the Spanish Empire, 1783–1829* (Chapel Hill, 1998); Malcolm J. Rohrbough, *The Trans-Appalachian Frontier: People, Societies, and Institutions, 1775–1850* (New York, 1978), chs. 8, 10–12.

2. Adam Rothman, "The Expansion of Slavery in the Deep South, 1720–1820" (Ph.D. diss, Columbia University, 2000), ch. 3; Thomas D. Clark and John W. Guice, *The Old Southwest, 1795–1830: Frontiers in Conflict* (Norman, OK, 1996); Frank L. Owsley, Jr., *Struggle for the Gulf Borderlands: The Creek War and the Battle of New Orleans, 1812–1815* (Gainesville, FL, 1981); James W. Covington, "The Negro Fort," *Gulf Coast Historical Review,* 5 (1996), 78–91.

3. Daniel H. Usner, Jr., *American Indians in the Lower Mississippi Valley: Social and Economic Histories* (Lincoln, NE, 1998), esp. chs. 4–5; Claudio Saunt, *A New Order of Things: Property, Power, and the Transformation of the Creek Indians, 1733–1816* (Cambridge, UK, 1999); Mary E. Young, *Redskins, Ruffleshirts, and Rednecks: Indian Allotments in Alabama and Mississippi, 1830–1860* (Norman, OK, 1961); J. Leitch Wright, Jr., *The Only Land They Knew: The Tragic Story of the American Indians of the Old South* (New York, 1981); James H. Merrill, "The Racial Education of the Catawba Indians," *JSoH,* 50 (1984), 263–284; Kathleen E. Holland Braund, "The Creek Indians, Blacks, and Slavery," *JSoH,* 57 (1991), 607–618; Theda Perdue, *Slavery and the Evolution of Cherokee Society, 1540–1866* (Knoxville, 1979).

4. Malcolm J. Rohrbough, *The Land Office Business: The Settlement and Adminis-*

tration of American Public Lands, 1789–1837 (New York, 1986); Rothman, "The Expansion of Slavery," ch. 6. For a classic case, Gordon T. Chappell, "John Coffee: Land Speculator and Planter," *AR,* 20 (1969), 24–43.

5. Joseph P. Reidy, *From Slavery to Agrarian Capitalism in the Cotton Plantation South: Central Georgia, 1800–1880* (Chapel Hill, 1992), ch. 1; Ralph B. Flanders, *Plantation Slavery in Georgia* (Chapel Hill, 1933), 55–64; Christopher Morris, *Becoming Southern: The Evolution of a Way of Life, Warren County, Vicksburg, Mississippi, 1770–1860* (New York, 1995), ch. 2; Daniel S. Dupree, *Transforming the Cotton Frontier: Madison County, Alabama, 1800–1840* (Baton Rouge, 1997), ch. 1; Donald P. McNeilly, *Old South Frontier: Cotton Plantations and the Formation of Arkansas Society, 1819–1861* (Fayetteville, AR, 2000), ch. 1.

6. For Virginia and Kentucky, see Samuel Shepherd, comp., *The Statutes at Large of Virginia, from October Session 1792, to December Session 1806,* 3 vols. (Richmond, 1835–1836), 1:122–130; and *Laws of Kentucky . . .* (Lexington, KY, 1799), 105–116; North Carolina and Tennessee, see John Haywood, comp., *A Revisal of all the Public Acts of the State of North Carolina and of the State of Tennessee Now in Force in the State of Tennessee* (Nashville, 1809), and Haywood, comp., *Public Acts of the General Assembly of North-Carolina and Tennessee, Enacted from 1715 to 1813, in Force in Tennessee* (Nashville, 1815), 64–80; for Georgia and Mississippi, see Horatio Marbury and William H. Crawford, comps., *Digest of the Laws of the State of Georgia* (Savannah, 1802), 426–444, and A. Hutchinson, comp., *Code of Mississippi . . .* (Jackson, 1848), 512–525.

7. Stuart Bruchey, *Cotton and the Growth of the American Economy, 1790–1860* (New York, 1967), 14–17, table 3A.

8. Frederic Bancroft, *Slave-Trading in the Old South* (Baltimore, 1931), 398, estimates that about 30 percent of slaves were carried by traders. Robert William Fogel and Stanley L. Engerman, *Time on the Cross: The Economics of American Negro Slavery,* 2 vols. (Boston, 1974), 1:47–49, increase that proportion to 50 percent, and Tadman, *Speculators and Slaves,* 22–41, in an extensive critique of Fogel and Engerman, puts the proportion carried by traders between 60 and 80 percent. A recent re-estimate by Jonathan B. Pritchett, "Quantitative Estimates of the United States Interregional Slave Trade, 1820–1860," presented at the Social Science History Association Conference, Chicago, 1998, lowers Tadman's estimate to about 50 percent.

9. Kulikoff, "Uprooted Peoples," 149; W. E. B. DuBois, *The Suppression of the African Slave Trade, 1638–1870* (Cambridge, MA, 1896), 108–130, 136–150; Robinson, *Slavery in American Politics,* 338–346; Gene A. Smith, "U.S. Navy Gun-

boats and the Slave Trade in Louisiana Waters, 1808–1811," *MHW,* 23 (1963), 135–147; Judd Scott Harmon, "Suppress and Protect: The United States Navy, the African Slave Trade, and Maritime Commerce, 1794–1862" (Ph.D. diss., College of William and Mary, 1977), chs. 3, 5; Frank L. Owsley, Jr., and Gene Smith, *Filibusters and Expansionists: Jeffersonian Manifest Destiny, 1800–1821* (Tuscaloosa, 1997), 118–140; Francis J. Stafford, "Illegal Importations: Enforcement of the Slave Trade Laws along the Florida Coast, 1810–1828," *FHQ,* 46 (1967), 124–133; Royce Gordon Shingleton, "David Byrdie Mitchell and the African Importation Case of 1820," *JNH,* 58 (1973), 327–340.

10. Jesse Torrey, *A Portraiture of Domestic Slavery in the United States* (Philadelphia, 1817, rpt. 1970), 49–58; Carol Wilson, *Freedom at Risk: The Kidnapping of Free Blacks in America, 1780–1865* (Lexington, KY, 1994); Patience Essah, *A House Divided: Slavery and Emancipation in Delaware, 1638–1865* (Charlottesville, 1996), 83–86, 121–123; Bogger, *Free Blacks in Norfolk,* 99–101; Frances D. Pingeon, "An Abominable Business: The New Jersey Slave Trade, 1818," *NJH* 109 (1991), 15–35; Nash, *Forging Freedom,* 242–245; Rothman, "The Expansion of Slavery," 303–327; Matthew Mason, "The Rain between the Storms: The Politics and Ideology of Slavery in the United States, 1809–1821" (Ph.D. diss., University of Maryland, 2002), 277–297; Nell Irvin Painter, *Sojourner Truth: A Life, A Symbol* (New York, 1996), 33–35.

11. Steven Deyle, "The Irony of Liberty: The Origins of the Domestic Slave Trade," *JER,* 12 (1992), 37–62.

12. Bancroft, *Slave Trading in the Old South;* Wendell H. Stephenson, *Isaac Franklin: Slave Trader and Planter of the Old South* (Baton Rouge, 1938); Tadman, *Speculators and Slaves;* Walter Johnson, *Soul by Soul: Life Inside the Antebellum Slave Market* (Cambridge, MA, 1999); Edmund Drago, *Broke by the War: Letters of a Slave Trader* (Columbia, SC, 1991); Edward E. Baptist, "Cuffy, Fancy Maids, and One-Eyed Men: Rape, Commodification, and the Domestic Slave Trade in the United States," *AHR* (2001), 1619–1650.

13. Like the number of slaves who crossed the Atlantic in the First Middle Passage, the number of slaves transported to the southern interior also is contested. Fogel and Engerman, *Time on the Cross,* 47, estimate it at 835,000 between 1790 and 1860. Herbert G. Gutman and Richard Sutch, "The Slave Family: Protected Agent of Capitalist Masters or Victim of the Slave Trade?" in Paul A. David et al., eds., *Reckoning with Slavery: A Critical Study in the Quantitative History of American Negro Slavery* (New York, 1976), 99, put the total at "more than a million"; Michael Tadman, *Speculators and Slaves,* ch. 2 and 237–247, estimates that interregional movement averaged some 200,000

slaves each decade between 1820–1860 and that the total for the period be-
tween 1790 and 1820 was at least 200,000. Also see Peter McClelland and
Richard Zeckhauser, *Demographic Dimensions of the New Republic: American
Interregional Migration, Vital Statistics and Manumissions, 1800–1860* (New
York, 1982), 159–164.

14. Tadman, *Speculators and Slaves*, 12; quotation in James C. Cobb, *The Most
Southern Place on Earth: The Mississippi Delta and the Roots of Region Identity*
(New York, 1992), 12.

15. Tadman, *Speculators and Slaves*, 132–178, 296–302; quotation in Steven F.
Miller, "Plantation Labor Organization and Slave Life on the Cotton Frontier:
The Alabama-Mississippi Black Belt, 1815–1840," in Berlin and Morgan, eds.,
Cultivation and Culture, 157; Reidy, *Slavery to Agrarian Capitalism*, 23.

16. Quotations in U. B. Phillips, ed., *Plantation and Frontier*, 2 vols. (Cleveland,
1909), 2:68; Miller, "Plantation Labor Organization and Slave Life," 157;
Charles S. Sydnor, *Slavery in Mississippi* (New York, 1933), 162–171; Randy J.
Sparks, "Religion in Amite County, Mississippi," in John B. Boles, ed., *Masters
and Slaves in the House of the Lord: Race and Religion in the American South,
1740–1870* (Lexington, KY, 1988), 59.

17. Tadman, *Speculators and Slaves*; 25–31; McClelland and Zeckhauser, *Demographic Dimensions*, 8; Jonathan P. B. Pritchett and Herman Freudenberger, "A
Peculiar Sample: The Selection of Slaves for the New Orleans Market," *JEH*,
52 (1992), 110; Miller, "Plantation Labor Organization and Slave Life," 157.
Computed from the published U.S. census: *Census for 1820* (Washington, DC,
1821); *Fifth Census of the United States 1830* (Washington, DC, 1832); *Sixth Census . . . 1840* (Washington, DC, 1841); *Seventh Census . . . 1850* (Washington,
DC, 1853); *Population of the United States in 1860* (Washington, DC, 1862).

18. John Hope Franklin and Loren Schweninger, *Runaway Slaves: Rebels on the
Plantation* (New York, 1999), 225, 398. George P. Rawick, comp., *The American
Slave: A Composite Autobiography*, 41 vols. (Westport, CT, 1972–1979), ser. 2,
vol. 16, pt. 1, 116.

19. Todd H. Barnett, "Virginians Moving West: The Early Evolution of Slavery in
the Bluegrass," *FCHQ*, 73 (1999), 221–223, 239–243.

20. Rawick, ed., *American Slave*, supp., ser. 2, vol. 7B, 2800; also *ibid.*, supp., ser.
2, vol. 3, 800. G. W. Featherstonhaugh, *Excursions through the Slave States*, 2
vols. (New York, 1844), 1:119–123, 169; Charles Ball, *Fifty Years in Chains* (New
York, 1858), 29–30.

21. Rawick, ed., *American Slave*, supp., ser. 1, vol. 5, 284–285; *ibid.*, supp., ser. 1,
vol. 5, 320–321; Tadman, *Speculators and Slaves*, 68–70, 237–238, 298–300.

After more than a century of decline, the slave mortality rate began increasing in the second and third decade of the nineteenth century. Fogel, *Without Consent or Contract,* 128–129.

22. Torrey, *A Portraiture of Domestic Slavery,* 55–56, 61, 67; Rawick, ed., *American Slave,* supp., ser. 2, vol. 7B, 2464; William Wells Brown, *Narrative of William W. Brown, A Fugitive Slave,* ed. Williams Andrews (New York, 1993), 45; Ball, *Fifty Years in Chains,* 30; E. S. Abdy, *Journal of a Residence and Tour in the United States,* 3 vols. (London, 1835), 2:179–180; Carl David Arfwedson, *The United States and Canada in 1832, 1833, and 1834,* 2 vols. (London, 1834), 2:429. One Arkansas planter found her slaves were deeply depressed and "so dissatisfied that they lost all ambition for almost anything." Quotation in McNeilly, *Old South Frontier,* 51.

23. Edward D. Jervey and C. Harold Huber, "The *Creole* Affair," *JNH,* 65 (1980), 196–211; Howard Jones, "The Peculiar Institution and National Honor: The Case of the *Creole* Slave Revolt," *CWH,* 21 (1975), 28–50; Charles S. Syndor, *Slavery in Mississippi* (New York, 1933), 149–150; Featherstonhaugh, *Excursions through the Slave States,* 37; Robert H. Gudmestad, "A Troublesome Commerce: The Interstate Slave Trade, 1808–1840" (Ph.D. diss., Louisiana State University, 1999), ch. 6; Franklin and Schweninger, *Runaway Slaves,* 55–56.

24. Joan E. Cashin, *A Family Venture: Men and Women on the Southern Frontier* (New York, 1991), 72; quotations in T. Lindsay Baker and Julie P. Baker, eds., *The WPA Oklahoma Narratives* (Norman, OK, 1996), 82; Rawick, ed., *American Slave,* vol. 4, pt. 2, 115, also supp., ser. 2, vol. 5A, 1762–1763; McNeilly, *Old South Frontier,* 31.

25. Morris, *Becoming Southern,* 65–67; Fletcher M. Green, ed., *The Lides Go South . . . and West: The Record of a Planter Migration in 1835* (Columbia, SC, 1952), 17–19.

26. Quotation in Miller, "Plantation Labor Organization and Slave Life," 165–166.

27. Stampp, *Peculiar Institution,* ch. 4.

28. Quotation in Carter, ed., *Territorial Papers,* 6:299; Miller, "Plantation Labor Organization and Slave Life," 157–159; H. R. Howard, *The Life and Adventures of John A. Murrell: The Great Western Land Pirate* (New York, 1847); Franklin and Schweninger, *Runaway Slaves,* 86–89, 102–103.

29. Baker and Baker, eds., *The WPA Oklahoma Narratives,* 82; *Southern Agriculturalist,* 7 (1834), 404; Rawick, ed., *American Slave,* ser. 1, vol. 6, 172–173; Morris, *Becoming Southern,* 74–75; McNeilly, *Old South Frontier,* ch. 5.

30. Gray, *So. Ag.,* 2:689–705; John Hebron Moore, *The Emergence of the Cotton Kingdom in the Old Southwest: Mississippi, 1770–1860* (Baton Rouge, 1988), chs.

2–5; Cashin, *Family Venture,* 112–118; Rawick, ed., *American Slave,* ser. 1, vol. 6, pt. 1, 172–173; supp., ser. 2, vol. 5A, 183; Ball, *Fifty Years in Chains,* 131–133, 146–149; Frederick Law Olmsted, *A Journey in the Back Country* (New York, 1860), 81, and Olmsted, *The Cotton Kingdom: A Traveller's Observations on Cotton and Slavery in the American States,* ed. Arthur M. Schlesinger (New York, 1953), 439.

31. Joseph P. Reidy, "Obligation and Right: Patterns of Labor, Subsistence, and Exchange in the Cotton Belt of Georgia, 1790–1860," Berlin and Morgan, eds., *Cultivation and Culture,* 141; Cashin, *Family Venture,* 114–117; Cobb, *Most Southern Place on Earth,* 19–22; Robert William Fogel, *Without Consent or Contract: The Rise and Fall of American Slavery* (New York, 1989), 77–79, emphasizes the speed up as well as the unremitting nature of gang labor.

32. John W. Blassingame, ed., *Slave Testimony: Two Centuries of Letters, Speeches, Interviews, and Autobiographies* (Baton Rouge, 1975), 132; Ball, *Fifty Years in Chains,* 149–150; for the transformation of the slaves' economy with changes in tandem in the staple economy, see John Campbell, "As 'A Kind of Freeman'?: Slaves' Market-Related Activities in the South Carolina Up Country, 1800–1860," Berlin and Morgan, eds., *Cultivation and Culture,* 243–274.

33. Miller, "Plantation Labor Organization and Slave Life on the Cotton Frontier," 163–164; Scarborough, "Heartland of the Cotton Kingdom," in Richard A. McLemore, *A History of Mississippi,* 3 vols. (Hattiesburg, MS, 1973), 1:337–338; William K. Scarborough, *The Overseer: Plantation Management in the Old South* (Baton Rouge, 1966); Genovese, *Roll, Jordan, Roll,* 3–25; Fogel, *Without Consent or Contract,* 52; Franklin and Schweninger, *Runaway Slaves,* 2–3, 9–11.

34. Michael P. Johnson, "Work, Culture, and the Slave Community: Slave Occupations in the Cotton Belt in 1860," *LHist,* 27 (1986), 325–355; Fogel, *Without Consent or Contract,* ch. 2.

35. Cashin, *Family Venture,* 67–68, 114–115, quotation on 114; in the 1850s, Olmsted found "the plowing, both with single and double mule teams, was generally performed by women, and very well performed, too." *A Journey to the Back Country,* 81, but see Fogel, *Without Consent or Contract,* 45–46; Deborah Gray White, *Ar'n't I a Woman? Female Slaves in the Plantation South* (New York, 1985), 69, 120–121, 129; Jacqueline Jones, *Labor of Love, Labor of Sorrow: Black Women, Work, and the Family from Slavery to the Present* (New York, 1985), 15–21.

36. Computed from the published U.S. census: *Census for 1820; Fifth Census . . . 1830; Sixth Census . . . 1840; Population of the United States in 1860.* In identifying the sugar parishes, I have followed Sarah Paradise Russell, "Cultural

Conflicts and Common Interests: The Making of the Sugar Planter Class in Louisiana" (Ph.D. diss., University of Maryland, 2000).

37. Johnson, *Soul by Soul;* Tadman, *Speculators and Slaves,* 22–23, 64–71; Michael Tadman, "The Demographic Cost of Sugar: Debates on Slave Societies and Natural Increase in the Americas," *AHR,* 105 (2000), 1534–1575; Herman Freudenberger and Jonathan B. Pritchett, "The Domestic United States Slave Trade: New Evidence," *JIH,* 21 (1991), 452; Freudenberger and Pritchett, "A Peculiar Sample," 110; Ann Patton Malone, *Sweet Chariot: Slave Family and Household Structure in Nineteenth-Century Louisian*a (Chapel Hill, 1992), 54–55. Computed from the *Fifth Census . . . 1830.*

38. J. Carlyle Sitterson, *Sugar Country: The Cane Sugar Industry in the South* (Lexington, KY, 1953), 28–50, 112–156; Gray, *So. Ag.,* 2: 750–751; John C. Rodrigue, *Reconstruction in the Cane Fields: From Slavery to Free Labor in Louisiana's Sugar Parishes, 1862–1880* (Baton Rouge, 2001), ch. 1; Tadman, "The Demographic Cost of Sugar," 1534–1575; Walter Prichard, "Routine on a Louisiana Sugar Plantation under the Slavery Regime," *MVHR,* 14 (1927), 168–178; Featherstonhaugh, *Excursions through the Slave States* 1:120; quotation in Solomon Northup, *Twelve Years a Slave,* ed. Sue Eakin and Joseph Logdson (Baton Rouge, 1968), 149.

39. John A. Heitman, *The Modernization of the Louisiana Sugar Industry, 1830–1910* (Baton Rouge, 1987), chs. 1–2; quotations in Thomas Hamilton, *Men and Manners in America,* 2 vols. (Edinburgh, 1833), 2: 229; Northup, *Twelve Years a Slave,* 148.

40. Tadman, *Speculators and Slaves,* 68, and Tadman, "The Demographic Cost of Sugar," 1534–1575; Richard H. Steckel, "The Fertility of American Slaves," *Research in Economic History,* 7 (1982), 266–267; John Campbell, "Work, Pregnancy, and Infant Mortality among Southern Slaves," *JIH,* 14 (1984), 793–812. In 1850 the number of slave children under four years per slave woman age fifteen to forty years was .54 compared to .78 and .92, respectively, for slave women in Dallas and Greene counties, Alabama. Computed from *Seventh Census of the United States 1850.*

41. Some did so permanently, translating frontier opportunities into freedom. See, for example, the entrepreneurial Free Frank, Juliet K. Walker, "Pioneer Slave Entrepreneurship—Patterns, Processes, and Perspectives: The Case of Free Frank on the Kentucky Pennyroyal, 1795–1819," *JNH,* 68 (1983), 289–308; also Basil Hall, *Travels in North America in the Years 1827–1828,* 2 vols. (Philadelphia, 1829), 2:260. Quotation in William Littell, comp., *The Statute Law of*

Kentucky to 1816, 5 vols. (Frankfort, KY, 1809–1819), 2:114; Rawick, ed., *American Slave,* supp., ser. 2, vol. 5, 41–43.

42. Leland W. Meyer, *The Life and Times of Colonel Richard Mentor Johnson of Kentucky* (New York, 1932), 317–321; also see Willard B. Gatewood, "Sunnyside: The Evolution of an Arkansas Plantation, 1840–1945," in Jeannie M. Whayne, *Shadows over Sunnyside: An Arkansas Plantation in Transition, 1830–1945* (Fayetteville, AR, 1993), 4–5; James M. O'Toole, *Passing for White: Race, Religion, and the Healy Family, 1820–1920* (Amherst, MA, 2002); John R. Kern et al., "Sharpley's Bottom Historical Sites," Report to U.S. National Park Service (C-54039 [80]), 1982, 43–44; William Ransom Hogan and Edwin Adams Davis, eds., *William Johnson's Natchez: The Ante-Bellum Diary of a Free Negro* (Baton Rouge, 1951), 597n. Although they were never as visible and probably not as numerous, the frontier also allowed for similar relations between black men and white women; see, for example, Loren Schweninger, ed., *The Southern Debate over Slavery: Petitions to Southern Legislatures, 1778–1864* (Urbana, IL, 2001), 88–89; Martha Hodes, *White Women, Black Men: Illicit Sex in the Nineteenth Century* (New Haven, 1997), chs. 2–5. Forced sexual relations between slave master and slaves, of course, were much more frequent; see Cashin, *A Family Venture,* 106–108.

43. For an exception see Michael P. Johnson and James L. Roark, *Black Masters: A Free Family of Color in the Old South* (New York, 1984). The general condition of rural free people of color is discussed in Berlin, *Slaves without Masters.*

44. Bell, *Revolution, Romanticism, and the Afro-Creole Protest Tradition,* chs. 4–6; Michael Eggart, "Anniversary Address" [1844], in Michael P. Johnson and James L. Roark, eds., "'A Middle Ground': Free Mulattoes and the Friendly Moralist Society of Antebellum Charleston," *SS,* 21 (1982), 246–266, quotations on 263.

45. Campbell, "As 'A Kind of Freeman'?" 243–274.

46. McDonald, *The Economy and Material Culture of Slaves,* ch. 2; Frederick Law Olmsted, *A Journey in the Seaboard Slave States* (New York, 1856), 327.

47. Reidy, *Slavery to Agrarian Capitalism,* 36–37, 41–42; Morgan, "Task and Gang Systems," 205–206; Drew Gilpin Faust, *James Henry Hammond and the Old South: A Design For Mastery* (Baton Rouge, 1982), ch. 5; Olmsted, *Journey through the Seaboard Slave States,* 327.

48. Campbell, "As 'A Kind of Freeman'?" 243–274, and Roderick A. McDonald, "Independent Economic Production by Slaves on Antebellum Louisiana Sugar Plantations," in Berlin and Morgan, eds., *Cultivation and Culture,* 275–302;

Charles S. Sydnor, *A Gentleman of the Old Natchez Region, Benjamin L. C. Wailes* (Westport, CT, 1970, rpt. 1938), 101–104; Morris, *Becoming Southern*, 75–76; Ball, *Fifty Years in Chains*, 147–148.

49. Campbell, "As 'A Kind of Freeman'?" 243–274; McDonald, "Independent Economic Production," 275–302; Reidy, *Slavery to Agrarian Capitalism*, 69–73. See R. H. Clark et al., comps., *The Code of the State of Georgia* (Atlanta, 1861), 368–370, for the legal right of slaves to hold property and trade with the slaveowners' permission.

50. Computed from the published U.S. census: *Fifth Census . . . 1830; Sixth Census . . . 1840; Seventh Census of the United States 1850*. Also see Scarborough, "Heartland of the Cotton Kingdom," in McLemore, *A History of Mississippi*, 1:326–328.

51. Morris, *Becoming Southern*, 68–70.

52. Mullin, ed., *American Negro Slavery*, 214–215, quotation on 214; Cashin, *Family Venture*, 70 (quotation), 74, 116; Pheobia and Cash to Mr. Delions, 17 March 1857, in Robert S. Starobin, ed., *Blacks in Bondage: Letters of American Slaves* (New York, 1974), 57. A similar "cultural nostalgia" informed the African victims of the First Middle Passage; for the phrase and the concept see Joseph C. Miller, "Central Africa during the Era of the Slave Trade, c. 1490s," in Heywood, ed., *Central Africans and Cultural Transformations*, 43.

53. Hawkins Wilson to the Chief of the Freedmen's Bureau at Richmond, 11 May 1867, enclosing Hawkins Wilson to Sister Jane, Letters Received, ser. 3892, Bowling Green VA Assistant Commissioner, RG 105, NA; Rawick, ed., *American Slave*, ser. 1, vol. 7, 81.

54. Ball, *Fifty Years in Chains*, 168–169.

55. Herbert G. Gutman, *The Black Family in Slavery and Freedom, 1750–1925* (New York, 1976); Malone, *Sweet Chariot*.

56. In 1864 and 1865, when officers of the Freedmen's Bureau registered the marriages of Mississippi slaves, approximately one-third of slaves over 40 years of age had a marriage broken by force. Gutman, *Black Family*, 18–20; Cashin, *Family Venture*, esp. ch. 3.

57. Rawick, ed., *American Slave*, ser. 1, vol. 4, pt. 1–2, 215.

58. Ball, *Fifty Years in Chains*, 131–133, quotation on 131.

59. Gutman, *Black Family*, chs. 2, 5; Cheryll Ann Cody, "Naming, Kinship, and Estate Dispersal: Notes on Slave Family Life on a South Carolina Plantation, 1786 to 1833," *WMQ*, 39 (1982), 192–211; Morris, *Becoming Southern*, 68–83.

60. Sylvia Frey and Betty Wood, *Come Shouting to Zion: African-American Protestantism in the American South and the British Caribbean to 1830* (Chapel Hill,

1998), chs. 6–7, quotation on 162; Randy Sparks, *On Jordan's Stormy Banks: Evangelism in Mississippi, 1773–1876* (Athens, GA, 1994), chs. 4–5; Boles, ed., *Masters and Slaves in the House of the Lord,* chs. 2–5.

61. Frey and Wood, *Come Shouting to Zion,* ch. 6, esp. 161–163; Lawrence W. Levine, *Black Consciousness: Afro-American Folk Thought from Slavery to Freedom* (New York, 1977), 32–124; Albert J. Raboteau, *Slave Religion: The "Invisible Institution" in the Antebellum South* (New York, 1978); Sparks, *On Jordan's Stormy Banks,* ch. 4; Donald G. Mathews, *Religion in the Old South* (Chicago, 1977); Reidy, *Slavery to Agrarian Capitalism,* 26; quotation in Charles Colcock Jones, *The Religious Instruction of the Negroes in the United States* (Savannah, 1842), 125.

62. Gray, *So. Ag.,* 2:888–908; Moore, *Emergence of the Cotton Kingdom,* chs. 3–5; Carville Earle, "The Myth of the Southern Soil Miner: Macrohistory, Agricultural Innovation, and Environmental Change," in *Geographical Inquiry and American Historical Problems* (Palo Alto, 1992), 258–299; William L. Barney, "Towards the Civil War: The Dynamic of Change in a Black Belt County," in Orville Vernon Burton and Robert C. McMath, Jr., eds., *Class, Conflict, and Consensus: Antebellum Southern Community Studies* (Westport, CT, 1982), 146–172; Reidy, *Slavery to Agrarian Capitalism,* 83–85; Cobb, *Most Southern Place,* 9–14; Gavin Wright, "'Economic Democracy' and the Concentration of Agricultural Wealth in the Cotton South, 1850–1860," *Agricultural History,* 44 (1970), 63–93; Randolph B. Campbell, "Intermediate Slave Ownership: Texas as a Test Case," and the continuing controversy between James Oakes and Campbell, *JSoH,* 51 (1985), 15–30; Joseph K. Menn, *The Large Slaveholders of Louisiana, 1860* (New Orleans, 1964). For the growing reliance on overseers, see Fogel, *Without Consent or Contract,* 52.

63. Cobb, *Most Southern Place,* 16–20; Dupree, *Transforming the Cotton Frontier,* ch. 3; John Michael Vlach, *The Planter's Prospect: Privilege and Slavery in Plantation Painting* (Chapel Hill, 2002).

64. John Michael Vlach, *Back of the Big House: The Architecture of Plantation Slavery* (Chapel Hill, 1993); Vlach, *The Planters' Prospect: Privilege and Slavery in Plantation Paintings* (Chapel Hill, 2002).

65. See note 62 and especially Reidy, *Slavery to Agrarian Capitalism,* 83–85; Morris, *Becoming Southern,* 158–160, 163–164; Cobb, *The Most Southern Place,* 9–14; Gavin Wright, "'Economic Democracy' and the Concentration of Agricultural Wealth in the Cotton South, 1850–1860," *AgH,* 44 (1970), 63–93; James C. Bonner, "Profile of a Late Ante-bellum Community," *AHR,* 49 (1944), 663–680; Sellers, *Slavery in Alabama,* 42; Barney, "Towards the Civil War," 147; Jo-

seph Karl Menn, *The Large Slaveholders of Louisiana—1860* (New Orleans, 1964); Rodrigue, *Reconstruction in the Cane Fields,* 20–24, 61–63; Richard J. Follett, "The Sugar Masters: Slavery, Economic Development, and Modernization on Louisiana Sugar Plantations, 1820–1860" (Ph.D. diss., Louisiana State University, 1997), 92–95, 224–225.

66. The variety can be seen, for example, in Carol H. Moneyhan, *The Impact of the Civil War and Reconstruction on Arkansas: Persistence in the Midst of Ruin* (Baton Rouge, 1994), chs. 1–3; John C. Inscoe, *Mountain Masters: Slavery and the Sectional Crisis in Western North Carolina* (Knoxville, 1989); Wilma A. Dunaway, *The First American Frontier: Transition to Capitalism in Southern Appalachia, 1700–1860* (Chapel Hill, 1996); R. Douglas Hurt, *Agriculture and Slavery in Missouri's Little Dixie* (Columbia, MO, 1992), esp. chs. 9–10.

67. In a few cases, black "wives" won out over their white competitors. Elisha Worthington, founder of the gigantic Sunnyside plantation in Arkansas, maintained his relationship with his slave mistress, and his white wife eventually returned to her parent's home in Tennessee and had the marriage annulled. Worthington then educated his black children at Oberlin, sending his son on to France. Gatewood, "Sunnyside: The Evolution of an Arkansas Plantation," 4–7. Adele Logan Alexander, *Ambiguous Lives: Free Women of Color in Rural Georgia, 1789–1879* (Fayetteville, AR, 1991), 62–95. Also Catterall, ed., *Judicial Cases,* 3:342.

68. Berlin, *Slaves without Masters,* ch. 10.

69. *Southern Cultivator* (March 1846), 43; *DeBow's Review* (Aug. 1852), 192–194 (quotation), (Oct. 1854), 421–426 ; James O. Breeden, ed., *Advice among Masters: The Ideal in Slave Management in the Old South* (Westport, CT, 1980), 58, 240, 242, 249; McNeilly, *Old South Frontier,* 135–136 (quotation on 136); quotation in Olmsted, *Journey through the Seaboard Slave States,* 332–333; Emily West, "Masters and Marriages, Profits and Paternalism: Slave Owners' Perspectives on Cross-Plantation Unions in Antebellum South Carolina," *S&A,* 21 (2000), 56–72; Anthony E. Kaye, "Neighbourhoods and Solidarity in the Natchez District of Mississippi: Rethinking the Antebellum Slave Community," *S&A,* 23 (2002), 1–24; Reidy, *Slavery to Capitalism,* 43, 84.

70. Quotation in McNeilly, *Old South Frontier,* 135.

71. For the persistent fear of insurrection, see Edwin A. Miles, "The Mississippi Slave Insurrection Scare of 1835," *JNH,* 42 (1957), 46–60; Christopher Morris, "An Event in Community Organization: The Mississippi Slave Insurrection Scare of 1835," *JSH* (1988), 93–111; Michael Wayne, *Death of an Overseer: Reopening a Murder Investigation from the Plantation South* (New York, 2001);

Winthrop D. Jordan, *Tumult and Silence at Second Creek: An Inquiry into a Civil War Slave Conspiracy* (Baton Rouge, 1993).

72. Mark M. Smith, *Mastered by the Clock: Time, Slavery, and Freedom in the American South* (Chapel Hill, 1997), also Breeden, *Advice among Masters.* For a different view of reform, see Genovese, *Roll, Jordan, Roll,* 49–70.

73. *DeBow's Review* (March 1851), 325–333, quotation on 328.

74. Eugene D. Genovese, later joined by Elizabeth Fox-Genovese, has made the fullest case for planter paternalism or seignorialism in the nineteenth-century American South, hinging its development on the closing of the African slave trade and close relations between resident masters and slaves. Genovese, *Roll, Jordan, Roll;* Fox-Genovese, *Within the Plantation Household.* Others have traced its origins to the colonial period, alternately as a product of monarchical ideologies or evangelical revivalism. Olwell, *Masters, Slaves, and Subjects,* and Allan Gallay, "Origins of Planter Paternalism." Philip D. Morgan and others have distinguished eighteenth-century patriarchalism from the nineteenth-century paternalism. While not always addressing the controversy directly, a number of scholars have recently noted how the planters increased interventions under the head of paternalism—on matters of religion, family, medical practice, diet, and sanitation—created new struggles between masters and slaves. Janet Duitsman Cornelius, *Slave Missions and the Black Church in the Antebellum South* (Columbia, SC, 1999), Marie Jenkins Schwartz, *Born in Bondage: Growing Up Enslaved in the Antebellum South* (Cambridge, MA, 2000); Sharon M. Fett, *Working Cure: Healing, Health, and Power on Southern Slave Plantations* (Chapel Hill, 2002).

75. The *Southern Cultivator* provides a sample of the reformist debate. On work: 24 June 1844, 16 (quotation); Oct. 1844, 155. On health and diet: Aug. 1846, 127; Jan. 1850, 4; Apr. 1851, 51. On housing: Apr. 1847, 55; Feb. 1852, 41. On sanitation: July 1849, 103; Sept. 1849, 135. On religion: Nov. 1850, 164; June 1851, 86–87.

76. Frey and Wood, *Come Shouting to Zion,* chs. 5–6; Sparks, *On Jordan's Stormy Banks,* ch. 4; Raboteau, *Slave Religion,* ch. 4; Genovese, *Roll, Jordan, Roll,* 232–255; Anne Loveland, *Southern Evangelicals and the Social Order, 1800–1860* (Baton Rouge, 1980), ch.8; Donald G. Mathews, "Charles Colcock Jones and the Southern Evangelical Crusade to Form a Biracial community," *JSoH,* 41 (1975).

77. Quotations in Loveland, *Southern Evangelicals and the Social Order,* 252; Ball, *Fifty Years in Chains,* 150; quotation in Rawick, ed., *American Slave,* ser. 1, vol. 7, 42. For a thoughtful analysis of how the slaves' appropriation of the Exodus narrative became "a language among African-Americans as well as a metaphor-

ical framework for underlying the middle passage, enslavement, and quests of emancipation," see Eddie S. Glaude, Jr., *Exodus! Religion, Race, and Nation in Early Nineteenth-Century Black America* (Chicago, 2000), 3.

78. Frey and Wood, *Come Shouting to Zion*, ch. 6; Boles, *Masters and Slaves in the House of the Lord;* Mathews, *Religion in the Old South;* Genovese, *Roll, Jordan, Roll;* Gayraud S. Wilmore, *Black Religion and Black Radicalism: An Interpretaton of the Religious History of Afro-American People* (Maryknoll, NY, 1983).

79. Rawick, ed., *American Slave,* supp., ser. 1, vol. 7A, 372–373.

80. Coclanis, *The Shadow of a Dream,* ch. 4; Dusinberre, *Them Dark Days,* ix, xi, 4, ch. 15; Charles W. Joyner, *Down by the Riverside: A South Carolina Slave Community* (Urbana, IL, 1984), 34–36.

81. Dusinberre, *Them Dark Days,* ix, xi, 4, ch. 15; Joyner, *Down by the Riverside,* ch. 2; Hilliard, "Antebellum Tidewater Rice Culture," 91–115; Morgan, "Task and Gang Systems," 197–212; James Scott Strickland, "'No More Mud Work': The Struggle for the Control of Labor and Production in Low Country South Carolina," in Walter J. Fraser and Winfred B. Moore, eds., *The Southern Enigma* (Westport, CT, 1983), 43–62; Richard H. Steckel, "Birth Weights and Infant Mortality among American Slaves," *EEH,* 23 (1986), 173–199; Steckel, "The Fertility of American Slaves," 266 and "A Dreadful Childhood: The Excess Mortality of American Slaves," *SSH,* 10 (1986), 447.

82. Olmsted, *Cotton Kingdom,* 187–194; Morgan, "Task and Gang Systems," 197, 212; Joyner, *Down by the Riverside,* 43–45, 51–55; Dusinberre, *Them Dark Days,* 180–187, 317, esp. 128–130 (on workhouse); Richard Wade, *Slavery in the Cities: The South, 1820–1860* (New York, 1964), 95–96. For the strength of the slaves' internal economy, see Wood, *Women's Work, Men's Work.*

83. Gray, *So. Ag.,* 2:752–887; John T. Schlotterbeck, "The 'Social Economy' of an Upper South Community: Orange and Greene Counties Virginia, 1815–1860," in Burton and McMath, Jr., eds., *Class, Conflict, and Consensus,* 3–28; Dunaway, *The First Frontier;* Fogel, *Without Consent,* 65, 270; Stevenson, *Life in Black and White,* 172–173.

84. Tadman, *Speculators and Slaves,* 12. For laws banning exports, see Bancroft, *Slave-Trading in the Old South,* 269–275; Winfield H. Collins, *The Domestic Slave Trade of the Southern States* (New York, 1904), ch. 17.

85. Computed from the published U.S. census: *Census for 1820;* Stevenson, *Life in Black and White,* 177–178.

86. David L. Lightner, "The Interstate Slave Trade in Antislavery Politics," *CWH,* 36 (1990), 119–136; Tadman, *Speculators and Slaves,* 180–184, 212–216. On slave

breeding, Richard Sutch, "The Breeding of Slaves for Sale and the Westward Expansion of Slavery, 1830–1860," in Stanley Engerman and Eugene D. Genovese, eds., *Race and Slavery in the Western Hemisphere: Quantitative Studies* (Princeton, 1975), 173–210; Robert W. Fogel and Stanley L. Engerman, "The Slave Breeding Thesis," in Fogel and Engerman, eds., *Without Consent or Contract: The Rise and Fall of American Slavery: Technical Papers,* 2 vols (New York, 1992), 2:455–472.

87. Tadman, *Speculators and Slaves,* 211–212; Gutman, *Black Family in Slavery and Freedom,* 145–148; Cheryll Ann Cody, "Sale and Separation: Four Crises for Enslaved Women on the Ball Plantation, 1764–1854," in Larry Hudson, Jr., *Working toward Freedom: Slave Society and the Domestic Economy of the American South* (Rochester, NY, 1994), 119–142.

88. Rawick, ed., *American Slave,* ser. 2, vol. 14, 71.

89. Nicholas B. Wainwright, ed., *A Philadelphia Perspective: The Diary of Sidney George Fisher Covering the Years 1834–1871* (Philadelphia, 1967), 188–189; Rawick, ed., *American Slave,* ser. 1, vol. 6, 72.

90. Gutman, *Black Family in Slavery and Freedom,* 145–148; also Emily West, "Surviving Separation: Cross-Plantation Marriages and the Slave Trade in Antebellum South Carolina," *Journal of Family History,* 24 (1999), 212–231.

91. Rawick, ed., *American Slave,* supp., ser. 2, vol. 1A, 319; ser. 2, vol. 14, 354–355; also see Stevenson, *Life in Black and White,* 179.

92. Rawick, ed., *American Slave,* supp., ser. 2, vol. 1A, 319; ser. 2, vol. 14, 354–355; ser. 1, vol. 12, 335; Ulrich B. Phillips, *Life and Labor in the Old South* (Boston, 1929), 212; John Tomlin to Benjamin Brand, 6 Jan. 1809, Benjamin Brand Papers, VaHS; Stevenson, *Life in Black and White,* 179; Minutes of the First Baptist Church of Richmond, 19 Apr. 1823, VBHS; James Williams, *Narrative of James Williams, an American Slave* (Boston, 1838), 32–33; Nehemiah Adams, *A South-Side View of Slavery* (Boston, 1854), 73; Charles Lyell, *A Second Visit to the United States of North America,* 2 vols. (New York, 1849), 1:209–210. For slave flight in the wake of sale, see Franklin and Schweninger, *Runaway Slaves,* ch. 3, and for slaves who ran away in order to be sold, *ibid.,* 104–105.

93. Rawick, ed., *American Slave,* vol. 18, 156–57, 288; also ser. 1, vol., 7, 302.

94. Rawick, ed., *American Slave,* supp., ser. 2, vol. 3, 87–89; also Sterling, *We Are Your Sisters,* 50.

95. Walter Johnson, *Soul by Soul,* 176–187; Joseph Holt Ingraham, *The South-West, by a Yankee,* 2 vols. (New York, 1835), 2:195–197.

96. Blassingame, ed., *Slave Testimony,* 22–23; Starobin, ed., *Blacks in Bondage,* 58; Rawick, ed., *American Slave,* ser. 1, vol. 6, 72–73; ser. 2, vol. 15, 248–249;

Hawkins Wilson to the Chief of the Freedmen's Bureau at Richmond, 11 May 1867, enclosing Hawkins Wilson to Sister Jane, Letters Received, ser. 3892, Bowling Green VA Assistant Commissioner, RG 105, NA.

97. Quotations in Terry, "Sustaining the Bonds of Kinship in the Trans-Appalachian Migration," 464; Joyner, *Down by the Riverside,* 24–25; Ball, *Fifty Years in Chains,* 12–14.

98. Frederick Douglass, *Narrative of the Life of Frederick Douglass,* ed. David Blight (Boston, 1993, rpt. of 1845), 65–66; Richard S. Dunn, "A Tale of Two Plantations: Slave Life at Mesopotamia in Jamaica and Mount Airy in Virginia, 1799 to 1828," *WMQ,* 24 (1977), 32–65.

99. Quoted in Levine, *Black Culture and Black Consciousness,* 15, 39–40; also speaking to the same experience, a stanza of "Michael Rowed the Boat Ashore": "I wonder where my mudder ben / See my mudder on de rock gwine home. / On de rock gwine home / in Jesus' home. / Sister, help for trim dat boat. / Jordan stream is wide and deep. / Jesus stand on t' oder side. / I wonder if my maussa deh. / My fader gone to unknown land." William Francis Allen et al., *Slave Songs of the United States* (New York, 1965, rpt. of 1867), 45–46.

100. Jacob Stroyer, *My Life in the South* (Salem, MA, 1898), 39–43; Rawick, ed., *American Slave,* supp., ser. 2, vol. 5A, 1637.

101. Clement Eaton, "Slave-Hiring in the Upper South: A Step toward Freedom," *MVHR,* 46 (1960), 663–678; Genovese, *Roll, Jordan Roll,* 390–391, estimates that hired slaves made up 5 to 10 percent of all southern slaves in the late antebellum period; Fogel and Engerman, *Time on the Cross,* 56, judge the proportion in 1860 to be 7.5 percent for all slaves, but 31 percent for urban slaves and more than 50 percent in industrial cities like Richmond; Brenda Stevenson, studying rural Loudoun County, Virginia, calculates that more than one-third of slaves were hired in 1860. *Life in Black and White,* 184. Wilma A. Dunaway, "Diaspora, Death, and Sexual Exploitation: Slave Families at Risk in the Mountain South," *Appalachian Journal,* 26 (1999), 137, "estimates the proportion of hired slaves at between one quarter and one fifth of [the] slave population." Richard Wade, *Slavery in the Cities: The South, 1820–1860* (New York, 1964), 38–54; Claudia Dale Goldin, *Urban Slavery in the American South, 1820–1860* (Chicago, 1976), 35–42, 69–75; Charles B. Dew, *Bond of Iron: Master and Slave at Buffalo Forge* (New York, 1994); Robert S. Starobin, *Industrial Slavery in the Old South* (New York, 1970); Jonathan Martin, *Divided Mastery: Slave Hiring in the Colonial and Antebellum South* (Cambridge, MA, forthcoming).

102. Blassingame, ed., *Slave Testimony,* 535; H. C. Bruce, *The New Man: Twenty Years a Slave, Twenty-Nine Years a Free Man* (Lincoln, NE, 1996), 13–21; Har-

riet A. Jacobs, *Incidents in the Life of a Slave Girl, Written by Herself,* ed. Jean
Fagan Yellin (Cambridge, MA, 1987), 15, 27–28, 118; Perdue, Baden, and
Philips, eds., *Weevils in the Wheat,* 135, 318. Andrew Fede, "Legitimized Violent
Abuse in the American South, 1619–1865: A Case Study of Law and Social
Change in Six Southern States," *AJLH,* 29 (1985), 138–146. The general point
is made by Barbara Jeanne Fields, *Slavery and Freedom on the Middle Ground:
Maryland during the Nineteenth Century* (New Haven, 1985), 27, who notes
that "hire arrangements worked vast mischief in the personal lives of slaves."

103. Douglass, *Narrative,* 91–92; Northup, *Twelve Years a Slave,* 92.

104. Starobin, *Industrial Slavery,* 110–111; quotation in *Southern Planter* (Dec. 1852),
376–379.

105. *Ibid.,* esp. 376–377; Douglass, *Narrative,* 95–97; Blassingame, ed., *Slave Testimony,* 216, 469, 440; Richard B. Morris, "The Measure of Bondage in the
Slave States," *MVHR,* 41 (1954), 220; Eaton, "Slave-Hiring in the Upper
South," 663; Loren Schweninger, "The Underside of Slavery: The Internal
Economy, Self-Hire, and Quasi-Freedom, 1780–1865," *S&A,* 12 (1991), 10–21;
quotation in Alfred Steele to Mary Steele, 15 Nov. 1835, John Steele Papers,
Southern History Collection, University of North Carolina, Chapel Hill.

106. See, for example, William A. Byrne, "The Hiring of Woodson, Slave Carpenter of Savannah," *GHQ,* 77 (1993), 254–263; John Hebron Moore, "Simon
Gray, Riverman: A Slave Who Was Almost Free," *MVHR,* 49 (1962), 472–484;
Randolph B. Campbell, "Research Note: Slave Hiring in Texas," *AHR,* 93
(1988), 107–114.

107. Quotation in *Southern Planter* (Dec. 1852), 377.

108. See, for example, Loren Schweninger, "The Free Slave Phenomenon: James P.
Thomas and the Black Community in Antebellum Nashville," *CWH,* 22
(1976), 293–307. For the growth of term slavery, see Whitman, *Price of Freedom.* In 1817, Maryland prohibited the sale of slaves from the state, and Delaware banned the export of any slave. *Ibid.,* 78; Essah, *House Divided,* 40–42.

109. *Population of the United States in 1860,* 598–605.

110. Berlin, *Slaves without Masters,* ch. 11.

111. Stevenson, *Life in Black and White,* chs. 7–8; Gutman, *Black Family,* ch. 9; Herbert Gutman, *Slavery and the Numbers Game: A Critique of Time on the Cross*
(Urbana, IL, 1975), 105, 141, 130–137; Gutman and Sutch, "The Slave Family,"
103–105; West, "Cross-Plantation Marriages," 217; Richard H. Steckel, *The
Economics of U.S. Slave and Southern White Fertility* (New York, 1985), 227–228.

112. Frey and Wood, *Come Shouting to Zion,* chs. 4–5; Luther P. Jackson, "Religious
Instruction of the Negro in Virginia from 1760–1830," *JNH,* 16 (1931), 198–

239; Elizabeth Russey, "The Right Hand of Fellowship: African-Americans and the Baptist Church, 1820–1830" (Masters thesis, University of Maryland, 2002).

113. John C. Willis, "From the Dictates of Pride to the Paths of Righteousness: Slave Honor and Christianity in Antebellum Virginia," in Edward L. Ayers and John C. Willis, eds., *The Edge of the South: Life in Nineteenth-Century Virginia* (Charlottesville, 1991), 37–39.

114. Quotations in *Minutes of the Rappahannock Baptist Association*, 1850, p. 11; Minutes of the Fork Baptist Church, 1825–1873, June 1845, VBHS. Also Minutes of the First Baptist Church of Richmond, 3, 7 July 1829, 30 June, 16 Sept. 1830, VBHS.

115. Minutes of the First African Baptist Church, VBHS; John T. O'Brien, "Factory, Church, and Community: Blacks in Antebellum Richmond," *JSoH*, 44 (1978), 509–536; Berlin, *Slaves without Masters*, 306–315, quotation on 311.

116. Frederick Douglass, *The Life and Writings of Frederick Douglass*, 5 vols. (New York, 1950), 1:157.

117. White, *Somewhat More Independent*, 53–54; Paul Finkelman, *Slavery and the Founders: Race and Liberty in the Age of Jefferson*, 2nd ed. (Armonk, NY, 2001), chs. 2–3; David Brion Davis, *In the Image of God: Religion, Moral Values, and Our Heritage of Slavery* (New Haven, CT, 2001), 200–201; James Simeone, *Democracy and Slavery in Frontier Illinois: The Bottomland Republic* (Dekalb, IL, 2000); David A. Gerber, *Black Ohio and the Color Line, 1860–1915* (Urbana, IL, 1976), 10–11.

118. Leon F. Litwack, *North of Slavery: The Negro in the Free States, 1790–1860* (Chicago, 1961), chs. 2–3; Leonard P. Curry, *The Free Black in Urban America, 1800–1850: The Shadow of the Dream* (Chicago, 1981), chs. 2–5; Gerber, *Black Ohio*, 3–4; Melish, *Disowning Slavery*, chs. 2, 5; Paul Finkelman, "Prelude to the Fourteenth Amendment: Black Legal Rights in the Antebellum North," *Rutgers Law Journal*, 17 (1986), 415–482; Eugene H. Berwanger, *The Frontier against Slavery: Western Anti-Negro Prejudice and the Slavery Extension Controversy* (Urbana, IL, 1971); Charles Wesley, "Negro Suffrage in the Period of Constitution-Making, 1787–1865," *JNH*, 32 (1947), 143–168.

119. Litwack, *North of Slavery*, ch. 5; Horton and Horton, *In Hope of Liberty*, ch. 5; Curry, *The Free Black in Urban America*, chs. 5–6; P. J. Staudenraus, *The African Colonization Movement, 1816–1865* (New York, 1961); Floyd J. Miller, *The Search for a Black Nationality: Black Emigration and Colonization, 1787–1863* (Urbana, IL, 1975); Ruth Herndon, *Unwelcome Americans: Living on the Margins in Early New England* (Philadelphia, 2001).

120. Melish, *Disowning Slavery,* chs. 4–6; Nash, *Forging Freedom,* chs. 6–8; George M. Fredrickson, *The Black Image in the White Mind: The Debate on Afro-American Character and Destiny, 1817–1914* (New York, 1971), chs. 3–5; William R. Stanton, *The Leopard's Spots: Scientific Attitudes toward Race in America, 1815–59* (Chicago, 1960).

121. Alexander Saxton, *The Rise and Fall of the White Republic: Class, Politics and Mass Culture in Nineteenth-Century America* (London, 1990); David Roediger, *The Wages of Whiteness: Race and the Making of the American Working Class* (London, 1991).

122. Fehrenbacher, *The Slaveholding Republic.*

123. Quotation in C. Peter Ripley et al., eds., *Witness for Freedom: African-American Voices on Race, Slavery and Emancipation* (Chapel Hill, 1993), 19.

124. Curry, *The Free Black in Urban America,* 249; Gerber, *Black Ohio,* 15–19; J. D. B. DeBow, *Statistical View of the United States . . . Being a Compendium of the Seventh Census* (Washington, DC, 1854), 78–80; *Population of the United States in 1860,* 612.

125. Patrick Rael, *Black Identity and Black Protest in the Antebellum North* (Chapel Hill, 2002), 27–29; Theodore Hershberg, "Free Blacks in Antebellum Philadelphia: A Study of Ex-Slave, Freeborn, and Socio-Economic Decline," *JSH,* 5 (1971), 183–209; and Hershberg and Henry Williams, "Mulattoes and Blacks: Intra-Group Color Differences and Social Stratification in Nineteenth-Century Philadelphia," in Hershberg, *Philadelphia: Work, Space, Family, and Group Experience in the Nineteenth Century* (New York, 1981), 392–434.

126. Quotation in Rael, *Black Identity and Black Protest,* 27.

127. Paul Finkelman, "The Kidnapping of John Davis and the Adoption of the Fugitive Slave Law of 1793," *JSoH,* 56 (1990), 397–422; Wilson, *Freedom at Risk,* 106–108; Peter P. Hinks, "'Frequently Plunged into Slavery': Free Blacks and Kidnapping in Antebellum Boston," *HJM,* 20 (1992), 16–31; Wilson, *Freedom at Risk,* 106–108; Franklin and Schweninger, *Runaway Slaves,* ch. 8, 272–274; Philip J. Schwarz, *Migrants against Slavery: Virginians and the Nation* (Charlottesville, 2001), 25.

128. Nash, "Forging Freedom," 27–40; Horton and Horton, *In Hope of Liberty,* ch. 4; Paul Lammermeier, "The Urban Black Family of the Nineteenth Century," *Journal of Marriage and the Family,* 35 (1973), 440–455.

129. Will Gravely, "The Rise of African Churches in America (1786–1822): Reexamining the Contexts," *Journal of Religious Thought,* 41 (1984), 58–73; Nash, *Forging Freedom,* ch. 4; Carol V. R. George, *Segregated Sabbaths: Richard Allen and the Emergence of the Independent Black Churches, 1760–1840* (New York,

1973); C. Eric Lincoln and Lawrence H. Mamiya, *The Black Church in the African-American Experience* (Durham, 1990); Jon Butler, *Awash in a Sea of Faith* (Cambridge, MA, 1990), 280.

130. Quotation in Benjamin Quarles, *Black Abolitionists* (New York, 1969), 69.

131. For the lower orders, see Shane White and Graham White, *Stylin': American Expressive Culture from Its Beginning to the Zoot Suit* (Ithaca, 1998), esp. chs. 1–4; Leslie M. Harris, *In the Shadow of Slavery: African-Americans in New York City, 1626–1863* (Chicago, forthcoming); for the respectables, see Julie Winch, *Philadelphia's Black Elite: Activism, Acccommodation, and the Struggle for Autonomy, 1787–1848* (Philadelphia, 1988); Emma J. Lapsansky, "Friends, Wives, and Strivings: Networks and Community Values among Nineteenth-Century Philadelphia Afro-American Elites," *PMHB*, 108 (1984), 3–24; Joseph Wilson, *Sketches of the Higher Classes of Colored Society in Philadelphia* (Philadelphia, 1841), and Frank J. Webb, *The Garies and Their Friends* (New York, 1857). Quotation in Ripley et al., eds., *Witness for Freedom*, 7.

132. James O. Horton, *Free People of Color: Inside the African-American Community* (Washington, DC, 1993), ch. 6; Rael, *Black Identity and Black Protest*, 49.

133. Rael, *Black Identity and Black Protest*, chs. 2–7; Miller, *The Search for a Black Nationality;* Quarles, *Black Abolitionists*. The debates among northern blacks can be followed in the debates at the national conventions. See Howard Bell, ed., *Minutes of the Proceedings of the National Negro Conventions, 1830–1864* (New York, 1969).

134. *The Rights of All*, 18 Sept. 1829.

135. Thomas D. Lamont, *Rise to Be a People: A Biography of Paul Cuffe* (Urbana, IL, 1986); Miller, *Search for Black Nationality*, ch. 2; Richard J. M. Blackett, *Building an Anti-Slavery Wall: Black Americans in the Atlantic Abolitionist Movement, 1830–1860* (Baton Rouge, 1983); C. Peter Ripley et al., *The Black Abolitionist Papers*, 5 vols. (Chapel Hill, 1985–1992), vol. 4.

136. Quarles, *The Black Abolitionists;* Ripley et al., eds., *Black Abolitionist Papers*.

137. James Henry Hammond, *Selections from the Letters and Speeches of the Hon. James H. Hammond, of South Carolina* (New York, 1866), 38–39.

138. Larry Gara, *The Liberty Line: The Legend of the Underground Railroad* (Lexington, KY, 1961); William Still, *The Underground Rail Road: A Record of Facts, Authentic Narratives, Letters* (Philadelphia, 1872); Stanley W. Campbell, *The Slave Catchers: Enforcement of the Fugitive Slave Law, 1850–1860* (Chapel Hill, 1970); Schwarz, *Migrants against Slavery*, ch. 1; Henry Box Brown, *Narrative of Henry Box Brown Who Escaped from Slavery Enclosed in a Box 3 Feet Long and 2 Wide* (Boston, 1849); William Craft, *Running a Thousand Miles for Free-*

dom (London, 1860); R. J. M. Blackett, *Beating against the Barriers: The Lives of Six Nineteenth-Century Afro-Americans* (Baton Rouge, 1986), 87–137; Thomas P. Slaughter, *Bloody Dawn: The Christiana Riot and Racial Violence in the Antebellum North* (New York, 1991).

139. Blassingame, ed., *Slave Testimony,* 118–119.

140. Olmsted, *Cotton Kingdom,* 321; Dusinberre, *Them Dark Days,* 155; Merton L. Dillon, *Slavery Attacked: Southern Slaves and Their Allies, 1619–1865* (Baton Rouge, 1990), 240–242; Clarence L. Mohr, *On the Threshold of Freedom: Masters and Slaves in Civil War Georgia* (Athens, GA, 1986), ch. 2.

EPILOGUE: FREEDOM GENERATIONS

1. Blassingame, *Slave Testimony,* 377; Rawick, ed., *The American Slave,* ser. 2, vol. 15, pt. 2, 246.

2. Ira Berlin et al., *Free at Last: A Documentary History of Slavery, Freedom, and the Civil War* (New York, 1992), 518.

3. *Freedom,* ser. 2, docs. 17–20.

4. Mary Boykin Chesnut, *A Diary from Dixie,* ed. Ben Ames Williams (Boston, 1949), 38–39; *Freedom,* ser. 2, doc. 113, see also doc. 114.

5. U.S. War Department, *The War of the Rebellion: A Compilation of the Official Records of the Union and Confederate Armies,* 128 vols. (Washington, DC, 1880–1901), ser. 2, vol. 1, 750; John Q. Anderson, ed., *Brokenburn: The Journal of Kate Stone, 1861–1868* (Baton Rouge, 1972), 37.

6. *Freedom,* ser. 1, vol. 1, 9–15, 59–60, 159–160, 331–334, 395–397, 664–665.

7. *Freedom,* ser. 1, vol. 1, 12–22, 60–64, 104, 161–164, and esp. docs. 1A–C.

8. *Freedom,* ser. 1, vol. 1, 32, 64–67, 105–110, 251–258.

9. See, for example, *Freedom,* ser. 1, vol. 1, doc. 17.

10. *Freedom,* ser. 1, vol. 3, 455–456. For black life in contraband camps, see *Freedom,* ser. 1, vol. 2–3; Louis S. Gerteis, *From Contraband to Freedman: Federal Policy toward Southern Blacks, 1861–1870* (Westport, CT, 1973).

11. *Freedom,* ser. 1, vol. 3, ch. 3; Lawrence N. Powell, *New Masters: Northern Planters during the Civil War and Reconstruction* (New Haven, 1980); Willie Lee Rose, *Rehearsal for Reconstruction: The Port Royal Experiment* (Indianapolis, IN, 1964).

12. Dudley T. Cornish, "The Union Army as a School for Negroes," *JNH,* 37 (1952), 368–382; Herbert G. Gutman, *Power and Culture: Essays on the American Working Class* (New York, 1987), ch. 6; Joseph T. Glatthaar, *Forged in Battle: The Civil War Alliance of Black Soldiers and White Officers* (New York, 1990), 226–227; Ronald E. Butchart, *Northern Schools, Southern Blacks, and Re-*

construction: Freedmen's Education, 1862–1865 (Westport, CT, 1980); *Freedom*, ser. 2, ch. 14, quotation in Berlin et al., *Free at Last*, 518.

13. Dudley T. Cornish, *The Sable Arm: Negro Troops in the Union Army, 1861–1865* (New York, 1956), chs. 2–5; James M. McPherson, *The Negro's Civil War: How American Negroes Felt and Acted During the War for Union* (New York, 1965), ch. 11; quotation in Leon F. Litwack, *Been in the Storm So Long: The Aftermath of Slavery* (New York, 1979), 72.

14. *Freedom*, ser. 2, 7–14, esp. chs. 2–3; Cornish, *Sable Arm*, 105–111, ch. 6.

15. *Freedom*, ser. 2, 12–16, esp. chs. 2–4.

16. Cornish, *Sable Arm*, 181–196; McPherson, *The Negro's Civil War*, ch. 14; Litwack, *Been in the Storm So Long*, 79–86; *Freedom*, ser. 2, chs. 10–11, quotation in doc. 291.

17. *Freedom*, ser. 2, ch. 9, quotation on 618.

18. W. E. B. DuBois, *Black Reconstruction, 1860–1880* (New York, 1935), ch. 4; James L. Roark, *Masters without Slaves: Southern Planters in the Civil War and Reconstruction* (New York, 1977), chs. 1–3; C. Peter Ripley, *Slaves and Freedmen in Civil War Louisiana* (Baton Rouge, 1976), 22–23, 44, 200; *Freedom*, ser. 1, vol. 1; "Diary of John Houston Bill," May–June, 1863, Southern History Collection, University of North Carolina, Chapel Hill.

19. William F. Messner, *Freedmen and the Ideology of Free Labor: Louisiana, 1862–1865* (LaFayette, LA, 1978), 35; quotation in Litwack, *Been in the Storm So Long*, 148. For the slaveholders' disillusionments see Genovese, *Roll, Jordan, Roll*, 97–112.

20. Col. J. P. S. Gobin to Major General Gilmore, 12 Aug. 1865, G-23 1865, Letters Received, ser. 15, Washington Hdqrs., RG 105, NA; Litwack, *Been in the Storm So Long*, 249.

21. Joel Williamson, *After Slavery: The Negro in South Carolina during Reconstruction, 1861–1877* (Chapel Hill, 1865), 309–311; Litwack, *Been in the Storm So Long*, 247–251; Eric Foner, *Reconstruction: America's Unfinished Revolution, 1863–1877* (New York, 1988), 79; *Freedom*, ser. 1, vol. 1, doc. 231.

22. *Freedom*, ser. 3, vol. 1, ch. 2, forthcoming; Foner, *Reconstruction*, 80–84; Litwack, *Been in the Storm So Long*, ch. 6; John T. O'Brien, "Reconstruction in Richmond: White Restoration and Black Protest," *VMHB*, 89 (1981), 259–281.

23. Gutman, *Black Family*, 61–62, 141–145, 225–228, 417–420; Litwack, *Been in the Storm So Long*, 229–247; Ira Berlin and Leslie S. Rowland, eds., *Families and Freedom: A Documentary History of African-American Kinship in the Civil War Era* (New York, 1997), 231–233.

24. Quotation in Foner, *Reconstruction*, 90.

25. Charles E. Johnson to Capt. A. S. Flagg, 26 Oct. 1865, Letters & Orders Received, Asst. Subasst. Comr, Norfolk, ser. 4180, RG 105, NA [A-7946].

26. Claude F. Oubre, *Forty Acres and a Mule: The Freedmen's Bureau and Black Land Ownership* (Baton Rouge, 1978); Litwack, *Been in the Storm So Long*, 392–404; quotation in Olmsted, *Cotton Kingdom*, 83.

27. FSSP E-98.

28. Philip Smith to Freedom Bureau, 5 Apr. 1866, Unregistered Letters Received, ser. 9, Alabama Ass't Comr., RG 105, NA [A-1777]; *Freedom*, ser. 3, vol. 1, forthcoming; Ronald L. F. Davis, *Good and Faithful Labor: From Slavery to Sharecropping in the Natchez District, 1860–1890* (Westport, CT, 1982); Foner, *Reconstruction*, chs. 3–4; Gerald D. Jaynes, *Branches without Roots: Genesis of the Black Working Class in the American South, 1862–1882* (New York, 1986), ch. 4; Litwack, *Been in the Storm So Long*, chs. 4–8; Roger Ransom and Richard Sutch, *One Kind of Freedom: The Economic Consequences of Emancipation* (Cambridge, UK, 1977); Reidy, *From Slavery to Agrarian Capitalism*, ch. 6; Julie Saville, *The Work of Reconstruction: From Slave to Wage Laborer in South Carolina, 1860–1870* (Cambridge, UK, 1994); Gavin Wright, *Old South, New South: Revolutions in the Southern Economy since the Civil War* (New York, 1986).

29. Foner, *Reconstruction*, 28; Gerber, *Black Ohio*, 32–40.

30. *Freedom*, ser. 2, doc. 275; Petition of Prince Murell et al., 17 Dec. 1865, Unregistered Letters Received, ser. 9, Alabama Ass't Comr., RG 105, NA [A-1632]; H. Crawford to Mr. Andrew Johnson, 5 Nov. 1865, filed as P-35, Letters Received, ser. 15, Washington Hdqrs, RG 105, NA [A-5190]; Colored People of Florida to Major General Foster, 20 Mar. 1866, M-61 1866, Letter Received, ser. 1691, Dept. of Fla., RG 393 Pt. 1, NA [C-322].

31. Many Colored Citerzens to Hon. W. H. Seward, 25 Jan. 1866, C-67 1866, Registered Letters Received, ser. 15, Washington Hdqrs., RG 105, NA [A-1539]; *Freedom*, ser. 2, 811–816, quotation on 814; Foner, *Reconstruction*, 110–119.

32. Jacqueline Jones, *Soldiers of Light and Love: Northern Teachers and Georgia Blacks, 1865–1873* (Chapel Hill, 1980); Henry Lee Swint, *The Northern Teacher in the South, 1862–1870* (Nashville, TN, 1941); Clarence G. Walker, *A Rock in a Weary Land: The African Methodist Church during the Civil War and Reconstruction* (Baton Rouge, 1982); Joe M. Richardson, *Christian Reconstruction: The American Missionary Association and Southern Blacks, 1861–1890* (Athens, GA, 1986).

33. Thomas C. Holt, *Black over White: Negro Political Leadership in South Carolina*

during Reconstruction (Urbana, IL, 1977); Charles Vincent, *Black Legislators in Louisiana during Reconstruction* (Baton Rouge, 1977); Eric Foner, *Freedom's Lawmakers: A Directory of Black Officeholders during Reconstruction* (New York, 1993).

34. Ira Berlin et al., "The Terrain of Freedom: The Struggle over the Meaning of Free Labor in the U.S. South," *History Workshop Journal,* 22 (1986), 109–130, quotations on 125, 128.

ACKNOWLEDGMENTS

Generations of Captivity grows out of generations of scholarship which have made the historiography of slavery one of unrivalled richness. I have acknowledged my debt to that long tradition—and the men and women who made it—in the footnotes, which for reasons that confound logic no longer reside at the foot of the page. But, at critical moments, I have received support from friends and colleagues that go beyond this ancient—if now mangled—form of scholarly recognition.

My colleagues at the University of Maryland's Freedmen and Southern Society Project—particularly Anthony Kaye, Steven Miller, Susan O'Donovan, and Leslie Rowland—have been a continued source of collegial and intellectual companionship. Again and again, I have drawn upon their deep engagement with the history of emancipation to reflect back upon slavery's evolution. Like Cynthia Kennedy, Matthew Mason, and Marie Schwartz—former students who now have students of their own—they provided a sounding board for a host of ideas which have found their way onto these pages.

In the last stages of completing this volume, I had the great good fortune to read Steven Hahn's path-breaking study of African-American politics between the Civil War and World War I. Hahn's work forced me to rethink the nature of the society that could produce such a rich, complex political tradition. In addition, portions of what is now Chapter 4 were presented to the Milan Group, the Institut Charles V, Université Paris VII, the History Department at the University of Virginia, and the Center for Historical Studies at my own University of Maryland. I would especially like to thank the members of those diverse audiences for broadening my conception of this project.

When the project neared completion, Eric Foner and Steven Hahn read the entire manuscript. Ronald Hoffman, Walter Johnson, Matthew Mason, Sally Mason, Marie Schwartz, Shane White, and Steven Whitman read Chapters 4 and 5 and saved me from numerous howlers. Linda Noel, Linda Sargent, and Jonathan White assisted in some of the preliminary research and helped track down numerous fugitive citations. As the project was going to press, Peter Kolchin reviewed the entire manuscript with his usual care.

Finally, to return to first causes, my editor at Harvard University Press, Joyce Seltzer, suggested—and when I resisted—insisted that I extend my earlier work on slavery in the seventeenth and eighteenth centuries into the nineteenth. Her persistence and good sense have sent me on a venture that is just beginning. With good cheer and an uncanny ability for smoothing the roughest sentence, plucking out the ill-fitting word, and killing—without the slightest hint of compassion—any metaphor that dared to meander, Susan Wallace Boehmer magically transformed manuscript into book. I'm grateful.

This book is dedicated to my brothers, whose loving companionship has smoothed the bumps and made the ride more interesting.

INDEX

Free people of color *(continued)*
during plantation revolution, 66–67; in the North, 85, 88, 102–111, 118–119, 121, 122, 135, 136, 137, 138, 183, 230–244, 247, 249, 267; attitudes toward slavery among, 105–106, 235–236, 239, 240–244, 260, 269–270; family life of, 108–109, 121–122, 236–237, 247, 262–263; institutions of, 109, 123, 139–140, 183–184, 228–230, 236–238, 244, 247, 263–264; egalitarian ideology among, 109–110; attitudes toward freedom among, 109–110, 121, 243–244, 248–249, 253–255, 259–261, 266–270; opposition to slavery among, 109–110, 138, 183, 266–268; African identity among, 110–111, 123; and skin color, 119, 139–140, 143, 183–184, 238; as skilled workers, 122, 182, 232; Christianity among, 123, 228–230, 237–238, 247, 263–264; churches of, 123, 228–230, 237–238, 247, 263–264; in Lower South, 135–140, 183–184; in Charles Town/Charleston, 138–139, 183–184; during Second Middle Passage, 162, 167, 182–184, 199–200, 224–226; in Southern interior, 182–184; class divisions among, 238–239; political activism among, 239–240, 266–270; during Civil War, 247, 249, 253–257, 267; military service during Civil War, 255–257, 267; after Civil War, 259–270; relations with white nonslaveholders, 263, 267; land sought by, 264–265, 270
French Revolution, 99, 155; Declaration of the Rights of Man, 11, 100, 154
Fugitive slaves, 43–46, 111–112, 119–120, 124–126, 142, 161, 175–176, 234–236, 241–242, 249–251, 253–254; and Underground Railroad, 241; Fugitive Slave Act, 242. *See also* Maroons

Gang labor, 63–64, 87, 132, 149, 150, 177–178, 185, 211. *See also* Working conditions
Garrison, William Lloyd, 202
Genovese, Eugene D., 16, 18
Georgia: plantation revolution in, 6, 55, 67, 68, 71, 96, 165, 166, 198, 199; rice cultivation in, 6, 55, 129–130, 211; Savannah, 79, 125, 126, 135; cotton cultivation in, 127, 130; slave population of, 127, 135, 187, 198; free people of color in, 135; slave code in, 166; during Second Middle Passage, 167, 168, 187, 210, 213, 220. *See also* South, Lower; South, seaboard
Grant, Sarah, 215–216
Green, James, 217

Haitian Revolution, 11, 43, 99, 106, 128–129, 142, 146, 152, 154, 156, 188; Toussaint L'Ouverture, 101, 129, 153, 155, 202–203
Hall, Prince, 122
Hammond, James Henry, 185, 240
Hemp cultivation, 113, 162
Heywood, Nathaniel, 210
Hiring out/rental of slaves, 90–91, 114, 118, 221–224, 225, 266. *See also* Working conditions
Hope, Ceasar, 122
Howard, Emma, 219
Humane Brotherhood, 140
Hunt, Susan, 199

Ideology: egalitarianism, 6, 8, 11, 13, 14, 16–17, 96, 99–101, 103–104, 107–108, 109–110, 111, 117, 142, 153–154, 193–194, 240, 248; of slaveholders, 10–11, 17, 18, 63, 64, 200, 204–205
Igbos, 83, 170
Illinois, 231
Indentured servants, 10, 34, 55, 61, 62, 81, 88, 99, 104–105, 119, 231
Indians. *See* Native Americans
Indigo cultivation: in lower Mississippi Valley, 42, 89, 146; in South Carolina, 67; in Lower South, 67, 71–72, 77, 126–127; in seaboard South, 210. *See also* Plantation revolution
Insurrections, slave: Bacon's rebellion, 10, 55; Natchez rebellion, 42, 88, 93, 141, 145, 153; Stono rebellion, 47, 74; Pointe Coupée conspiracy, 154, 157; St. John the Baptist Parish rebellion, 164, 188; Nat Turner's rebellion, 203, 206, 217, 228; Denmark Vesey's conspiracy, 203, 217
Islam, 27–28

Jackson, Andrew, 13–14, 164
Jamaica, 12, 17, 29, 56
Jamestown, Va., 56
Jefferson, Thomas, 3, 13–14, 103, 163, 231, 243
Jeremiah, Thomas, 125, 137
Jerónimo (Wolof slave), 30
Johnson, Andrew, 265, 268
Johnson, Anthony, 36–38, 53
Johnson, Richard Mentor, 182

Kentucky, 111, 113, 181, 224, 231; during Second Middle Passage, 162, 163, 166, 168, 210, 212,